CONSTITUTIONAL
CONSTRUCTION

CONSTITUTIONAL CONSTRUCTION

Divided Powers and Constitutional Meaning

Keith E. Whittington

Harvard University Press

Cambridge, Massachusetts, and London, England | 1999

Library of Congress Cataloging-in-Publication Data

Whittington, Keith E.
    Constitutional construction : divided powers and constitutional
meaning / Keith E. Whittington.
    p. cm.
    Includes index.
    ISBN 0-674-16541-1 (alk. paper)
    1. Constitutional law—United States.   2. Separation of powers—
United States.   3. Law and politics.
KF4552.W48   1999
342.73'02—dc21   98-42668

For Tracey

CONTENTS

PREFACE

The Constitution has a multifaceted nature. Constitutional theory, however, has too often focused on a single facet to the exclusion of the rest. By recapturing the complexity of the Constitution, we can bring all its parts into better focus and demonstrate how they interact to produce a total governing document that both controls and informs American politics. Most scholarly work focuses on the aspect of the Constitution that produces constitutional law. Specifically, such work explores how the Constitution is designed to limit governmental actions and how the judiciary is to enforce those constraints.

This book is concerned with another facet of the Constitution, one that is not primarily legal but political. In this context, the document does not provide external constraints on governmental action to be imposed by a neutral enforcer of the constitutional will. Rather, the political Constitution operates within politics to empower and to bind political actors in the very process of making government policy. Operating in this dimension, the Constitution is dependent on political actors, whether government officials or active citizens, both to formulate authoritative constitutional requirements and to enforce those fundamental settlements in the future. Constitutional meaning is shaped within politics at the same time that politics is shaped by the Constitution. The result is not simply the elimination of the Constitution as a binding force, but rather is a recognition of the changing nature of constitutional meaning. Political actors can be expected to bring a different set of concerns and interests to bear on the Constitution, leading to a much more contested and rather different process of constitutional deliberation than a simple reliance on judicial interpretation would allow. The political constitution is not the same as the legal constitution, either in substantive content or in practical operation. Constitutional meaning, in this sense, is dynamic. When relatively closed, the Constitution prevents certain government actions from being considered or adopted through a structuring of the ideological and institutional environment of governmental decisionmaking. When relatively open, political actors must determine for themselves what the Constitution will mean, and in doing so they engage in the elemental task of politics and take on the highest responsibilities of self-governance. Constitutional meaning is not simply the province of the courts.

Many scholars have responded helpfully to the ideas presented in this book. In particular, I thank Herman Belz, Terri Bimes, J. Budziszewski, Robby George, Howard Gillman, Marissa Golden, Mark Graber, Sandy Levinson, Joe Mink, Walter Murphy, Karen Orren, Corey Robin, Tracey Storey, and Jeff Tulis.

I owe a special debt of gratitude to David Mayhew, Stephen Skowronek, and Rogers Smith for their untiring efforts to correct my errors and to encourage further thought. David Mayhew's immediate understanding of my project was invaluable to the articulation of my overarching theory of how the Constitution is given meaning. My understanding of American politics and the relationship between history and politics would be radically different if not for Stephen Skowronek's example and teaching. He confirmed my belief that the understanding of history is critical to the understanding of politics and convinced me that American politics is a field worth studying. Rogers Smith generously dedicated more time and effort to me and to this manuscript than any student could expect or deserve. His knowledge of American politics, constitutional law, and political theory are reflected throughout this work in points large and small.

In addition, I must extend my appreciation to the faculty and staff of Yale University, Bowling Green State University, and Catholic University of America, who have made my research and writing much easier. Completion of this manuscript was made possible by financial and administrative support from the Social Philosophy and Policy Center, Bowling Green State University. Delay in the completion of this manuscript was engineered by my wife, who continually persuaded me that there is more to life than constitutional theory.

An earlier version of Chapter 2 appeared in *Studies in American Political Development* 9:1 (Spring 1995): 55–116. Parts of Chapter 3 appeared in *Publius: The Journal of Federalism* 26 (Spring 1996): 1–24. Material from those journals is used here by permission.

We may rest assured it is no less true in politics than in theology, that the power which creates can alone preserve—and that preservation is perpetual creation.

—JOHN C. CALHOUN, "SOUTH CAROLINA EXPOSITION"

1

The Political Constitution

The Constitution is a governing document. It defines and constrains the way government operates and politics is conducted in the United States. The process by which the Constitution does this, however, is not entirely clear. There is a tendency to regard the Constitution as primarily a legal document: constitutional law substitutes for the Constitution, and the exercise of judicial review is regarded as tantamount to constitutionalism itself; the Constitution is considered relevant to politics as a consequence of and only to the extent that the judiciary is willing to enforce its terms and block the actions of government officials. This image, though dominant, obscures too much.[1] The Constitution penetrates politics, shaping it from the inside and altering the outcomes. Along the way, the Constitution is also made subject to politics.

Constitutional construction is the method of elaborating constitutional meaning in this political realm. Constitutional meaning can be partially determined by relatively technical and traditional interpretive instruments, such as text and structure, framers' intent, and precedent. But such "modalities" elucidate only a portion of the Constitution's meaning.[2] Additional meaning cannot be discovered in the text through more skillful application of legal tools; it must be constructed from the political melding of the document with external interests and principles. This essentially creative task does not expose a failing in the constitutional design; it represents a working constitutional system.

After a long period of almost exclusive concern with the normative questions of judicial review, constitutional scholars are beginning to recognize the importance of nonjudicial actors for construing constitutional meaning. Although scholars such as Stephen Griffin, Bruce Ackerman, and Wayne Moore are deeply concerned with the judicial elaboration of constitutional law, they also recognize that nonjudicial actors are likely to bring

1

different concerns and perspectives to bear on the Constitution and the problems of determining its meaning.[3] These nonjudicial actors struggle to reconfigure, challenge, or depart from judicial efforts to define constitutional meaning.

This book is concerned with clarifying the concept of constitutional construction, how constructions have worked in American history, and their importance to American politics. Scrutiny of the concept of construction will illuminate how the Constitution operates in practice and how constitutional meaning changes. Although the history and practice of judicial review have obviously influenced the effect of the Constitution on politics, the Constitution also operates more directly on political actors, without the mediation of the courts or the creation of amendments. The jurisprudential model of constitutional interpretation not only has drawn our attention to the legal arena; it also has shaped the assumptions that we bring to our examination of judicial review. We cannot fully understand the Court itself without better analytical tools that can recognize the political aspects of the judiciary's work without abandoning its genuine concern with the constitutional. Not everything that courts do is consistent with the ideal of interpretation. Not everything that elaborates constitutional meaning is interpretation.

The possibility of constitutional construction indicates that not all changes in effective constitutional meaning should be regarded as analogous to textual amendments. Bruce Ackerman, in his effort to integrate constitutional theory with American political development, has posited the existence of informal constitutional amendments. In Ackerman's view, "constitutional moments" have two primary characteristics: they are legitimated by sustained electoral support, and they are enforced by judicial review.[4] Although both characteristics are consistent with an amendment-based theory of constitutional change, neither is consistent with the cases of constitutive politics examined here. These constructions were never directly put before the voters, and their success, substantive development, and legitimacy did not depend on subsequent "ratifying" elections. Elections were more likely to serve as catalysts for political change than to determine or legitimate particular outcomes.[5] Nor do these constructions depend on judicial review for their enforcement. The constructions considered here altered constitutional practices but barely affected judicial doctrine.

The notion of construction also elucidates the relationship of political agents to the Constitution. Too often, judges are assumed to possess a monopoly on constitutional understanding and deliberative capacity. Other government officials are seen as irrelevant to constitutional development at best and as threats to the constitutional order at worst.[6] But the practice of construction is held in common by the various branches of government, and its recognition allows for empirical analysis of the constitutional deliberations of political actors without unduly weighting the scales in favor of the prerogatives and practices of the judiciary. Uncritical acceptance of the jurisprudential model often leads to regarding political actors as responsible constitutional interpreters only to the extent that they adequately engage in a rationalistic dialogue over constitutional meaning and refrain from immoderate rhetoric, institutional and partisan bickering, or emotional appeals.[7] Similarly, the Constitution is "real" within the legislative arena only to the extent that political actors regard it as a fixed, external constraint on their actions.[8] But all parts of the government are crucial to the realization of the promise of the Constitution. Examination of political efforts to construct constitutional meaning reveals that the governing Constitution is a synthesis of legal doctrines, institutional practices, and political norms.[9] Constitutional constructions capture this second dimension of constitutional elaboration, showing the degree to which the Constitution operates through and with elected representatives and their actions.

Interpreting Constructions

Constitutional construction is one mechanism by which constitutional meaning is elaborated. It supplements other methods of determining constitutional meaning and provides a more complete and workable governing instrument. Clarification of this practice help us better understand how our Constitution operates.

Deliberation on constitutions can be analyzed in terms of the extent to which constitutional structures and principles are considered and modified. At one extreme, the constitution may be written anew. Two forms of such constitutional transformation are possible: revolution and creation. (See Table 1.1) A constitutional revolution abandons the old text *in toto* in order to replace it with a new one. The authority for such a radical revision of the old order must necessarily be external to the old constitution, since none of the old constitution survives the revolution. In substance, however, constitutional revolutions need not be radical. The United States Constitution of 1787 supplanted the Articles of Confedera-

Table 1.1. Levels of constitutional deliberation

Level of deliberation	Characteristics
Policymaking	Assumes consensus on fundamental principle
	Settles only immediate political action
	Specifies individuals and actions of governance
Interpretation	Allows "dialogue" between judiciary and other branches
	Searches for discoverable meaning
	Develops in evolutionary fashion
	Relies on legal norms
	Assumes ratification by judicial recognition of results
	Specifies rules for government action
Construction	Considers fundamental political principles
	Structures future political practice
	Occurs at moments of unsettled understanding
	Develops in interstices of discoverable textual meaning
	Provides standards for political conduct
Creation	Specifies new political principles
	Alters of current textual requirements
	Authorizes final judicial action
	Stabilizes constitutional meaning
Revolution	Abandons existing constitutional text
	Establishes new constitution
	Depends on authority external to existing constitution

tion, but retained a basic commitment to the British common law inheritance. Nonetheless, the new constitution abandoned its predecessor as irredeemably flawed, and brought forth a new government that did not simply build upon the old. Less radically, constitutional creation involves the addition of new text; the old constitution is not rejected, but simply amended. Moreover, the authority to amend flows from original constitution itself, and the supplement is as authoritative as the original, joining with the old text to form a new whole.[10] In either case the founders who draft the new text stand in a unique position in the history of the polity, as their decisions are authoritative.

At the other extreme of constitutional deliberation is policymaking. Policy may fulfill the promise of a constitution in governmental practice, yet it does not extend the meaning of the constitution itself. Policy initiatives may help solidify constitutional understandings and stability or help destabilize inherited constitutional arrangements by hastening fundamental crisis, but they elaborate on constitutional forms only indirectly. Policy decisions determine the specific personnel of government office and the particular actions of an operating government, yet they assume an underlying consensus on what offices exist and which actions the government may take. Not all important political decisions are constitutional in nature; policy changes may cause severe alterations in the existing distribution of social resources, benefiting some social interests at the expense of others, elevating some claims over others. Normal politics need not be uneventful.[11] Nonetheless, policy concerns are eminently contemporary, setting a particular course that will undoubtedly have implications for the future but without claiming any authority over it. Later policymakers have as much, and as little, authority to determine the actions of government as their predecessors.

Between these extremes, in which the constitution is either produced or assumed, lie efforts to elaborate the inherited text. Currently the only analytical model for this activity is jurisprudential and focuses on interpretation. Interpretation, however, covers a range of quite different activities and biases the analysis of constitutional meaning toward accepted legal forms.[12] The jurisprudential model needs to be supplemented with a more explicitly political one that describes a distinct effort to understand and rework the meaning of a received constitutional text. That more political model is one of constitutional construction. Both interpretation and construction assume a fidelity to the existing text. Both seek to elaborate a meaning somehow already present in the text, making constitutional meaning more explicit without altering the terms of the text itself. As such, both methods of constitutional elaboration are subordinate to the text, which is understood as prior and more fundamental.[13] Interpretations and constructions can be abandoned without abandoning the text, and if a correct understanding of the text is seen as being in conflict with prior efforts at interpretation or construction, it is the earlier elaborations that must give way.

Unlike jurisprudential interpretation, construction provides for an element of creativity in construing constitutional meaning.[14] Constructions do not pursue a preexisting if deeply hidden meaning in the founding document; rather, they elucidate the text in the interstices of discoverable, interpretive meaning, where the text is so broad or so underdetermined as to be incapable of faithful but exhaustive reduction to legal rules. In such cases, the interpretive task is to limit the possibilities of textual meaning, even as some indeterminacies remain.

It is a necessary and essentially political task, regardless of the particular institution exercising that function, to construct a determinate constitutional meaning to guide government practice. Something external to the text—whether political principle, social interest, or partisan consideration—must be alloyed with it in order for the text to have a determinate and controlling meaning within a given governing context. As a result, constitutional constructions are often made in the context of political debate, but to the degree that they are successful they constrain future political debate. As the jurisprudential model emphasizes, interpretation is understood to be a more technical activity, concerned with employing a set of analytical tools to unearth the meaning inherent in the constitutional text. Although constitutional interpretation may be more of a craft than a science, and its practitioners lawyers not machines, its results are immediately justified in terms that are internal to the Constitution itself. The tools of interpretation may not be limited to the "four corners" of the document itself, but such aids as precedent, history, and constitutional structure are meant to illuminate the text, not to alter or add to it.[15] If construction employs the "imaginative vision" of politics, interpretation is limited to the "discerning wit" of primarily judicial judgment.[16]

Allowing for both interpretation and construction expands the field of constitutional elaboration without shrinking the range of interpretation. One need not accept an overly confining view of interpretation in order to accept a supplemental category of construction. Addressing hard cases—questions for which the legal constitution does not seem to provide answers—is a deeply political activity.[17] It transcends the widely accepted but narrow "analogy between a constitution and ordinary law,"[21] which provides disproportionate support for the practice of judicial review, and relieves us of the dubious burden of "defin[ing] the difference between the Constitution and politics as the difference between law and politics."[18] The cases examined in the following chapters demonstrate that government officials have sought to gain political mileage by portraying their understandings as "legal" and "technical" interpretations of the constitutional text. Drawing a distinction between interpretation and construction addresses the political dimension of American constitutionalism, while maintaining our ability to analyze our historic experience of a legalistic constitution.

The concept of constitutional construction allows a full range of interpretive methods and also opens other areas of the Constitution. Notably, it allows us to abandon an exclusive focus on the Bill of Rights and to take into account political institutions and public purposes. Additionally, the idea of construction makes way for new types of constitutional arguments and activities that were previously excluded as entirely outside the scope of constitutionalism. Constitutional arguments derived from abstract normative theory must somehow be reconciled and integrated with legalistic elements such as textual language or inherited precedent, and interpretations based on a national "ethos" must struggle with the appropriate level of abstraction in the moral theories that are recognized in the constitutional text.[19] When political actors systematically make such arguments with little regard for balancing such textual components, it makes more sense to recognize that they are engaged in a different activity than to accuse them of making "bad" interpretations. We need a conceptual scheme that can account both for purely political arguments based on either moral theory or pragmatic calculation and for narrowly technical arguments based on precedent or historical intentions. Moreover, we need an analytical model that can incorporate political practices and not just judicial opinions. Political practice helps define what we understand the Constitution to mean, but it does not arise through anything like interpretive argument and does not exist in the form of constitutional law. The idea of construction helps us understand how constitutional meaning is elaborated even when government officials do not seem to be talking about the Constitution, or are not saying anything at all.

Interpretation and construction not only bear rather different relations to the constitutional text; they also take somewhat different approaches to the Constitution and produce different kinds of results. The model of interpretation has always been a somewhat idealized version of judicial practice, carrying with it a prescriptive standard as well as an element of description.[20] This model asserts that constitutional meaning should be understood through the rationalistic production of legally binding rules. Ideally interpreters set aside their own interests in the case at hand in order to pursue an objectively demonstrable, correct outcome, the interpretation emerges from a process of careful argumentation and incremental application. Although any given effort at interpretation may be flawed, interpretive results are largely evolutionary, with errors being exposed and corrected through extended analysis and new applications. A complementary model is needed to clarify an understanding of constitutional meaning through the political construction of authoritative norms and governing institutions. Government officeholders and constitutional commentators often find themselves engaged in constructing constitutional meaning from an indeterminate text. In this context, the Constitution is often understood less as a set of binding rules than as a source of authoritative norms of political behavior and as the foundation of governing institutions; it permeates the substance of political action, establishing not only the boundaries of permissible action but also the standards of action. The Constitution not only constrains; it also empowers. As a consequence of the indeterminacy of the constitutional text, the inherently compromised nature of a successful construction reflects not a flaw in the process, but rather the balancing and synthesis of competing social interests and external ideologies with the partial directives of the foundational document. The construction gains its authority less from its unassailable derivation from textual imperatives than from its capacity to give practical meaning to constitutional concerns.

Several factors are likely to lead even conscientious political actors to turn to construction to supplement their interpretive understandings of the Constitution.[21] Traditional tools of interpretive analysis can be exhausted without providing a constitutional meaning that is sufficiently clear to guide government action.[22] The text may specify a principle that is itself identifiable but is nonetheless indeterminate in its application to a particular situation. Either the principle itself may break down in a specific context, or the facts at issue may be deeply controversial.[23] Alternatively, the principle established by the text may be unclear: the text may contain contradictory requirements with little or no indication of how to weigh the different values at stake or how much force to give to particular, atypical requirements; there may not be sufficient information for an interpreter to arbitrate among contested meanings; or the text may be simply silent on issues that are nonetheless substantively constitutional.[24]

Beyond such problems of textual ambiguity lies the complex nature of the Constitution itself. The jurisprudential model of interpretation largely assumes a legal text providing clear specifications of duties and rights, but the Constitution is also a political text. As such, the Constitution also expresses normative sensibilities. An act may be constitutionally permitted and still not be constitutionally appropriate.[25] The political construction of constitutional meaning helps close the gap between legal requirements and constitutional sensibilities, speaking with the authority of the Constitution even where the text does not seem determinative. Similarly, construction helps transform constitutional theory into constitutional practice. Constitutional mandates are often not self-enforcing, nor are the concrete instruments for their realization always readily at hand. Efforts to make the text concrete draw upon the Constitution's authority and impetus, but supplement its actual terms. The embodiment of an "independent judiciary" or the legislature's "power of the purse" depends on a myriad of specific practices that are intimately connected with the founding document but that cannot be completely subsumed by it. In such cases, interpretation need not give way to construction, but construction will be necessary to elaborate fully the governing Constitution.

Recognizing Constructions

Moving beyond the jurisprudential model of interpretation requires further definition of the content of constructions. The formal nature of interpretation makes it relatively easy to identify and analyze. Explicit discussions of the constitutional text and the use of familiar tools of analysis help distinguish efforts at constitutional interpretation from the mass of political activity. In many ways, it is the striking presence of a written constitutional text that has blinded us to the complexity of our constitutional discourse. The jurisprudential model takes the text as its touchstone, such that dissection of the text becomes synonymous with constitutional elaboration.[26] Nonetheless, not all constitutional activity in the United States deals so explicitly and obsessively with the terms of the document itself. The Constitution is not just a form of "literary theory"; it is a fundamental and independent part of politics.[27]

The defining features of constitutional constructions are that they resolve textual indeterminacies and that they address constitutional subject matter. Thus, some political debates are properly characterized as constitutive even if explicit references to the terms of a specific written constitution are rare or nonexistent. Consideration of both our own various written constitutions and the British tradition of nontextual constitutionalism provides a representative list of constitutional subjects.[28] Such a list would include organic structures, the distribution of political powers, individual and collective rights, structures of political participation/citizenship, jurisdiction, the role of domestic government, and international posture. The organic structures of government include the various governmental institutions created under the Constitution to initiate and implement government policy. The Constitution is organized around these structures, establishing a federal legislature, executive, and judiciary and recognizing the existence and function of the states. Further, the Constitution is self-referential, naming procedures for its own ratification and amendment and naming itself as the supreme law of the land. In instituting these various organic structures, the Constitution also distributes political powers among them through enumeration, designation, prohibition and reservation, all of which are means of specifying the functioning of political institutions. Individual and collective rights are provided for in both the original Constitution and its several amendments, and those rights define the limits of political power relative to the people as opposed to other political institutions.

In addition to specifying government institutions, their powers and limits, constitutions must specify who participates in those institutions and to whom their powers are applied. Thus, citizenship and structures of political participation specify who is to participate in making government policy and how they are to participate. Most narrowly, these citizenship issues include who will hold government office and how they will be selected, but they may also include mechanisms for influencing those officeholders.[29] Similarly, the application of government power is defined through issues of jurisdiction. In the modern state, jurisdiction is defined almost entirely by territory. American federalism provides for two fundamental levels of government to have jurisdiction over a single territory. The American constitutional order also provides for the existence of a district, land, and territories to be administered exclusively by the federal government. In addition, jurisdictional issues must define how these territories are to be acquired, governed, and ceded.[30]

The final two substantive issues on this list are the role of domestic government and international posture.[31] These issues are both less familiar and more difficult to define as distinctly constitutional. Their inclusion is based on three considerations. First, constitutionalism is concerned not only with the identification of political structures, but also with the principles underlying their operation. The very definition of those institutions and their powers remains unclear without some notion of the political values that are given substance through their actions and their place in the context of the regime as a whole.

Second, the American constitutional tradition specifically recognizes a role for principles in defining the purposes of government and the nature of the American republic. The most familiar of these is the preamble to the federal Constitution, which lists in general terms the purposes of the Constitution.[32] These goals not only provide the context within which the rest of the document is to be understood, but also represent a public statement as to the nature of American society and government. The continuing process of constructing a specific meaning out of such general terms as promoting the "general Welfare" and securing a more "perfect Union" reconstructs the nature of the political nation and shapes public attitudes about the appropriateness of specific policy proposals and particular textual constructions. The Constitution helps create a national identity, as well as a blueprint for government. The articulation of general governing principles is not limited to the preamble, however, but is also embodied in specific sections throughout the text. Through such securities as the "guarantee" and the "necessary and proper" clauses, the Constitution seeks to characterize the United States as a republican regime and to define the political spirit and culture of the nation.[33]

Finally, considerations of general principle help fill in the "penumbras" of the text's many clauses. In defining the extent and nature of delegated powers, a construction stretches across many aspects of the text, drawing the whole together in order to determine the document's general spirit. This general concern with the spirit of the document cuts across the several substantive areas considered above, contributing to their definition individually but existing above them as something more. Thus, for example, the American shift in international posture as marked by the Spanish-American War left the country with permanent noncontiguous, ethnically distinct territories that were not seen as being held in a temporary status until population growth and political organization should allow a transition to statehood. This construction not only affected the size and nature of the territorial jurisdiction of the federal government, but also redefined the nature of citizenship and contributed to shifts in the distribution of powers among branches and levels of government, the nature of the organic structures of government, and the considerations that defined individual rights.[34] The shift in American international posture from an expansionist republic in the Western Hemisphere to an interventionist global empire remade the nature of the United States as a political entity, and did so in a manner that directly affected multiple individual substantive categories. Such broad shifts in the American regime require us to give them distinct consideration as constitutional issues, but they also require particular caution in their identification and in distinguishing them from normal policy debates.

In addition to dealing with such substantive issues, constructions may themselves be either broad or narrow. As Table 1.2 indicates, the universe of constructions is quite large. Though this list only scratches the surface of historical constructions, it does suggest their nature and range. A broad

Table 1.2. Selected constructions

Organic structures
creation of the Executive Office of the President
creation of civil service
creation of military colleges
creation of independent regulatory commissions
creation of executive departments
creation of inferior federal courts
elimination of federal courts
specification of size of Supreme Court
no implicit time limit on amendment ratification
set time limit on amendment ratification
congressional committee system
formalization of cabinet system
creation of independent counsels

Delegation and distribution of political powers
independent presidential treaty negotiation
"fast track" treaty authorization
senatorial courtesy
peacetime blockade
embargo power
protective tariffs
no protective tariffs
federal incorporation of banks
no federal incorporation of banks
federal appellate jurisdiction from state courts
federal grants-in-aid to states
presidential policy veto
limitations on presidential pocket veto
executive agreements
federal military draft
judicial review
federal sedition power
creation of federal land-grant colleges
congressional subpoena power
congressional contempt power
federal price control authority
federal mandates to state governments
legislative veto
nationalization of fugitive-slave procedures
judicial refusal to issue advisory opinions

Individual and collective rights
no right to secession
truth as a defense in seditious libel prosecutions
limitations on discrimination on basis of physical
    disability
limitations on private discrimination on basis of
    race
prohibition of racial exclusions from jury service
protection of secrecy of membership in associations
federal regulation of unionization
federal exclusionary rule
limitations on federal wiretapping authority
federal military draft

Structures of political participation/citizenship
congressional term limits
state adoption of direct election of U.S. senators
state adoption of Australian ballot
state regulation of political parties
development of nonpartisan governmental agencies
citizen advisory committee requirements
open meeting requirements
judicial regulation of amicus curiae briefs
federal naturalization procedures
registration of foreign lobbyists
specification of single member U.S. House districts
specification of a single date for national elections
capping the total number of members of the U.S.
    House
regulation of campaign financing

Jurisdiction
Louisiana Purchase
state annexation through treaty
home rule of the District of Columbia
federal restriction of slavery in the territories
extension of coastal national waters
Hawaiian statehood

Domestic governmental role
centralized presidential budgeting
federal macroeconomic responsibility
national bankruptcy law
protective tariff for "infant industries"
general protective tariff
rejection of any protective tariff
establishment of the Federal Reserve System
creation of independent treasury
authorization of railroad rate regulation
development of the "welfare state"

International posture
mediation of Russo-Japanese Treaty of Portsmouth
expansion of Spanish-American War to Philippines
acquisition of Pacific territories
entrance into NATO
entrance into United Nations
entrance into Organization of American States
diplomatic recognition of the Soviet Union
attendance at the 1826 Panama Conference
rejection of the League of Nations

construction not only addresses a substantive constitutional issue, resolving a particular question of textual meaning, but also is productive of additional constructions across other issues. The same process is familiar in the judicial consideration of the Constitution. Given cases are recognized as landmarks of constitutional law not only because they address a particularly crucial issue themselves, but also because they are representative of an approach to constitutional interpretation that can be applied to several issues and several situations. Thus, the *Lochner* era is known for a single case, not because a great deal hinged on whether the due process clause allowed state legislatures to limit the number of hours bakers might work, but because it was exemplary of an approach to several constitutional issues.[35] Similarly, the broad claims in *Brown* marked the culmination of a series of more narrow specifications of the requirements of the equal protection clause and guided an additional and subsequent series of narrow applications of the clause.[36] Constructions operate in much the same way, with numerous relatively limited ones elucidating narrow issues or elaborating the path marked by an earlier landmark.[37] Broad constructions may be expected to spark more popular interest and more explicitly constitutional deliberations, while establishing firmer and more encompassing boundaries for future political debate. Substantive characteristics may be affected as well by a construction's breadth, as a given construction "leaks" across substantive categories and reorients our understanding of multiple constitutional issues.

Not only do constructions range across a variety of substantive categories or a series of debates, but they may also deal with more or less critical features of our constitutional system. Such distinctions are familiar in the judicial arena and in the history of constitutional amendments. Just as most amendments subsequent to the founding period itself have dealt with relatively unimportant details of the constitutional scheme, many constructions must also be concerned with the technical mechanics of governing. Only a few constructions rise above such concerns to reshape the constitutional framework in a substantial way. Just as the Fourteenth Amendment represents a fundamental change in the constitutional system and is of clearly greater significance than the Eleventh, so Lincoln's refusal to recognize a right to secession was more important than Jefferson's decision to avoid personally delivering his annual messages to Congress.

The boundaries of constitutional construction are not rigidly marked. (See Figure 1.1.) In practice, the process of constitutional creation may not be wholly separate from the process of construction, for example.

Although different constructions will be plausible in different political contexts, and such shifts are appropriate, some proffered constitutional values will not be consistent with the constructed text. The availability of formal amendments institutionalizes this possibility, marking the fact that the text is not infinitely malleable or expansive. Creations may begin as constitutional constructions, however, as the momentum of a political movement carries it beyond the plausible meaning of the inherited text. On the other hand, the proffered constructions may have never seemed plausible, or sufficiently plausible, in the first place, and a reform movement may be forced to amendment politics from the outset. In either case, the ultimate constitutional creation is tied politically to constitutional construction, and though the two stages are analytically distinct they may not be held as separate enterprises by those involved. A successful movement to amend the Constitution may be surrounded by constructions of other aspects of the same text.[38]

The potential synchronicity of constitutional interpretation, construction, and creation highlights the difficulty in distinguishing among them. Further, the ambiguous quality of constructions makes them difficult to separate from the policy debates that normally surround them. Time alone may be able to bring into focus the full image of a construction. Historical perspective can clarify both the contours of a construction and its relative success. The political context of a debate over construction may fray the

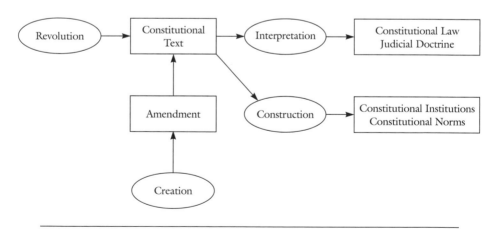

Figure 1.1. The process of constitutional elaboration

boundaries of constitutional and policy disputes as speakers rise to address the same government action but struggle on different argumentative planes. Some separation from the issues involved may be necessary in order to be able to perceive that principled rhetoric was more than mere rhetoric but was offered with sincerity, insight, and a solemn intention to affect the course of the republic, or to see that the same principles were being employed in several forums and across a range of narrow policy disputes. Similarly, only time can demonstrate the stability of a constitutional settlement. Though an argument may seem to sweep all before it and an issue may seem to be laid to rest, the next electoral cycle may find the entire dispute being resurrected. Few political movements achieve "overnight success," and a low-level conflict over constitutional meaning may persist for years before culminating in a decisive construction. Likewise, a rearguard action may have to be fought for some time to secure the gains previously achieved. Time is necessary to demonstrate whether these conflicts are significant enough to be considered major battles or whether they are merely continued skirmishes, though even short-lived constructions may be significant.

Distinguishing among different forms of constitutional elaboration is not necessary for this approach.[39] Constructions do not depend on contemporary recognition in order to be effective. Indeed, contemporary actors may well fail to distinguish between their own creative efforts at settling an indeterminate constitutional meaning and the necessary requirements of the original text or fail to realize the constitutional nature of their actions. Constructions never leave the realm of politics; they do not become a higher law to be recognized and applied from above. The terms and authority of a construction are subject to future political struggle, just as the Constitution itself is. The value of a model of constitutional constructions is in understanding constitutional development. An understanding of past constructions, won, lost, and deferred, may shed light on less distinct efforts in the present.

Getting Down to Cases

The following chapters consider in detail four episodes of constitutional construction, three from the nineteenth century and one from the twentieth. They are varied in their breadth, in their degree of success, and in the issues they address. In three the president played a leading role; in one, court decisions intervened at crucial times. Although all the episodes involved appeals to popular support in electoral outcomes, only two show evidence of significant efforts at mass mobilization, and only one served as the defining conflict in an electoral campaign. Although each episode is cohesive, each also involves several interdependent cases of construction.[40]

As indicated in Table 1.2, constructions range in importance, breadth, and complexity. Similarly, the constructions considered here arise from a variety of sources and reflect myriad origins and pressures that cannot be easily captured under a single ordering rubric.[41] Although these cases of construction are obviously not exhaustive of the category—none of them directly addresses the determination of individual rights, for example— they demonstrate how political action becomes constitutive of the political order, reshaping how political problems are conceptualized and restructuring what government actions are possible.[42]

The selected instances of constitutional construction are representative of the variety and nature of constructions as a class throughout our history. Though presented in chronological order, the cases do not form a linear progression along a single constitutional dimension. Some of these constructions are related to one another, but they do not describe a single evolutionary development. These cases also indicate the diversity of actors who participate in constitutional constructions.[43] No single governmental branch has dominated our constitutional discourse, and the state itself is not the locus of all significant constitutional politics, though constructions most often reach their culmination in those political institutions. Additionally, these cases are drawn from numerous substantive categories and represent the levels of complexity that individual constructions may display. They reveal the mix of policy and principle involved in constructing constitutional meaning, and the kinds of factors that must be considered in providing that meaning. Finally, in their varying degrees of success these cases open up the ambiguous nature of constitutional settlements characteristic of political conflict.

In other respects these cases are purposefully not representative. All are relatively important constructions, and thus also highly visible. Although some of the most significant constructions in our history—such as Lincoln's rejection of the right of secession, the federal government's acceptance of responsibility for the country's macroeconomic performance, or the American rise to the status of a global superpower—are not discussed, the included cases substantially shaped American constitutional and political development. Moreover, they were particularly bitter political conflicts and thus do not reflect the degree of consensus and moderation that can and often does accompany constructions.

Skewing the sample in these respects serves several useful purposes. To the degree that these cases are no longer strictly or wholly representative, they illuminate the practice of constitutional politics. As "politics by other means," these constructions reveal not a single model but rather a shifting, multilayered process. These cases also have the advantage of possessing an independent substantive interest beyond their utility in elucidating the analytical model. A proper appreciation of their constitutional dimensions will give us additional insights into these important and formative moments in American history.

Each of the following chapters considers a distinct historical episode, and each offers different insights into the process of constitutional construction and the complex nature of constitutional governance. Chapter 2 examines the impeachment of Associate Justice Samuel Chase. This episode displays the involvement of the judiciary as a political institution in the formation of our constitutional understandings, while highlighting congressional leadership in that process. In addition, the outcome of the Chase impeachment offers a perspective on the constitutive effect of political action on governing norms and ideological commitments. The impeachment helped establish our subsequent understanding of the purpose and limits of the federal impeachment power and reshaped our dominant conceptions of the appropriate use of the judicial power in American politics.

Chapter 3 explores the nullification crisis of the winter of 1832–33. The crisis features the states as significant actors in reshaping the meaning of the federal constitution, as well as presidential involvement in the constitutional dispute. The nullification debates addressed important constitutional subjects, setting the boundaries of government power as well as dealing with the distribution of institutional functions. As a shifting and multilateral conflict over constitutional meaning, the crisis highlights the interaction of policy interests and constitutional principle in constructions, and the use of statutory instruments to consolidate the new understandings. Although the specific mechanism of nullification was ultimately rejected, the crisis promoted more decentralizing conceptions of federalism, and the protective tariffs that instigated the crisis were abandoned for the remainder of the antebellum period.

Chapter 4 considers the impeachment of President Andrew Johnson.

The debates surrounding this impeachment provide a substantive contrast to many of those surrounding the Chase impeachment. Presidential challenges to received constitutional commitments sparked a direct conflict between the president and Congress over relative powers and institutional commitments. The episode highlights the unintended consequences of constructive activity and the compromised nature of possible outcomes. In this instance Congress reaffirmed earlier understandings of the impeachment power, crushed Johnson's efforts to strengthen the postbellum presidency, and put the spoils system on the defensive.

Chapter 5 examines a similar conflict between Congress and President Richard Nixon. The Watergate crisis provides the broad context of an activist judiciary and the modern presidency for more specific struggles over the direction of American politics and the control of the modern state apparatus. These conflicts highlight the interrelationship between institutional struggles and substantive political goals. The resolution of the conflicts also illustrates the role of institution building in constructive activity. In such areas as budgeting, war powers, and intelligence, Congress sought greater presidential responsiveness in policymaking rather than to displace or weaken the presidency or the modern state that he led.

The historical range of these cases—from the patrician period of Thomas Jefferson to the party period of the mid-nineteenth century to the bureaucratization of the Nixon era—allows us to see how the very different political resources available to the relevant actors affected the dynamics and outcomes of the constructions. The use of these resources reveals the close connection between constitutional construction and normal political activity, and the relative distance between constructions and the dominant jurisprudential model of interpretation.

Chapter 6 draws several implications from these cases as a whole. In particular, it explores the mechanisms employed by political actors to maintain their constitutional settlements over time, the influences on and instruments of constitutional construction, and the theoretical implications for our understanding of constitutional governance and American politics.

Together these chapters make it clear that the Constitution is a substantive document and not merely the formal background against which policymaking is conducted. The Constitution empowers political actors to alter their social and institutional environment. The meaning of the Constitution is also a very real prize of political struggle.

This study suggests the need for a more complex understanding of the separation of powers. The various branches of government not only share overlapping powers—a constitutional defect requiring reform and evasions;[44] they also possess distinctive perspectives, resources, and capacities that help to shape political outcomes. The constitutional division of powers contributes to a unique and unpredictable dynamic that can feed government action, encourage institutional development, and foster political and constitutional deliberation.[45]

Constitutional constructions are often highly partisan, messy, bitter disputes, in which the losers are driven from the public stage. New constructions emerge when the existing ideologies and institutions are at their weakest and alternatives are open for consideration. As successful constructions close off some alternatives, they open the path for others. It is at these moments that the republic is most open to change and to dissenting voices. To the extent that such fundamental issues of the American republic have been opened to public debate, Jefferson's goal of reconsidering the Constitution from time to time has been partially achieved,[46] perhaps against the goals of those founders who hoped through the Constitution to limit political debate within a controlled arena.

2

The Chase Impeachment and Shaping the Federal Judiciary

Only one United States Supreme Court justice has ever been impeached. In January 1804 the House of Representatives began a formal inquiry into the official conduct of Associate Justice Samuel Chase and in November of that year approved eight articles of impeachment. The Senate held a trial of the justice in February 1805, which concluded with his acquittal on March 1. On the final article of impeachment, Chase escaped removal by four votes.

This chapter examines the constitutional constructions developed through the Chase impeachment, as they relate both to Congress and its powers of impeachment and removal and to the judiciary and its "judicial power." The Chase impeachment helped set our understanding of the impeachment power as a weapon against abuse of office as well as criminal activity. The impeachment also helped redefine the role of the judiciary within the new constitutional system, such that judicial independence was to be dependent on the depoliticization of the judiciary. The Chase impeachment is critical not simply because it was "early." The federal judiciary had been in operation for some sixteen years at the time and had already adopted, implicitly or explicitly, a large number of conventions, many of which were rooted in the prior history of state and British courts. Further, the limits of judicial power have been continually tested over the past two centuries, suggesting that institutional norms are rarely completely fixed. Even such a basic issue as the proper method of constitutional interpretation remains unsettled. The Chase episode stands in contrast to most judicial impeachments, which have been fairly routine; the impeachment of such judges as Harry Claiborne in 1986 for willfully underreporting his income taxes and of Robert Archbald in 1912 for misusing his office for private, financial gain raised few difficult issues of constitutional meaning.[1] The proceedings against Justice Chase, on the other hand, tested the boundaries of the impeachment mechanism and raised substantive constitutional questions over the nature of the judiciary.

Samuel Chase was a leading Maryland patriot during the Revolution. He was a signer of the Declaration of Independence, had been a member of the state assembly and the Continental Congress, and had served as a state judge in Maryland for eight years. Chase's time on the state bench had not been without pitfalls, and he narrowly missed being removed by the state legislature. Although he had opposed ratification of the federal Constitution, George Washington appointed him to the Supreme Court in 1796.[2]

At the time of his appointment, the justices of the Supreme Court "rode circuit" and participated as trial court judges, which is where Chase made most of his memorable rulings.[3] As the election of 1800 approached, as tensions with France escalated, and as Congress took action to repress political opposition with the passage of the Alien and Sedition Acts in 1798, Chase became increasingly belligerent.[4] In August 1800 he invited substantial criticism for causing the Court to delay the opening of its term for lack of a quorum as he campaigned for John Adams.[5] His circuit ride of 1800 had already made him a favorite target of Republican criticism, and set the basis for his later impeachment.[6] The justice's difficulties began while sitting with Judge Richard Peters in Philadelphia on a sedition case against Thomas Cooper, a prominent Republican pamphleteer. Though the case did not appear in the official records of the impeachment, Chase took a prosecutorial tone throughout. His conduct was widely reported, in part through the efforts of Cooper himself, which fed the notoriety of both the Sedition Act and Justice Chase.[7]

While still in Philadelphia, Chase sat for the second treason trial of John Fries, who was charged with leading a Bethlehem mob that had helped free a number of tax resisters. Fries's first conviction was overturned on the grounds of jury bias, resulting in a second trial before Chase.[8] Knowing that the defense strategy was to admit the facts of the case but to argue that Fries's actions did not meet the constitutional definition of treason, Chase issued an opinion at the opening of the trial upholding a broad interpretation of treason.[9] After a sharp exchange with the defense and an *ex parte* meeting with Peters and the prosecutor, Chase offered to withdraw his opinion and allow the defense counsel to proceed with their case; however, the defense withdrew, leaving Fries at the mercy of the court.[10] The Fries trial served as the basis for the first article of impeachment.

From Philadelphia, Chase traveled to Richmond, where he intended to prosecute another Republican, James Callender, for a book that had been helpfully underlined and sent to him by Luther Martin. Eventually the federal marshal found Callender and brought him before Chase and District Judge Cyrus Griffin. Several irregularities occurred during the Callender trial, all of which were heavily publicized in the local press. Chase began by wrangling with the defense over the timing of the trial and by minimizing efforts to exclude biased jurors. During the trial the justice gave immunity, on his own initiative, to witnesses who might be disposed to remain silent on constitutional grounds, excluded defense witnesses who could not individually prove to Chase's satisfaction that both parts of a two-part charge in the indictment were false, required the defense before any examination to present its questions to witnesses to Chase in writing, announced in another prepared opinion that the defense could not present arguments against the constitutionality of the Sedition Act to the jury, and so badgered the attorneys during their presentations such that they withdrew from the case.[11] The Callender trial furnished another five articles of impeachment. Chase then traveled to Delaware, where he held over a grand jury and suggested prosecuting a local printer for sedition. The prosecutor and grand jury found nothing out of the ordinary except for a pointed criticism of Chase himself, and the justice dropped the issue. Despite the lack of results, his zeal in promoting a prosecution and stooping "to the level of an informer" resulted in another impeachment charge.[12]

After the election Chase abstained from public comments against the new administration, but in May 1803 he abandoned his low profile.[13] While opening his circuit term in his home state, Chase delivered a general charge to the grand jury that went beyond setting out the court business and ventured into recent political conflicts in both Maryland and Congress. The justice alluded to his opposition to the repeal of the Judiciary Act of 1801, suggested that the authors of that repeal should be replaced at the next election, and denounced "universal suffrage" and the proposed alterations in the state judiciary, which threatened to unleash a "mobocracy" and "take away all security for property and personal liberty."[14] These comments not only grounded the final article of impeachment but also served as the instigation for the entire proceeding. In a letter to Congressman Joseph Nicholson, Jefferson sent a published copy of Chase's charge to the Baltimore grand jury, suggesting that Nicholson take appropriate action. After consulting with Speaker of the House

Nathaniel Macon, Nicholson declined to take any action. John Randolph, Republican chairman of the Ways and Means Committee, determined to bring the justice before the House himself.[15]

Randolph asked for a formal investigation of Chase the day after District Judge John Pickering was removed from the bench by the Senate. Pickering was the first judge ever impeached by the House, and the first to be removed by the Senate. The New Hampshire Federalist had shown signs of encroaching insanity before being elevated to the federal bench from the state supreme court, and his condition had rapidly deteriorated in his new post. Finally, his summary judgment and drunken tirade in a politically charged seizure case came to the attention of the administration. After local Federalists refused to usher Pickering quietly off the bench for fear of a Republican successor, Jefferson formally sent a file on the judge to the House for its consideration. Under the leadership of Nicholson and Randolph, Pickering was quickly impeached. Carefully limiting testimony to the judge's behavior, the Senate voted to remove him against a solid Federalist minority and a handful of Republican abstentions.[16] The difficulty of removing even such an obviously incompetent judge, as well as his own unpleasant experience with impeachments, led Jefferson to complain to a Federalist senator from New Hampshire that impeachment was "a *bungling way*" to remove a judge; still, Senator Plumer refused to take the hint and seek a less formal alternative.[17]

The Chase impeachment was a contest over political principle and not just the trial of a single judge. The groundwork for a major confrontation was laid by the Federalist hostility to the new administration and open reliance on the judiciary as "ramparts" and "anchors" against Republican policies,[18] the partisan tone adopted by the Federalists during the Pickering impeachment, and the desire of some Republicans to restructure the judiciary and the Constitution. Much of the commentary surrounding the Chase impeachment has focused on evaluating whether Chase's acquittal was justified. Thus, the impeachment has been understood in the legalistic terms emphasized by the Federalists; that is, whether Chase was guilty of "high crimes and misdemeanors" and whether the acquittal was a just vindication of Chase or a miscarriage of justice. Like any other trial, the impeachment is measured in terms of its winners and losers, being marked by the Republicans' failure to convict Chase.[19] Surprisingly little attention has been paid to John Randolph's stated political concern, of changing the principles of the federal government, not the men who occupied office.[20] Such a political, rather than legal, perspective results in a more complicated understanding of the impeachment and the constitutional issues at stake.

Often quoting (out of context) Republican Senate leader William Branch Giles's remark to John Quincy Adams that the impeachment proceedings against federal judges were a statement that *"We want your offices,"* commentators have judged the success of the Chase impeachment by the extent to which the Republicans managed a turnover of personnel on the federal bench. Thus, Senator Adams commented in his diary that "the whole bench of the Supreme Court [is] to be swept away, because *their offices are wanted,"* thereby transforming the Chase impeachment into an extension of presidential patronage policy, as the Republicans had earlier accused the Adams administration of doing with the Judiciary Act.[21] Similarly, in his biography of Randolph, Henry Adams observed that "Randolph's victory would have made impeachment as useless as his defeat made it, for there never sat on the Supreme Bench another judge rash enough to imitate Chase by laying himself open to such a charge."[22] The irony of Adams' position emerges if the impeachment is considered as part of a successful construction, rather than a matter of preserving a single judge on the bench.

In attempting to measure the nature and success of the constitutional construction involved in the impeachment, it is best to focus not simply on the Senate's verdict in the case, but also on the attitudes, expectations, and principles conveyed in taking the drastic step of impeaching a Supreme Court justice. As a recent defender of Justice Chase pointed out, simply attributing Chase's later, more subdued behavior to a "broken spirit" or encroaching age renders the event in too personalistic terms.[23] It seems more likely that a judge who had already survived a lifetime of scandal and criticism and faced his federal impeachment with stern defiance was not broken by an acquittal. Rather, he recognized the changed political and constitutional environment that existed after the impeachment. Although we should be wary of drawing too much from British impeachment practices, they serve as a useful model of how constitutional constructions occur. Thus, during the heyday of British impeachments the Commons often used this device as a political tool and did not bother to prosecute impeached officials in the House of Lords; instead it let the impeachment itself serve as warning to the opponents of the Commons to curb their behavior. Later, impeachment was reserved for high officials who had committed serious political crimes. This approach allowed minor officials to be removed for lesser offenses through the ordinary means of indict-ment.[24] The Chase impeachment is of political significance because it ranks with only a handful of impeachments of such high federal officials as presi-dents, cabinet secretaries, and senators. In those times, congressional in-vestigation carried heavy symbolic overtones, regardless of the particular outcome. Chase achieved a personal victory in his acquittal in the Senate. For his vision of an elitist and politically active American judiciary, how-ever, his victory must be regarded as Pyrrhic.

The constitutional constructions involved in the Chase impeachment are best divided into procedural and substantive categories. The very use of the impeachment mechanism as a means to other ends encountered sub-stantial resistance and had to be defended on its own terms. The second construction involved a cluster of issues defining the meaning of the "judi-cial power" delegated to the courts in the Constitution. Like many other aspects of the text, this sweeping delegation of power was underdeter-mined and subject to substantial controversy. The Chase impeachment was the culmination of a movement to define the nature of the federal courts under the Constitution and how judges were to conduct themselves and their courtrooms in a republic. The Republicans were fairly successful in both areas, expanding the impeachment power to serve as a mechanism for disciplining the judicial branch while constraining judges from engaging in political disputes.

Constructing Impeachments

The Constitution provides that the House of Representatives "shall have the sole Power of Impeachment"; that the Senate "shall have the sole Power to try all Impeachments," the penalty for which is limited to re-moval from office, and that the "President, Vice President and all Civil Officers of the United States, shall be removed from Office on Impeach-ment for, and Conviction of, Treason, Bribery, or other high Crimes and Misdemeanors." These grants of power are complicated somewhat by the additional proviso that judges "shall hold their Offices during good Behav-ior."[25] Several features of these clauses make them particularly apt for construction. Given the specification of the two chambers of Congress as the "sole" agents responsible for impeachments, there is a strong textual bias against judicial review of a House determination to impeach or a Senate decision to convict.[26] In any case, the judiciary has so far remained out of the impeachment process, though it has helped the investigative process along, leaving uncontested a broad field of discretion open to the Congress to determine the meaning of these aspects of the Constitution.[27] The predominance of the political branches in elucidating these clauses invites noninterpretive considerations to enter into congressional deliberations, despite their legalistic tone.[28]

The space for construction is further expanded by the limited possibility of decisive interpretation. The textual references to impeachment are few, vague, and contradictory. For example, the Constitution limits the Senate's power to punish impeached officials for "high crimes and misdemeanors" but allows for criminal indictments that can carry additional penalties, despite the Fifth Amendment's prohibition of double jeopardy. Similarly, the Senate is given the "sole" power to "try" impeachments, yet the Sixth Amendment guarantees a trial by "impartial jury" in "all criminal prosecutions." Such terminology suggests that impeachment both is and is not a criminal prosecution. Although the specification of "high crimes and misdemeanors" suggests common law language with relatively determinate meaning, the American and British histories of impeachments prior to constitutional ratification undermine the specificity and technicality of such formulas. Similarly, the history of the drafting, ratification, and early exposition of these clauses provides relatively little information about their meaning.[29]

Despite the lack of such legal aids as binding precedent and clearly defined doctrinal rules, federal impeachments have shown a remarkable consistency over time, at least in the cases of lower court judges.[30] The failure of the Senate to abide by such rules reflects not an unfortunate oversight on the part of an inadequately trained political body, but a conscious construction of its own powers and the nature of the impeachment process, which renders such devices superfluous. As the first significant impeachment, the case of Samuel Chase shaped how Congress would approach later impeachments and the extent to which it would conduct itself as a political, and not just a narrowly legal, institution.

Criminal Indictments and "High Crimes and Misdemeanors"

The earlier impeachments of the former Republican Senator William Blount by the Federalist-controlled House and of Judge Pickering worked around the edges of the meaning of the impeachment clauses, specifically the grounds for removing government officials. Since Blount had already resigned his government position, his trial immediately turned to the touchy issue of whether the Senate could convict a private citizen and bar him from future office. The risks of such a construction were clear, as was its tenuous textual base, and the first federal impeachment quickly concluded without a conviction. The Pickering inquiry was similarly limited, for all sides recognized Pickering's inadequacy for office and the undesirability of impeaching someone for a mental defect, and thus the trial turned on whether evidence of the judge's insanity was to be admitted.[31] By contrast, Justice Chase was willing and able to attend his trial and to offer a vigorous defense of his actions as not only correct but unimpeachable, thus forcing a confrontation over the very core of the impeachment power. Chase centered his defense on the contention that the impeachment initiated a full criminal trial, with the Senate being held to the highest standards of legal procedures. The effect of this perspective was to give a very narrow reading of the grounds for impeachment, one that would exclude Chase's own behavior.[32]

Chase struck the legal theme with his opening statement, denying "with a few exceptions, the acts with which I am charged; I shall contend, that all acts admitted to have been done by me, were *legal;* I deny, in every instance, the *improper* intentions with which the acts charged, are alleged to have been done, and in which their supposed criminality altogether consists." It was, Chase contended, upon the illegality and criminality of his actions that the articles of impeachment must be tried. Chase concluded his response with the flip side of this claim, that he was being prosecuted for nothing more than his political opinions. The justice argued that he was simply the victim of a changing political climate that now rejected the views it had once accepted, and which he continued to espouse.[33]

Between these two basic points, Chase laid out the essentials of his case that impeachment proceedings were equivalent to a criminal trial. After his blanket denial of wrongdoing, Chase went through the articles of impeachment point by point, characterizing them in his own terms. To this end, Chase insisted on regarding the articles as a legal indictment, while complaining that they were badly written for this purpose. Given this failing on the part of the House, the justice declined to answer any "general accusation, too vague in itself for reply." Having directed the Senate to disregard the political and rhetorical aspects of the impeachment, Chase proceeded to establish the standards by which the remaining charges were to be evaluated. First, the Senate was not to sit as a court of appeals over the judicial branch. Because it was the constitutional duty of the judiciary alone to interpret the laws, any legal errors Chase might have made in conducting his circuit duties could be corrected only by the judiciary. Incompetence per se was insufficient grounds for an impeachment. Such a limitation became particularly important for Chase, for although he insisted that he was "free from intentional impropriety," he admitted to lacking "sufficient caution and self-command" and that "his indignation had been strongly excited" by some of these cases. But "intentions and feelings" were irrelevant without misconduct, and he would admit only the strong feelings.[34]

The possibility of some errors in judgment, and perhaps some failings in his judicial temperament, could not carry the case anyway. For not only must an impeached judge have displayed corrupt motives; he must also have committed indictable crimes in order to sustain an impeachment. "No civil officer of the United States can be impeached, except for some offense for which he may be indicted at law," Chase argued, and the same rules of evidence should be applied as at a criminal trial. One component of an indictable offense, of course, is that the action must be "in violation of some law," and a law containing criminal penalties at that. The same considerations of fairness that control the criminal law generally demand such a standard. A second implication of such a standard, however, was that even admitted judicial misconduct may not justify an impeachment. After all, Chase reminded the senators, "there are many improper and very dangerous acts, which not being forbidden by law cannot be punished."[35]

In making this case, Chase could rely upon certain assumptions that had previously been articulated by the Federalists, as well as some shared by many of the Republicans. In developing such an "indictable offense" construction of the impeachment power, Chase could build upon the existing text, which clearly referred to such things as "trials" and "crimes and misdemeanors." But he also needed to connect such terms to a specific vision of the judicial office.[36] Although the term "high crimes and misdemeanors" was borrowed from British practice, the full impeachment mechanism supporting that phrase had been left behind. Unlike the British House of Lords, which had the power to impose any criminal penalty, including death, the Senate was explicitly limited to removing an impeached official from office. It was up to the criminal courts to pursue, if applicable, a separate indictment, trial, and criminal punishment for the offense.[37] All would admit that such guarantees as prohibitions on *ex post facto* laws must apply to criminal prosecutions; however, it was not immediately clear that removal from office should be considered a true "punishment" of the same class as fine, imprisonment, or death. In order to appeal successfully to due process guarantees, therefore, Chase had to assume that at least part of his audience would regard them as relevant.

The debate surrounding the Judiciary Act of 1801 suggested the basis for their relevance. Jefferson wrote to Madison that he dreaded the judiciary bill "above all the measures meditated [by the Federalist Congress], because appointments in the nature of freehold render it difficult to undo what is done."[38] Unlike the soldiers in the New Army and the excise men hired to collect the new federal taxes, judges could not simply or easily be removed from their offices. The Constitution's guarantee of their continuation in office during "good behavior" gave judges something akin to a property interest in those offices—a point the Federalists had emphasized.[39] If judges were not simply public servants, but in fact owned their offices within certain conditions, then removal from office was a type of criminal punishment, depriving the judge of property, and all of the usual guarantees should apply, including that the reasons for removal conform to a legal standard and be "capable of precise proof and of a clear defense." Luther Martin, another Chase defender and a member of the constitutional convention in Philadelphia, bolstered that view by informing the Senate that the power to try impeachments had been given to the upper house in recognition of its more deliberative, judicial character, not as a corollary of its executive role in filling offices in the first place.[40]

The strong claim that impeachable "high crimes and misdemeanors" were limited to indictable criminal offenses put Chase in the best position, while working within a political context already established by the Federalist reaction to both the repeal of the Judiciary Act and the Pickering impeachment. Senator Plumer feared what he took to be the implication of Pickering's removal, that absent a showing of a crime, judges would hold their offices "not by tenure of *good behavior*, but the *pleasure of the legislature*," to the detriment of separation of powers. Similarly, Republican Senator William Cocke protested that he knew "*of no law that makes derangement criminal*."[41] Without the fixed standard of criminal law to guide and constrain impeachments, the personnel of the judicial branch would fluctuate with every party victory.[42]

For the Federalists, with their more general conception of the Constitution, the criminal law served as a convenient hook on which to hang the impeachment of Chase. The Federalists had already been split by the Blount impeachment between their desire to fashion a new weapon to use against the Republicans and their realization that impeachments were essentially another check on the power of government. The latter fear proved the stronger, and Chase's defenders were put in the awkward position of urging a "strict construction" of the Constitution when it came to the impeachment power. Unlike the Jeffersonians, for whom strict construction served as a political framework for limiting the power of the federal government generally, the Federalists hoped to emphasize the Constitution's status as a legal instrument. Constructing the Constitution as law meant recognizing that its terms had well-defined "legal and technical" meanings requiring legal interpretive skills to understand and apply properly. Therefore, the House, a political institution, did not have the freedom to define impeachable offenses, for they were already defined in law. Any acts that were truly harmful were indictable by the "pure and wholesome mandate of that common law."[43] Such an understanding of the Constitution also had the virtue of shifting constitutional discourse and power from the popular branches of government to the judiciary.

The construction of constitutional provisions as primarily legal, rather than political, led Chase's defenders to pursue highly interpretive approaches to elucidating constitutional meaning. If the text had a "technical" meaning embedded in the common law, then proper investigation could uncover the fixed meaning of those terms. To this end, the defense counsel explored the lexical and grammatical possibilities of the impeachment clauses, minutely parsing the relevant passages and comparing definitions of the words in multiple dictionaries and legal commentaries. Counsel brought forward personal knowledge of debates during the drafting convention and interpretations from the ratification debates. British common law precedents were cited, though Chase's counsel disagreed among themselves whether the practice of the states was useful precedent because those impeachments were legalistic in their terminology or bad examples because they were corrupted by politics.[44]

These efforts at interpretation, however, were grounded on the prior constructive claim that the meaning of the impeachment clauses had to be determined by reference to the law. This link was made by combining the freehold conception of the judicial office with a political concern for limiting the exercise of the impeachment power. Federalists complained that opening impeachment proceedings to crimes not defined in the common law not only cleared a path to unfair and unpredictable prosecutions, but also threatened the security of the judicial branch. For the Federalists, abandoning the legal standard necessarily made impeachment easy. If easy, impeachments would undoubtedly be used for political purposes. Political attacks on judges in particular called into question the objectivity of law, suggesting that the application of law depended on the individuals holding office.[45] The ever-present temptations for Congress to act from political motives had to be resisted by its binding itself closely to a fixed rule.

The Federalists did not want to see judges and other officials subjected to impeachment proceedings for relatively minor violations of even well established laws. Thus they insisted that the adjective "high" must be understood as applying to both "crimes and misdemeanors." This grammatical interpretation, however, was clearly insufficient by itself to eliminate the ambiguity, so Chase's counsel also made appeals to the nature of the event. Impeachments had to be weighty and rare occurrences if government officials were to be able to perform their duties in accord with their best judgment. The Senate could not be expected to sit in judgment on every little deficiency discovered in the other branches. This focus also suggested the utility of collapsing "high misdemeanors" into the category of "high crimes." After all, misdemeanors were simply defined in law as a type of crime, and therefore carried all the same attributes of high crimes more generally.[46] To denigrate the charges contained in the impeachment and to emphasize the height of the hurdles the House managers would have to jump, Chase's counsel repeatedly asserted that the Senate could not monitor and correct mere deficiencies in courtesy. "Is the Senate of the United States solemnly convened and held together in the presence of the nation to fix a standard of politeness in a judge, and mark the precincts of judicial decorum?" Such concerns were not only below the dignity of the Senate and unlikely to do any real damage, but were also "vague and changing" and, as the defense implied, too closely tied to politics.[47]

Abuse of Office and "Good Behavior"

Whereas Chase began from the clear and strong position that impeachments must be limited to indictable crimes, the Republicans were less consistent in offering their alternative construction of the impeachment power. The Federalist-controlled judiciary was a prime source of irritation, even before Jefferson took office, and William Branch Giles wrote the president-elect that he favored "an absolute repeal of the whole Judiciary and terminating the present offices and creating a new system." The repeal of the Judiciary Act satisfied most Republicans, but some remained convinced that additional removals could be managed through the impeachment power. Certainly some Federalists were convinced that the Pickering impeachment was an opening wedge, in which "the process of impeachment is to be considered in effect as *a mode of removal,* and not as a charge and conviction of high crimes and misdemeanors."[48]

There was some support for this extreme view of the impeachment power. Giles extended his antagonism toward the judiciary into a sweeping theory of impeachment "without limitation," arguing that

> it was the undoubted right of the House of Representatives to impeach [the justices], and of the Senate to remove them, for giving such opinions [as threatening to issue a *mandamus* to the secretary of state or to declare an act of Congress unconstitutional], however honest or sincere they may have been in entertaining them. Impeachment was not a criminal prosecution; it was no prosecution at all . . . A trial and removal of a judge upon impeachment need not imply any criminality or corruption in him . . . And a removal by impeachment was nothing more than a declaration by Congress to this effect: You hold dangerous opinions, and if you are suffered to carry them into effect you will work the destruction of the nation.[49]

Others, including James Monroe, had made similar, though more limited, suggestions.[50]

Such a construction did not extend so far as to challenge Chase's distinction between a court of impeachment and a court of appeals, but it did contend that judges were responsible for false or dangerous constitutional interpretations. If the judicial office included the power of interpretation, then a judge's incorrect approach to that task was at least as dangerous to the republic as any criminal mischief. Judges were still not to be removed for every minor error committed in office, but a persistent and serious breach of official duty required correction. Denying that a political constitution could not be constraining, Randolph emphasized to the House that impeachment, like the power to declare war, was only to be "exercised under a high responsibility." Madison had hinted as much in a speech to the First Congress, in which he declared that Congress might impeach an "unworthy man" holding executive office and that the president himself could be removed for a serious "act of maladministration." Ultimately, such disagreements "must be adjusted by the departments themselves," and if they could not resolve it themselves, then "there is no resource left but the will of the community."[51] Not only was the impeachment power broad enough to reach beyond indictable crimes; it was essentially a political question, not a legal one.[52]

While Giles's extreme construction filled the Federalists with fear for the whole judiciary, Republican opinion was divided over how far the impeachment power should extend. George Clinton, the vice-president elect, observed that several Republican senators thought that Chase's actions had to be prohibited by "express and positive law" in order for him to be removed. Another Republican, Israel Smith of Vermont, answered Giles that an "honest error of opinion" by a judge could not justify an impeachment, for the result would be a "tyranny over opinions."[53] The result of this division of opinion was an immediate moderation of the extreme Republican construction, represented in the mixture of charges contained in the articles of impeachment passed by the House. Observing the articles presented, Henry Adams concluded with some overstatement that Randolph was forced "at the outset to abandon his own theory of impeachment" and adopt the "whole paraphernalia of the law." The articles of impeachment "withdrew the trial from the region of politics, and involved it beyond extrication in the meshes of legal methods and maxims." Even so, Adams criticized the articles for inadequately narrowing the "field of dispute, . . . exclud[ing] doubtful points of law, and avoid[ing] cumulative charges," as would have been expected in a court of law.[54] Rather than giving the ground over to Chase, as Adams claimed, Randolph, in modifying his proffered construction, still offered an alternative to Chase's rigid standard of indictable crimes. Though involving himself in some legal points in order to establish the facts justifying the impeachment, his construction of the impeachment clause itself was purely political. The deeply legalistic assumptions of the Federalist construction, shared by Henry Adams, provided no tools for even understanding the force of the Republican arguments. Thus, Plumer noted that Randolph's opening speech, which outlined the political nature of the impeachment powers, "is the most feeble—the most incorrect that I ever heard him make."[55]

As the lead manager representing the House on the impeachments, Randolph provided the initial response to Chase's answer to the articles. He expressly asserted that the constitutional requirement of impeachment could be met without a showing that Chase had committed any indictable crimes. A mere showing that Chase had abused his office was sufficient to carry the charges and support his removal. The various articles with their multiple subparts were designed to be a "chain of evidence indissolubly linked," showing a pattern of misconduct that added up to a whole greater than the parts of the individual charges.[56] The inclusion of relatively minor errors in law and judgment that did not themselves constitute a "high crime" helped create a picture of official abuse and dereliction of duty that rendered Chase unfit for office. As Adams observed, such a scattershot approach was clearly inadequate as a legal charge, but politically such an argument was both common and effective.

In their closing arguments, the managers developed more thoroughly their construction of the impeachment power. George Campbell began by pushing the construction toward the extreme, by contending that impeachment was "a kind of inquest into the conduct of an officer . . . more in the nature of a civil investigation, than of a criminal prosecution." Not only was actual criminal indictability unnecessary, but so was illegal action of any kind. The key to an impeachment, unlike any criminal trial to which an officer might also be subject, was the "breach and violation of official duty." While pushing the impeachment power away from the indictable offense standard, Campbell avoided defining the extent to which the power could be taken. Implicitly, Campbell suggested that mere errors in law were not impeachable, but his arguments did not rule this out.[57]

Campbell supported his extension of the impeachment power by turning the same considerations of legal due process against Chase. Campbell was willing to concede the principles of legal fairness that ought to hold in a republican system, but the constitutional text did not provide for them in impeachments. Viewing impeachment proceedings as a civil inquest into official conduct explained the lack of appropriate legal protections, such as the waiver of double jeopardy and the possibility of conviction in absentia.[58] Of course, this view required that judges not possess a freehold in their office for their own private benefit, but be removable in accord with the public good. Though recognizing the importance of a relatively stable and independent judiciary, few Jeffersonians were willing to admit into the republic a kind of aristocracy for whom public offices were held like private property. Judges were public officers like all others, and held their offices in public trust only.[59]

The disagreement among the House managers was demonstrated when Joseph Nicholson took the floor and immediately distanced himself from the extreme construction advocated by Campbell. But Nicholson's concession was more rhetorical than real. Even as he denounced the language of the extreme construction, the congressman maintained the distinction between the House and Chase, for the managers "do not contend that this is a criminal prosecution . . . We do contend that to sustain an impeachment, it is not necessary to show that the offenses charged are of such a nature as to subject the party to an indictment."[60]

If a violation of the criminal law was not necessary for an impeachment,

Nicholson still maintained that impeachment was not an act of pure political will. The managers were willing to grant that mere errors in law or insignificant offenses were insufficient to support an impeachment. In contrast to the Federalists' elaborate investigation of the British criminal law and history of impeachments, however, the managers insisted that political principle was essential to understanding the impeachment power. The Constitution required "not an English construction, but one purely and entirely American," in which principles and not mere legal words were at stake. The Federalist attempt to center the debate on issues of legal interpretation was intended to avoid the principled conflict at the heart of Chase's actions and impeachment.[61]

On this basis, the managers moved away from Chase's emphasis on the constitutional grounds of impeachment for "high crimes and misdemeanors" to the constitutional specification that the judicial tenure would last for "good behavior." The legal determination of the meaning of "high crimes" was subject to endless confusion. Not only was British common law unclear, but each state had further modified the common law in its own ways and had added statutory crimes as well. Further, the federal government did not explicitly recognize the common law and had defined few statutory crimes. Federal impeachments had to center on their own standards, which were amply contained in the notion of good behavior.[62] A "good behavior" standard met Chase's argument based on legal principle by providing an independently known and preexisting standard for impeachment, and it also had the advantage of being grounded in the public good and a fitness for office. By interpreting "high crimes and misdemeanors" in light of the requirement for "good behavior" and construing "good behavior" in terms of republican political principles, the managers were able to offer a plausible, and yet broad, construction of the impeachment power.

Consideration of good behavior provided responses to some of the difficulties that the impeachment of Chase had raised. Not only did it move the impeachment away from strictly legal considerations and into a more political realm, but also it provided the basis for considering a string of questionable, but probably not criminal, activities. What Chase's defenders characterized as minor issues of demeanor, the managers were able to represent as evidence of a "breach of trust," a "flagrant breach of duty," and "gross impropriety of conduct in the discharge of his official duties." Moreover, far from being the retroactive application of a new political doctrine, the "good behavior" standard was the "law of truth and justice

. . . It is written on the heart of man in indelible character, by the hand his Creator, and is known and felt by every human being."[63] Such duties were certainly greater than the minimal conditions of the criminal law, but were nonetheless known and obvious to anyone likely to hold office.

The impeachment mechanism was a different form of security for republican government from the criminal law, which punished private harms. Impeachments ensured that all public officials were accountable for their actions. All government officials were charged to use state power *"with a sound discretion and under high responsibility, for the general good."* If they abused that discretion, they remained responsible for the public good. Accountability, and thus the public good, would be rendered nugatory if "sound common sense were to be confounded by technical jargon," such that "conduct at which the plain sense of every honest man would revolt" would be excused by being unindictable at the common law. "This honorable body must have a standard of their own," which need not be "minutely specified and described" in the "particular provisions" of the "black lettered lore."[64] The Constitution represented a set of principles, not a legal code, and the conduct of the judges operating under it was to be measured by those republican principles.

Thus, the moderate Republican construction developed by the House managers during the Chase impeachment slid from being a political inquest into a judge's general fitness for office to being a trial for abuse of office. The first formulation suggested the radical construction urged by various Republicans such as Giles, Monroe, and Randolph in private, but it was nonetheless not sharply inconsistent with the second formulation. Individual managers apparently saw no contradiction in referring to the impeachment as both a "grand inquest" and a "criminal proceeding."[65] In either case, civil officers could not be removed through impeachment simply for holding the wrong political opinions or for making minor errors in judgment, but they could and should be removed for systematically engaging in activities that were inconsistent with their station. As one commentator observed, the "Republicans' extreme view of impeachment, though probable, did not have its origins in the document itself."[66] Unlike the Federalist counsel for Chase, the Republicans' understanding of impeachment grew out of a distrust of all political power and was conveyed not through a close textual analysis of the law, but through a broad consideration of political principle. In this view, officials could be removed only in accord with fixed standards, but those standards encompassed more than narrow legal rules.

Though often portrayed as such, Chase's acquittal was a clear victory for neither the justice nor the Federalist construction of the impeachment power. A majority of the Senate returned guilty verdicts on three of the eight articles of impeachment and narrowly missed a majority on a fourth, though the Senate never achieved the constitutionally required supermajority necessary for removal. The voting pattern on the various articles reflected the relative success of the constructions offered during the Chase impeachment. Though the Federalists voted as a bloc against every article, no Republican voted guilty on every article, and only four supported seven of the eight. Thus, the impeachment was not a strict party vote, but seemed to reflect individual judgments on the merits of the various charges. This was the conclusion of both Republican and Federalist observers.[67]

No senator voted guilty on the fifth article, and only four supported the sixth. This poor showing can be partially explained by the weakness of the evidence supporting the two charges. These articles were unique in charging Chase only with technical errors in his application of the Virginia law in the Callender case, and thus that Chase's actions were "contrary to law."[68] The charges tended to support the claim that Chase was biased against Callender and arrogant in his attitude toward the state of Virginia. It seems likely that this was the purpose of including these articles in the impeachment, though the Federalists suspected more sinister motives.[69] In themselves, these charges did not amount to either an abuse of office or a violation of the criminal law. The Senate's overwhelming rejection of them indicates the complete failure of the largely undefended contention that judges could be removed for mere legal error.[70]

The rejection of these two articles also contributed to the clear failure of the privately defended view that judges could be impeached and removed at will. The form of the articles themselves already suggested that the House was unwilling to defend such a construction. The articles did charge a violation of law, even if only a technical error, and nowhere claimed that Chase could be removed simply for his obnoxious political opinions or in order to create a beneficial vacancy on the Court. Even Giles, the purported defender of the removal-at-will construction, voted against these two articles. Moreover, the House managers, in their arguments to the Senate, were clearly unwilling to maintain such a construction. The managers not only reminded the Senate that it was to act as an impartial judicial body, but also repeatedly asserted that Chase had not been impeached and should not be tried for his private political views, but only for the public conduct of his office.[71]

If the extreme Republican construction was decisively rejected during the Chase impeachment, the very limited construction of the impeachment powers offered by Chase was unsuccessful as well. As Chase's defenders pointed out, none of the charges specified a violation of any criminal law, let alone proved criminal intent. Nonetheless, only fifteen senators voted not guilty on all eight charges, with six Republicans joining the nine Federalists. Though the vote totals alone cannot fully represent the reasoning behind the votes, it is apparent that the very narrow reading of the impeachment power won over a sizable minority of the Senate, including several Republicans. The Federalist construction was ameliorated somewhat, however, by the fact that as the trial wore on, even Chase's counsel became less insistent that impeachment could be justified only for indictable crimes. By the end, the defense's primary concern was that Chase not be removed for behavior that had been previously regarded as largely acceptable, if indecorous.[72]

The primary result for the impeachment power that emerged from the trial of Samuel Chase was that removals should be limited to serious offenses that violated the duties of the office, though such offenses could be essentially political in nature. This construction is reflected in the voting. The eighth charge garnered guilty votes from every senator except the fifteen who voted not guilty across the board, and came just four votes short of removal. This article, which was based on Chase's charge to the Baltimore grand jury, was among the furthest from the Federalist standard of criminal indictability. It had the advantage of being both current and relatively undisputed in the presentation of the evidence, and thus probably lost no votes to doubts about the facts or timing of the charge. Although it did not allege a violation of the criminal law, it did demonstrate that Chase purposefully chose to take on the administration politically and in a manner that heightened state fears of encroaching central power. With his Baltimore charge, Chase had entered the political arena, and the votes against him showed that to the extent that judges entered that domain, they were vulnerable. Likewise, the third and fourth articles, which garnered only one less guilty vote than the eighth, indicated that Chase's intemperate behavior at the Callender trial, when suggesting more than an innocent legal error in a case before the court, was a removable offense as a breach of duty and a violation of the strictures of office.

Having failed to remove Chase, the Republicans made no serious attempts to remove any other Federalist judges, even as the Federalist numbers in Congress continued to dwindle. There was some loose talk of impeaching Chief Justice John Marshall for his conduct of the treason trial of Aaron Burr, but charges were never pursued. Notably, calls for Marshall's impeachment relied upon similar charges as those in the Chase impeachment, that the justice had manipulated the outcome of a criminal trial for political reasons. But Marshall's courtroom behavior was a model of decorum in comparison with Chase's, and as Adams observed, no other judges were foolish enough to engage in the type of behavior that brought Chase before the bar in the first place.[73] Thus the cessation of the Jeffersonian impeachments can be credited as much to altered judicial behavior as to the failure of the Republican construction. No major Republicans disavowed the moderate construction after the Chase acquittal, nor were its proponents driven from office or public life. As the primary advocate of the extreme construction, Randolph was not so lucky; his influence with both the administration and the Congress was sharply curtailed after the Chase episode. The Federalists gained nothing politically from Chase's "success," and their influence in national politics continued to decline after the verdict. The Chase episode was not the last time that the judiciary came under political attack, but subsequent efforts at "court curbing" have generally had to rely on mechanisms other than the impeachment power.[74]

The subsequent history of federal impeachments suggests that the moderate Republican construction was both successful and stable over time. Though the Federalist construction would clearly have required rejecting the precedent of the Pickering impeachment, gross incompetence remained plausible grounds for impeachment after Chase, and no Republican regarded the Chase acquittal as a rebuke for the actions against Pickering. Moreover, federal judges have been routinely impeached and removed from office over relatively vague charges that included abuse of office and violations of public trust but no commission of indictable criminal offenses. Overall, the historical usage of "high crimes and misdemeanors" has not been limited to criminal activity, but has extended to "serious, probably persistent, misconduct that brings the office into disrepute," essentially the moderate Republican construction.[75] The success of the construction cannot be regarded as total, however. There was significant dissent in favor of an even more narrow construction at the time of the Chase impeachment, and subsequent defendants before the Senate have continued to raise limiting arguments against the impeachment power. Such a defense has been most vigorous and successful when the factual charges have seemed weakest. For example, one defender raised the indictable-crimes standard in the next impeachment, that of Judge James Peck in 1830, but the impeachment depended on a single factually dubious charge of a wrongfully imposed contempt citation.[76] In such instances, the defense has highlighted both the inability of the impeachers to meet even the modest standard established with Chase and the danger that the trial itself become a sham event obscuring the real political motivations at work. When impeachment advocates have been able to produce credible charges of abuse of office, judges have not been able to rely on an indictable-crime defense to protect them and have rarely sought its shelter.

Reconsidering the Judicial Power

In addition to construing the impeachment power, the Chase impeachment marked the culmination of several arguments over the nature of the judiciary in a federal republic. These substantive concerns, loosely collected under the rubric of judicial temperament and good behavior in office, propelled the particular attack on Chase and the justification for his removal from the bench. The impeachment served as a useful vehicle for consolidating these several grievances with the contemporary operation of the judiciary and establishing an alternative construction to temper judicial behavior. Accordingly, the impeachment prosecution went far beyond what would have been necessary to support narrow charges of legal error and judicial partiality in cases before the court. These substantive concerns have been largely ignored in the subsequent commentary on the impeachment, which has sought to determine whether a conviction was justified when considered at the level of isolated acts. This individualistic focus neglects the larger constitutional forces at work in the impeachment and ignores the Republicans' own statements that this single impeachment should have repercussions throughout the judicial branch. To the extent that historians have considered the broader implications of the Chase impeachment, they have usually adopted the Federalist assumption that Chase was an opening wedge for an attempt to subject the judiciary to political control. This sharp dichotomy between noble defenders of modern judicial independence and party-mad democrats seeking to eliminate separation of powers obscures the more complicated positions at stake in the impeachment.[77] These several substantive constructions involve three issues: depoliticizing of the judiciary, defining the power of the judge in the courtroom, and determining the meaning of judicial independence.

Depoliticizing the Judiciary

The perceived Federalist politicization of the judicial branch was one of the primary complaints carried before the electorate by the Republicans at the end of the eighteenth century. It was Chase's politicized grand jury charge that drove Jefferson to suggest the impeachment and led to the greatest number of guilty votes, and several of the additional charges were supported with references to Chase's partisanship on the bench. The willingness of the House to impeach was sufficient to signal to the judiciary, still largely controlled by Federalist appointees, that partisanship in the conduct of their official duties would not be tolerated, and federal judges rapidly and obviously moved to a more neutral position relative to "political" conflicts.[78]

The propriety of political neutrality of judges may seem fairly obvious to modern observers, but this relatively secure modern consensus is due in no small part to the early construction of judicial behavior secured by the Republicans. Before the Chase impeachment, the politicization of the federal judiciary was actively urged by some and assumed by many more. The apparent national consensus on politics during George Washington's first term was reflected in the judiciary as well, which maintained a careful distance from politically controversial issues and a limited view of its own jurisdiction. As the consensus broke down within the administration and the future Republican party began to take shape, both Washington and Adams were careful to select only committed Federalists to the bench, and judges became increasingly willing to involve themselves in political controversies on the side of the Federalist party. Even as Jefferson and the Republicans won a sweeping victory over the Federalists in 1800, the new chief justice did not hide his contempt for Jefferson, the Republicans, and their policies.[79]

The Federalists' willingness to employ the judiciary as an arm of the party was grounded in their refusal to recognize the legitimacy of any political opposition, especially the Jeffersonian Republicans. Given such an assumption, the use of the judiciary to aid in putting down an unacceptable political faction was a natural extension of government policy. The Federalists in Congress expressed their approval of a politicized judiciary through the passage of the Judiciary Act of 1801 and the Sedition Act of 1798. Although both measures were motivated in part by public-spirited concerns and contained some beneficial and needed provisions, they also represented the Federalists' understanding of the proper conduct of judges and how they were to serve the government.[80]

The Judiciary Act began with a judicial reform bill considered in the Senate as early as March 1798, but did not receive the support necessary for passage until after the outcome of the election of 1800 was certain and the Federalists knew that they would soon lose control of the elected

branches of the federal government. After the Virginia and Kentucky resolutions showed that there was serious opposition to Federalist policy, Alexander Hamilton recommended the formation of a permanent army and an
expanded federal judiciary to "disconcert the schemes of [the Constitution's] enemies." Later in the year, the soon-to-be House Speaker Theodore Sedgwick expressed the belief that the judiciary could be sent into
Republican strongholds to "overawe the licentious, and to punish the
guilty." Delay in Congress prevented passage of the bill in time to help the
Federalists in the 1800 elections, and thus a new concern came to the fore.
Judicial reform could be delayed no longer, for "the close of the Executive's authority was at hand," and "the Importance of filling these Seats
with federal characters, must be obvious." Given the "heavy gale" about to
be faced by the Federalists, who could blame them "for casting as many
anchors to hold their ship through the storm"?[81] Robert Harper, later a
Chase defender, was reported to have said that the Judiciary Act was "as
good to the party as an election."[82] The judiciary was to be the Federalists'
bastion in the federal government during the Republican interregnum.

The partisan utility of the federal judiciary had been made even plainer
with the Sedition Act. Nominally justified by the hostilities with France,
the Alien and Sedition Acts were designed to strike at Republican constituencies and operatives and were set to expire with the election.[83] While the
Alien Act placed the power to expel suspicious aliens in the hands of the
executive, the Sedition Act authorized the judiciary to engage in a partisan
persecution of Republican writers. As one Federalist paper editorialized,
"Whatever American is a friend to the present administration of the American government, is undoubtedly a true republican, a true patriot . . . Whatever American opposes the administration is an anarchist, a jacobin and
a traitor . . . It is *Patriotism* to write in favor of our government—it is
Sedition to write against it." In order to enforce this view, the Senate
defined as a federal crime any writing intending to create in the citizenry
the belief that a federal law was "hostile to Constitution, or liberties, and
happiness of the people," or defaming the president, Congress, or the
judiciary, or criticizing "their motives in any official transaction." Somewhat more generously, the House proposed only to outlaw any "false,
scandalous, and malicious writing or writings against the Government"
tending to bring any elected federal official into "contempt or disrepute;
or to excite against them . . . the hatred of the good people of the United
States," leaving it to the judiciary to enforce these provisions in a manner
consistent with the First Amendment.[84] The passage of a federal sedition

law was a direct result of the undependability of federal common law prosecutions and a Federalist distrust of state courts that could not be adequately controlled.[85]

The partisan intentions of the Federalist Congress were understood and accepted by the judiciary, and Chase's enthusiasm for persecuting Republicans made him exemplary of the partisan judiciary as a whole.[86] One Federalist editor, dissatisfied with the efforts of Judge Bushrod Washington, turned to Chase, "that sworn enemy of free democrats" who "would have made you a real example, to terrify democratic printers from insolently avowing opinions contrary to the ruling powers." Similarly, Judge Peters complained that Chase "was forever getting into some intemperate and unnecessary squabble."[87] Chase earned such a reputation, especially in the sedition trials of 1800 for which he was unwilling to wait for the Federalist prosecutorial machine to bring defendants to him, but actively initiated and aided prosecutions.[88]

Even as Marshall avoided retribution by denying himself jurisdiction in the *Marbury* case, he used the occasion to issue a lengthy rebuke to the administration, sparking criticism in the Republican press for his political *dicta*.[89] Before the election several judges actively used the Sedition Act to silence the Republican press. It was common for the judges to use their charges to the grand jury to make political statements, which the Federalists considered as part of the educative function of the judiciary. One charge by James Iredell lauding the Adams administration garnered praise from the newspapers for being "replete with sound principles and the very essence of Federalism" and containing "much *political* and *constitutional* knowledge." Although most federal judges managed to make their court appearances, Chase was not alone in actively campaigning for Adams.[90]

It soon became an article of faith among Republicans that the judiciary was a partisan institution under the Federalists. Giles wrote that the Federalists had chosen the judiciary "in which they could entrench themselves," and that that branch had been "filled with men who had manifested the most indecorous zeal in favor of the principles of the Federal party."[91] Jefferson for one needed little convincing, thinking the Federalists "more disposed to coerce [public opinion] than to court it." From the judiciary, Jefferson wrote, "the remains of federalism are to be preserved and fed from the treasury, and from that battery all the works of republicanism are to be beaten down and erased."[92] When they were under his immediate control, Jefferson was willing to remove partisan judges. He did not hesitate to withhold undelivered commissions to District of Columbia justices of the peace such as William Marbury. However, Jefferson did retain twenty-five of Adams' justice-of-the-peace appointees. Similarly, concerned about the partisan judiciary, Jefferson excepted federal attorneys and marshals from his general removal policy and immediately replaced them all with his own appointees, since "the courts being so decidedly federal & irremovable" they were "indispensably necessary as a shield to the republican part of our fellow citizens."[93]

The Republican view of the judiciary as partisan also fed into the repeal of the Judiciary Act and the condemnation of the Sedition Act. The congressional debate over the repeal of the Judiciary Act was replete with accusations that the Federalists had expanded the judiciary in order to continue to use it for partisan purposes against the Jefferson administration. Most vocally, Giles, at this point still in the House, battered his Federalist opponents with accusations that "we have seen judges, who ought to have been independent, converted into political partisans, and like Executive missionaries, pronouncing political harangues throughout the United States!" Responding to Federalist criticisms of the repeal, Randolph disavowed any effort to replace "one set of men, from whom you differ in political opinion, with a view to introducing others" who possessed a more favorable political affiliation. Any such bill, Randolph agreed, would be unconstitutional and an abuse of legislative power, but the repeal measure simply reduced the total number of judges without balancing the political interests of the remainder.[94] No Federalist congressman in 1802 ventured to defend a partisan judiciary.

The rejection of the principles contained in the Sedition Act was a key aspect of the Republican "Revolution of 1800." Along with the raising of a standing army, the persecution of the press and concurrent expansion of the judiciary marked for the Republicans the decay of constitutional principles and a threat to the maintenance of a free government. The Virginia and Kentucky resolutions were essential statements of the Republican vision, and in addition to maintaining that the Constitution established a decentralized political system, they asserted the necessity of a press free from political prosecutions. In opposing the Sedition Act, the Republicans developed a construction of the freedom of the press that completely excluded the federal government from sedition prosecutions and sharply curtailed the justifications for any such prosecutions in a republican government.[95]

The Republicans saw the hostilities with France as a cover for the Federalists' real aim, which was to stay in power. Not only were the laws directly repressive of Republicans, but, as John Nicholas declared, "to restrict the press, would be to destroy the elective principle." An unrestricted press was necessary to convey information to the electorate and foster deliberation on the current administration. Whereas the British common law allowed sedition prosecutions, such a governmental power was outmoded in the republican system established by the Constitution. The Constitution had to be construed in accord with its own political principles, not imported law. A republic had to accept political disagreement and criticism of current political officials if those officials were to be held accountable and if the government, and particularly the judiciary, were to avoid being drawn into a vortex of political oppression.[96] To these criticisms the Federalists responded directly by denying that the power to prosecute sedition would lead to abuse, for harmful speech could be readily distinguished from legitimate speech. The political speech thought necessary by the Federalists, however, was sharply limited, and they suggested that allowing free debate within Congress itself would provide all the criticism of the government that republican principles, and the Constitution, required.[97]

In Pennsylvania, the judicial abuse of the sedition power had already sparked an impeachment attempt, and excessive partisanship by another judge led to a successful impeachment. The Republicans similarly grounded the impeachment of Chase in his partisan zeal while conducting his duties.[98] The eighth article of impeachment was based explicitly on the inappropriateness of Chase's political activities on the bench. In criticizing recent state and federal laws, policies, and constitutional changes during his charge to the grand jury, Chase was "disregarding the duties and dignity of his judicial character" in order to "pervert his official right and duty to address the grand jury" with an "intemperate and inflammatory political harangue." Moreover, the particular criticisms of state laws and constitutions offered by Chase "were peculiarly indecent and unbecoming in a judge of the supreme court of the United States," and his opinion "against the government of the United States . . . even if the judicial authority were competent to their expression, on a suitable occasion and in a proper manner, were at that time and as delivered by him, highly indecent, extra-judicial, and tending to prostitute the high judicial character with which he was invested, to the low purposes of an electioneering partizan." Although the eighth was the most explicitly concerned with partisanship, other articles depended on similar complaints.[99]

Randolph concluded his opening statement for the House managers with the basis of the entire impeachment. The accumulation of evidence from all the articles would ultimately demonstrate, promised Randolph, that "through the whole tenor of his judicial conduct runs the spirit of party." It was for this mixture of official action and partisanship that Chase should be removed from office. The evidence from the Callender trial built the case that Chase's trial conduct was infected with political partisanship. While traveling by carriage to Virginia, Chase had told a fellow passenger that he was taking Callender's book to Virginia as "a proper subject for prosecution" and that "before he left Richmond, he would teach the people to distinguish between liberty and licentiousness of the press" and "would certainly punish Callender" if the state was not too "depraved" to provide a right-thinking jury. Similarly, Richmond attorney John Heath testified that he had heard Chase instruct the federal marshal that if he had "any of those creatures called democrats" on the jury, he should "strike them off." Although Heath's account seems doubtful, the Callender jury was composed exclusively of known Federalists, and the House managers clearly thought it important to their case against the justice to show the confluence of partisanship and Chase's judicial conduct, though no specific charge turned on Heath's testimony. Similarly, the House introduced testimony that Chase had directed the Delaware grand jury to a Republican press that "in times like these" displayed a "seditious temper or spirit that pervades too many of our presses [and] should be discouraged or repressed."[100]

In their summations, the House managers took care to conclude with Chase's partisanship. Peter Early expressed offense that "he who was seated on the judgment seat of the nation to execute the laws of the union" had attacked the "very government under whose authority he was sitting, and whose laws he was sworn to execute." Similarly, Campbell found that Chase had converted the "judicial power . . . into an engine of political oppression," and that the "same spirit of persecution and oppression" motivated all of Chase's actions. He was guided by "a mind inflamed by party spirit and political intolerance," the result being that the "judicial authority was prostituted to party purposes."[101]

Having established Chase's particular actions, the final speeches by the managers made the construction contained in the impeachment clear. Caesar Rodney stated forthrightly that the managers "wish to teach a lesson of instruction to future judges, that when intoxicated by the spirit of party, they may recollect the scale of power may one day turn, and preserve the scales of justice equal." The threat of impeachment was not to replace one set of partisan judges with another, but to indicate that partisanship of any kind was not to be tolerated in the courts. Because partisan passions

could infect even judges and interfere with their capacity to treat defendants and apply the laws equally, "party and party spirit should be banished
from every court." Although a judge, like anyone else, must be allowed to
hold any form of political opinion in his private capacity, "in his judicial
character" he must be scrupulously nonpolitical. Certainly, he should not
use the bench to "preach political sermons, and impose his private dogmas
on the people under the garb of administering the laws." To this degree,
the managers offered the same standard of official conduct that Jefferson
had offered to lower executive-branch officers, that private political opinions were not grounds for removal, as long as they did not affect the
officer's duties.[102]

With regard to the eighth article of impeachment, Chase's counsel offered a limited defense of Chase's conduct. Their first tactic, which was
consistent with their construction of the impeachment power itself, was to
divert attention to the partisan nature of the Congress. The impeachment
proceedings themselves were apt to fall into fits of party passion, and by
comparison the judiciary seemed relatively stable and objective. Indeed,
the threat of impeachment was likely to make judges even more partisan as
they sought to please the legislative majority. Refusing to address the
substantive construction represented by the impeachment and in the process implicitly granting the Republican point, the Federalists concluded that
the removal of a judge would imply that the law was not objective, but
dependent upon majority will.[103]

Despite these apparent concessions, the Federalists also sought positively to defend the justice's actions. Chase insisted that judges could not
be punished for their political opinions even if they engaged in seditious
speech. The independence of the judicial branch was too important to
place judges at risk for their political views. In any case, it was a judge's
prerogative and duty as a high public officer to endeavor "to convince the
public that [a law] is improper," and such political debate should never be
restricted. Chase claimed the right to address the grand jury in any manner
he wished, as a "right sanctioned by the universal practice of this country,
and by acquiescence of its various legislative authorities." In other words,
the construction of judicial behavior was already complete, and the judge's
role as political actor was established. Chase's attorneys likewise pointed to
the persistent practice of the Federalist judiciary as justifying not only
Chase's own grand jury charge, but even active electioneering. A capacity
to engage in political activity might even be necessary to sustaining federal
policy in the face of opposition.[104]

Ultimately, the Federalists could not sustain a persuasive defense of

Chase's actions. Chase's advocates wavered among several conflicting responses to the charge of judicial partisanship, variously denying it as untrue, dismissing it as trivial, and defending it as appropriate. When arguing over the scope of the impeachment power, the Federalists hoped to contrast the partisanship of Congress with the nonpolitical nature of the judiciary. But the evidence of Chase's own actions on the bench undermined the assumptions of that argument. In the end, the justice's allies seemed to claim that judicial partisanship was tolerable precisely because it was not very significant, the harmless affectation of an old patriot. This was an inherently weak defense, and it was incapable of addressing the central Republican charge: an innocuous judicial tradition of "educating" the citizenry had taken a distinctly dangerous turn with the partisan prosecutions and agitation of the Adams-era judiciary.

The Republicans successfully held Chase up as an exemplar of the partisan judiciary. The impeachment provided an opportunity not only to reconstruct the norms of judicial behavior, but also to conclude the delegitimation of the federal sedition power that the quiet expiration of the Sedition Act had not allowed. In order to achieve this goal, it was not necessary to remove Chase from the bench. The strong vote by the Senate against Chase, especially on the eighth article, combined with the virtual Federalist admission of the inappropriateness of future judicial politicking, sent the necessary signal to the judicial branch, which was the true objective of the trial. Subsequently, Republicans hoped that the acquittal itself would "have a tendency to mitigate the irritation of party spirit." Though Chase was not removed for behavior "sanctioned by the practice of other judges," future conduct of a like nature was nonetheless effectively proscribed. Chase himself "never again actively participated in politics," and a subsequent jury charge was described as "short and pertinent . . . pointed, modest and well applied."[105]

The more moderate Marshall represented the future of Federalist judges. Marshall's actions were undoubtedly ideological, but they were not "political" in the partisan sense of Chase's. Marshall strained to distinguish between law and politics, even as he actively defended his understanding of the fundamental law from the bench and in the press. Marshall's jurisprudence carefully construed judicial questions as specifically legal, even as the law itself drew upon basic political principles of right. In an extreme but symbolic gesture, the chief justice pointedly refused even to vote in presidential elections. The postimpeachment judiciary could debate questions of constitutional and legal meaning, but it could not engage in day-to-day partisan political contests.[106] One result of this change was to secure certain ideological positions as superficially "nonpolitical," but it also reduced the justifications available for politicizing the criminal law.[107]

Even as the Republican construction led to depoliticization of the judicial branch, so the other branches conformed to that construction by largely refusing to draw the judiciary into a partisan political struggle, at least until the rise of modern warfare and radical political philosophies once again challenged that construction.[108] The construction was concerned primarily with official conduct. Individual judges maintained friendships and informal ties with other political actors, but the impeachment shifted understandings to recognize a boundary between their official duties and their private lives, forcing judges to curb their behavior and to offer explanations for apparent conflicts. The elimination of partisanship did not necessarily exclude judges from all "political" activities. Certain actions in the public sphere, such as consideration of institutional features of the judiciary itself, have been regarded as consistent with the judicial station, though the boundaries between the public and the partisan required additional elaboration.[109] John Taylor of South Carolina, for example, wrote to Justice William Johnson during the nullification controversy that it would be improper for a sitting judge to "come and mix in the common fight," especially given the likelihood of future litigation.[110] Participation in political conventions would be inappropriate to the extent that it impinged on official duties. Such standards did not prevent judges from hosting political discussions in their homes or even from entertaining presidential ambitions, as long as such activities were not reflected on the bench.[111] Chief Justice Roger Taney maintained political correspondence but assured Andrew Jackson that "since I have been on the Bench I have abstained from taking part in political movements." Justice John Catron found it necessary to explain "on the Judgeship score" why it was acceptable for him to allow his old friend and presidential candidate James Polk to stay in the former's Nashville home and meet political supporters there.[112] Likewise, twentieth-century judges have been willing to offer private political advice to their friends and have been intermittently active on policy matters relating to the judiciary itself, such as new appointments and institutional structure.[113] The depoliticization of the judiciary required "only" its institutional removal from partisan conflicts and its disentanglement from administration politics.

The opprobrium attached to judicial partisanship was not reduced by the general acceptance of the legitimacy of parties and party government.[114] Undoubtedly, the power of the charges against Chase was enhanced by the republican distrust of the "spirit of party" wherever found. Nonetheless, the construction of the judiciary was institutionally specific, and thus relatively durable even against general environmental changes. The nature of the impeachment debates also suggests that more was at stake than a confirmation of generic antiparty ideology. Indeed, one possible implication of a general antipathy to party politics was the judicial prosecution of Republican partisans. Chase was not only accused of being partisan; he was also regarded as more broadly political. He not only aligned the judiciary with a corrupt faction of power-seekers; he also involved the courts in controversies toward which the judiciary should have remained scrupulously neutral. Similarly, Chase was charged with having erased the distinction between his private political opinions and his public administrative function. The Republicans did not denounce Chase's politics as illegitimate, but rather insisted that his office precluded his acting on those political views. The construction of the nonpartisan judiciary was distinct from the maintenance of consensus politics.

Defining the Power of the Judge in the Courtroom

The anti-Federalists had been deeply concerned about how criminal trials would be conducted under the proposed federal government. The original constitutional text had done little to define the range of the federal criminal law, criminal jurisdiction of the federal courts, and how those courts would actually operate. Unlike those provided for in many state constitutions, the federal judiciary was largely isolated from the people. Moreover, the federal marshals and attorneys who would be instrumental in operating the federal criminal justice system were not directly accountable to the people. The lack of provision for a federal jury system only seemed to confirm the new government's probable isolation from the people. In order to assuage such concerns, criminal justice guarantees were included in several of the first amendments, including a right to a jury trial, a right to a public trial, protection against self-incrimination, and a right to counsel.[115] Though giving some representation to the people in the courtroom, it remained to be decided just how extensive these inroads on judicial authority were to be. The Chase impeachment solidified aspects of the anti-Federalist construction of the meaning of those constitutional guarantees, securing the existence of a vibrant adversarial process in the criminal courts.

The Anglo-American tradition of adversarial, coordinated proceedings mixing both fact and law differed markedly from the more centralized, hierarchical, and administrative judicial style developing on the Continent. The American counterrevolutionary shift, represented by the ratification of the Constitution, toward a more centralized, distant authority at least suggested the possibility of a movement toward a more bureaucratic judicial system. Indeed, the Judiciary Act of 1801 was a significant step toward a more rationalized and active federal judiciary, with a clear hierarchical structure and systemic integrity. The repeal of the Judiciary Act as an unnecessary burden on the taxpayers stifled the capacity of the federal judiciary to assert itself fully and marked a Republican effort to prevent it from developing along a path independent of the state judicial systems.[116] The Chase impeachment represented the culmination of the Republican construction of the federal judiciary as a decentralized, institutionally open, and adversarial system.

Samuel Chase imported the legal and judicial habits developed in his home state into the federal judiciary. Maryland practice recognized a sharper division between law and fact and gave the judge much greater control over the former than in many other states, including Pennsylvania and Virginia, where he rode circuit in 1800. Chase developed a firm conviction that both attorneys and public owed deference to a judge sitting on the bench. The British "Court" model of the operation of the judiciary as a mechanism for maintaining government control over an unruly populace and sustaining a balance among governmental orders meshed well with Chase's own High Federalist beliefs that the alternative to firm order was social chaos.[117]

Chase was not alone in his belief in the need for popular deference to judges. Chief Justice Thomas McKean of Pennsylvania had in 1788 held a printer in contempt for his "address to the public" on the judge's handling of a case, contending that "assertions and imputations of this kind are certainly calculated to defeat and discredit the administration of justice." Judges could be "neither corrupted by favor to swerve from, nor influenced by fear to desert their duty," and public criticisms of their behavior were designed to influence justice in exactly these ways. The judge warned the printer that either "you shall bend to the law, or the law shall bend to you, [and] it is our duty to determine that the former shall be the case."[118] Federalist congressmen supported this view in defending the Sedition Act, on the grounds that political matters should be discussed only by those capable of proper deliberation. Federal judges' practice of delivering political sermons to grand juries was part of this effort to educate the public in proper political opinion, and reflected the elitist principles underlying the Federalist understanding of government.[119]

Such elitism extended beyond judicial politics to the conduct of legal affairs. Before the reforms of Fox's Libel Act in 1792, British judges' charges to juries excluded all questions of law, and even on the determination of the intent of the writer, the judge frequently commented to the jury on the appropriate decision. Some Federalist congressmen opposed giving juries the right to decide questions of law in sedition trials, for fear that doing so would allow the jury to determine the relevant law, that is, whether the Sedition Act was consistent with the Constitution. Justice William Paterson acted to quash this defense in the very first sedition trial, when Congressman Matthew Lyon attempted to argue for jury nullification in his trial.[120] The jury's involvement in the law was to be kept to a minimum.

Chase's own regard for juries, and the public that they represented, exemplified this position. For Chase, the adversarial process in the courtroom held little significance. Rather than relying on the attorneys before the court to bring to light the truth for the jury's deliberation, Chase thought it proper for the judge to intervene actively to make the proper result clear for the jury. Thus, Chase did not hesitate to interrupt to point out to the jury an added support for the prosecutor's case in Fries's treason trial. Similarly, when the prosecutor hesitated to deliver his closing for the jury in the absence of a defense attorney, Chase declared that if the prosecutor was unwilling to proceed the justice would apply the law to the facts for him.[121] In Virginia, Chase granted prosecutorial immunity to witnesses, without suggestion from or consultation with the federal prosecutor. The justice took a strong role in filtering the evidence presented to the jury, examining defense witnesses for relevancy, and requiring defense questions in writing in order to prevent the defense from attempting to "deceive the people." Chase was equally cavalier about even this limited role of defense attorneys, constantly interrupting their arguments with his disagreements. Upon driving the attorneys from the bar, he assured Fries that the "court will be your counsel, and will do you as much justice as those who were your counsel."[122]

Such a view of the dispensability of the adversarial process also left little role for the jury, which for Chase seemed primarily to invite prejudice, passion, and confusion into the courtroom. Not only was he active in excluding witnesses that might serve to confuse the jury, but he was equally concerned with preventing defense attorneys from arguing disputed points of law before the jury. For Chase, allowing the jury to determine the law would be equivalent to subjecting the law to politics, and thus freeing the populace from the constraining influence of law. Similarly, it was the exclusive role of the judge to interpret the Constitution, and the jury and Congress were equally excluded from any place in determining constitutional meaning. Even in the narrow space left for jury action, of applying the law to the facts, Chase felt compelled to offer his own conclusions for the jury's consideration. In delivering his jury charge, Chase informed them that with the same law and facts, a previous jury had already convicted Fries of treason. In addressing the Cooper jury, after having already denounced Cooper for his malicious intent in publishing criticisms of Adams so as to "mislead the ignorant, and inflame their minds . . . and to influence their votes on the next election," Chase assured the jury that it was "not necessary for me to go more minutely into an investigation of the defense."[123]

Chase defended his actions before the Senate in the name of administrative efficiency, legal certainty, and institutional prerogative. Chase avowed that in delivering a prewritten opinion disallowing the defense's legal arguments in the Fries case, he was primarily hoping to save time given a busy court docket. Time could be so readily saved, however, by the fact that the law could be and had been settled, and "it is the duty of every court in this country . . . to guard the jury against erroneous impressions respecting the laws of the land." To disallow the defense from challenging the judge's interpretation of the constitutional definition of treason was simply to prevent "an improper attempt, to mislead the jury in a matter of law." After all, attorneys had every incentive to mislead, and only the judge had an incentive to seek the truth, and therefore should maintain a tight rein on the adversarial process.[124]

Unlike the jury, the judge was well trained in the law, and this professional expertise was essential to determine the law. Moreover, the judge gained his position by being a particularly skilled attorney, and thus could hardly be expected to require the arguments of the attorneys at the bar to form an opinion on the law. A judge should not tolerate attorneys "impudently and insolently" suggesting that the judge had rendered an "erroneous opinion." By virtue of their training and institutional position, judges were also beyond partisanship and passion. Far from needing a jury to check such an incorruptible judge, it was the judge alone who provided the necessary counterpoint to the popular excesses of republican government. Such Herculean judges were particularly necessary in a republic to protect the people from the "violence of their own passions," their "vague and changing opinions," and their "political prejudice."[125]

In emphasizing the legal training of judges and contrasting such training with the wild passions of juries and legislatures, Chase's attorneys hoped to highlight a point that was useful to constructing both the impeachment and the judicial power. The law, unlike politics, was certain and easily determined by those trained to do so. There was neither room nor necessity for inviting public scrutiny or participation in the determination of law, or in judging its violators. In the context of the courtroom, this meant carefully circumscribing the role of the jury and enlarging the role of the judge. If the facts in the cases of Fries or Callender were not in dispute, rather than attempting to argue over the law, the defendants should have simply thrown themselves on the mercy of the court. It was "subversive of the order of things" to allow such pseudo-disputes before a jury, who could not be trusted to recognize or respect the clear contours of the law. In fact it was an error to regard the jury as having any role in determining the law at all. The jury must presume the existence of a clear and settled law, and only incidentally interpreted it in applying the law to the facts. The jury had no right to render a verdict contradicting the determination of the court.[126]

For the Republican House managers, it was arrogance to imagine that the law was ever completely closed. Although proper judgments could be made as to whether a law had been violated, such judgments depended less on extensive legal learning than on sound intelligence and common sense. This was especially true for constitutional meaning. Though Chase had cut off defense arguments over the meaning of the constitutional definition of treason and the extent of congressional power to regulate speech, the Republicans asserted that the Constitution could never be closed off from further investigation. The value of a written constitution was in its ability to be easily seen and to resist previous bad interpretations attributed to it. Though a string of judicial interpretations might be clear, constitutional meaning was not equivalent to these glosses, and the court should always be available to hear reargument and criticism of its precedents.[127]

The uncertainty of the law, as well as the inadequacy of legal training and institutional independence in guaranteeing virtue, required jury participation in the determination of the law, especially when a defendant's life and liberty were at issue. The judge too could be subject to party passion and plain error in judgment. Given such human failings, the judge could not be raised up to an unimpeachable position, even in the context of the courtroom. The jury served as a useful check on judicial excess and discretion. The broader public too could serve such a role, as Thomas Cooper argued in publishing his account of his own sedition trial. The court, Cooper contended, must be perfectly impartial in its charge to the jury, allowing the jurors to make up their own minds in accord with the arguments of counsel. If the judge erred in the course of a trial, not only might he be corrected in the courtroom, but he could also be brought "before the more solemn tribunal of the Public" for rebuke and correction. Chase, Randolph charged, relied upon an outdated understanding of the judicial role, appealing to such foreign precedents as the Star Chamber to justify his actions. The inappropriateness of such conceptions in a republic should be obvious; there could be no room for courts "assuming to themselves a more than papal infallibility" by claiming the right to engage in "the exclusive exposition and construction of the constitutions" and the law more broadly. Contrary to Federalist claims, relying on individual men in unaccountable positions opened the law up to an "ocean of uncertainty and contestation." In the long run, the jury and the public could be counted on to bring stability to the law.[128]

Far from simply excluding immaterial evidence and giving jurors appropriate advice on the law, the managers contended, Chase had subverted the nature of a jury trial. It was in fact a recent republican advance that gave juries adequate discretion over law and fact and trial lawyers sufficient latitude to contest the charges faced by the defendant. Yet the judge had taken it upon "*himself* substantially to decide the case by prejudging the law thereto." In doing so, "all of the privileges and all the benefits of that institution were swept at once from an American court of justice and scarcely the external form preserved. The law was predetermined by the judge, and the accused was debarred from pleading it to the jury. Of what avail is it, sirs, that the jury should be made judges of law and fact, when the law is not permitted to be expounded to them?" The judge must allow great scope to the attorneys to present all the arguments they thought relevant to trying the case. In such a full adversarial proceeding, the jury trial became a meaningful mechanism for community determination of the appropriateness of applying criminal penalties to the accused. The jury did not need to be protected from the attorneys at bar, for the adversarial proceedings themselves and the common sense of the jury were sufficient to ensure justice.[129]

The construction that emerged from the impeachment tended to be a compromise of the two positions urged by Chase and the House managers. After the political eighth article, the three articles of impeachment to receive the most guilty votes were those most closely connected with complaints about judicial interference with the workings of an adversarial, jury trial. The meaning of these votes was somewhat less clear than on the eighth article, for the Federalists gave little ground on the construction of the judicial role in the courtroom and raised several serious challenges to the factual evidence presented to support those articles. Outside the proceedings, however, other judges had not followed Chase as far down the road to a more administrative courtroom. In the Fries trial, which elicited the most complaints from the Republicans for Chase's conduct toward counsel and jury, Judge Peters had warned Chase against attempting to constrain the defense by issuing a prewritten opinion on the law of treason and against treating the Philadelphia bar with such high-handed disdain. The reaction of Fries's attorneys forced Chase to moderate his position, though grudgingly. Though Chase claimed to be following the precedent set in the first Fries trial, he actually had allowed much less discretion to the jury than earlier judges reluctantly had in that case and others.[130] The meaning of a federal jury trial was still unsettled at the time the Republicans came to power, and Chase was on the leading edge of adopting a more conservative position relative to the bar and the public.

Although the transition was not as sharp as with some other constructions, the Chase impeachment, combined with the repeal of the Judiciary and Sedition Acts and the division of power between a Republican executive and a Federalist judiciary, constrained judges from taking upon themselves the role of prosecutor and jury in order to initiate and determine prosecutions. The appropriate role of the judge in the courtroom evolved throughout the nineteenth century, especially in the states, where institutional forms were subject to greater experimentation and where trials were much more common and significant. The British common law inheritance gave substantial freedom to early American judges to comment on the facts of the case. At the state level, such freedom was gradually constrained by statute. At the federal level, such a prerogative fed fears of a distant and unaccountable judiciary, but judicial discretion was not so constrained and fixed in law. The Chase impeachment served as a sharp rebuke to the federal judiciary and as a warning against future abuse of the judge's position. In response, federal judges, including Chase himself, effectively surrendered the power to advise the jury on the proper application of the law to the evidence. The norms of judicial behavior militated against the judge's involvement in the realm of "facts," breaking from the common and accepted practice of the Federalist era.

Even as judges lost their authority to speak on the facts of a case, they solidified their roles in interpreting the written law and in limiting juries to the application of law. As the Republicans recognized, there was a certain value in the uniformity of law, and this division of power between judge and jury allowed public participation in protecting defendants against state power, but channeled that discretion within a known law. Federal judges occasionally told juries that they had the right to determine both the law and the facts of the case, as some Republicans desired, but the practice declined rapidly. Instead, juries were to determine the law only in applying it to the facts of a given case. The Republican curtailment of federal criminal prosecutions for sedition and treason reduced concern over this particular judicial practice. This expansion of the judge's authority to determine the law, however, depended on the avoidance of such partisan bias and "abuse" as Chase had displayed.[131] Judicial determination of the law was not to be accompanied by the extreme public deference to judges that Chase demanded. The overall result was a distinct democratization of the federal judiciary, but also a rejection of the wide-open legal forum envisioned by Republicans in their more extreme moments. The judge was to take on the role of an umpire in the courtroom, but was to shed any pretensions of being an active participant in the trial or the arbiter of its results.[132]

Determining the Meaning of Judicial Independence

The final construction pressed by the Republicans through the Chase impeachment concerned the nature of the judiciary in a system of separated powers. The Chase impeachment is perhaps most remembered as a battle over the independence of the judiciary, with the justice's acquittal preventing the judiciary from becoming pawns of the current political majority. The actual construction at issue was more complicated. Although there was a minority faction urging such an extreme rejection of judicial independence, the primary dispute concerned the nature of the independence appropriate to a judiciary in a republic and the terms under which such independence could be maintained.

The attempted removal of Justice Chase was the final step in a series of moves that defined the appropriate extent of judicial independence under the Constitution. The common reference to "judicial independence" begged two questions that the construction attempted to answer: independence from whom and independence for what? The answers to these questions were interrelated. With the advantage of knowing that the federal bench was solidly packed with allies, the Federalists mounted a defensive construction of the judicial power that asserted that judges should be viewed as independent of all other political institutions, particularly the legislature and, by implication, the people. For Chase and the Federalists, the very purpose of the judiciary was to provide a stable force to resist popular pressures. The judiciary was to be not only independent of the people, but also necessarily somewhat antagonistic to them.

Upon the repeal of the Judiciary Act, Chase emphasized the protections of judicial tenure to Marshall, arguing that the object of those protections was to preserve "Judges, and their Offices . . . independent of the Legislature." The Constitution was one of limited powers, and it was clear "that the *limitations* of the power of Congress can only be preserved by the *Judicial* power." Chase expressed similar sentiments, in more hyperbolic form, to the Baltimore grand jury, contending that the "independence of the national judiciary is already shaken to its foundation," and this state of affairs threatened that the nation would "sink into a mobocracy."[133]

Chase was echoing the opinions widely held by High Federalists and developed during earlier controversies. In urging the passage of the Judiciary Act, one Federalist paper warned that "If free government can ever be maintained without a *standing army* it can only be effected by a firm, independent, and extensive Judiciary." The alternative to an expanded federal bench was the continued reliance on state judges, who not only were more subject to legislative removal but, more importantly, were often hostile to Federalist initiatives. The Federalists argued for a firm and extensive judiciary filled "with federal characters." It was an error, Congressman James Bayard contended, "to leave too much power in the hands of men not immediately under the control of the government, nor liable to impeachment in case of misuse of that power."[134]

Emphasizing the need for an aristocratic element in every political system, Chase's defenders developed the strong claim that "the independence of judges were more essentially important" in a republic than in a monarchy. A republic was in particular need of a stabilizing force to uphold permanent principles and to guard the people from themselves, "to protect them from the violence of their own passions." The unelected judiciary, on the other hand, matched the Federalist conception of law itself. An independent judiciary guaranteed stability, certainty, skill, and virtue. These characteristics required that the judiciary be given broad and exclusive powers to construe constitutional meaning, that trial judges dominate the courtroom over juries and attorneys, and that all judges be free from public questioning of their actions.[135]

At the opposite extreme was the radical democratic position often attributed to the Republicans generally, that the judiciary was completely dependent on the legislative will. William Giles, according to John Quincy Adams, exemplified this approach. In appealing to another senator during the Chase impeachment, Giles "treated with the utmost contempt the idea of an *independent* judiciary—said there was not a word about such an independence in the Constitution, and that their pretensions to it were nothing more nor less than an attempt to establish an aristocratic despotism in themselves."[136] Without the notion of an independent judiciary embedded in the constitutional delegation of the judicial power, Congress' powers over the judiciary, such as impeachments and control over appellate jurisdiction, could be exercised without constraint. In defending the repeal of the Judiciary Act, some Republicans had gone so far as to denounce judicial review on these grounds. Mirroring the Federalist claim, they advocated a legislative supremacy in which the "Legislature have the exclusive right to interpret the Constitution in what regards the law-making power, and the Judges are bound to execute the laws they make." The people judged the public good through their elected representatives; thus, the judiciary must give way to the legislature when the two come into conflict.[137]

This radical Republican view informed the more general Republican construction, but did not constitute it. The Republicans also offered a more moderate construction of the judicial power that made a place for an independent judiciary, but put conditions on that independence. Primary among these conditions were the political neutrality of the judiciary (that is, "good behavior" as discussed above) and the separation of the judiciary from the executive branch. It was this moderate construction, not the Federalist or the radical Republican constructions, that was achieved through the Chase impeachment.

Dissatisfaction with the Constitution as defined by the Federalists led some to develop the true principles of republican government that ought to guide a new administration. John Taylor wrote Jefferson that constitutional amendments might be necessary to extend the suffrage, shorten the tenure of federal offices, and require the rotation of officers. Even short of an amendment, accountability in office was the guiding principle of the Republican construction of existing constitutional terms. During the Judiciary Act controversy, Taylor applied his logic specifically to the judiciary, arguing that judicial tenure was designed to serve the "public interest." Far from giving individual judges a special claim to their offices, the Constitution indicated that judges should be isolated from partisan political pressures and maintained in office during good behavior in order to secure "the honesty of Judges" and "counteract the influence" of the executive.[138]

Jefferson was sympathetic to these views, and though a mechanism for easy removal would have required changing the constitutional text, he agreed that such republican principles should determine the construction of the existing text. He later wrote that "Independence can be trusted nowhere but with the people in mass. They are inherently independent of all but moral law." Thus, any claims of judicial independence must be tempered by the recognition that all branches of government were ultimately responsible to the people. While recognizing that judges were not easily removable, he argued that they constituted a coordinate branch only and that their independence was always qualified.[139] Impeachment was to be regarded as a mechanism not for removing judges at the will of the legislature, but for holding judges accountable to the people. The very purpose of the degree of independence that judges did possess was to remove them from the partisan political sphere. To the extent that judges stepped into that sphere, they had subverted the purpose of independence and forfeited their claim to it. As the Richmond *Enquirer* noted after Chase's acquittal, the Republicans desired "a restricted but not a dependent Judiciary."[140]

Such an understanding of judicial independence was consistent with the administration's handling of federal offices generally. The Constitution includes judges with "all other Officers of the United States" for purposes of their method of appointment and removal by impeachment.[141] Like that of judges, the tenure of executive officers has been the subject of some dispute, and a "good behavior" standard has often been seen as appropriate for executive as well as judicial officers. Jefferson was particularly concerned with replacing all federal prosecutors and marshals in order to provide a buffer between the citizenry and the more independent Federalist judiciary. Nonetheless, Jefferson did not regard all executive officers as removable at will. Only officers "guilty of *official* malconduct are proper subjects of removal," and that criterion included those who allowed their private political opinions to interfere with the conduct of their offices. In the very letter in which Jefferson called Nicholson's attention to Chase's "seditious and official attack," he noted that some officials in the executive branch had been removed for "active and bitter opposition to the order of things which the public will had established." In the Republican view, it was a federal officer's duty to distinguish between his private partisan opinions and his official conduct, and to ensure that the latter was consistent with the expressed public will. Although judicial officers were more difficult to remove, the justification for their tenure of office was the same as that of other officers.[142]

The House managers applied such Jeffersonian reasoning to the judiciary. Far from seeking to make judges mere pawns of the legislature, as the Federalists contended, the Republicans insisted that they favored the "rational independence of the judiciary." Such "rational independence" was to be distinguished, however, from the "inviolability of judges," who "like a spoiled child" could not be questioned or held accountable for their actions. Accountability to the people was the touchstone of republican constitutionalism and extended to judges as well as other public officials. The particular mechanism for such accountability was strictly secondary to the larger principle. As the third constitutional branch of government, the judiciary was neither subordinate to the legislature, as Giles maintained, nor superior to it, as Chase implied, but equal and coordinate.[143]

If judges were to remain free from legislative interference, however, neither could they be pawns of the executive branch. The Federalist construction of the independent judiciary emphasized the necessity of insulating the judiciary from popular pressures conveyed through the legislative branch. The mingling of executive and judicial functions was not merely tolerated, but actively encouraged by the Federalists. Because the purpose of judicial independence was to provide a check on the people, there was little necessity of separating the two less popular branches of government. The Republicans, on the other hand, saw the government as a threat to the people, not vice versa. As such, the impartial administration of justice required a strict separation between executive and judicial functions in order to prevent political prosecutions. Jefferson's wholesale replacement of federal prosecutors and marshals was designed to disentangle the two branches by breaking up the close relationship between Federalist judges and prosecutors, and the Chase impeachment served to highlight the dangers of executive corruption of the judicial branch.

The Republican press had been highly critical of the close connection between the Federalist administration and the judicial branch. The press connected Chase's absence from the bench while campaigning for Adams to the absence of Chief Justice Oliver Ellsworth, whom the president had sent on a diplomatic mission to France. Ellsworth's predecessor, John Jay, had been sent as special envoy to England by President Washington, and did not resign his seat on the Court until elected to the governorship of

New York. Similarly, Ellsworth's replacement, John Marshall, continued to serve as Adams' secretary of state after taking up his new duties as chief justice. Such dual appointments severely undermined claims to judicial independence, at least from the executive branch, and Jefferson complained that the president "has been able to draw into this vortex the Judiciary branch . . . and by their expectancy of sharing the other offices in the Executive gift to make them auxiliary to the Executive in all its views."[144] Though Chase had not held executive office during his tenure on the bench, he exemplified the danger of a close connection between the executive and judicial branches. The justice had clearly identified himself with the Federalist administration. To the Republicans, he had claimed to be "almost beyond the reach of the people, though not beyond the immediate power and influence of the executive."[145]

The full establishment of republican separation of powers and "rational independence," however, also required the elimination of the federal common law of crimes. The early sedition prosecutions typified the perceived abuses inherent in the criminal common law. Not only did such prosecutions tend to entangle the judiciary with the executive as prosecutor and judge were drawn together to initiate, define, and execute the criminal prosecutions, but they also placed judges in the role of legislators in an area directly affecting personal liberty. Though Chase was not the best choice for highlighting the common law issue, since he had been slow to accept a federal common law and had not overseen any common law sedition prosecutions, his impeachment was the one opportunity for the Republicans to express their full construction of the federal judicial power.

The Federalist construction of a federal common law of crimes was clear and persistent. The justices had separately upheld common law prosecutions as natural extensions of political sovereignty. Federalist prosecutors did not hesitate to initiate common law prosecutions, and the Sedition Act was not passed until the Federalists doubted the future successes of such prosecutions before juries. Federalist congressmen agreed on the necessity of a federal criminal common law and thought a common law jurisdiction was inherent in the judicial power granted in Article III.[146]

The Federalist commitment to the common law permeated the defense of Chase. Chase's conduct in the treason and sedition trials of 1800 demonstrated the common law approach, as he had assumed a strong role for the judge in defining the law and determining relevant precedent. Far from being the result of political expression, Chase contended that the law was fixed and certain, but required technical legal skills in order to be discovered. Allowing the jury a role in determining the law in a case, the legislature a role in defining the meaning of treason, or the Senate a role in applying political standards to the impeachment all shared in the same error—that of introducing politics and uncertainty into an area that required only legal training in the case law of Britain.[147]

Though the primary attack on the common law was conducted in the states, the Republicans were also antagonistic to the relatively modest use of the criminal common law by the federal bench. Any abuses under the Sedition Act were equally attributable to the encroachment of the common law into the federal judicial system. Both represented the introduction of foreign principles into a republican political system, removing the lawmaking power from popular control, undermining the elective principle, and expanding the reach of the national government. The Chase impeachment served as the Republicans' instrument for decisively rejecting any future common law prosecutions, and thus fulfilled the terms of the judicial power delegated under the Constitution.[148]

The success of this particular construction was undoubtedly aided by the Republicans' ability to support it negatively by refraining from appointing any judges to executive posts or from initiating any common law prosecutions. Nonetheless, the positive act of impeaching a justice set the terms for future understandings of judicial independence. The impeachment also allowed the more moderate Republican construction to establish itself against both the Federalist vision and the extreme Republican alternative. If judges were to be held accountable to the people and freed from executive influence, they were also to be made independent of legislative interference. In contrast to the articles of impeachment alleging Chase's excessive partisanship and prosecutorial involvement, the Senate decisively rejected the articles that implied a congressional role in monitoring the courts for legal errors.[149]

Despite his ambivalence about the nature of judicial independence, Randolph, along with the other managers, was unwilling to assert a strong view of the impeachment power that would have undercut judicial independence completely. Trapped between their concern for changing constitutional principles and their immediate need to convict an individual judge, the managers personalized the conflict in such a way as to render further impeachments difficult. While making clear the behavior that they regarded as unacceptable, the Republicans also gave political cover to other individual judges, by making such judges as Peters and Griffin mere silent partners in Chase's misconduct and even cautiously approving of others such as Marshall. That the inadequacy of the extreme Republican construction lay with its content and not just with its consistency with the existing constitutional text is demonstrated by the fate of Randolph's effort to transform his construction into an act of creation. Immediately after the Senate's acquittal of Chase, Randolph introduced into the House a constitutional amendment allowing removal by address, but the administration disapproved of the measure, and the House quashed it by a large majority.[150]

The "rational independence" of the judiciary urged by the Republicans secured for the judiciary a separate position within the division of powers. The possibility of impeachment for abuse of office hovered over the judiciary as a reminder of its limited independence. Moreover, the depoliticization of the judiciary was indicative of the new terms under which the judicial power was to be exercised. Judicial independence was grounded in the judiciary's avoidance of partisan politics and was to be maintained not as a check on the people, but as a coordinate branch of government playing a primarily "legal" role. The implications of this redefinition were sweeping, affecting not only the grounds for impeachment but also other methods of constraining the judiciary and of the judiciary's own conception of its appropriate function. The judiciary was not to serve as the representative of an elite interest against the people, but as a specialized functionary within a popular government.[151] Even as judges were brought a step closer to the people, they were pushed further from the executive. The Republican administrations took on a more adversarial role relative to the still-Federalist judiciary, a role that was largely maintained even as judicial personnel turned over. The fairly regular practice of appointing judges to executive posts was substantially modified, restricting the extrajudicial activities of judges to informal contacts or relatively nonpartisan roles, such as Justice Robert Jackson's service as Nuremberg prosecutor, Chief Justice Earl Warren's chairmanship of the Kennedy assassination investigation, and several justices' service on the 1877 commission to resolve the disputed presidential election.[152] Judges were not to be independent of the people, but they could not be servants of either of the other two branches of government.

The Supreme Court itself made explicit the success of the Republican construction against a federal common law of crimes. In 1812 the Court for the first time addressed the issue of whether a federal criminal common law existed. Before briefly summarizing the substantive case against such a common law jurisdiction, Justice William Johnson noted that the issue was "long since settled in public opinion." Earlier political action had forced the "general acquiescence of legal men" and demonstrated the "prevalence of opinion" on the matter. The definition of "crimes against the state" was essentially a legislative power, and the constitutional delegation of the judicial power did not extend to such an authority.[153] If the separation of powers implied that judges could not be reduced to instruments of legislative or executive policy, it also limited the sphere of judicial activity and restricted judges from assuming a lawmaking function.

Conclusion

The Chase impeachment centered on two different general constructions, procedural and substantive. Stretching the bounds of both constitutional language and previous federal experience, the Republicans who sought to remove Justice Chase were forced to construct the impeachment power on favorable and relatively broad terms. In doing so, they established a power that allowed the removal of judges for more than narrowly criminal conduct, but not for simple political expediency. The newly constructed impeachment power extended to the abuse of public office in accord with an essentially political standard, but protected federal officers from removal by impeachment for mere technical errors in the conduct of their office, for private political sentiments, or simply for the purpose of creating vacancies.

In addition to defining the instrument of their attack on Chase, the Republicans initiated several substantive constructions of the nature of the judicial power itself. These substantive constructions not only indicated the basis for the desired removal of a single judge, but also served notice on the judicial branch as a whole that the constitutional nature of the judicial office was being redefined. To this degree, the impeachment was as much prospective as retrospective, sparked by the abuses of the past to construct new principles to govern the future. The substantive effects of the impeachment, therefore, were multiple. The Republicans succeeded in changing expectations of what constituted proper judicial behavior, thereby excluding overt partisan political activity. This effort at specifying proper judicial temperament also served to delegitimate the Sedition Act as co-opting the judiciary for the purpose of political persecution. Somewhat less successfully, the Republicans sought to restructure the role of the judge in the courtroom, so as to secure an open adversarial process and to expand the role of the jury. While this effort did halt a drift toward a more centralized, elitist, administrative criminal justice system, it contributed to a new compromise that ensured the right to counsel and a jury trial, but did so by clarifying the judge's role as a determiner of law, not as a trier of fact. Finally, the Republicans defined the "rational independence" of the judiciary that insisted that judges were separate from the normal operations of either the legislature or the executive, but were nonetheless representatives of and responsible to the people.

Randolph and the Republicans were frustrated in part by the tools they had chosen for making their construction. The use of the impeachment power created procedural diversions that absorbed the political energy available to make the desired substantive constructions. Even so, impeachment offered a mechanism by which the political stakes could be consolidated and quickly raised as attention was focused on a series of substantive constructions centering on the nature of the federal judiciary. Furthermore, the procedural device of impeachment highlighted many of the same themes developed in the substantive arguments. The very choice of the impeachment device emphasized the need for maintaining the accountability of all government officials and an acknowledgment that the popular branch of the government held the means for inquiring into and checking the activities of all others. The Republican arguments defending a relatively broad impeachment power melded easily with their arguments advocating a limited independence for the judiciary and the necessity of popular involvement in the law.

In addition to absorbing political capital as a relatively controversial and underdetermined constitutional weapon, the impeachment power also had the tendency of pitching constitutional debate at a personal level. By charging a single justice with high crimes and misdemeanors, the Republicans could document specific problems with current judicial behavior, but they risked losing the principled point in the morass of details about Chase as an individual. Even as Chase was made an exemplar of the Federalist judiciary, he was also made its scapegoat. Congress could not reasonably empty the bench one judge at a time, and in vilifying Chase, the Republicans made the remainder of the judges look better by comparison. In fact the Republicans did not need to remove each judge in turn; they did not even need to remove Chase from the bench, though they clearly wished to do so. The mere fact that they could initiate a sustained examination of judicial conduct and muster substantial political force behind their charges was sufficient largely to defeat the existing and proffered Federalist construction of the judicial power. The failure to win a conviction and remove Chase was a personal defeat for Randolph, but the systemic changes in the federal judiciary captured by the impeachment marked the success of the Republican constitutional construction. Although Chase won his legal battle, he largely lost the constitutional and political war.

Chase's concern with winning a "legal" battle in the Senate is indicative of the form of construction adopted by the Federalists. As such conservative nationalists as Daniel Webster would later do, the Federalists sought to oppose the new construction by drawing the debate into a legal context. The fact that Chase was on trial naturally served to introduce a legalistic element to the debate, but the federal impeachment power was not yet established as a primarily legal instrument. As we shall see, Webster was able to use a similar tactic in the different context of nullification. His ability to do so indicated that the legalism of Chase's defense was more a constructive strategy than a natural outgrowth of the impeachment proceeding itself.

In fact this legalistic turn reflected the substantive concerns of the Federalist construction. Whether defending a narrow reading of the grounds for impeachment, the common law in general, the extreme independence of the judiciary from the people, or the strong role of the judge in bringing uniformity and administrative efficiency to the courtroom, the Federalists continually built upon the idea that the realm of the law and the judge was one of certainty, technical precision, and reason. Although this concern with legality emphasized an interpretive approach to the Constitution, it was itself grounded on considerations of political principle external to the text. With Chase, both those political principles and their partisan uses were too close to the surface. Chase's willingness to depart from legal forms when it served his political purposes to do so emphasized simultaneously the legal nature of the Constitution and the political possibilities of the judiciary. John Marshall was both more consistent and more moderate in his efforts. Marshall was able to carve out a larger place for the judiciary by portraying judicial review as an essentially legal task, rather than as a political act of inquiry into the fundamental principles of the republic as others, including Chase, understood it to be.[154] Whereas Chase involved the judiciary in the alien disputes of politics and saw its role sharply curtailed, Marshall emphasized the Court's legalistic strengths and won a political victory. In both instances, judicial practice under the Constitution was determined by reference to larger political disputes and understandings, specifying one historically contingent alternative for institutional growth at the expense of others.

Whereas the Federalists sought to construe the Constitution as a type of law subject to traditional legal analysis, the Republicans emphasized the political principles contained in the document and the extent to which constitutional meaning turned on popularly understood principles of right and justice. Such arguments were not only necessary for expanding the impeachment power beyond narrow indictable crimes, but were also part of the larger Republican vision. They indicated why the judiciary was subject to political abuse and had to be hemmed in by checks and balances. In the end, the Republicans made relatively little effort to locate their construction in the known meaning of the text, but argued broadly from favored political principles and general understandings of republican government to establish their case.

Though each side offered and defended its construction in the context of a government authorized by a written constitution, both sides turned to external political principles to supplement what was discoverable in the text itself. Ultimately, the Constitution delegated to Congress a power to remove judicial officers without detailing the nature of that power and with only an uncertain reference to a deeply ambiguous practice developed in Britain and the states. The nature of the judicial branch of government and its place within a system of separated powers were, if anything, even less defined in the founding document and essentially depended on an evolving tradition of practice to flesh out the bare constitutional skeleton.

In order to give substance to the constitutional text, those involved in the Chase impeachment made use of interpretive tools and evidence when possible, but unabashedly grounded their arguments on external sources of political principle as well. Federalist defenders of Chase were obsessed with the dangers inherent in popular government and latched onto every available constitutional means to try to constrain those dangers. Jeffersonian prosecutors, on the other hand, relied on a relatively democratic and libertarian republicanism to challenge the power and influence of the unelected judiciary. Both believed that the Constitution was on their side. More importantly, they believed that correct political principle supported their own views, and they made little effort to distinguish the two in contemplating government action and the appropriate structure of the federal government.

As an opposition party, the Republicans were perhaps more explicit about the contingent nature of their understanding of constitutional meaning. Republican radicals such as Taylor and Pendleton suggested new amendments to make their conception of republican government clear and permanent, but once in power the Jeffersonians had little difficulty embodying many of these principles in the foundations of the government, even without an amended text. By their rejection of the constitutional amendment advocated by Randolph at the conclusion of the impeachment trial, they made clear that the perceived limits on their actions were not inherent in the text. The boundaries of this particular construction were drawn not by the original text, but by the political will of the dominant actors. Randolph was lacking more than textual support.

Moreover, not only were the political principles of the various constructions drawn from sources external to the constitutional text, but they were asserted and defended in a noninterpretive manner. Rhetorical strategies were critical to both sides. Thus, even as the managers strove to paint Chase as a tyrannical servant of party on the bench, the justice refused to respond directly to political charges at all, denying them any formal recognition in the proceedings. As the defense drew an image of a pristine and technical law being sullied by the passions and political interests of the mobs, the prosecution compared Chase to the most infamous figures in British history and threatened the return of the Star Chamber. Such invective not only vilified the opposition and its constitutional position, but also positively invoked the political context in which each side hoped to place itself. While such comparisons could serve a legitimate interpretive purpose in shedding light on the purposes and problems of the text, in the hands of the speakers on the floor of the Senate these examples served simply to mark out the distance separating the two sides and to tap into the political platforms that motivated the two national parties. Each side struggled to elevate the political branches occupied by its own forces, for explicitly instrumental as well as substantive reasons. Moreover, each side saw its own preconceived fears realized in the actions of the others, solidifying the perceived connection between political belief and constitutional necessity. For the Federalists, the attempt to remove Chase itself emphasized the need to secure an unassailable force within the government to secure Federalist principles. For the Republicans, Chase's behavior before and after the election simply confirmed that the federal experiment had gone awry and required drastic measures to refound the republic on correct principles. Ultimately, the relative independence and function of the judiciary depended far more on visions of proper government and perceived abuses than on any specific conception of what the constitutional text required.

The various constructions that emerged from the Chase impeachment are also notable for their lack of formalizable meaning. Although Chase's

own preferred construction of the meaning of "high crimes and misdemeanors" would have limited impeachments to a handful of clear legal
crimes, the success of the moderate Republican claim that the impeachment power could reach political abuses as well as narrowly criminal activity rendered the basis for removal purposefully vague. The managers could
provide examples of impeachable abuses, but could not and did not attempt to articulate a clear rule that would have satisfied a criminal court.
The standards for judicial behavior were left even more ambiguous.
Though the construction of the judicial power had real political force in
the following decades, its success did not require detailed rules. Political
norms were modified through the impeachment, but no new legal doctrines were codified either for the benefit of the participants in the impeachment itself or for their descendants. The new standards of behavior
established through the impeachment were not adhered to absolutely.
The boundaries of the new requirements were uncertain, leading to disputed actions on the margins of consensus understandings. Moreover,
some individuals, or some individuals in particular circumstances, could
violate established norms without provoking legal mechanisms of correction. Such exceptions and violations, however, indicate the strength as well
as the limits of the new constructions. Establishing a constitutional framework does not guarantee perfect compliance; rather, it structures political
behavior so as to alter predominant outcomes. Individual judges might
stretch the boundaries of acceptable behavior, but the boundaries themselves were still generally recognized and obeyed. The success of the Chase
impeachment was not in preventing a future judge from behaving in a
partisan fashion or a congressman from calling for a purely political impeachment, but in redefining such actions as inappropriate, exceptional,
and requiring justification. Chase's example has stood as a warning, not as
a paradigm.

The achievement of the construction that was offered during the Chase
impeachment was largely attitudinal. Institutionally, the Chase impeachment served as the capstone to a series of efforts at judicial revision. The
impeachment attached additional meaning and significance to such earlier
achievements as the election of Jefferson, the expiration of the Sedition
Act, the cessation of sedition prosecutions and pardoning of the previously
convicted, the wholesale replacement of federal prosecutors and marshals,
the cessation of filling executive offices with sitting judges, and the repeal
of the Judiciary Act. The impeachment represented the culmination of
these efforts and indicated that these measures were not simply transient

governmental policies but were part of a larger effort at constitutional reform. The impeachment succeeded despite its indirection by building on these previous conflicts and political understandings of the issues surrounding the judiciary, and thus making the investigation of Chase immediately recognizable as a construction of the judiciary as a whole. While not all of the proffered constructions were equally implicated in the impeachment or equally successful, the Republicans were able overall to invigorate the impeachment power as a political weapon and to reconstitute the judiciary on more limited and politically neutral grounds.

3

The Nullification Crisis and the Limits of National Power

In the winter of 1832–33, in the wake of Andrew Jackson's triumphant reelection, the state of South Carolina took up an untested political device in order to challenge the federal government and to reorient the direction of American constitutional politics. Those events have been aptly labeled a "prelude to civil war," for both the ferocity of the presidential response and the debate over the nature of the federal union which foreshadowed the controversies that would again surround South Carolina nearly three decades later.[1] At the national level, these debates centered on the premiere political figures of America's second generation, including John C. Calhoun, Andrew Jackson, Henry Clay, and Daniel Webster. Politically, they helped secure the Jacksonian legacy, revive Clay's flagging fortunes, and catapult Calhoun to the head of a unifying Southern section. Constitutionally, they marked the culmination of decades of agitating and theorizing on the nature of the federal union and laid the groundwork for several decades of additional consideration and development. The nullification controversy marks one of the central constructions to take place between the founding period and the Civil War, touching upon some of the most contentious issues and significant political agents of the period.

A brief summary of the main events provides a guide to the course and nature of the various arguments used to elucidate and dispose of the constitutional problems at stake in the conflict. As part of a general effort to secure his position for reelection, President Jackson took several actions to placate the more Jeffersonian wing of his constituency and to consolidate his economic program, including vetoing the rechartering of the Second National Bank; vetoing a prominent internal improvements bill sponsored by his chief rival, Henry Clay; and overseeing the passage of a compromise tariff that rolled back the duties imposed by a previous campaign measure, the "Tariff of Abominations" of 1828. Despite these ac-

72

tions and Jackson's subsequent success at the national polls, nullifiers won South Carolina's state elections and called a popular convention to meet in November 1832 to consider the constitutionality of recent federal actions and the appropriate response. The convention declared the protective tariff unconstitutional, resolved that it would not be enforced in the state after February 1, 1833, and authorized and required state officials to take the actions appropriate to carry out those resolutions. Though moderate in his fourth annual message, on December 11 Jackson issued a proclamation denouncing nullification, extolling national unity, and requesting support for his position. In January 1833 Jackson requested, through the "Force Bill," congressional authorization for using military force to collect the revenue in South Carolina and to put down any resistance to national authority. Additional reductions in the tariff had been proposed in December 1832 in the Verplank Bill, and in response to these two actions, South Carolina suspended the nullification ordinances until a congressional settlement could be reached. At the end of February, Henry Clay orchestrated a compromise measure that included the passage of the Force Bill, with Northern and Western support, and of a tariff that gradually brought duties to a revenue standard, with Southern and Western support.[2] Jackson signed the measures, and the South Carolina convention rescinded its earlier ordinances, passed a new nullification ordinance aimed at the now unneeded Force Bill, and thus brought the crisis to an end.

The nullification controversy involved several interrelated though distinguishable constructions. For purposes of analysis, these constructions may be divided into two subject areas. Within each area, the debate can again be divided into broad and narrow constructions. (See Table 3.1.) Each of the four constructions drew upon the understandings and arguments underlying the other three. Additionally, the outcome of each affected, but did not determine, the outcome of the others. The first subject area places nullification in the context of federal-state relations. Most narrowly, of course, a successful construction would have established state nullification as an accepted instrument for rendering effective judgments on the constitutionality of federal actions. More broadly, nullification would have added to the strength and significance of the states in the constitutional system and imbued the federal system with a relatively decentralized spirit. The second subject area regards South Carolina's actions as a means for affecting economic policy and the nature of the American domestic regime. In this context, the forum for airing the dispute was less significant than the substance of the dispute itself. At the narrowest level of analysis, South

Table 3.1. Constructions at issue in nullification crisis

Subject area	Narrow construction	Broad construction
Federalism	Nullification	Decentralized federalism
Tariffs	Free trade	Laissez-faire

Carolina sought to establish the unconstitutionality of the protective tariff, largely by determining the meaning of Congress' constitutional power "to lay and collect Taxes, Duties, Imposts and Excises, to pay the Debts and provide for the common Defence and general Welfare" of the country.[3] At a more general level, the nullifiers hoped to redefine the relationship between government and its citizens on their own terms.

Recent historical writings have emphasized the extent to which the nullification debates were really pretexts for disagreements over slavery or broader divergent economic interests.[4] Such hypotheses may shed useful light on the controversy, but they cannot exhaust its meaning. The debate was also conducted at the level of principled argument. These arguments illuminate the ideologies that shaped the political world in which these actors operated, and thus also shaped their political actions.[5] Jackson's understanding of union and the presidency helped determine his response to the nullification threat, for example. A theory of constitutional construction pulls various levels of analysis together and indicates the interrelations and patterns of feedback among them. The material undercurrents flowing through the nullification debates must be seen as one layer in the whole.

Nullification and the Structure of Federalism

The doctrine of nullification marked the culmination of some thirty years of political thought on the nature of states' rights in the context of a federal union. Although the nullifiers stood at one extreme of the federalist spectrum, they operated within a viable tradition of constitutional decentralization. Their failure to establish nullification as a regular mechanism of constitutional settlement was by no means foreordained, and their ability to capture the political mechanisms of a state and to provoke serious deliberation on the issue by mainstream political actors is testimony to the fact that their suggestions were not yet "beyond the pale" of American politics. Although the ratification of the Philadelphia Constitution clearly

closed off some political options, at least without constitutional amendment, it also left many issues regarding the nature of American federalism
unresolved and available for future debate.[6]

Nullification and the States' Rights Tradition

After ratification of the Constitution and the Bill of Rights, among the
first significant attempts to resist political consolidation were the Virginia
and Kentucky resolutions of 1798. Responding to the centralizing tendencies of the Federalist administrations, the resolutions were secretly drafted
by Madison and Jefferson and passed by the Virginia and Kentucky state
legislatures respectively.[7] Building from the premise that the Tenth
Amendment made explicit the limited powers of the general government,
the resolutions declared the sense of the legislatures that the Alien and
Sedition Acts were unconstitutional and requested that the other states
similarly condemn the acts and "require" their repeal in the next Congress.
A number of states responded with resolutions of their own, criticizing
Virginia and Kentucky and denying the authority of the states to pass
judgment on the constitutionality of federal actions; many cited the judiciary as the proper forum for such interpretive efforts.[8] Virginia and Kentucky responded to these attacks in a second set of resolutions, adopted in
1799, and a report drafted by Madison in 1800.[9]

Though the Virginia and Kentucky resolutions contained some interest-
ing differences, both began from the assumption that the Constitution was
a "compact" of the states, and that as the parties to that contract the states
had both a right and a duty to interpret and enforce its terms, including a
special duty to take notice of constitutional violations.[10] Any "indifference
. . . now shown to the palpable violation" of rights represented by the acts
"would mark a reproachful inconsistency and criminal degeneracy" on the
part of the state. Further, Jefferson contended, to regard the federal government as "the exclusive or final judge of the extent of the powers delegated to itself" would undermine the very notion of a limited government.
Instead, "as in all other cases of compact among powers having no common judge, each party has an equal right to judge for itself, as well of
infractions as of the mode and measure of redress."[11]

In what became known as their "sentinel" role, the state governments
were to serve as guardians against the general government, "jealous" of
liberty and unwilling to show any "confidence" in national officeholders.[12]
Like the judiciary's argument for the power of review, the state govern-

ments contended for the need for a disinterested judge to protect the parchment barriers of the constitutional text from aggressive actions by Congress or the president.[13] But to these arguments concerning the general nature of limited government, proponents of states' rights added particular historical considerations that favored the states as constitutional creators and that emphasized the close political relationship between state officials and their constituents, neither of which could be invoked by unelected federal judges. Though Jefferson wrote to a political collaborator that he would prefer "for the present" simply to make a public declaration and "reserve ourselves to shape our future measures or no measures, by the events which may happen," the resolutions carried an implicit threat of the use of state political power to "interpose" the state government between a citizen and the federal government that had "marked him as its prey" in order to prevent the operation of acts that were "unauthoritative, void, and of no force."[14] It was in part to this threat that the other states responded.[15]

Jefferson's election to the presidency effectively ended the controversy over the Virginia and Kentucky resolutions. Nonetheless, the less centralized understandings of federal-state relations represented by the resolutions persisted and spread beyond both the South and the strongholds of the Republican party, laying down strong roots in the Northern states where Calhoun would be educated. Numerous states, North and South, used legislative resolutions to reaffirm the compact theory of the Union, to express interpretations of the federal Constitution, and often to direct their U.S. senators to take designated steps to prevent or end unconstitutional federal actions.[16] During this period, states' rights sentiments found their strongest expression not in the South but in New England, where they culminated in the Hartford Convention, which met in opposition to the conduct of the War of 1812 and recommended that states resist any federal laws providing for conscription and proposed mechanisms for allowing the states to conduct the war separately.[17]

The growth of decentralizing tendencies fed into an increasing Southern sectionalism and accelerated after the financial panic of 1819, a series of nationalist decisions by the Marshall Supreme Court, and the Missouri crisis in 1820. The Southern disenchantment with growing federal power made itself felt in several arenas and on numerous issues.[18] Two such episodes are of particular interest: the response in Virginia to the Marshall Court, and Georgia's refusal to accept federal jurisdiction over Indian affairs. In 1815 the Virginia high court refused to act in accord with mandates issued by the U.S. Supreme Court, prompting a strongly worded rebuke by the Madison-appointed Justice Joseph Story.[19] Three years later, after the decision in *McCulloch v. Maryland,* the chief judge of the Virginia Court of Appeals took to the newspapers to rally the people of the state to oppose the consolidating tendencies expressed in Marshall's opinion. Relying on the ratification debates and Madison's report to make his case, Judge Spencer Roane emphasized that the Constitution was incomplete and neither addressed every possible political contingency nor provided the most satisfactory remedies for future political problems. In the absence of clearly known constitutional meaning and in the face of the federal government's interest in expanding its own powers, Roane argued, disputed powers had to be arbitrated by the states through political settlements. In the end, however, Roane put his faith in the federal government's bowing to an aroused public opinion.[20] On such states' rights principles Virginia and Kentucky made a series of official legislative protests to the intervention of the federal judiciary in state land dealings.[21]

During the late 1820s, the state of Georgia engaged in an extended dispute with the federal government over the state's right to extend its criminal laws and civil jurisdiction over the lands of Indian tribes residing within its territory. Early in the dispute, the state legislature relied upon a theory of state sovereignty to claim full authority over Indian lands and to denounce the threat of the use of federal military force against the state. Governor George Troup explicitly denied the jurisdiction of the Supreme Court over a dispute "involving rights of sovereignty between the States and the United States," and refused to send representatives of the state to argue cases brought before the Court on the issue. Such issues of sovereignty were a "matter for negotiation between the States and the United States," that is, subject to political discussion and compromise, not legal resolution. Nonetheless, the constitutional requirement that would govern the outcome of such discussions was clear to Georgia, for federal actions relative to the Creek Indians were "an invasion of our vested rights, offensive in its manner, and not warranted by any principle of justice," and relative to the Cherokees, the legislature contended that "the lands in question *belong* to Georgia—she *must* and she *will* have them."[22] Despite protests by New England, the election of Andrew Jackson proved beneficial for Georgia, and the administration and its allies acted swiftly during the nullification crisis to satisfy the state's concerns and to ensure Georgia's neutrality in the conflict with South Carolina.[23]

Georgia's example soon inspired those in South Carolina who viewed the protective tariff—a tariff designed to protect domestic producers rather than to raise revenue—to be an unconstitutional and intolerable burden upon the state. The particular mode of protest, as well as the vehemence of opposition to the tariff, depended upon a specific vision of the Union and the constitutional relation between the general government and the states. The localist vision of the Constitution already had deep roots by the time the nullifiers took it up, developed it, and forced it to the center of the national stage in an effort to reshape national understandings of the federal Union.[24] The process began with a series of essays by Robert Turnbull, writing under the pseudonym "Brutus," published in 1827 under the title *The Crisis.* Turnbull connected complaints against the tariff with fear of political centralization and undertook to define a more limited role for the general government. South Carolina, he asserted, "knew the general government, not by the kindnesses which it practises towards us, but by the taxes and the tribute money that it incessantly demands of us," and he placed this complaint within the context of a federal principle that "we are an united people it is true—but we are a family united only for external objects."[25]

Turnbull simultaneously emphasized that there were principled, and restrictive, limits to federal power and that the balance between the general government and the states was a rather murky political issue. One effect of this mix was that the judiciary could not adequately determine the constitutional meaning of federalism. Not only was the Supreme Court an interested party in any conflict between the general government and the states, but it also could not reduce the relevant constitutional principles to legal precision.[26] Without a neutral judge to arbitrate the conflict, it was up to the states to adopt "such measures to enforce such compacts as in their wisdom they shall judge fit." Given that the Constitution was a compact among the sovereign states, its meaning had to be understood as consistent with states' sovereignty, doubts resolved in favor of the states, and its terms ultimately determined by the states. When faced with a violation of the limits of federal constitutional power, the states must resist, with arms if necessary.[27]

Though Turnbull detailed numerous particular powers delegated to the general government under the Constitution, he also strove to define the principle that governed those delegations. This essential guiding principle was that the general government only had the power to act in those instances in which "the want of a common head" would "involve the whole in distress and ruin," which principally meant foreign affairs. Unless a given subject was crucial to the survival and prosperity of all the states, it was a purely local concern, and the exercise of national power was inappropriate. Turnbull emphatically rejected any possibility that the general welfare could "mean such interests, as a *majority* of the States might possess." The national interest must be held equally and directly by every state. Turnbull was also concerned that the state governments not be reduced to "petty corporations," little more than "repairers of parish roads and bridges." The states had "from time immemorial" exercised numerous essential political functions that were both constitutionally reserved and essential to their political power. Ultimately, the federal balance was a question of political influence. Through the accumulation of power over numerous local affairs, the general government, already entrusted with "important powers" and "physical strength," could easily tilt that balance in its own favor.[28]

John C. Calhoun developed the most sophisticated version of what may be called "radical federalism." A late convert to the states' rights cause, while serving as vice president Calhoun anonymously wrote the "Exposition and Protest," which was printed by the South Carolina legislature at the end of 1828. Under his own name, Calhoun later elaborated his theory of nullification in several public statements and on the floor of the Senate. Nullification sparked two alternative constructions of federalism. Daniel Webster led the development of a fully nationalist position. Andrew Jackson, with the aid notably of Secretary of State Edward Livingston, carved out a third position, which can be labeled "centrist federalism."[29] The conflict among these three versions of federalism peaked in the winter of 1832–33, when the nullifiers proved only partially successful in establishing their construction and managed to defer the other part of the issue.

Calhoun's proffered construction of federalism embodies the politically sustainable and fully articulated localist position during the controversy, and can largely be taken as representative of that position. He was actually concerned to defend his version of federalism against both more-nationalist sentiment from the North and West and extreme disunionist sentiment from the South. Moreover, even radical federalists who wished for the time being to remain in the Union questioned the constitutionality of nullification as a particular expression of the states' rights view. Nevertheless, Calhoun offers the best representation of the extreme states' rights position, for South Carolina ultimately chose to pursue nullification not secession in 1832, and he maneuvered himself to the head of the extremist forces.

Calhoun's exposition of the position emerged almost fully formed, incorporating Turnbull's escalation while reaffirming a commitment to the union and thereby isolating the secessionists.[30] He built his broad construction of radical federalism with and through a more narrow construction of nullification as a means for limiting the power of the general government. Repeatedly invoking the memory of Jefferson and the "spirit of '98," Calhoun portrayed nullification as the logical extension of the state interposition that lay at the base of Republican politics. Despite the appeal to precedent, nullification was clearly a step beyond the 1798 resolutions and their offspring, for South Carolina was the first to make explicit a state's right to prevent the enforcement of federal laws and to adopt measures to that end. Moreover, Calhoun added a clear innovation in requiring that a popular convention rather than a state legislature issue the nullification ordinance.[31] These developments not only required a new theoretical foundation to support them, but also provided firmer support for the political movement.

Nullification was presented as a necessary complement to the power of judicial review. Though the courts served as impartial arbiters in disputes between individuals or states, they were necessarily partial in any conflict between the general and state governments, ultimately influenced by the same factors as other federal institutions and incompetent to address many of the key issues on which federal-state relations turned. Further, if the states were to recognize in any branch of the general government the power to determine the limits of the states' reserved powers, then the same authority must exist in the other branches as well. The judiciary's power was coextensive with the powers of the general government, but did not extend farther. For the nullifiers, federal relations required political, not legal, settlements. In an intrinsically political dispute over the boundaries of federal power, the judiciary had no distinctive claim, so inviting judicial intervention would be tantamount to inviting any other form of federal political control over the states. Moreover, the successful resolution of such a political conflict from the states' perspective necessitated that the states have effective political influence. Federalism required that each state be able to look to its own interests and not rely on other agents and institutions to represent and respect those interests. By providing each state with a provisional veto over federal actions, nullification would elevate the state's power to interpret and enforce the limits of federal power delegated under the Constitution to a role similar to that already exercised by the courts and president.[32]

The particular mechanism of nullification was a corollary to a larger understanding of federalism, and it arose out of a creative process of continuing constitutional adjustment. Nullification was asserted to be a direct result of President Jackson's betrayal of Southern interests on the tariff issue and the tardy response of other Southern states to the need for action.[33] Constitutional meaning, in terms of both the eventual tilt of federal relations and the suggestion of the device of nullification, developed through and from political need. In explaining how such a procedure could be found in the Constitution, South Carolina followed the lead of *The Federalist* and grounded its argument in the nature of man and of political systems, minimizing the distinction between the task faced by the founders and that faced by their heirs. At least for Calhoun, maintenance of the founders' Constitution was dynamic and constructive.[34] Without nullification, the Constitution would be "in the end utterly subverted," and that was enough to demonstrate the constitutionality of the mechanism. It was the permanent hostility of the different sections and interests in the Union that made a constitution necessary, and if a check on the majority interests was the basis of the Constitution, then such an effective mechanism as nullification for achieving that goal must be a part of that document as well. The states' check on the general government flowed from the Constitution and its theory of government in the same fashion as the judiciary's, as a natural and necessary consequence implicit in the text.[35]

The permanent diversity of interests within the union grounded the construction of radical federalism. As Turnbull argued, the states represented a variety of local interests. In some instances, these same interests might exist within all the states, but in others, the interests might be unique to particular states and in opposition to the dominant interests of other states. South Carolina's concern with free trade was one such interest that would consistently be in opposition to the manufacturing interests of other states. For the nullifiers, political action rested on shared, not divergent, interests, and thus the federal role was limited to those activities that touched upon common interests. Those powers delegated to the general government were supposed to operate uniformly on all of the states, providing what each required without unduly burdening any. As a compact among equals, the Constitution and its agents must give equal concern to each of the states. The capacity of the general government to mobilize vast economic resources, however, gave some an interest in exploiting the others. The exercise of contested federal powers then became a struggle between those favoring power and those favoring liberty, and the necessity of resorting to force against a state in order to carry out federal policy was an indication that the federal system was out of balance and treating some states unequally.[36]

The character of the federal union was not only shaped by the current diversity of interests, however. It was also essentially determined by its origins. The history of the various states as independent colonies, member states in a loose confederation, separate ratifiers of the Constitution, and conservators of the undefined reserved powers all served to establish the case for radical federalism. The rights and powers held by the states were not concessions granted by the Constitution, but the document's central core, delimiting the general government's delegated powers. As Calhoun put it, "the truth is that the very idea of an American people, as constituting a single community, is a mere chimera. Such a community never, for a moment, existed, neither before, nor since the dec[laratio]n of Independence."[37] By appealing to the people of the states, Calhoun sought not only to strengthen the theoretical appeal of nullification, but also to undercut the political power of the general government. The sovereign people constituted the basis of both constitutional authority and political power. Indeed, the great threat of a consolidated government was not merely in the formal violation of constitutional divisions, but in the sapping of the popular influence of state governments.[38] As the nationalists recognized, and the nullifiers feared, a more active federal government, even within its own sphere, necessarily threatened the ties between the citizenry and their state governments. The political threat was the constitutional threat. Therefore, the radical federalists were forced to challenge not only attempts to exercise undelegated power but also the "abuse" of delegated powers. At a more formal level, the states must defend their special status as the sovereign creators of the original compact. As such, it was their right to interpret and fix the Constitution's terms and restrain its agents. Allowing that power to fall into disuse threatened the theoretical understanding of the Constitution itself, and thereby fostered greater federal abuses as not only the mechanisms of restraint and the very belief in restraints were abandoned.[39]

Daniel Webster and the Nationalist Alternative

The strongest response to this construction was Daniel Webster's. Webster was uniquely positioned to build the nationalist construction, for he stood as the premiere representative of the traditional center of nationalist sentiment, an architect of the economic system the nullifiers hoped to destroy, and the attorney instrumental in establishing several nationalistic Court decisions. Thus, it was Webster who first attacked nullification in the national legislature and ushered the Force Bill through Congress three years later. Although each participant in the struggle claimed to be developing constitutional meaning, Webster was perhaps most assertive in positioning himself as the defender of the status quo. Although the nullifiers could point to a states' rights tradition extending at least to 1798, they were also clearly initiating the crisis and a new construction. Despite the fact that Webster's extreme nationalism was not clearly the prior consensus either, he did defend existing government policies. Thus, Webster insisted to a New York audience that "this is the actual Constitution, this is the law of the land." Webster continually emphasized that the nullifiers were attempting to replace the existing Constitution and not simply interpret it.

> I shall not consent, Sir, to make any new constitution, or to establish another form of government. I will not undertake to say what a constitution for these United States ought to be. That question the people have decided for themselves; and I shall take the instrument as they have established it, and shall endeavor to maintain it, in its plain sense and meaning, against opinions and notions which, in my judgment, threaten its subversion.[40]

If the nullifiers succeeded in their construction, then the text "should not be denominated a constitution," but rather it should be called "a collection of topics, for everlasting controversy." Continued controversy over constitutional meaning, in Webster's view, could "not be a government." The people's role in forming the Constitution was over, and now "the thing is done," and the time to worry about continuing agreement to its terms or operation "is at an end."[41] In line with this vision of settled constitutional meaning, Webster referred all interpretive questions to the courts. The choice between "law" and "force" required the resort to judicial elaboration of constitutional meaning.[42]

Though hoping to turn constitutional disputes over to the Marshall Court, Webster was willing to offer his own vision of the "actual" Constitution. When dealing with the delegated powers of the general government, "if the law be within the fair meaning of the words in the grant of the power, its authority must be admitted until it is repealed." The courts should be highly deferential toward Congress in reviewing its legislation, but the understanding of the courts was the only available measure of constitutionality. In instances that could not be formulated as a judicial question, as the nullifiers contended the protective tariff and issues of state sovereignty could not, then Congress' own judgment as to its powers must necessarily remain unquestioned. The Constitution should be regarded as a full and generous trust, not as a jealous grant of power to the general government. If the general government stood on the same authority as the state governments, that is, on the sovereign people, then there should be no reason to be any more cautious of the one than of the other. In fact the general government might be even more trustworthy, for it had emerged out of the failure of the state governments during the confederation and represented the whole people. Regular elections were a sufficient check on federal action.[43]

The general government was not simply to preside over the foreign affairs of the Union, but should be active in forging a nation. In order to do so, there must be a central government capable of operating in its own right, with full taxation and enforcement power to use at its own discretion. Further, in order for the government to possess sufficient energy, "the judgment of the majority *must* stand as the judgment of the whole." The only alternative, in Webster's view, was anarchy, and then the Union would be nothing but "a rope of sand."[44] If the United States were understood to be a seamless whole, a true nation rather than a confederated union, then there would be little question as to whether unchecked majority rule was appropriate. Thus, against the nullifiers' vision of a contingent union, Webster contended that the states were not "strangers" to one another, but that a "bond of union" had always existed between them long before the present Constitution. Far from being a compact among separate states, the Constitution was ordained and established by the whole people of the nation. As a result, the Union was indissoluble; individuals could be free from the Constitution's authority only upon its destruction.[45] Within the union, "we should look upon the States as one," and federal powers should be exercised for the "general benefit" of that single unit. The general government should be active in taking measures that would bind the Union together and bring the interests of the states in line with the interests of the whole. The national debt, the federal revenue, and the national roads and canals all served to secure the advantage of general government, and Webster was quick to remind his Northern allies that every blow against his vision of the Union "strikes at the tenderest nerve of her interest and her happiness," which would bring their "own future prosperity into debate also," which was "but another mode of speaking of commercial ruin."[46] Constitutional meaning was not simply a function of abstract speculation or historical investigation, but one of current economic interest, which was itself a constitutional end.

Andrew Jackson and Centrist Federalism

Andrew Jackson, among others, carved out a middle position. This construction of centrist federalism sought to strike a balance between an appropriate concern for states' rights and a desire to preserve a permanent and supreme national government. The Jacksonian center pursued a Madisonian line, and encountered many of the same difficulties. On the one hand, the Jacksonians reasserted Madison's claim as Publius that the Constitution was partially national and partially federal, thus denying the absolutist position insisted on by both Calhoun and Webster.[47] On the other hand, Jackson, like Madison before him, wavered between nationalist and particularist statements, which could not be easily reconciled but could be used to build a political coalition.

Like Webster's nationalism, the centrist position developed first and most fully during the 1830 debates over the Foot Resolution.[48] Edward Livingston of Louisiana, like Jackson from the new Southwest, rose relatively late in the debate and noted that though the "recurrence which has necessarily been had to first principles is of incalculable use," he was of an opinion that differed, "in a greater or less degree, from all the Senators who have preceded me." Livingston thought the question had been divided between those who argued that the general government was "popular or consolidated" and those who argued that it was "federative." In fact, "we find traces of both these features."[49] Contrary to the nationalists, Livingston thought that the former colonies had existed independently of one another until bound together through the constitutional compacts. The nationalist difficulty, in his view, was that they rested their case on a shaky historical foundation and the preamble's reference to the people. As a corrective, Livingston sought to shift the foundation of federalism from the social basis disputed between Webster and Calhoun to a purely political basis. The centrist vision was grounded in governmental institutions, or the autonomous power of the state, not the people or the nation that supposedly stood behind them. Instead of emphasizing the unity of the people in a single nation, Livingston thought it was sufficient to establish the strength of the Union to emphasize the general government's power of enforcement, including the constitutional recognition of treason as a federal crime. The president was obliged to enforce the laws of the general government, and if any form of resistance to those laws was a reserved power of the state, then there should be a correlative federal duty to respect those rights laid out in the Constitution. Instead, the federal enforcement power was absolute. Sovereignty was not reserved to the states, but divided between the two governments.[50]

Even though the general government possessed a full right and duty to enforce its laws against the states, it should respect those subordinate governmental units. Repeating his early arguments for a stronger central government, the mostly retired Madison contended that the exercise of a right to nullification would disrupt the workings of the efficient administration of government and would subject the nation to delays, inconveniences, and expenses and weaken the "salutary veneration for a system requiring frequent interpositions." Thus, the mechanisms for checking the activities of the federal government must be internal. Among those internal checks should be a careful regard by federal officials for the limits of their authority. Jackson had pledged in his First Inaugural to be "animated by a proper respect for those sovereign members of our Union," and Livingston emphasized that no single national majority would emerge to overturn the place of the states in the federal system.[51] This concern for the states expressed itself partly through attempts to reclaim the authority of the Virginia and Kentucky resolutions for centrist federalism. Livingston was careful to assure his opponents that his views "coincide in the sentiments of those resolutions," and Madison engaged in an extensive effort to deny the nullifiers the authority of the resolutions.[52] More concretely, the centrists leaned toward resolving the dispute through concessions. If the general government had the right to enforce the laws against the states, it should also respect the opinions of those states and voluntarily work to meet their objections. Livingston asked the nationalists, "how can we hope for ready obedience to our laws, if the people are taught to believe in a permanent hostility of one part of the Union towards another?" Even if the government should occasionally be active to make its territory productive, it should not impose burdens on some in order to benefit the remainder.[53]

More than the competing alternatives, centrist federalism vacillated in its commitments. Although such logical tensions are not intrinsically debilitating, the particular centrist emphasis on the general government's power of enforcement fractured the construction in the face of active nullification. As Jackson and Livingston were driven by their institutional position to focus on the threat to the enforcement of federal laws, other centrists outside the executive branch grew increasingly concerned over the threatened expansion of national power inherent in the use of force against a state. Having built the centrist position on the governmental power of enforcement itself, the administration was in no position to be sensitive to such concerns. If the president flinched from his institutional capacity to enforce the law, then the entire centrist edifice of divided governmental sovereignty would collapse. Jackson could remain passive in the face of Georgia's recalcitrance to court orders, since Georgia's actions did not directly challenge presidential authority and were consistent with Jackson's own Indian policy. South Carolina, however, threatened to disrupt the revenue collection for which the president was directly responsible, and did so by directly and explicitly challenging federal political authority and preparing troops. It is not particularly surprising that Jackson would regard "the act of raising troops [as] positive treason."[54] Additionally, Jackson did not understand the Court to speak with the authority of the people, as Congress and the president did. A state challenge to political, as opposed to mere legal, authority called into question the existence of the general government as a sovereign entity, legitimated by the democratic voice of the majority of the people. Moreover, having no strong interest in tariff reduction, Jackson easily believed that "nullification is an effort of disappointed ambition, originating with unprincipled men who would rather rule in hell, than be subordinate in heaven" and a personally threatening *"monster."*[55] In the midst of the crisis, Livingston, through the voice of the president, could only strengthen his earlier assertions that the executive had no discretion in these matters and was obliged by oath and office to put down nullification. Thus, when the foundations of the centrist construction were challenged, its proponents retreated into the institutional and formal powers of the general government.[56]

This increasing concern with putting down what was taken to be a treasonable course of action so overshadowed all others that Jackson's special proclamation against nullification not only denounced it in the strongest terms, but also rebuilt his constitutional theory along more nationalist lines. Nullification was "subversive of [the] Constitution" and had "for its object the destruction of the Union"; it was a pure "invention," inconsistent with the Constitution's "every principle." From their earliest days, the colonies were "connected by common interest," and jointly constituted a nation at the outset of the Revolution. The general government was now the "safest depository of this discretionary power in the last resort," for it represented *"one people."* Now Jackson emphasized the care to be taken not in protecting states' rights, but rather in preventing the states from improperly interfering with the powers vested in the nation. Indeed, the states did not merely share sovereignty, but in fact were "no longer sovereign."[57] Such retrenchment could only be the expected result of a challenge to effective governmental authority upon which the centrist theory rested. The proclamation divided the centrists in the states. The governor of Virginia asserted his willingness to use force to prevent Jackson from marching on South Carolina, even if he was unwilling to embrace nullification.[58] Many others who were unwilling to endorse nullification as a constitutional remedy nonetheless accepted increasing portions of radical federalism, admitting that the states contained distinct and hostile interests and that the Union could exist only so long as the general government acted on interests that imposed no unequal burdens.[59]

Constructing "Jacksonian" Federalism

Along with the Compromise Tariff, the Force Bill came to a vote in the Congress at the end of February 1833. During the 1830 debates on the Foot Resolution, when Robert Hayne first raised the nullification issue in the Senate, a number of members expressed their support, including the chairman of the judiciary committee. By the end of the crisis, only one member, John Tyler of Virginia, was willing to vote against the Force Bill. In order to secure the Compromise, however, fourteen senators from Southern and border states, including Calhoun, abstained from the vote. In the House, forty members voted against the Force Bill, including several pro-administration Southerners.[60] In March the South Carolina convention reconvened, rescinded its earlier ordinance, and nullified the Force Bill. Although Virginia state judge and eventual U.S. Secretary of State Abel Upshur produced perhaps the most elaborate defense of nullification seven years later, few supported its use after 1833.[61] During the crisis, no state legislature had endorsed nullification, and even in the South several states had denounced it. Even Calhoun made little mention of it after 1833.[62] The specific argument for nullification had clearly failed.

The broader construction of radical federalism was less clearly a failure, however. It rather served to create a compromise position between the centrist and radical positions, until even more extreme constructions gained support later in the antebellum period. Jackson's Second Inaugural, delivered days after passage of the Compromise, emphasized two points of domestic policy, "the preservation of the rights of the several states and the integrity of the Union."[63] This dual concern, with the tribute to the states voiced first, tempered the strident nationalism of the proclamation. Instead of his earlier cautions that the federal government should be careful of the states in pursuing its own policies and interests, Jackson now stressed his willingness energetically to defend the states and their interests. The president offered only a minimal warning against disunion, betraying his continuing preoccupation with secession. If his political flirtation with Webster was short-lived, however, Jackson's personal break from Calhoun was complete. By the middle of Jackson's first term, both he and Calhoun were telling political associates that they had "dissolved all ties, political or otherwise . . . forever."[64] The relative independence available to Calhoun as a result actually helped secure the new construction, as the states' rights faction played a swing role that kept both the Democratic and Whig parties from drifting away from decentralist principles. While nationalist and secessionist sentiment continued in the North and the South, a new center solidified between them that dominated state and national politics.[65]

Upon Jackson's departure from office, Calhoun swung the support of the "states' rights" party behind the president's more orthodox successor, Martin Van Buren, who had carefully avoided antagonizing the nullifiers during the crisis and remained highly solicitous of states' rights concerns.[66] A mere five years after the Compromise, Calhoun introduced test resolutions in the Senate designed to force explicit recognition of the compact theory of federalism in relation to debates over the receipt of abolition petitions. Though not directly comparable, the contrast between the test resolutions and the discussions of the Foot Resolution and the Force Bill is instructive. With relatively little debate, Calhoun's resolutions passed by large majorities, indicating the partial success of the broader construction. To little avail Webster protested that Calhoun and remarkably Henry Clay "have attempted in 1838, what they attempted in 1833, *to make a new Constitution*," but Webster failed to recognize that 1833 had seen a new construction of the Constitution and that 1838 was merely a confirmation of that new understanding. Though the panic of 1837 restricted Van Buren to a single term, the limits of the Whig victory in 1840 were apparent as John Tyler, the only senator to vote against the Force Bill, soon rose to the presidency and Calhoun served as his secretary of state. The Democratic Polk's 1845 inaugural indicated the stability of the localist construction; in it he emphasized the boundary between federal and state powers, recognized the different interests of the various states, denied the federal government's authority to intervene in local affairs, and noted the significance of minority rights against national majorities.[67]

The judicial rhetoric of the period provides another illustration of this shift in constitutional understandings. The constitutional settlement of 1833 formed the intellectual and political context for the federalism cases of the antebellum period, shaping both the nature of the legal controversies and the concerns expressed in the opinions.[68] Under the leadership of Chief Justice Roger Taney, Jackson's attorney general during the crisis, the Court shifted away from the strongly nationalist position of Marshall to a more centrist position consistent with the post-nullification settlement.[69]

Chief Justice Marshall had expressed his nationalist sentiments in any number of judicial opinions, especially in the decade before nullification. In determining the congressional power to incorporate a national bank in *McCulloch*, Marshall largely accepted the nationalist construal of the founding. The Constitution was derived from a national citizenry, and thus the federal government was the expression of their collective will. The general government was "a government of the people. In form and substance it emanates from them. Its powers are granted by them, and are to be exercised directly on them, and for their benefit." Marshall then tied the popular roots of the federal government with its supremacy, providing the nationalist significance of his analysis. Though acknowledging that the powers of the federal government were limited, Marshall emphasized that it "is supreme within its sphere of action . . . It is the government of all; its powers are delegated by all; it represents all, and acts for all." The government was not simply popular, it was national, and therefore superior.[70]

Marshall later expanded on the implications of this reading of the federal government's constitutional nature. The powers of the general government were to be construed expansively, as a generous grant by the people for their own benefit, because the Constitution was "an investment of power for the general advantage."[71] As a result, Marshall recognized no distinct interests residing in the states. The Constitution took cognizance only of the "general advantage" of the collective people and did not recognize distinctions among them. Powers were left to the states for the sake of practical efficiency in administration, not in respect of any fundamental values or differing concerns. Marshall even flirted with the strong position that the commerce clause was a grant of exclusive power to Congress, such that the states could never regulate objects that fell within its domain even in the absence of congressional action.[72] He did not make this position explicit, however, and subsequently qualified it with the notion that the commerce power could be "dormant" when Congress had not acted. In those cases, the Court must exercise its own discretion in order to ensure that the states did not trench on the delegated, if unused, powers of the federal government.[73]

As would be expected given the failure of the radical federalism construction, the Taney Court did not completely reverse Marshall's nationalism in order to move in the opposite direction, but rather limited his precedents and adopted a less centralizing perspective.[74] The new attitude emerged in a number of areas. Unlike Marshall, Taney gave full support to the states' rights history of the founding, emphasizing that in the revolutionary period and during the Confederation the Union was composed of "thirteen separate, sovereign, independent States," and Congress was little more than a meeting of "separate sovereignties." The founding itself was done "by the people of the United States," but for Taney this meant "by those who were members of the different political communities in the several States" and those "people of the several States [remained] absolutely and unconditionally sovereign" after ratification.[75] Ultimately, however, Taney committed himself to the "divided sovereignties" interpretation of this history, which was more consistent with the moderate position.[76]

As in Congress and the presidency, in the Court the adoption of a different constitutional logic had practical implications. For example, the states were given both a larger sphere of control and a firmer basis for the exercise of that control over interstate commerce. Against Marshall's suggestion and Webster's and Story's advocacy, Taney thought that states could regulate commerce even up to the point that state regulations came into direct conflict with congressional law. The rationale for such deference to the states was that the reservation of powers by the states was of more than administrative convenience. The state power to regulate commerce was exercised "according to its own judgment and upon it own views of the interest and well-being of its citizens."[77] Taney grounded himself on the key decentralizing claim, that the states had distinct and contradictory interests that required constitutional recognition. The federal government was excluded from intervening in all areas of economic life not simply because it was inconvenient to do so, but because in some areas there was no "national interest" but only antagonistic local ones that were equally respectable. In a different context, Taney articulated the rationale for strict construction of federal powers, for a "state ought never to be presumed to surrender this power, because, like the taxing power, the whole community have an interest in preserving it undiminished." Any government power that was necessary "to promote the happiness and prosperity of the community" was to be considered by the courts as vital to that government.[78] As a result, the state's regulatory powers were as essential to their reserved sovereignty as their power to tax or to determine their own seat of government. For Taney, the federal government was not the only government exercising powers at the behest of and to the advantage of the people.

Although "they are sovereign states," there was also an "intimate union of these states, as members of the same great political family" sharing certain "deep and vital interests." The familial metaphor sufficiently extended the comity relationship between the states that the Court adopted the presumption that states recognized the legal actions of other states. There are two significant points to note about Taney's stance. First, Taney reserved to the states the right to override the judicial comity presumption. A nationalist reading would have barred the states from ever refusing to recognize out-of-state corporations, since such divisions could not be tolerated within a seamless nation. Taney's federalism recognized a state's right to protect its own domestic interests, only requiring that it do so consciously and explicitly. The union of states was a presumption only; it could always be rescinded. Second, Taney used the metaphor in dealing with state-chartered corporations. As a dissenting justice pointed out, the effect of Taney's decision was to give each state an "imputed national power" to impart an extraterritorial application to its laws.[79] In Taney's hands, the "intimate union" empowered the state governments, not the general government.[80] In line with the presumptions of the radical federalists, Taney repeatedly respected the role of state officials in construing and enforcing provisions of the federal Constitution. In recognition of the states' independent responsibility for maintaining their constitutional faith, Taney emphasized that the Constitution did not fearfully take power away from the states, but expressed the sovereign states' own commitment to union. As a result, the states must be given the leeway to exercise their own constitutional responsibilities in accord with their own constitutional judgments.[81]

Taney portrayed the federal government as an arbiter of interstate conflicts and a servant of their interests, not as an independent actor pursuing overarching national goals.[82] Taney reaffirmed existing precedent, but did so by refounding it on a decentralizing logic. Whereas Marshall was driven by the fear of state encroachment on federal powers, Taney emphasized the danger of federal encroachment on the states. Throughout the government, post-nullification political actors were emphasizing their duty to protect the states from the consolidating tendencies of the general government. In the judicial context, this claim reflected a willingness to respect the settlement reached in the political sphere.[83] In the political context, it required greater care on the part of national officials and an active effort on the part of state officials to exercise their own extensive constitutional responsibilities.

Protectionism and the Struggle for Free Trade

Like nullification, South Carolina's construction of the protective tariff drew upon several years of gradually increasing protest and discussion. Unlike the debate over the nature of federalism, however, the constitutionality of the protective tariff turned on a much more specific textual base and drew upon a younger controversy. Doubts about the constitutionality of the protective tariff did not emerge until relatively late in the life of the republic, and they could not depend so heavily on the vague reserved rights of the states. Despite these disadvantages, the specific construction of the unconstitutionality of the protective tariff was remarkably successful in 1833 and helped solidify a broader construction limiting the role of the federal government in actively shaping the domestic economy.

Providing the general government with the means to collect its own revenue and to regulate trade among the states and between the states and other nations was a primary goal in the movement to replace the Articles of Confederation. Appropriately, a tariff was among the first measures taken up by the new Congress that met under the Constitution. With relatively little principled objection, Madison ushered through Congress the Tariff Act of 1789 for the collection of revenue and "the encouragement and protection of manufactures." More ambitious proposals by Alexander Hamilton and others to aid manufacturers met with greater opposition and helped establish the basis of the first national party division. Similarly, the Jeffersonian embargo sparked vigorous protest by the commercial states, but little debate over the power to raise protective barriers per se. The conclusion of the War of 1812 and the subsequent nationalist outburst led to the passage of the protective Tariff of 1816, advocated by a young Calhoun among others.[84] The first serious suggestion that a protective tariff might be unconstitutional was raised in 1820.[85]

In 1820 a representative from Maine briefly questioned whether the Constitution provided for the encouragement of manufacturers. Daniel Webster was the first to elaborate this point. In a speech at Faneuil Hall, which he excluded from his collected papers, Webster argued that it would be "somewhat against the spirit and intention of the Constitution" to exercise "a power to control essentially the pursuits and occupations of individuals in their private concerns." Webster was willing to accept any incidental protective effects of a revenue tariff, but "he doubted whether Congress fairly possessed the power of turning the *incident* into the *principal*," and purposefully arranging tax burdens in order to benefit one economic class at the expense of others. Webster remained tentative in his assertions, thinking that the constitutional issue was a fair question for Congress to deliberate upon, but the meeting approved more emphatic resolutions asserting that the protective tariff was *"equally inconsistent with the principles of our Constitution, and with sound judgment."*[86] Southern politicians, speakers, and writers picked up this broad argument by the time of the debates over the 1824 tariff, even as Webster dropped it as the New England states shifted from commercial to manufacturing pursuits.

At least three memorials to Congress, presented by groups representing Charleston, New York City, and Virginia, made use of constitutional arguments in their denunciations of the tariff. The Charleston memorial especially was willing to grant that the constitutional text gave broad authority to Congress on the tariff issue, but that nonetheless the text should be construed narrowly in order to conform to the antiprotectionist spirit of the Constitution. The New York memorial, on the other hand, employed a limited view of the "general welfare" clause in order to emphasize that federal fiscal policy must be for the true shared, common good, rather than the good of particular interests at the expense of others.[87] These outside arguments were reflected in congressional debates, though there were also some distinct claims made. Protective tariffs, by manipulating private economic pursuits and market prices, were seen as a violation of property rights, which the Constitution broadly sought to secure. Senator John Taylor, author of a significant 1822 book dissecting the protectionist system, argued that republican and representative government required that political actions have generally equal effects if all citizens were to be represented and not effectively disfranchised by the unconstrained actions of a majority faction.[88]

South Carolina's Robert Hayne developed the most extensive arguments against the protective tariff on constitutional grounds. Hayne granted that by 1824, precedent already existed for the protective tariff, and yet this tariff was an innovation. Previously, Hayne contended, protective tariffs had been advocated as temporary measures necessary to foster nationally important infant industries. In 1824, however, the protective tariff took on a more ominous aspect, as part of a permanent "American System" that was to become a persistent feature of federal policy in order to prop up favored industries in perpetuity. The desire to prepare for war that motivated the 1816 tariff, Hayne asserted, was not the same as a system of economic manipulation by the government for the sake of private profits. Similarly, the power to regulate commerce could not be appropriately used to reduce commerce in order to expand manufacturing.[89] If the protective tariff was to be defended, it had to be justified under the revenue clause, and on that basis, Hayne believed, such justifications failed. He was forced to admit that the literal terms of the grant of the impost power did not prohibit its use to protect manufactures, but the indeterminate text itself could not be controlling. The clear implication of the clause was that imposts were to be levied for revenue purposes.

The remainder of the construction had to be drawn from nontextual material. The entire purpose of the Revolution and the Constitution was to expand American freedom, including freedom from colonial and confederation restraints on trade. Thus, any doubts about constitutional delegations of power should be resolved in favor of freedom. Although this sort of principle could not be formulated in terms of fixed rules, sharply marking the boundary between permissible revenue and impermissible protection, it was fully constitutional and binding on Congress. Hayne concluded that the passage of this strictly protectionist tariff was an exercise of naked power on the part of the majority, and without an accepted principle governing the matter, he warned, "we shall feel ourselves justified in embracing the very first opportunity of repealing all such laws as may be passed for the promotion of these objects . . . we will not hold ourselves bound to maintain the system," regardless of the economic interests that might grow up around it.[90]

In the 1820 legislative debates, Henry Clay had not bothered to respond to constitutional objections.[91] In 1824 the expansion of the argument demanded his limited attention. Clay pointed out that the revenue clause contained no explicit restrictions except that duties be geographically uniform. Without more explicit limits on federal power, its use was left to congressional discretion. But more important for Clay was the commerce clause, for this "grant is plenary, without any limitations whatever," and allowed every possible limitation on commerce up to and including total prohibition. In line with the nationalist construction elaborated above, congressional power was to be exercised to the fullest, and any constitutional limitations on that power must be explicit in the text. Indeterminacies were always to be resolved in the favor of a power that could be exercised for the public good and in favor of political discretion— that is, an indeterminate constitutional text removed the issue from a constitutional context into a purely political context. The impossibility of distinguishing sharply between revenue and protective tariffs was taken as indicative of the constitutional irrelevance of the issue, for inquiring into the legislative mind to impugn motives had "too much subtlety and refinement to be just."[92] The judiciary, and thus the Constitution, could not investigate into the usage of a discretionary power.

Though the constitutional argument against the protective tariff gained more adherents over time, it did not significantly develop. As Clay's dismissive attitude indicates, the antiprotectionist forces had as much difficulty convincing opponents that this was a constitutional issue as they had that their particular determination of constitutional meaning was correct. Not only did the narrow construction of the revenue clause connect with a broader construction of the federal domestic regime, as nullification connected to federalism, but the tariff construction mingled with a recognized and preexisting policy debate. Just as Webster's most effective tactic in the debate over the nature of the Union was to deny radical federalism any constitutional foothold, so Clay's approach in the tariff controversy was to refuse to allow the debate to be carried onto a constitutional plane.

Clay's approach was benefited not only by a history of debate on protection as a purely nonconstitutional issue, but also by the recent decisions of other political figures to deconstitutionalize the issue. The federal power to restrict trade gained substantial credibility from President Jefferson's decision to employ an embargo against the European powers. Although the tremendously unpopular embargo was clearly a foreign-policy tool, its use also reflected domestic concerns over the continued dependence of the American economy on foreign powers, especially the British, and corrupting luxuries. These policies weakened the connection between trade policy and the Republican constitutional vision inaugurated in the "Revolution of 1800" and laid the groundwork for Clay's expansive concerns for the development of a "home market" in the 1820s.[93]

The continuing legacy of the Jeffersonian concession to trade restrictions can be seen in Madison's justifications for the protective tariff during the nullification crisis. Madison had taken the lead in publishing defenses of the Jefferson administration's trade policy and was willing to repeat and develop those arguments as South Carolina increased the pressure on the protective tariff. Hardly an advocate of the American System, Madison thought that there was no justification for the perpetual system of support envisioned by Clay. Nonetheless, for Madison the protective system could at most be "an abuse, not . . . a usurpation of power," and he thought this distinction crucial. For Madison, mere questions of abuse of delegated powers could be ameliorated through the exercise of the suffrage and political accommodations. Only usurpations, such as the Federalists' nationalization of the reserved power to prosecute seditious libel, could justify taking other measures to strike out the power completely. He could not imagine that even Jefferson would have "intended to reject *altogether* such a power" as the protective tariff. Thus, he would leave the subject to the discretion of Congress as a difficult political issue, not a constitutional issue on a par with the actions of the Federalists in the 1790s. Even given an indeterminacy in textual meaning, Madison thought that "a course of practice of sufficient uniformity and duration to carry with it the public sanction [could] settle doubtful or contested meanings," and the protective tariff had gained the approval of "a uniform interpretation by all the successive authorities under [the Constitution], commencing at its birth, and continued for a long period, thro' the varied state of political contests, or the opinion of every new Legislature." The alternative was that "every new Legislative opinion might make a new Constitution."[94] Thus, while recognizing the limitations of legitimate interpretation of constitutional terms, Madison still hoped to restrict constitution making to the founding period. Ultimately, constitutional meaning was closed and not properly subject to continuing public debate.

The Supreme Court had adopted a similar view of the constitutional powers of the general government at the inception of the American System. Though addressing the National Bank, not the tariff, and thus considering the "necessary and proper" clause rather than the revenue or commerce clauses, the Court in the 1819 *McCulloch* decision adopted the sweeping nationalist vision advocated by the Bank's attorney, Daniel Webster. In doing so, it not only withdrew itself from monitoring the economic policy of the general government, but also fostered the view that the government's operation in that sphere was beyond constitutional question. Thus, *McCulloch* was not just a victory for the nationalist under-standing of the union. It also provided support for the legalistic concep-tion of constitutionalism adopted by the nationalists in order to deny the relevance of the Constitution to the tariff dispute.

The latter opinion was generated in part by the Court's sweeping claims for its own authority with which it began the opinion, insisting that the Constitution had given the "important duty" of authoritatively determin-ing constitutional meaning to "this tribunal alone."[95] Thus, the Court laid claim to the entire sphere of constitutional meaning. Presumably, if it was the Court alone that could render a final decision on constitutional mean-ing and uniquely possessed the duty to interpret that text, then if the Court did not or could not act on a given issue, the Constitution must not be implicated. As all sides recognized, the tariff could not be easily formu-lated as a judicial question and subjected to legal examination, for the distinction between protective and revenue tariffs could not be fixed and depended on legislative motives not readily visible on the face of a statute.

The Court further deconstitutionalized such issues as the protective tariff by its broad understanding of the powers delegated to the general government. Though the Constitution created a limited government whose boundaries the Court would enforce, the text could not detail "all the subdivisions of which its great powers will admit, and of all the means by which they may be carried into execution." To do so would have converted the Constitution into a mere legal code, an instrument con-cerned with policy not principle. Within the "great outlines" of federal power, Congress had been entrusted with "a choice of means" to be used as the "exigencies of the nation may require." The Constitution "does not profess to enumerate" those means. Congressional discretion within the plenary powers was outside the context of the Constitution and within the realm of politics and the public trust. Further, as Madison would also conclude, the Court asserted that in doubtful cases, the judiciary must defer to the consistent actions of successive legislatures, especially when the issue was merely one of federal power rather than "the great principles of liberty."[96] The necessary effect of such a decision was not simply to bolster the claims of nationalists such as Webster, but also to subsume constitutional disputes about the powers of the federal government under the rubric of expediency.

The Jacksonian war on the Bank and the Carolinian attack on the tariff must be seen as analogous in their efforts to recover this aspect of the Constitution and to reintroduce constitutionalism into these political debates. To this extent, both denied that either precedent or judicial sanction could render a political institution beyond constitutional question. Further, both denied that these economic decisions were outside the range of constitutional interest. South Carolina's willingness repeatedly to challenge the constitutionality of the protective system helped maintain an opening that Jackson could exploit in order to attack the Bank. Similarly, Jackson's general understanding of the domestic regime, though not highlighting tariff reform, supported the nullifiers' own understanding and willingness to act.

Jackson's centrist laissez-faire vision drew naturally on many of the same ideological sources as the antiprotectionists'. In his First Inaugural Jackson pledged to "observe a strict and faithful economy" in public expenditures as part of an effort to eliminate the national debt and "public and private profligacy." Many Southerners hoped that the final amortization of the national debt would create an unstoppable political pressure for tariff reform, and to this degree Jackson's goals appeared to coincide with those of the antiprotectionists. Moreover, Jackson's understanding of the role of government in society seemed to lend support to the antiprotectionist position. For both, public money appeared to have been manipulated for the benefit of an advantaged few. In his Bank veto message, Jackson contended that the great danger was that "many of our rich men have not been content with equal protection and equal benefits, but have besought to make them richer by act of Congress."[97] For the nullifiers, among others, the protective tariff operated to the same effect, and the movement to eradicate the revenue leg of the American System was at one with the movement to dismantle its financial leg.

Although Jackson's popularity was grounded in part on Southern opposition to the tariff, he did not include the elimination of the protective tariff as part of his vision of a newly revitalized republic. In fact the protective tariff had an important, if limited, role to play in the Jacksonian polity. The Jacksonians orchestrated the 1828 "Tariff of Abominations" in order to force the Adams-Clay coalition to reject its oppressive duties. If Adams were forced to reject a tariff on the eve of the election, then Jackson could plausibly compete with him for the protectionist vote. To everyone's surprise, the administration swallowed even this tariff, and the repercussions were felt by his successor. Even as this tactic failed, however, Jackson hoped that carefully worded statements waffling on the tariff issue would win protectionist votes without losing Southern support. His public statements on the subject voiced his advocacy of and support for a protective tariff to secure "the means of national defense and independence," but he also thought that protection should be used so that "our own manufactories and laborers may be placed on a fair competition with those of Europe" and "with an eye to the proper distribution of labor, and to revenue." As to the dangers of the tariff, he judged them more "fanciful than real."[98]

These concerns were reflected in President Jackson's first annual message to Congress, which insisted that the protective tariff was necessary for American independence, to guarantee "fair competition" and military preparedness, but that it should be adjusted as possible to account for the "general interest of the whole." The reduction of the national debt made this adjustment possible, and Jackson suggested that duties be reduced on noncompeting necessities, preserving protection but reducing taxes. Beyond that, Jackson hoped to distribute any surplus revenue to the states. As pressure from the South increased, Jackson defended the constitutionality of the protective tariff as a useful power approved by uniform precedent, but assured opponents that the suffrage would prevent excessive taxation. Even in the midst of the nullification crisis, when Jackson finally advocated the reduction of the tariff to the revenue standard, he maintained that the harms of the tariff had been exaggerated, and the primary detriment he was willing to assign to protectionism was its tendency to foster public discontent. It was only in the context of internal improvements that Jackson admitted that the Constitution withheld from the general government "power to regulate the great mass of the business and concerns of the people," and suggested that federal action could be constitutional only if a "general and well-defined principle" could be established to identify genuine national interests.[99] Jackson was not merely agnostic on the tariff issue, but was a proponent of protectionism, though to a lesser degree than some others. The elimination of the protective tariff from the Jacksonian system was the result of outside pressures, not of his own determination of the political agenda.

The nullifiers' task, therefore, was to place the attack on the protective tariff on a constitutional footing, and in doing so to reorient the broader Jacksonian construction of the domestic regime to include the fiscal operations of the protective system. This construction necessitated the rejection of the Marshall Court's understanding of the implications of expounding a constitution. Whereas Marshall had taken this as an injunction to read political powers broadly so as to maximize the sphere of political discretion, Calhoun insisted that constitutions were about limits on power, and thus every positive use of power was a constitutional issue. The particular expansion of the power to lay imposts placed all constitutional limitations at risk, for once fiscal policy could be turned to unauthorized uses, the enumerated powers were nugatory.[100]

The nature of the issue, especially as structured by the *McCulloch* ruling, required the opponents of the protective tariff to develop the intimate connection between so-called policy issues and constitutionality. Although some attempted to answer Clay on narrowly interpretive and textual grounds, most elaborated how protectionism perverted the spirit and broader meaning of the Constitution even as it remained within the confines of its terms.[101] Notably, the attack on the protective tariff during the crisis was not grounded primarily in the agrarianism that had characterized much of the early Jeffersonian regime. Instead, while accepting the existence and value of manufacturing, the nullifiers focused more particularly on the protective tariff.[102] The protectionist system operated as "a system of plunder" benefiting particular local interests.[103] This understanding was related to the nullifiers' commitment to radical federalism. The tariff necessarily expanded federal powers, not only by weakening the constitutional limits of the enumerated powers but also by increasing the political and economic influence of the general government. Additionally, the constitutional requirement that the tariff be uniform was not simply the technical requirement that Clay and his allies thought, but expressed a larger constitutional vision. All the powers of the general government were supposed to be exercised for the common interest, and therefore would "act uniformly on all the parts." The need for permanent support of Northern industries was indicative of the local and essentially private nature of the interests at stake and of the tendency to create a parasitic class permanently dependent upon public largesse.[104] Of course, this view of the effect of protection was also grounded in economic theories regarding international trade and the operations of labor and capital markets that were popular in the South.

Even as opponents denounced the constitutionalization of the protection issue as excessively rigid, nullifiers such as Calhoun articulated an understanding of a more flexible Constitution. In a public letter to Calhoun, William Henry Harrison pleaded with the South to understand that the North could not yield on a constitutional issue, for to do so would be "to cut our own throats" and lose the benefits of protection completely and forever. Such views, noted Calhoun, made it "hard to find a mid[d]le position . . . It involves not the question of concession, but surrender, on one side, or the other."[105] But such a view was unnecessary. South Carolina accepted that once brought down to a revenue standard, the tariff could provide incidental protection. In private, Calhoun even thought that it might be possible to "single out some of the most important articles" for "liberal protection" within an otherwise revenue-oriented tariff, while gratifying the West with internal improvements. Such support should be temporary and anomalous, however, and he rejected the "*permanent* adjustment" sought by the administration in 1832 that increased the unequal effects of the protective system and further consolidated the principle of protection. Calhoun was also willing to accept adjustments in the tariff structure that might be necessary to accord with the exigencies of war and peace, but linking the tariff to such external and transitory policy considerations was distinct from abandoning constitutional principles and committing to "that system of oppression."[106]

By agreement, Southern congressmen largely held silent during the debates over the Compromise Tariff of 1833, as they had in 1828. The exposition of the tariff's purpose was left to Clay and the North. In introducing the Compromise, Clay indicated that it established stability in tariff policy, giving protection for a reasonable but limited period. Second, the Compromise would "bring the rate of duties to that revenue standard for which our opponents have so long contended." In doing so, Clay acted out of fear for the interests dependent on protection, but recognized that most of the union was apparently against the protective system. The "protective principle must be said to be, in some measure, relinquished at the end of eight years and a half," but Clay insisted that the power was only dormant and not fully abandoned. As the debate wore on, Clay became increasingly shrill in insisting that the protective power could not be forever abandoned, for it was a necessary attribute of government. Nevertheless, Clay's list of acceptable modes of protection in the future, of admitted constitutional powers, did not include protective duties without regard to revenue.[107] Despite Clay's assurances, Northern members repeatedly asserted that the tariff abandoned protection as both principle and system. The Compromise did embrace uniform duties, the Southern touchstone of a revenue tariff. Webster predicted that the people would mobilize to overturn the Compromise as a policy failure. But Clay pointed out that even Webster had to admit that tariff reduction was imminent, and his ultimate formulation of the Compromise was that it considered "revenue the first object, and protection the second"—that is, incidental protection.[108]

In addition to the substantive commitments of the Compromise, Clay had to struggle with the binding nature of the legislation. If the compromise measures were passed, Clay contended that Congress would have settled the great questions that had agitated the country, and that the settlement could be broken only in the case of such an emergency as war. The act was admittedly prospective, seeking to bind successor congresses and creating "a species of public faith which would not rashly be broken" and would "be adhered to by all parties." The promises extracted during the controversy might not be enforceable in the courts against future legislatures, but "there were other pledges which men of honor are bound by, besides those of which the law can take cognizance."[109] The pledges exchanged not only would be self-enforcing through the honor of the contracting parties, but public opinion and political and economic interests would all act to sustain the Compromise into the future. As far as Clay was concerned, the tariff issue was settled at least until 1842, the last year specifically included in the law's tariff schedule. Again and again, Clay alluded to the similarity between the ratification of the Constitution and the passage of the Compromise. In both cases, the contending parties accepted the terms as a whole in the interest of structuring the political future, and thus transcended contemporary and persistent difficulties; the great issues at stake and the solemn occasion that produced the pact would ensure its survival, just as they ensured the survival of the Constitution itself.[110]

In fact the construction marked by the Compromise was remarkably successful. Despite Northern and Western resistance to recognizing the explicitly constitutional position taken by the South on the protective tariff, the settlement reached in 1833 achieved a binding quality that did largely remove from politics one of the most contentious issues of the period. As Calhoun had advocated, the ultimate settlement achieved a virtual political consensus around incidental protection, effectively abandoning protection as the primary object of the tariff, though the South would have preferred the simpler and more orthodox abandonment of any purposeful protection. Moreover, the nullifiers' actions reorganized the priorities of Jackson's own construction of the domestic regime, pushing the president toward a more laissez-faire and localist position than he was otherwise taking on his own. By portraying federal fiscal policy as operating in the same way that Jackson was already representing federal financial policy as functioning, the nullifiers broadened and changed Jackson's agenda, elevating fiscal policy to a prime place in the new regime and further limiting the economic role of the general government. These new priorities are evident in Jackson's new attitude toward revenue distribution schemes in his last annual message and in his new hardline approach to internal improvements as no longer realistic after the Compromise.[111]

The 1833 settlement continued to affect consideration of the issue long after Jackson's term of office. In 1837 Clay squelched initiatives to modify the tariff by insisting that the Compromise was binding and should be regarded like the Constitution itself. In 1838 Webster complained that Jackson had been elected with support from protective interests and that the Compromise was an "attempt to make a new constitution; to introduce a new fundamental law, above the power of Congress, and which should control the discretion of Congress, in all time to come." Despite his objections to these goals, even Webster was forced to admit that the agreement was binding given the "important and agitating subject," and could be set aside only under "clear necessity."[112] The true viability of the construction is indicated, however, by its fate after the technical expiration of the Compromise in 1842. The Whig electoral success in 1840 posed a superficial challenge to the continuation of the Jacksonian regime, and the passage of the protectionist "Black Tariff" of 1842 suggests the limits of the particular tariff construction. Nonetheless, several factors in favor of the construction are decisive. Though the 1842 tariff was clearly protectionist, its passage depended on a genuine revenue shortfall that required an increase in duties. Additionally, in contrast to past measures the tariff had remarkably little popular support and was initiated and passed almost entirely at the behest of Whig congressional leaders. Third, the tariff fight in 1842 helped fracture the Whig party, splitting the congressional delegation sectionally and from the president, the tenuous Whig Tyler, who regarded the Compromise of 1833 as a constitutional principle. This fragmented party suffered a devastating reversal in the midterm congressional elections of 1842 and was forced from office in 1844. The new tariff passed in 1846 vindicated the revenue principle and marked the last major tariff revision of the antebellum period.[113] Finally, the Compromise, though officially over, continued to influence the congressional debate in 1842 and 1846, and protectionists were forced to justify themselves in terms of that agreement and its constitutional principles. A Northern congressmen exposed the secret understandings of the Compromise, in which Clay was said to have assured the North that the Compromise would not be binding. Others immediately responded that the Compromise was no mere law, but occupied a special place in American politics between law and the constitutional text itself. In any case, Clay's public expressions and assurances were the relevant features of the agreement, not any possible hidden intentions. Throughout the 1842 debate, opposition speakers repeated the constitutional and political understandings of the 1833 construction, insisting that the spirit and understandings of the Compromise outlived the strictures of the act itself. Once again, Southern speakers insisted that the tariff was an exercise in sheer majority power, and as such would be repealed at the first opportunity.[114]

Upon regaining political control, the Democrats reasserted the principles of the Compromise. Unlike the Whigs, the Democrats were willing to campaign on the tariff issue, explicitly committing themselves to the revenue tariff with only incidental protection.[115] They denied that the 1842 tariff established any precedent for a return to protection after the expiration of the 1833 act, insisting instead that the Compromise ended protection forever and established the true constitutional principles, from which 1842 marked an aberration and a fiscal emergency. Speaking in the Senate in 1846, the vice president explicitly identified the Compromise with a distinct constitutional vision that had become the decided majority and general will of the nation, and the secretary of the Treasury defended the revenue tariff on constitutional grounds. The 1846 return to the revenue tariff was defended not simply as the appropriate policy decision, or even as a party measure, but rather as the vindication of principles entered into by all parties in a sacred compact. Free trade was not only the principle of the 1833 agreement, but also the original vision of the Constitution itself, of equal position with personal freedom and religious liberty.[116] The protective tariff was not reintroduced into American politics until the Civil War, when the lame-duck rump Congress passed the Morrill Tariff in 1861. Even the early Civil War tariffs were ambiguously justified, however, as the Republican party adopted a weak protectionist position on the tariff issue and congressmen justified tariff adjustments as needed for revenue and to compensate manufacturers for the extraordinary wartime internal taxes.[117] Meanwhile, the secessionists adhered to their constitutional understandings and textualized its requirements. In the Confederate constitution, which largely followed the model of the federal Constitution, a clause was added explicitly barring the introduction of protective tariffs in the independent South.[118] By the end of the war, the dominance of the Northern Republican constitutional vision had rejected the commitment to free trade. As internal taxes and duties on noncompeting goods were dismantled or lowered after the war, protectionist duties were actually increased. Tariff rates did not approach post-Compromise levels again until after World War I, and low rates were not sustained until the United States dedicated itself to a free trade regime after World War II.

Table 3.2 indicates the effects of the Compromise, for 1833 marks a clear break in average duties imposed. Though the average rates themselves are not conclusive evidence of the abandonment of protection, as Calhoun's complaint about the 1832 tariff and the fact that the protectionist 1816 tariff actually reduced rates from wartime heights indicate, such a marked shift is suggestive of a different policy course. Such a conclusion is confirmed by the nature of the arguments made for the tariffs before and after the Compromise, the structure of the rates imposed, and the frequency of adjustment of the duties. During the seventeen years from 1816 to 1833, there were five major tariff revisions, not including the 1820 tariff that was defeated in the Senate by a single vote and the 1827 tariff defeated in the Senate by the deciding vote of then Vice President Calhoun. In the twenty-seven years between the Compromise and secession, there were only three.[119] During that time, neither party supported the protective tariff as a primary campaign issue, and even the Whigs made little reference to it after 1844.

Table 3.2. Average tariff rates, 1821–1870

Years	Duties as a percentage of dutiable imports
1821–1824	44.62
1825–1828	50.29
1829–1832	51.55
1833–1842	35.08
1843–1846	33.47
1847–1857	26.22
1858–1861	20.13
1862–1865	38.27
1866–1870	47.64

Source: U.S. Bureau of the Census, *Historical Statistics of the United States, Colonial Times to 1970* (Washington, D.C.: U.S. Government Printing Office, 1975), Series U 207-212. Data are not available before 1821.

Note: The antebellum years are grouped according to different tariff laws. Because tariff legislation was in greater flux during the war years and afterward, the years after 1861 merely reflect wartime and postbellum rates.

Conclusion

None of the four identified constructions developed in a way fully consistent with our traditional understanding of constitutional law. Undoubtedly it is in part the failure of traditional models that has led commentators to neglect the constitutional aspects of the nullification crisis in favor of more "mundane" matters such as economic and slavery interests, party and personal politics, or even pure ideology. But constitutional constructions are part and parcel of larger political struggles. The Constitution is not simply used as political cover, nor are constitutional arguments employed in a purely cynical manner as yet another tactical weapon available to disputants. Rather, outside the realm of narrow interpretation, the constitutional text is provided meaning by the success of political movements in relating the document to current political life.

The very tone of the debates surrounding the nullification crisis is inconsistent with our expectations of constitutional elaboration. These debates were often conducted in highly personal terms and can hardly be characterized as moderate. Examining how the Constitution is actually debated in a political context reveals that considerations of constitutional meaning are not the sole province of technical or professional expertise, but are also and perhaps primarily fundamental to defining the nature of the polity and its citizenry. Even congressional speakers who couched their attacks in the traditional etiquette of the legislature nonetheless made their feelings known not only about opposing arguments but also about opposing speakers. Calhoun, among other Southern speakers, pointedly accused the president of betraying both Southern interests and his public faith. Clay suggested that Thomas Cooper, the president of South Carolina College and a prominent nullifier, was a traitor to his adopted country and should go back to Europe. The president of the United States repeatedly asserted that the nullifiers were traitors and pledged to march on South Carolina with two hundred thousand men to put them down with the sword and arrest the leaders of the nullification movement.[120] All the major figures in the debate spent substantial portions of their public statements exchanging and defending themselves against charges of personal inconsistency and heresy. Personalizing the debate and vilifying the opposition were intrinsic to the process of determining constitutional meaning on these issues. Similarly, claims of political authority, such as those invoking the name of Jefferson, secured a political place and a base of support. Such attacks helped define the positions at stake, as well as their significance, and the success or failure of personal accusations contributed to the ultimate fate of those positions.

The importance of such immoderate language is particularly manifest in the first-order struggle of the nullification construction, to win recognition as being about constitutional meaning. Despite the political openings provided for nullification by a states' rights tradition, Jackson's electoral success, and the economic distress of the cotton-growing South, nullification met sustained resistance from those who wished to label it as beyond the pale of acceptable debate. The Court's attempt to monopolize constitutional discourse while favoring expansive readings of congressional powers, combined with the political power of economic and political nationalists, laid the foundation for a plausible case that both federalism and the protective tariff had already been determined by the constitutional text. Nullification's success in winning support from a state legislature and prominent political figures, as well as the nationalist admission that the relevant text was indeterminate, belied both Jackson's and Webster's claims that a truly new constitution was in the offing. Additionally, the opponents of the nullifiers' construction operated within the context of a vague text with broad grants of power. To construe such grants as necessarily open to the discretion of Congress was itself to posit how the open-ended text could be transformed into concrete action. Nonetheless, such claims allowed the nationalists to attempt to transfer the ground of debate from one of political construction to one of judicial interpretation, and further to denounce their opponents in the strongest possible terms.

Similarly, the nullifiers did not clash with their opponents on every point and seek to refute every charge, but often simply ignored opposing arguments in order to shift the debate onto more favorable terms. Thus, Clay's insistence that the protective tariff fell under the commerce rather than the revenue clause was largely ignored by the nullifiers, who preferred to speak in broad terms about the spirit of the Constitution and the nature of republican politics. They bypassed what they saw as inadequate arguments about known or discoverable textual meaning in order to fill the document with the meaning of American politics more generally. In the case of the tariff, the unfamiliarity of constitutional constructions under a written constitution also served to confuse the debate, as congressmen simultaneously pledged their allegiance to a solemn pact that depoliticized key issues and questioned the obligations imposed by a legislative settlement. Even so, the understandings contained in the 1833 construction survived with relatively minor challenge until the late 1850s.

The anomalous nature of constructions is emphasized by the role of external factors in giving them meaning. Interested economic, political, and institutional considerations were critical not only in motivating the active parties, but also in forming the construction itself. It seems doubtful, for example, that nullification would have taken the shape it did if Calhoun's ties to the Jackson administration had not been frayed to the breaking point and his political base in South Carolina had not moved so far toward acceptance of disunion. Unlike Madison's Virginia, South Carolina seemed to have little success while relying on the national suffrage, shaping the constitutional arguments made. Moreover, rather than burying such issues in the background as inessential concerns of motivation and history, Calhoun and the nullifiers embedded them in the construction itself. Nullification was constitutional *because* it was a necessary political tool. Radical federalism was proper *because* contemporary federal actions undercut the political influence of the states. The protective tariff was unconstitutional *because* of the array of economic and political interests in the nation, and it could become constitutional if those interests changed. Indeed it was this feature that helped make protectionism nonjusticiable, for it was not simply the tariff law itself that was taken as unconstitutional. The protective tariff became unconstitutional, in the nullifiers' argument, only once it was placed in the context of the American System and both its redistributive taxation effects and its role in supporting a redistributive system of expenditures were taken into account. The judicial examination of a tariff law in isolation would achieve little in terms of clarifying why protectionism was illegitimate.

Consistent with this mixing of traditional policy considerations with constitutional concerns, the eventual settlement was itself a compromise measure. The nationalist contention that no fixed and clear rule could be drawn to distinguish between the roles of the general and state governments or a protective and revenue tariff tended to remove such issues from constitutional adjudication by the courts, but it also served as the basis for the development of Southern arguments. The lack of a clear rule did not preclude the existence of distinct principles. The imposition of a single tariff rate for all goods was at best an approximation of a revenue standard, but it served to guide the practical judgments as to the nature of the tax system. Outside the context of sharp breaks between constitutional and unconstitutional actions, principle could be satisfied with incidental protection and a schedule of gradually reduced rates. Political motivation, popular understanding, and political and economic effects were all essential to forming both the standard for judging constitutional violations and the particular judgment of those violations on the subjects of federalism and the tariff.

Like the Constitution itself, the construction initiated by nullification was subject to interpretation. Even after passage of the Compromise Tariff, doubts remained as to particular effects of legislation, its broader meaning, and its duration. Similarly, the requirements of the newly constructed federalism were not entirely clear and had to be further elaborated in the context of the congressional acceptance of abolition petitions, the distribution of federal revenue, and the administration of the territories. As Clay noted, some pledges were not binding in a court of law and had to be maintained through the continued support of active political interests and public understanding. Some, such as Webster, failed to recognize the existence of the new understanding even as they became increasingly isolated politically. Others, such as Clay, tested the limits and strength of the construction, requiring further demonstrations of its continued viability and dominance. Occasionally such challenges took the form of judicial inquiries, but more often they remained within the political sphere.[121] Although the construction of the tariff power received statutory embodiment, including a detailed schedule of duties and timetable for their reduction, the constructions settled by the Compromise were not fully formalized. Even in the case of the tariff, both the duration and larger meaning of the Compromise depended on broader political understandings that could not be reduced to legal rules, statutory language, or procedural requirements. The specific tariff duties were an indication of the construction, but did not exhaust its meaning. This limitation was recognized by those involved at the time, who noted the inadequacy of the specific legislation as a guide to correct principle even as they drafted and passed it. The proper conception of federalism was even more abstract. Contextualized political judgment would still be necessary to extend and apply federalist principles in the future.

The ultimate resolution did not fully satisfy any of the major figures in the struggle. Yet it did structure the nature of future political debate on the distribution of political power and the role of the general government in the economy and received the compliance of government officials. Such compliance did not always come easily, and the reinforcement of the free trade position with the election of Polk and the passage of the 1846 tariff required substantial political resources. Still, it was the Compromise that structured those later events, politically and ideologically. Ultimately, it

was Hayne's claims that violations of the construction were taken as illegitimate acts of political will that were vindicated, not Webster's prediction
that the people would reject the construction.

Success in this construction was not derived directly from electoral victory or legitimation. As Webster noted, Jackson's presidential campaigns
had purposefully obscured his position on the tariff and certainly had not
prepared the nation for abandonment of the protective system during his
administration. Despite attempts by all sides to bolster their proffered
constructions with expressions of popular support, through memorials to
Congress, political rallies, public speeches, published pamphlets and newspapers, and individual campaigns for state and national office, no national
election before or after the Compromise turned on the tariff or nullification issues. Only South Carolina put the issue directly to the voters. The
construction did benefit, however, from its reconstitution of the partisan
politics of the period. Embedding free trade within the Jacksonian regime
both contributed to Democratic electoral success and ensured the continuity of free trade policies. The free trade construction was maintained
through partisan means, but it was neither legitimated nor instigated by a
prior critical election.

Both the construction and the settlement reached went against the constitutional understandings of Marshall, Madison, and Jackson. For all three
of these figures, who explicitly addressed the place of political practice in
filling in constitutional meaning in doubtful cases, the weight of uniform
precedent served to establish a federal power within a constitutional grant.
This approach instituted a certain ratcheting effect, as additional powers
accumulated in the federal sphere without any mechanism for removing
them once established. Even Jackson did not question this function of
precedent, but rather challenged Marshall's view of the uniformity of
precedent on the particular issue of the Bank.[122] In emphasizing states'
rights and the limited enumeration of federal powers, Calhoun and the
nullifiers challenged the growth and stability of federal powers by rolling
back the protective tariff that had been in operation continuously since at
least 1816, and confirmed by multiple laws under four administrations.
Their success indicates that constitutional debate can subtract from as well
as add to the powers of the government and its institutions, and that a
history of institutional practice is neither necessary nor sufficient for a
successful construction.

In order to reach the complex settlement represented by the Compromise of 1833, South Carolina initiated several interrelated constructions,

both broad and narrow. Not all were equally successful. The narrow construction supporting the use of nullification as a means of resolving constitutional disputes was decisively rejected, even as the broad construction of radical federalism was partially accepted and the substantive goals that nullification was meant to advance achieved an even more substantial success. The same constitutional understandings that supported radical federalism fed into the arguments against the protective tariff, including conceptions of the diversity of interests in the Union, the constitutional requirement that the states be treated as equal and independent, and the concern about the concentration of central power. The uncertain borders between these different constitutional positions allowed a certain degree of movement and compromise that could retain elements of different constructions and sever unsuccessful constructions from those that could win a greater degree of support. Although not all the participants in these debates were fully conscious of the task in which they were engaged, their actions provide a robust example of a significant, contested, and influential constitutional decision.

4

Andrew Johnson and Executive Construction

Andrew Johnson long had the distinction of being the only U.S. president to be impeached by the House of Representatives and brought to trial before the Senate. Historians have been particularly drawn to the first Johnson presidency not only because of his infamy as the only impeached president, but also for his role in the struggle to impose Reconstruction on the South after the Civil War and his status as the first vice president to become chief executive as a result of the violent death of his predecessor. Not only did Johnson have to struggle with the difficult task of managing the peace after an internecine war; he also had the unenviable task of following the great wartime president Abraham Lincoln, whose martyrdom largely erased the criticisms that had plagued the president during his lifetime. None of these features is unrelated to the defining moment of the Johnson presidency, his impeachment eight months before the presidential election of 1868. That impeachment served as the focal point for a series of constructions that redefined the nature of the presidency in the division of powers and ushered in the era of congressional government. The Johnson impeachment defined the extent of presidential leadership of the federal government, helped undermine the spoils system and the politicization of the executive branch, and reaffirmed earlier understandings of the impeachment power in the context of the presidency.

Despite his Democratic and slave-owning background, Johnson opposed secession while serving as senator from Tennessee and refused to join his home state when it did secede.[1] After Union armies captured Tennessee, Lincoln appointed Johnson as its "military governor." Johnson gained a reputation for his zeal for the task and his oft-repeated declaration that "treason is a crime and must be made odious." Needing to project the image that the war was a nonpartisan and national measure, the Republicans, who had won the presidency in 1860 with only 40 percent of the popular vote, manufactured a new "National Union" ticket of Lincoln and Johnson for the 1864 contest. Lincoln's assassination in April 1865 elevated the pro-Union Democrat to the presidency days after Lee's surrender at Appomattox.

The Northern Radicals initially welcomed Johnson's ascendancy, but their hopes were dashed as a presidential reconstruction based on Lincoln's plans was begun during the congressional recess. Fueled by his own experiences in Tennessee and Lincoln's earlier arguments, Johnson contended that the Southern states had never left the Union. Their normal operation had merely been temporarily disrupted by a massive conspiracy of traitors. Johnson gave the state political machinery to the Southern loyalists while securing the capitulation of the secessionists for a rapid restoration of the Union and a return to normalcy. By the time Congress reconvened at the end of 1865, Johnson was able to declare the end of hostilities and of slavery and to present the South's new constitutions, governments, and federal representatives.

The Republican caucus denied seating to the Southern congressional delegations, which included such political notables as the former vice president of the Confederacy. The Joint Committee on Reconstruction was formed to make its own recommendations. On February 17, 1866, the Joint Committee refused to readmit Tennessee to the Union without additional conditions. Two days later the president surprised Congress by vetoing the first major piece of Reconstruction legislation, the Freedmen's Bureau Bill. On February 22, in a speech commemorating Washington's Birthday, Johnson denounced Radical congressmen by name as extremists comparable to the secessionist leaders. In March Johnson vetoed the Civil Rights Bill, but the Senate for the first time in its history overrode, by a single vote, a presidential veto on a major piece of legislation.[2] Over presidential opposition, Congress drafted the Fourteenth Amendment and sent it to the states for ratification.

Johnson took an active part in the midterm elections of 1866. In a "Swing around the Circle" he toured the country denouncing his congressional opponents and campaigning for his own favorites, while using the executive patronage to punish his adversaries. Nonetheless, the Radicals gained significant victories across the North.[3] In March 1867 Congress passed the Reconstruction Act, which dismantled Johnson's restored governments in the South and divided the South into five military districts; the Army Appropriation Act, which required that military orders go through General Ulysses Grant, who was protected from removal or transfer; and the Tenure of Office Act, which prohibited the president from removing civilian officials without Senate consent. Thus Congress gained effective control over both the design and the execution of Reconstruction.

Throughout 1867, Radicals in the House failed in three impeachment investigations of Johnson. Then, in February 1868, Johnson for the second time "removed" his Secretary of War Edwin Stanton and appointed a retired general, Lorenzo Thomas, to act as interim secretary. Johnson had already tried to remove Stanton once, appointing Grant to exercise the secretary's powers in his stead, but after passage of the Tenure Act the Senate had refused to concur in the removal, and Grant had returned the office to Stanton, who barricaded himself inside. The second Stanton removal tested the limits of the Tenure Act, and at the beginning of March the House for the first time was able to muster the votes to impeach. The first nine articles of impeachment dealt with the events surrounding the Stanton removal. The next day the Radicals included two additional articles, one censuring Johnson's speeches on his 1866 tour and the other a catchall charging general political resistance to the Congress. Despite Radical efforts to rush, the trial dragged on. At the end of May only three of the articles had been considered, and each had fallen short by one vote. The Senate then took a recess, during which the Republican convention nominated the moderate Grant for the presidency and endorsed the impeachment while refusing to condemn the seven dissenting Republican senators. Johnson's third-party hopes had long since been dashed, and the Democrats passed over him, nominating the morose Copperhead governor of New York, Horatio Seymour. With minimal resistance Johnson completed the rest of his term, and Grant was elected president in a relatively easy election in the fall of 1868.

The Johnson impeachment has proved particularly difficult to explain not only because of the continuing legacy of race in American political culture, but also because of the evident awkwardness of Congress' taking the drastic step of removing a president mere months before a presidential election. Explanations have tended either to demonize one of the parties involved or to attribute the entire affair to mass hysteria.[4] Some light can be shed on the conflict, however, by considering the impeachment in the context of the president's role in the constitutional and political system more generally and not simply in the context of immediate Reconstruction politics.

As Stephen Skowronek has recently observed, presidential authority has not developed in a simple linear progression, but has cycled in accord with movements in a larger political order.[5] The power at the executive's disposal after Lincoln's tenure allowed Johnson to embark on an ambitious program of unilaterally disfranchising and then pardoning huge numbers of Southern citizens, forcing Southern ratification of the Thirteenth Amendment and the repudiation of Confederate debt, and destroying and reconstituting the Southern state governments. Even as Johnson wielded these formal weapons, however, he lost authority over the government he directed. Once the pressure of war was released, the fractures in the Union alliance became evident. Notably, Johnson believed not only in the "Union as it was," but also in the strong Jacksonian presidency.[6] Although the Republican party was not united on what to do once the secessionist threat was overcome, few thought that the immediate restoration of the Southern Democracy under presidential leadership fitted the apparent mandate of the costly war. As Johnson exercised his available powers to bring about his vision of the restored South, he encountered a Northern polity committed to broader goals. In addition, focusing on the tenth article of impeachment, Jeffrey Tulis has argued that the Johnson presidency represents a failed attempt to break out of the original system of legislative deliberation in favor of a more modern presidential leadership of a popular, plebiscitary politics.[7]

The impeachment centered squarely on the relative power and roles of the legislative and executive branches of the federal government.[8] After Lincoln's wartime expansion of the presidency, Congress was eager to institute the Whiggish conception of the presidency that the Republican party had inherited, while Andrew Johnson hoped to expand the claims of the enlarged presidency on the national political process. The impeachment of Andrew Johnson holds the answer to Theodore Lowi's recent question, "if Lincoln somehow built upon a Jackson legacy, then what happened by 1900 that left us with what Woodrow Wilson called 'congressional government' and with what Lord Bryce characterized as a dreary parade of weak presidents?" If the conditions "favoring growth of executive power in a 'new American state' were all in place," why did they sustain not even a trace "from Lincoln's record?"[9] The withdrawal from the possibilities of a Lincolnian modern presidency was neither accidental nor foreordained, but was the outcome of a deliberate constitutional struggle between advocates of presidential power and proponents of congressional government who squared off over the future of the South and of postbellum America.

Reconfiguring the Presidency and Executive Powers

Like most significant impeachments, the Johnson impeachment was a means to other ends. The impeachment was the defining moment in a conflict between two visions of the president's place in the constitutional system. Presidential powers had been asserted and abandoned, strained and moderated from Washington to Lincoln, and the invigorated office inherited and extended by Johnson was neither clearly authorized by the Constitution nor fixed in the dominant political norms. The immediate political issues motivating the impeachment, such as overcoming Johnson's opposition to congressional policy in the South and determining the parameters of the 1868 presidential election, played into longer-term considerations of the growth in executive power and influence that had already become a concern under Lincoln and the threat of future continued interference with congressional policymaking. Regardless of the outcome of the 1868 elections, Johnson's institutional legacy threatened to shift political power to the White House.[10]

The eventual resolution prevented the president from centralizing power over the executive branch as his own political resource. Yet in defeating Johnson's political aspirations, the congressional Republicans advanced the cause of the administrative state and the ultimate reduction of party power. More broadly, Congress redefined itself as the central figure in the government, relegating the presidency to a distinctly secondary position as executor of the legislative will.

Setting the Conflict

The successful impeachment of Johnson came after a series of skirmishes between the executive and legislative branches at the end of the Civil War. This history of conflict framed the specific charges, helped the Radicals justify the necessity of an impeachment, and established the resources and arguments that would be employed later. Ultimately, these earlier battles allowed both sides to claim that the specific articles of impeachment were only the symbols of a dispute over the nature of the executive power and the separation of powers more broadly.

Concern over the strength of the presidency emerged almost immediately after the inauguration of Abraham Lincoln. Lincoln used the timing of the secession crisis during a congressional recess to take personal control of the political and military situation. Unlike his predecessor, Lincoln did not question the president's authority to act independently of Congress, let alone the authority of the federal government itself to act against seceding states.[11] Early in the conflict, Lincoln touched on the meaning of the war and the future of the peace when he rescinded Radical general John Frémont's emancipation order in Missouri and stripped him of command, while elevating the Democratic George McClellan to the head of the army. Congress soon reacted by forming the Joint Committee on the Conduct of the War to examine Lincoln's war policy and to control army personnel. Republican Senator Charles Sumner insisted that the Constitution gave Congress "all that belongs to any government in the exercise of the right of war" and made the president "only the instrument of the Congress."[12] Despite growing congressional opposition, Lincoln's wartime powers remained largely unchecked.[13] Similarly, dissension over the difficult and divisive task of Reconstruction was apparent but contained. The Radicals denounced Lincoln for "dictatorial usurpation," but the 1864 elections and the assassination prevented a more expansive conflict until Johnson tried to extend Lincoln's proposals throughout the South.[14]

Through sweeping use of his pardoning power and control over the military, Johnson embarked on a program of Southern "restoration" that secured the ratification of the Thirteenth Amendment and the creation of new state constitutions and governments. Following Lincoln, Johnson used presidential proclamations and pardons to make policy for the Southern states. By construing the war as primarily a problem of civil insurrection and disloyalty, Johnson could strategically use his exclusive constitutional power to issue pardons to undercut prior congressional policies and to force Southern politicians, property holders, and voters to follow his will in preparing the states for renewed participation in the Union.[15]

Mirroring Johnson's use of exclusive powers to implement Reconstruction, Congress immediately developed its own constitutional powers in December 1865 to establish its authority over Southern policy. Though Johnson undoubtedly regarded the seating of the Southern representatives as *pro forma,* the Republican caucus realized that it was nonetheless a wholly legislative function. Thus, not only did the caucus direct the House clerk to exclude the Southerners from the roll call, allowing Congress to constitute its Northern majority to deliberate on Southern policy, but it then organized a Joint Committee on Reconstruction to which it referred "without debate" "all papers which may be offered relative to the representation of the late so-called Confederate States of America," excluding those members "until Congress shall declare such States or either of them entitled to representation."[16] The exclusion of Southern members emphasized that Congress possessed exclusive constitutional tools of its own with which to determine when Reconstruction was complete. The formation of the Joint Committee attempted to secure for the Congress the institutional tools to ensure that it could control Reconstruction. The Committee not only circumvented the existing instruments of congressional policymaking and attempted to confine policy deliberation on this divisive issue to a small group of legislators, but it also gave Congress a similitude of administrative capacity, allowing it to monitor and respond to events in the South. It was this threat of legislative organization, unity, and energy that led Johnson to denounce the Joint Committee as "an irresponsible central directory."[17] The committee's very capacity to imitate executive strengths made it seem both unusual and dangerous.

The Joint Committee's June 1866 report on the Southern states concluded that Reconstruction was a congressional responsibility. To the extent that the president had any authority in the South at all, it was merely to secure the peace. Having done so,

> it was not for him to decide upon the nature or effect of any system of government which the people of these States might see fit to adopt. This power is lodged by the Constitution in the Congress of the United States, that branch of the government in which is vested the authority to fix the political relations of the States to the Union, whose duty is to guarantee to each State a republican form of government, and to protect each and all of them against foreign or domestic violence, and against each other.

The president could only advise Congress that, in his judgment as commander-in-chief, troops could safely be removed from the South.[18] Whether the states were regarded as conquered provinces, disorganized territories, or states in need of republican governments, Congress alone had constitutional authority to determine their status and reorganize their governments. The president had presented the war as a criminal and military problem; Congress now insisted that it was a territorial and political question and thus subject to exclusive legislative determination.[19]

Congress did indicate that it was not antagonistic to executive power per se. Though not contemplating extensive new administrative structures to control domestic affairs in the South or elsewhere, in its first Reconstruction measure Congress did seek to extend and expand the wartime Freedmen's Bureau for peacetime operation. The first Freedmen's Bureau bill was successfully vetoed in February 1866. Not only did the bill delegate substantial authority to an executive agency to provide for the freedmen, but it also specifically involved the president in the activities of that agency. By contrast, the second Freedmen's Bureau bill, passed over a presidential veto in July 1866, sharply curtailed executive discretion in implementing freedmen policy and largely removed the president from involvement in those activities. In March 1867 Congress insulated the military from the commander-in-chief by requiring the president to issue all military orders through General Grant and prohibiting Johnson from transferring Grant or relieving him of command.[20] Congress was willing to utilize the executive branch, and the military specifically, to implement congressional policy in the South, but it was determined that administrative acts would adhere closely to legislative will.

The override of the Civil Rights veto in March 1866 marked not only the beginning of congressional control over Reconstruction, but also the first time a presidential veto was overridden on a major piece of legislation.[21] Johnson's defeat emphasized the contingent nature of presidential vetoes and laid the basis for eliminating the president entirely from the legislative process on significant issues. Nonetheless, Johnson continued to use the veto power to a greater degree than any previous president had. Even as Congress cheapened the value of the veto by casually overriding them, often on the same day as Johnson issued his message, Johnson expanded the veto from being a seldom-used ultimate symbol of presidential prerogative to being a regular aspect of legislative activity. Johnson not only issued more vetoes than any previous president had done, and had more vetoes overridden than any president before or since, but Johnson's example of frequent resort to the veto power has been emulated by his successors. The sixteen presidents before Johnson averaged under 4 vetoes apiece, with an average of .375 overrides. The twenty-four presidents following Lincoln averaged over 100 vetoes and four overrides apiece.[22] The quantity of vetoes is not itself fully explanatory of the nature of those vetoes or the power of the president issuing them, but the dramatic shift in the frequency of vetoes is indicative of the power Johnson carved out for the presidential office.[23]

These skirmishes over the relative prerogatives of the executive and legislative branches were comparatively minor and did not play directly into the Johnson impeachment and trial. They did, however, set the context for that culminating struggle, and defense counsel Thomas Nelson invoked this context in characterizing the president as nothing but "a democrat of the straightest of strict constructionists; an old Jacksonian, Jeffersonian democrat."[24] Johnson had acted on a political philosophy taken from the Democratic party of Andrew Jackson, recognizing a limited nationalism and a powerful presidency to sustain that nation. The Republican Congress, willing to tolerate Lincoln as a temporary expedient, was not so generous with an heir of Jackson seeking to establish his own administration. These conflicts over executive power demonstrated the growing significance of the presidency, as well as an intensified congressional reaction once the pressures of war and the presidential benefits of military leadership were reduced.[25] As policy disagreements intensified, each of the two branches developed its particular institutional prerogatives in order to gain as much control over the design and implementation of Reconstruction as possible, while shouldering the other branch aside as superfluous and secondary.[26]

Appointments, Removals, and the Chief Executive

The concerns over the relative power of the two branches culminated during the impeachment in an effort to construct the locus of the removal power, specifically, and the control of the executive branch, more broadly. The political core of the executive branch remained its civilian component, and the dispute over the control of these officers forced Congress to address one of the most entrenched and problematic political practices of the time, the spoils system.

Both the second Freedmen's Bureau bill and the military appropriations rider indicated that Congress was not committed to an ideal of the executive branch as a unitary entity. The military appropriations bill excluded from the constitutional powers of the commander-in-chief the right to transfer or demote personnel, to determine the chain of command, or to issue orders directly to subordinate military officers. Although the bill did not attempt to transfer control over the military directly to the Congress, it did construct the military as a partially autonomous institution within the executive branch. Similarly, the second Freedmen's Bureau bill removed discretion from the executive branch and limited its officials to performing purely ministerial functions, reducing the necessity and possibility of presidential supervision of the bureau's activities.

These tendencies were most fully articulated in the Tenure of Office Act, which became law on March 2, 1867, the same day as the military appropriations bill and the first Reconstruction Act. The Tenure Act provided that each executive-branch civilian official confirmed by the Senate was secure in office until a successor was confirmed by the Senate. In doing so, the act abandoned the precedent established in the First Congress that the president acting alone had the power to remove executive-branch officials. Besides the provision for impeachment, the Constitution does not explicitly assign a power to remove officers, but despite occasional challenge subsequent legislatures had largely adhered to the construction of the First Congress until the Tenure Act.[27]

In addition to posing the narrow issue of the removal power, the impeachment also forced a construction of the broader issue of presidential control over the executive branch. This settlement indicated not only whether the president was truly to be the chief executive of a united, hierarchical executive branch, but also whether the offices of the executive branch were to be a base of political power for the president to influence elections and legislation. The president and the Radicals in Congress staked out two extreme positions on both issues, with the former claiming full authority over the executive branch and the latter regarding the executive branch as an instrument of the legislature. Between these two extremes, a number of moderates favored separating the two issues, dividing administrative responsibility and political influence.[28]

The president initially defended his removal power in his Tenure Act veto message. Though the message was substantively limited, relying primarily on the authority of long precedent, Johnson did assert that both precedent and constitutional principle required that the removal power be vested in the president alone. He warned that constitutional principles could be preserved only "by a constant adherence to them through the various vicissitudes of national existence," and thus Congress should refrain from challenging a long-held and apparently successful practice. Moreover, the existence of an "efficient Executive" and the effective execution of "the legitimate action of this Government" required that the president be able to remove ineffective or questionable officers at will.[29]

The president's defense further developed the administrative justification for an exclusive power of removal at the impeachment trial. Johnson asserted that the removal power was among "the necessary means and instruments of performing the executive duty expressly imposed on him by the Constitution of taking care that the laws be faithfully executed." The president alone was responsible for the execution of the laws, and thus he must have the powers to fulfill that responsibility. The constitutional grant of the "executive power" to the president carried its own set of implied powers necessary to carry out the explicit duties imposed by Article II, and the decision by the First Congress was merely declaratory of an inherent power. Congress was powerless to alter a removal power incident to the executive power.[30]

The implied power of executive removal lent substance to the broader claim that the president was the head of a unified executive branch of government. As commander-in-chief, the president's directives were "entitled to respect and obedience" regardless of the channels of communication or the actions of Congress. The president's power was similarly absolute and exclusive over civilian officials. Inferior officers owed the president a duty to obey, but high political officials, such as cabinet members, owed not merely obedience, but agreement. To Johnson, Stanton's "defiance" of the president and the secretary's "loss of confidence in his superior," who was responsible for the secretary's conduct, was itself "official misconduct." The members of the cabinet had a constitutional duty to render advice to the president, but this responsibility required the "mutual confidence" of the president and the secretary. The cabinet was not composed of independent advisers representing party, congressional, or administrative factions, but rather was composed of subordinate officials who were to aid the president in the design and implementation of executive policy. Any difference of opinion within the cabinet could only "impair the efficiency of any administration." Indeed, cabinet members were merely agents of the president "as head of the executive department," and their actions had no independent existence but were "presumed to be made by the President himself."[31]

In Johnson's construction, there could be only one executive power. The Constitution created a distinct executive branch in order to ensure a single executive will, and thus energy, in the enforcement of the laws. The "personally and politically" hostile Secretary Stanton "was really a new Executive," for he was "administering the duties of his department without recognizing even the President's name." By insulating the cabinet and inferior officers from presidential control, Congress threatened to divide the executive power into separate, uncoordinated, and possibly antagonistic pieces—an unendurable situation.[32]

As Johnson's concern with the loyalty of his secretary indicates, the president was also aware of the political dimension of his constitutional power over the executive branch. Thomas Jefferson recognized the need to represent the Republican party in government in making his executive removals, but his primary interest was in official conduct. Thus, most Federalists were secure in their offices as long as their political commitments did not interfere with their government duties. Upon gaining the presidency, Andrew Jackson had gone beyond Jefferson's statements to defend a system of political spoils, in which the entire executive branch was to be regarded as available for appointments to political supporters.[33] The spoils system had gradually increased until a policy of four-year rotation was adopted, in which James Buchanan replaced the holdovers from his predecessor and fellow Democrat, John Pierce. One observer noted that "Pierce men are hunted down like wild beasts," indicating that even as the late Jacksonian presidents were losing control over their appointments to congressionally centered parties, executive appointments were increasingly being viewed in terms of personal administrations and not just in terms of party.[34] In 1860 Buchanan actively used the federal patronage to secure his own nomination, turning the executive branch against his own Democrats in order to build a presidential party.[35] Lincoln was somewhat more constrained by the Whig ideology of his party and by his own weak political position, and thus began his term by carefully distributing the patronage to satisfy all factions in the Republican party. Nonetheless, he also used executive patronage not only to secure his renomination, but also increasingly to punish his congressional enemies, notably the Radicals.[36]

It was Johnson, however, with his marginal position in the Republican party and his strident disagreement with Congress over Reconstruction, who sharpened executive patronage into a tangible threat to congressional power.[37] At the very outset of Johnson's administration, the president was warned that patronage was being used by congressmen to defeat administration policy, and several appointments were delayed until the administration had time to "know who is who and what we are doing to fortify ourselves and the cause of right." As his vetoes were overridden, the president began replacing officials with his own loyalists, regardless of formal party affiliation.[38] Johnson made his position public in his Washington's Birthday speech, telling his audience that "I am free to say to you, as your Executive," that he opposed the Joint Committee on Reconstruction. Having thus threatened to block his own party's legislation, Johnson went on to list by name leading congressional Radicals whom he considered equivalent to the secessionists in their opposition to the Constitution. Finally, calling upon the electorate, he predicted that "there is an earthquake approaching, there is a groundswell coming, of popular judgment and indignation" that would remove Johnson's congressional foes.[39] As a student of Johnson's presidency observed, "by naming names and calling attention . . . to a deep division of conviction between himself and the Legislative branch, he had done something which was beyond the power of any other single individual to do: he had accorded official recognition to a split in the government."[40] Not only had Johnson advanced the idea that the government was not a unitary entity; he had also broken with his own party and publicly intervened in the legislative process. The president no longer represented himself as a dissatisfied partner in the government. The presidency was to be an alternative center of government.

As the 1866 midterm election approached, it became evident that Johnson's only hope of winning his own term of office in the White House was to build an alternative to the Republican party. This plan was most fully realized in the ill-fated National Union party that gathered in convention in August. Johnson praised the convention's resolutions as a second Declaration of Independence and Emancipation Proclamation, freeing the nation from the Congress. The president made selective use of the removal and patronage power throughout the spring and summer, filling the press and Congress with patronage discussions and complaints. A panicky Congress considered a measure to check removals, but it was defeated on the theory that Johnson's removals were not an immediate threat to congressional power. Embarking on his anti-Congress campaign tour, Johnson used the accouterments of the presidential office to enhance his political position, posing General Grant and Admiral David Farragut on the stage with him and, at least initially, receiving formal introductions from local officials. Republican fund-raising circulars portrayed the tour as the president's personal effort at "cutting off the heads of Republicans, and 'kicking' them out of office because they remain loyal to the principles of the loyal party."[41] Late in the Swing, Johnson berated Congress and the Republican party for its policies and its patronage. The Republicans had fattened congressional party power through public offices, and the president contended that it was time to "take the nipple out of their mouths."

How are these men to be got out—[Voice, "Kick 'em out!" Cheers and laughter.]—unless your Executive can put them out, unless you can teach them through the President? Congress says he shall not turn them out, and they are trying to pass laws to prevent it being done. Well, let me say to you, if you will stand by me in this action, [cheers,] . . . God being willing, I will kick them out. I will kick them out just as fast as I can.[42]

Johnson's efforts to defeat Congress in 1866 were unsuccessful, but his explicit attack on the Congress and his attempt to create a presidential party to shift political influence from the legislative to the executive branch built upon trends and possibilities that had already been apparent in previous administrations.[43] Johnson's success in constructing the removal power as an exclusive presidential instrument to consolidate the executive branch under a single leader would have represented a serious threat to existing political norms and division of powers.

Despite the passage of the Tenure Act, the Republicans in Congress did not agree on the nature of the removal power. The Radical construction asserted in the impeachment placed the removal power under exclusive congressional control, as set by statute. This specific claim was part of a larger theory that questioned whether the president was truly a "chief executive" of a unified executive branch. The Radicals suggested instead that the executive branch was an expression of legislative will and needs, and therefore need not possess any unified organizational structure nor any distinguishable executive will. The critical question for the Republicans was not whether the president was to have full authority over the executive branch, but whether the executive was to continue to be a congressional political tool or was to become a nonpartisan administrative device. In either case, neither the removal power nor the executive power was to be allowed to become a political instrument for the consolidation of presidential power.

In his report advocating impeachment, George Boutwell made clear the threat that the Radicals saw in the removal power. Boutwell admitted that the removal power had been used to supply patronage for political support in the past, but contended that Johnson had essentially changed the system, and in doing so had usurped powers and committed a constitutional offense. Johnson's abuse of the patronage was to turn it against the Congress in order to support an independent presidential policy and party.[44] Benjamin Butler, a House manager and previously an infamous Radical general, contended that the issue in the impeachment was whether "the President, under the Constitution, [had] the more than kingly prerogative at will to remove from office and suspend from office indefinitely, all executive officers of the United States . . . at any and all times, and fill the vacancies with creatures of his own appointment, for his own purposes, without any restraint whatever?" Indeed, "the momentous question, here and now, is raised whether the *presidential office itself (if it has the prerogatives and power claimed for it) ought, in fact, to exist as a part of the constitutional government of a free people.*"[45] While such rhetoric has led commentators either to dismiss the managers as wildly unrealistic or to condemn them for seeking to destroy the executive branch of the government, Butler's point was not that there should be no president but that there should be no chief executive. In contrast to the assumptions underlying the modern presidency of the twentieth century, the Republican presidency was not the chief of anything at all.[46] The executive branch was not to be a responsive hierarchy at the command of the president, but a set of tools of the congressional will. If the existence of a chief executive implied that the president had the capacity to remove officers at will in order to fill offices with his own partisans, then Butler was willing to reduce the president to a more limited, and isolated, capacity.

The managers argued that Johnson's conception of the presidential role as chief executive was inconsistent with the nature of the constitutional separation of powers. Far from being a general grant of executive power, Article II was strictly limited. The president would have no power of removal at all without positive statutory authority to grant and define that power. Only Congress possessed implied powers through its "necessary and proper" clause, and thus only Congress could supply by law the removal power that the constitutional text did not explicitly delegate. The legislature was the repository of ultimate power, with the authority to speak for the people to supplement the people's fundamental text. In initially creating the executive departments, the first Congress had only delegated the removal power to the president. As a delegation of congressionally controlled power, a later Congress had as much authority to modify the settlement as the original Congress had to delegate the power in the first place.[47]

The possibility of a united executive branch beholden to the president suggested a threat to the republic, and congressional power, reminiscent of the British monarchy. Congress had already sought to limit presidential influence over the military, but the risk of Johnson's using military force against Congress seemed to be a recurrent fear. Indeed, the managers urged haste on the senators in part because the president continued to hold military power during the trial, and Johnson's public addresses were seen as particularly dangerous because they came from the commander-in-chief. The cabinet posed a more subtle threat to congressional power. Granting a close relationship between the president and the cabinet seemed to open the door to the formation of a miniature legislature within the executive to deliberate together and make policy for the federal government. The cabinet served as the most visible display of what the president hoped to do to the entire executive branch, creating "a cabal to discuss party politics, and devise ways to perpetuate their tenure by securing the re-election of their chief." By refusing to advise Johnson further, Stanton had simply done his duty of maintaining his official relationship with Congress and the laws he was to execute, while refusing to participate in the formation of a centralized executive.[48]

At the lower levels of the executive branch, Congress noted that the quality of Johnson's appointments was inadequate, but by far the greater concern was Johnson's use of the removal power to promote his own political ends. The Senate's participation in the removal and appointment powers served as an essential check on the president to prevent him from "supplanting [faithful officers] with his own tools and confederates." The Tenure Act had served to stop Johnson, who had already "removed hundreds of faithful and patriotic public officers." His goal in making these removals, the managers charged, was to advance his own political ambitions, corrupt Congress and the electorate, and gain control over the execution of the laws.[49]

As such charges indicate, Congress was torn over the alternative to presidential removal. The spoils system risked shifting power to the presidency, but it had also been an important support to congressional power. The Tenure Act had made removals of any kind difficult, and therefore ultimately hampered the distribution of political patronage. The Republicans were unable to settle on a clear alternative to Johnson's claim to full discretion over the executive branch. The impeachment established that the removal power was under the control of Congress, but also that it was no longer fully discretionary. Through the remainder of the nineteenth century, further attempts to extend congressional power over removals and appointments beyond this understanding were defeated as the nonpartisan administrative function of the executive branch was formalized.

That the majority of the Senate was willing to vote for conviction of Johnson indicated the general rejection of any construction that lodged a fully discretionary removal power in the executive alone. Although some senators followed the House managers in relying on the "necessary and proper" clause to demonstrate the full authority of the Congress over executive powers as a whole, the senators more generally argued that the Senate and the president held a joint executive power, as indicated by the shared power of appointment. Even if the president had the legal power to remove officers at will, he did not have the constitutional and political authority to do so without cause. The president remained impeachable for "a wanton, corrupt, or malicious exercise of the power" to remove officers. Given the size and power of the executive branch after the war, removal policies that might once have been acceptable were no longer sufficient. The "corrupt and corrupting influences of executive patronage" were now too great.[50] As a result, the Senate established a new political norm that constrained executive discretion. But because of its vagueness and dependence on presidential motivations and political context, the new standard could not possibly be formalized or enforced by external, neutral agents.

By recognizing a joint power, rather than an exclusive congressional power, to control appointments and removals, the Senate weakened the strong construction advocated by the managers, but strengthened the position of the Senate relative to the House. A joint power to confirm and remove elevated the Senate's executive responsibilities, but undercut the House's interest in patronage appointments. Moreover, in order to condemn the president's use of executive patronage for his own political gains, the advocates of impeachment were forced to criticize the spoils system itself. Joseph Fowler, a Republican who voted to acquit the president, expressed the views of a more conservative bloc in doubting that the Senate, if given exclusive or primary control over removals, could refrain from using it for its own, merely political ends. All four of the Republicans who voted to acquit and survived until 1872, including Fowler, joined the Liberal Republican reform movement, which prominently advocated the end of the spoils system and the establishment of a civil service system.[51]

The construction that emerged from the impeachment was that the removal power was shared, but more importantly that it was to be used by the executive to enhance the administration of the laws. The executive branch was not to be the political tool of either the president or the Congress. The advocates of civil service reform split on the Johnson impeachment, being uncertain as to whether the removal of Johnson would help or hinder the cause of reform.[52] While some, such as Fowler, feared that the Senate would gain power at the president's expense and continue the congressionally dominated spoils system, others emphasized that Johnson's abuse of the patronage opened a political opportunity to depoliticize the executive branch. Though the reformers were not satisfied with the immediate results, their swing vote on the impeachment limited the construction that was available to Congress and forced a moderate stance that favored a reduction in the spoils system generally. The reformers were able to use the impeachment to strike a blow at the spoils, but were also able to pull the impeachment short so as not to emasculate the presidency and give the victory to congressional spoilsmen.

Commentators outside Congress were driven to the same conclusion. John Norton Pomeroy, who was generally sympathetic to the impeachment, nonetheless thought that the removal power had to be lodged in the president to secure effective enforcement of the laws. For him, however, the legal power to remove necessarily created an opportunity for abuse of that discretion. The appropriate response to this dilemma was not to change the beneficiaries of the abuse, but to change the operative norms of executive removals. Congress could do this by statute through civil service reforms, but more importantly it could also begin to change the political and constitutional norms under which the political system operated by making the "appointment of an unfit person, or the removal of a meritorious one . . . an impeachable offense." A change in practice was more important than a change in law for ensuring that executive officials held their positions during good behavior.[53] Alfred Conkling, whose brother would be defeated trying to resurrect congressional spoils under presidents Hayes and Garfield, came to similar conclusions. By turning the spoils against Congress and his own party, Johnson's example not only weakened the practice "impelling us onward to destruction, but affords a promise of future good." The removal power, though formally unlimited, was nonetheless constitutionally limited to its proper purposes and "invests its possessor with no right, in exercising it, to look an inch beyond the public weal." Again, Conkling advocated impeachment, not civil service reform, as the primary vehicle for reestablishing correct constitutional norms to govern the removal power and the administration of the executive branch.[54]

Though some reformist commentators feared that the focus on Andrew Johnson as an individual would miss the fundamental problem of a politicized executive branch, the impeachment did in fact change political norms, though it took decades to work out the implications and particulars. The Tenure Act itself was a particularly targeted version of civil service reform, which gained political support as a result of congressional opposition to Johnson. Its partial repeal during the Grant administration did not return power to the president, but rather removed what was seen as a temporary and clumsy statutory device. Although any version of a civil service weakened the presidency relative to the construction defended by Johnson, the absence of a statutory system did not indicate that the president controlled the executive branch.[55] Advocates of presidential power such as Henry Adams desired civil service reform only if it was self-imposed, by the president's own authority. But he recognized that control of the executive branch had decisively shifted away from the president and that Congress controlled the nature and pace of reform. Grant adhered to the new informal rules by vowing not to use executive offices to reward supporters and by studiously avoiding politics in appointing a decidedly administrative cabinet.[56] Although Grant retained a fair degree of discretion as to the individuals to appoint, that discretion could be exercised only within firm boundaries.

The construction established by the impeachment itself did not eliminate congressional influence from the distribution of executive offices. Grant and subsequent presidents were still occasionally forced to accept purely political appointments. Moreover, the president's ability to choose a large number of administrative officers remained dependent on the informational base of Congress to bring individuals to the administration's attention. Nonetheless, the impeachment did reverse the growing presidential construction that made the executive branch the political tool of the chief executive, and largely eliminated the notion of implied executive powers until reinvigorated by Theodore Roosevelt.[57] The executive power was diminished as a political and policy tool and redefined as primarily ministerial.

In defeating this presidential construction, however, the impeachment restricted use of the spoils system by Congress as well. In order to prevent the president from using his position to his own partisan benefit, the impeachers redefined the inferior offices of the executive branch as nonpolitical and administrative. This additional implication of the impeachment was not intended by all of those favoring Johnson's removal, but was nonetheless contained in the logic of congressional action. The tilt of the new construction was clarified as later legislators tried to diminish the president further by placing and protecting purely political appointments in executive offices. The administrative slant in the new construction of the removal powers gave later nineteenth-century presidents the authority to resist such efforts. The final defeat of Roscoe Conkling and the spoilsmen in Congress was not a victory for the president per se, but a further defeat for those seeking to gain partisan control over the executive branch. The administrative impetus set in motion by the impeachment eventually led to extensive civil service reform in the 1883 Pendleton Act.[58] The effects of the construction were still in evidence in the twentieth century. Even as the presidency was being expanded and strengthened to administer the newly constructed New Deal state, Congress again depoliticized a growing executive branch with the Hatch Act of 1939.[59] If the immediate executive office was to become a source of political power for the modern presidency, the administrative bureaucracy was not.

Separated Powers and the Constitutional Basis of the Presidency

The president and his congressional opponents also struggled over the definition of the presidential office, the meaning of the federal separation of powers, and the constitutional basis of the presidency. The result of that struggle would not so much determine the fate of a particular statute or instrument of political power as it would shape the way in which the two elected branches of the federal government would approach each other, and the electorate, in all of their activities. Johnson sought to establish the president as a full representative of the American people, equal to if not greater than the legislature. Such status would entail not only the direct relationship between the president and the people represented by the 1866 tour, but also the regular inclusion of the president in the policymaking process, the establishment of the executive branch as a source of independent policy formulation, and the recognition of a vigorous departmentalism that would authorize the president to refuse to execute at least some laws he deemed unconstitutional. Johnson was building on the examples of Lincoln and Jackson, but doing so in very different circumstances. As for Congress, a successful construction would recognize the primacy of the legislature in the federal system as the only legitimate representative of the sovereign people, reducing the president to a ministerial role. Although Congress did not completely achieve its desired construction, it was largely successful in securing its vision of the separation of powers at least through the remainder of the nineteenth century.

For Johnson, sustaining the status of the executive as an independent branch required grounding the presidency in a constitutional and political base as authoritative as that which empowered Congress. Johnson took the initial step in his first veto, declaring that the "President of the United States stands towards the country in a somewhat different attitude from that of any member of Congress." Whereas congressional representatives were chosen by small parts of the nation, only the president "is chosen by the people of all the States." Necessarily, therefore, congressmen took a narrow and partial view of the national interests; the president alone possessed the perspective of a national officer. Not only could he see beyond the confines of a single state or district, but more significantly "it would seem to be his duty" to defend the "just claims" of those citizens not represented in Congress at all, notably the loyal citizens of the Southern states excluded from congressional representation. As his relations with Congress deteriorated, Johnson declared himself the "Tribune of the people," resisting the abuses of the rump and internally divided Congress.[60]

Johnson's claim was radical not only because he himself had risen to the presidency through a wartime election and the death of his predecessor, but also because he offered it at a time when candidates had minimal contact with the electorate. During the party period initiated by Jackson and his foes, the public identities of presidential candidates were subsumed by their parties. With minimal direct campaigning by the presidential candidates themselves, the parties competed to elevate their representative to the White House.[61] By building a party around his own candidacy and policy views, Johnson threatened to reestablish the presidency on a new popular foundation. The president would be not only the enforcer of the national will but also the center of political deliberation. Johnson sought to back up his claim by taking his case directly to the people, engaging them in various public occasions in the capital and approaching them in the country at large explicitly in order to gain their support in an electoral contest.

Grounded in his constitutional authority as the head of an independent branch of government, and bolstered by the support of the people, Johnson did not hesitate to develop a set of policies separate from those being developed by the party caucus or Congress. Indeed, as a national officer faced with a partial legislature, the president felt a particular duty to be vigilant against any congressional usurpation. Independence risked conflict for Johnson. In order to resolve the conflict the president hoped to ground his position firmly in the Constitution, ultimately ensuring presidential victory. Lincoln had already indicated the president's willingness to intervene in the legislative process, proactively threatening to use his veto power against proposed legislation unless specific changes were made in the bill.[62] Though Johnson's first vetoes came as a surprise to Congress, he actively used his veto power to resist congressional policy. In the president's view, the Southern governments had already been restored through executive action, and both constitutional propriety and the national interest required that Congress accept his policy as completed. As Congress developed its own alternative, Johnson publicly condemned it for ignoring the presidential reports and recommendations and pursuing its own investigations. The president was willing to "cheerfully co-operate with Congress," but only if the latter abandoned its policy. In the meantime the president, as "the representative of another department of Government" having taken an "opposite doctrine," from Congress was obliged "to call the attention of my countrymen to their proceedings."[63] The president retained not only an independent voice in policy, but also an independent relation with the people and was obliged to appeal directly to them in order to check and influence Congress.

The ultimate expression of this elevated status of the presidency was Johnson's claim to the right to designate and refuse to execute unconstitutional laws. Johnson's particular version of departmentalism elevated the presidency primarily at the expense of Congress. Again, he built on the foundations laid by his model, Jackson, and his predecessor, Lincoln. Beyond his probably apocryphal declaration that Chief Justice John Marshall could enforce his own decision on Indian removal, Jackson had publicly defended the president's obligation to make an independent judgment on the constitutionality of a statute in exercising his own powers. In his first inaugural, Lincoln had defended the right of the other branches of government to limit the effect of Court decisions and to work to overturn the judicial reasoning. More quietly, Lincoln had ignored court orders in a habeas corpus case.[64] Both presidents, however, augmented congressional power over the Court at the same time that they enhanced executive power. Johnson, on the other hand, claimed that the president could refuse to execute a statute he believed to be unconstitutional, placing the president against Congress', not the Court's, judgment as to constitutional meaning. Moreover, Johnson emphasized his specific challenge to the legislature by arguing that he violated the Tenure Act only in order to bring the case before the Court. He counterpoised the constitutional judgment of both the president and the Court to that of Congress.[65]

The president's claim was a substantial expansion of executive prerogative, but Johnson's counsel was careful to limit its effects and application. Benjamin Curtis did not attempt to ground the legitimate violation of congressional statute in some particular aspect of presidential duty, but rather claimed it to be the "high and patriotic duty" of every citizen "to raise a question whether a law is within the Constitution of the country." Ironically, this sweeping claim to a general duty to question legislation severely threatened congressional supremacy without correspondingly increasing executive authority. In fact, Curtis assured the Senate that he did not intend to "occupy any extreme ground" to the effect that the president could "erect himself into a judicial court." Generally, the president could "only" agitate against unconstitutional laws and encourage the people to act at the polls. But if the law specifically encroached upon presidential prerogatives, then the president had the right and duty to violate the law in order to allow the judiciary to arbitrate between the two elected branches.[66]

For the president, the Constitution was a body of laws binding government officials, including the Congress. The law of the Constitution bound the president before the law of Congress did. In carrying out his duties "as the chief executive officer of the land," the president was "entitled to form a judgment . . . was compelled to form it," and thus had to follow his own interpretation of the Constitution to the exclusion of any congressional gloss on the document. Not only did presidential duty require him to construe his own constitutionally delegated powers, but his duty to enforce the law required him to determine what the law was, which included determining whether statutory law was consistent with constitutional law and thus authoritative.[67]

In developing this argument, the defense was too struck by its similarity to Marshall's reasoning in establishing judicial review to maintain a strict separation of executive and judicial functions. Nelson explicitly portrayed those two branches as allies in checking the arbitrary power of Congress. The president was not the "passive instrument of Congress," but rather

> under the Constitution there are living, moving, acting powers and duties vested in and imposed upon the President of the United States, and . . . he must, of necessity, have the right, in cases appropriately belonging to his department of the government, to exercise something like judicial discretion . . . he must act on his own authority and upon his own construction of the Constitution; and when he thus acts in reference to the removal of an officer or anything else, I maintain that it is different from the action of a private individual.[68]

The Constitution carefully created three departments of government, each with its own powers and duties. "They are independent of each other. No one is responsible to the other. They are responsible to the people or to the States." Moreover, each was enjoined "to take care of its prerogative" and to observe "with the utmost fidelity the provisions of the written Constitution." The president held an independent place in the constitutional system, and as a coordinate branch of government could not defer to congressional judgment as to constitutional meaning. The president possessed a direct link to both the people and the Constitution, and his perception of their goals was unmediated by congressional claims.[69]

The fundamental issue at stake for the defense was whether the executive was to be reduced to being subordinate to the legislature. The fact that Johnson had been elevated to the White House from the vice presidency served here to emphasize the stakes, for Johnson's own replacement could only be the leader of the Senate, who had never stood for executive office before the people. Benjamin Wade's ascension would result in the presidency's being "annexed to some other office" and in depriving "the nation of a President and [vesting] the office in the Senate." A branch of the government would be reduced to being an extension of the Congress. Far from being too strong, the presidency was in fact relatively weak, with only limited tenure and powers. The president was easily restrained by the suffrage, but the diversity of congressional membership and the significance of legislative powers ensured that Congress would be institutionally grasping and irresponsible. Only by strengthening the president's control over the full powers of the executive could Congress be checked and the national interest preserved.[70]

Congress, represented by the House managers, struck at Johnson with an expansive understanding of the legislative role under the Constitution. Only Congress possessed the full authority of the Constitution, and the impeachment and trial symbolized the close identification between the legislature and the sovereign people. With the crisis of war over, the managers contended that the time was ripe for reducing the power of the presidency and once again elevating Congress to the central place in political affairs. Though generally careful not to implicate Lincoln in Johnson's abuses, the House was clearly concerned with a general growth in executive influence. Congressional invective repeatedly cast the president in the role of a monarch and dictator, thus placing the legislature alternately in the role of the American patriots, the Parliament of the Glorious Revolution, or the people themselves. The spirit of republican government mandated a weak executive office unable to oppose the will of the legislature.[71]

Johnson had to be removed not simply because he violated a law, but because in doing so he had been defiant toward the expressed will of Congress. Johnson's technical violation of the Tenure Act was of far less importance than the attitude expressed by it, the evidence it provided that the president was developing an independent political will. The suspension of Stanton was merely one instance of this defiance, and Johnson's persistent use of the veto power, his reluctant execution of congressional Reconstruction, and his public speeches were all equally dangerous and equally indicative of his unwillingness to recognize the paramount authority of Congress. The ultimate result of such divisions could not be the mutual cooperation of equal and coordinate branches of government, but rather must be the eventual supremacy of one branch or another, the reestablishment of a single political will. Moreover, that will would be debased and corrupted, as presidential demagoguery and factionalism undermined deliberation.[72]

Within the construction offered by the managers, Johnson's actions were intolerable because Congress was identified with both the people and the Constitution. Rather than being an independent entity authorizing all of the branches of government, the managers contended that the Constitution was largely equivalent to the congressional will. Similarly, the legislature was the unique representative of the people in the federal government, and thus the Congress and the people were largely interchangeable terms. Representative James Wilson bluntly asserted that the national will could be known only "through the enactments of the legislative department of the government." The laws were not simply the policy pronouncements of one political unit, but were direct representations of the popular will. Legislative superiority was in fact unavoidable, in addition to being desirable, for the legislative powers were such that they must be the active force in government, and the legislature's special relationship to the people necessitated that in a free government the legislature would be dominant. After all, the Constitution created a government "*of* the people, *for the people*," which required a tighter union of the states and the reduction of the nonlegislative branches of government to popular accountability. That accountability was achieved by giving the Congress, as the representative of the people, the "controlling influence . . . even to regulating the executive and judiciary." Indeed, it was in the impeachment proceedings that Congress reached the fullest expression of its nature, "Here, at least, it may be said: '*Vox populi vox Dei*'—'the voice of the people is the voice of God.'"[73]

As the managers reflected on the responsibility and power of the impeachment, they were drawn inexorably to the conclusion that Congress was the living manifestation of the people in their sovereignty. Surveying the implications of the recent war and Reconstruction, Thaddeus Stevens affirmed that the "sovereign power in this republic is the Congress of the United States." The suffrage of the people was sufficient to ensure that the actions of Congress were consistent with the "people's will." It was this identification of Congress with the sovereign people that gave meaning to the "necessary and proper" clause particularly, and the legislative power more generally. It was to the Congress that the people had given powers "ample for all the necessities of national life" and to "adapt the administration of affairs to the changing conditions of national life." Contrary to the rigid set of laws envisioned by Johnson, the managers posited a Constitution that was constantly evolving and adapting, with Congress acting as the agent of change. The president was acting on a fundamental misconception of the nature of Congress in arguing that he must interpose himself as a check on its powers, for "it is not to be presumed, even for the purpose of argument, that they would wantonly disregard the obligations of their oath" to uphold the Constitution.[74] Ultimately, the conflict between Congress and the president was the continuation of a struggle between different forms of government, between self-government and dictatorship.[75]

The construction of congressional supremacy carried a number of implications. Most immediately, Johnson should be convicted for usurpation of power. In addition, the executive should be reduced to a ministerial function, and Johnson's claims about departmentalism were ungrounded. The impeachment was a conflict between the "Chief Executive Magistrate" and the "people of the United States." The continual characterization of Johnson by his critics as a drunkard, an image always linked to his public speeches, not only undermined his role as executor of the national will, but also made laughable his bid to participate in the deliberative process of policymaking. Moreover, to Congress, Johnson's claims to control his department heads only indicated his desire to transfer political deliberation from a legislative to a cabinet government, either supplanting or challenging the legislature's political will.[76] The president's defining function was to "follow and enforce the legislative will," without "uncertainties" or "discretion unless it is conceded to him by express enactment" of Congress. The president bore a special burden to defend the law, both in speech and action, for "he is its minister."[77]

To the managers, Congress was tantamount to the people and the Constitution, and thus there could be no plausible claim that its actions were unconstitutional. Johnson's constant cries of unconstitutionality were disingenuous and revolutionary. By questioning legislative authority, Johnson undermined the rule of law. By refusing to enforce, he stepped outside the bounds of law entirely. For the chief law enforcer to question the binding quality of congressional statute was to invite lawlessness throughout society; the president had no institutional claim that could distinguish him from any other citizen in this respect. The president was distinguished from the ordinary citizen, however, in the power at his command. Presidential disobedience in particular was tantamount to anarchy, undermining the unity of will that every government must possess.[78]

Johnson's antagonism toward Congress made him willing to challenge the legislature directly for control over the government. Until stopped by his advisers, Johnson was prepared to stand trial physically in the Senate and directly engage his congressional foes. Before the impeachment Johnson was defiant, telling his secretary that his thoughts were on "war." Boutwell, on the other hand, assured the Senate that a guilty vote was a vote for "peace," both from the sectional war and from the interdepartmental strife advocated by the president. The aftermath of the impeachment was to be the peace of both a Northern and a legislative hegemony over the nation, not the continuation of a raucous and divisive conflict of different interests. Though Johnson escaped conviction, he served the remainder of his term in irrelevance, and his successor gained the Republican party nomination in the midst of the impeachment beseeching his colleagues, "Let us have peace."[79]

The opinions of the senators endorsed the congressional construction of departmental relations, and Grant solidified the construction with a particularly passive term of office. To many senators, Johnson's technical violation of a statute gained its significance by being part of a continuing effort by the president to erect the executive branch into an independent policymaking entity.[80] As the trial approached, Senator Samuel Pomeroy sent word to the president that he could avoid conviction by turning over control of the cabinet to the Senate. Though rejecting Pomeroy's offer, Johnson did reach out to Republican moderates during the trial, accepting Stanton's immediate administration of the War Department, nominating a moderate replacement, securing Grant's authority in the South, advancing congressional Reconstruction, and sending assurances that if acquitted he would faithfully execute all laws.[81] Thus, moderate Republicans could satisfy their concerns for the formal separation of powers while being assured of the triumph of the Whig construction of the presidency and the success of their policies.

In accepting the nomination, Grant assured the Republican convention that he would "administer all laws in good faith" and that he regarded the presidency as "a purely administrative officer." In his inaugural he asserted that he retained a veto power, but assured Congress that "all laws will be faithfully executed whether they meet my approval or not." The president had no policy "to enforce against the will of the people."[82] Though later presidents had to be somewhat more assertive in defending executive prerogative against further erosion, the Whig conception of the presidency dominated. Presidential appearances before the public continued, but the remaining nineteenth-century presidents returned to the pre-Johnson pattern of being a figurehead in public, not a political partisan or policymaker. The primary limit on congressional control over the government was the lack of internal legislative organization, a defect gradually remedied by the congressional leadership. Even for the Democratic Grover Cleveland, heir of Jackson and Johnson, the conception of three independent branches of government now meant that Congress should legislate without interference from the executive. Late-century advocates of presidential power such as Woodrow Wilson and Henry Adams could only bemoan the existence of "congressional government."[83] The success of the congressional construction was so complete that even proponents of congressional power began to fear that the executive had been too weakened.[84]

Reconstructing Impeachments

The discoverable meaning of the impeachment clause is frustratingly ambiguous. Purely interpretive effort could shed little more light on the impeachment powers by the time of the Reconstruction era than at the time of the impeachment of Justice Chase. Moreover, even as historical precedent and interpretive conventions were canvassed to help clarify the issue, postbellum commentators were even more assertive of the exclusivity of Congress' power to settle on a controlling meaning. As with Chase, the Johnson impeachment was unique in calling one of the nation's highest government officials before the bar of the Senate. As a result, the limited number of precedents available could be regarded as even less settled than they might have been in a less momentous case. Nonetheless, the Johnson impeachment concluded with results quite similar to those reached with Chase, even if somewhat different paths were taken to that end.

Congressional Discretion and Abuse of Office

At the time of the Johnson impeachment, no executive official had ever been impeached, there had been no attempted impeachment of an elected official other than the abortive trial of the former senator William Blount. The case of Judge West Humphreys, who was removed in 1862 for accepting a judicial position in the Confederacy while formally retaining his seat on the federal bench in Tennessee, had resuscitated the impeachment mechanism after three decades of disuse. The specific charges against Humphreys had included several elaborately presented considerations of his public support for secessionist principles.[85] Six years later, impeachment for political offenses remained a plausible option.

The constitutional and political significance of the Chase impeachment assured that it too would receive renewed attention. The arguments of the Jeffersonian Republican managers were often highlighted by Johnson's foes as the true construction of the impeachment power, but the Johnson case was not presented simply as an application of established precedent. From a comparative perspective, the Johnson impeachment is of interest not only for how it paralleled the Chase proceedings but also in how it differed, as new arguments were developed and brought to bear to explain the impeachment power in terms of a different type of official and a different substantive dispute. Where the Chase impeachment focused on the appropriate nature of the judiciary, the Johnson impeachment focused on the place of Congress in the constitutional system.

The Lincolnian Republican impeachers were also concerned with establishing that the Senate should not be viewed strictly as a court, but they were perhaps more explicit than their predecessors in indicating the implications of that argument. Rather than being analogous to normal judicial forums, the Senate served as a final tribunal to judge political principle. In response to Johnson's desire to test the constitutionality of the Tenure Act, House manager James Wilson declared that "we will gratify his desire to carrying his case to the highest court known to the Constitution of the Republic, the high court of impeachment." In such a court, normal legal procedures were less important than political principle. In fact, on the eve of the impeachment, Timothy Farrar wrote that the Senate was established as "a higher tribunal" above the Supreme Court specifically to provide a political alternative to the narrow legalism of the normal courts.[86]

The result of removing the impeachment proceedings from a courtroom context was to free the Senate both from the judicial function of applying preexisting law and from legal procedures and guarantees. The articles of impeachment were not a narrow legal indictment, but rather a mechanism for bringing the larger political issues behind the impeachment before the Senate. The managers, therefore, were free from actually having to prove the details of the charges, and instead could focus on the larger spirit of the proceedings. The "great question" to be settled could be found only "far above and below and beyond these mere technical offenses."[87]

If the charges could be flexible and vague, so too could other procedural requirements, such as rules of evidence and judicial impartiality. Fortunately for the House, Butler asserted, "we are in the presence of the Senate of the United States convened as a constitutional tribunal," which "has no analogy to that of a court." The senators were "a law unto yourselves," bound only by the goal of serving the public good. The argument cut both ways, for if the legal rules of evidence did not apply, then the defense could also expect to introduce whatever evidence might exculpate the president. Indeed, Senator Charles Sumner, who strongly agreed with the managers, unsuccessfully moved to admit practically all evidence, leaving the Senate to weigh its value. On the other hand, the managers, led by Butler, pilloried the defense with motions to suppress evidence, most of which were upheld largely by the same senators who would ultimately vote guilty.[88] Political trials were not necessarily fair.

Politics was understood to be both a legitimate factor in construing the impeachment clause and the natural result of successfully establishing the broad construction. The subversion of fundamental principles and the threat to public safety required both Johnson's removal and the broad power to remove. Campaigning for the Senate, Simon Cameron put the case for impeachment in the most personal of terms, telling his Pennsylvanian audience that "I did not believe the *low* white of the South was fit to become President . . . Why suffer him to remain there if we can put him out? I am no lawyer, but if I were there, I would be the first to impeach him and put him out."[89] The fact that Cameron was not a lawyer bolstered his point, for the prospective senator was already committing his vote despite, and perhaps regardless of, his ignorance of the legal requirements for impeachment. Although few other influential Republicans were willing to express their rationale for removing Johnson in quite those terms, many agreed that Johnson's fundamental unfitness for office justified an impeachment.

The particulars of the Johnson case seemed to indicate that no legal crime was necessary to initiate an impeachment. Future manager George Boutwell had perhaps done the most in the House to argue that the impeachment mechanism was available to remove the "unfit" from a place of "public trust." The inability of the House to establish that Johnson had conspired to murder the president, bribed public officials, or committed treason by aiding Confederate officials only demonstrated the need for a broader conception of the impeachment powers in order to remove an antagonistic president. Johnson's possible violation of the Tenure Act, which pointedly specified that violation of its terms would constitute a "high misdemeanor," seemed to provide cover for the impeachment.[90] But such a statutory definition itself required a broad construction of the impeachment power, allowing Congress to characterize a political act as an indictable crime for the sake of impeaching the president. Moreover, the inclusion of the final two articles in the impeachment clearly cut the House loose from the narrow construction and required a defense of removals for noncriminal activity.

The extraordinary powers exercised by the government during wartime, as well as the exclusion of the conservative South, resuscitated an approach to the Constitution that emphasized its provisions to provide, rather than limit, power. Thus, Farrar reversed traditional assumptions and looked to what powers were not expressly prohibited rather than to what powers the Constitution delegated. In terms of the impeachment clause, this meant that "high crimes and misdemeanors" could be construed as something for which officials must be removed, but that Congress retained discretion to impeach for lesser charges.[91] Somewhat less ambitiously, other impeachment advocates emphasized that impeachment was a discretionary power of Congress. Congress was free to determine for itself what would constitute a sufficient "crime" to justify removal. The belief in the benefits of government power justified reading the impeachment clause broadly.[92] John Norton Pomeroy was dismissive of the possibility that Congress would abuse a broadly constructed impeachment power, for the Constitution was "full of grants which may be abused," and the benefits of active political power outweighed the limited potential for abuse.[93]

The postbellum Constitution freed Congress from constraint even as it remained a check on other government officials. If the broad construction of the Chase impeachment developed around a concern to check the aristocratic potential of the judiciary, a new broad construction similarly developed during Reconstruction around the threat of executive despotism. Boutwell continuously warned his colleagues that Johnson's real crime consisted not in a technical violation of either statute or common law, but in a whole series of "systematic" events potentially minor in themselves but tending to undercut the authority of Congress in favor of a "more than kingly power." The subtlety of presidential abuse of discretionary power as well as the danger of executive usurpation made a broad impeachment power necessary.[94]

Rather than requiring narrow criminal activity, the Constitution's standard of "high crimes and misdemeanors" was construed as including political abuses. From the perspective of legislative-executive conflict, British history seemed to offer an alternative definition to the term "high crimes and misdemeanors" provided by the *"lex parliamentaria,"* or the practices of Parliament rather than the judge-made common law. Parliamentary law provided the constitutional text with a semblance of relatively fixed meaning, undercutting concerns that the broad construction would set the power free from all constraints. At the same time, however, it denied the authority of judicial or legalistic interpretations of the text. The impeachment power was fundamentally what Congress made of it, just as it had been what the Parliament had made of it. Even while acting within the Constitution, Congress was literally free from law, even its own, though it was still constrained by political norms.[95]

The House welcomed this distinction between parliamentary and common law, and the managers pressed the claim that the constitutional limitation on the congressional power to punish merely emphasized this distinction. Butler asserted that "any malversation in office, highly prejudicial to the public interest, or subversive of some fundamental principle of government by which the safety of a people may be in danger, is a high crime against the nation, as the term is used in parliamentary law."[96] This doctrine was not so broad as to allow Congress simply to remove unpopular presidents, for it required definitive actions on the part of the president to justify his removal as a subversion of fundamental principles, but it did open a wide range of presidential actions to congressional scrutiny. The judicial oath only made explicit what was already present in the constitutional scheme, as "the power of impeachment, so far as the President is concerned, was inserted in the Constitution to secure 'good behavior,' to punish 'misconduct.'" Violation of the president's political duties under the laws and the Constitution could justify his removal, even if his actions were legally allowed.[97]

Congressional discretion over the extent of the impeachment power preserved executive accountability, which if not necessarily secured in the details of the constitutional text was necessarily "in strict harmony with the general design of the organic law." The necessity of preventing executive misuse of power extended even so far as to making innocent errors impeachable. Though technical errors were clearly excluded as a result of the

Chase impeachment, the impeachers of Johnson did not face the difficulty of accounting for the Senate's serving the same functions as an appellate court. Other than the impeachment power, there were no mechanisms to check presidential error or to act upon executive disability. The potential damage of bad executive actions was so severe that the president had to be restrained from committing, even with good intentions, potentially serious and uncorrectable errors.[98]

Similarly, the political standard vitiated the presumptions of innocence appropriate to criminal law. The purely personal consequence to Johnson was meaningless in a political context. With only political issues at stake, Congress had to err on the side of correct political principle. Though impeachable acts were necessary to initiate the proceedings, Congress was obliged to consider the president's entire character to determine the appropriateness of his continuing in office, to estimate his likely future conduct, and to determine the appropriate signals to be sent to other political officials. It was not only the character of the acts, but also the character of the actor that determined whether political principles were being subverted. What might be tolerable acts by one president could be impeachable when committed by another in a different context. The goal of the impeachment power was to protect the state from bad men and bad principles, regardless of whether those were already proscribed by law or custom.[99]

Crimes and Courts

Though willing to challenge the managers on principled, as well as evidentiary, ground, Johnson's defenders gave somewhat limited attention to the nature of the impeachment power itself.[100] The most extensive discussions of the narrow construction of the impeachment power emerged before the impeachment itself. The advocates of the broad construction were the ones who felt less secure in their task and thus repeatedly returned to the issue in order to bolster their claims that the impeachment was legitimately political.

Johnson's counsel immediately recognized that the Senate could not be regarded as an ordinary court. Delicate political and constitutional issues were at stake, and the defense complained that these were "to be treated as if it were a case before a police court, to be put through with railroad speed." If the proceedings were uniquely weighty, however, they were still judicial in character. In appealing for time to prepare a reply, Nelson denied that the defense expected all of the normal procedures and protections found in common-law courts, but he did insist that, in the context of a broad review of the evidence and arguments, the Senate should decide in a manner appropriate to the courts. Notably, it must be prepared to deliberate on the issues at hand. In order to do so, the Senate must consider the case "not as mere party questions, but as the grand tribunal of the nation, disposed to dispense justice equally between two of the greatest powers [the president and Congress] . . . in the land." To the defense, it was the judiciary that was the special province of deliberation, and the great challenge was to force the Senate to give up its normal manner of rushed decisionmaking and one-sided investigations.[101]

The defense opened with former Supreme Court justice Benjamin Curtis reminding the Senate of its judicial character. The defense was present in order "to speak to the Senate of the United States sitting in its judicial capacity" only; "party spirit, political schemes, foregone conclusions, outrageous biases can have no fit operation" in that court. One implication of this judicial character became immediately apparent as Curtis began parsing the terms of the Tenure Act, discovering that no "judicial interpretation" of the law could make it apply to Secretary Stanton. In pointed contrast to the House managers, Curtis insisted that the Senate was now acting as the "expounder of this law judicially," and thus could not now exercise its "legislative power" to make the law fit the crime. The Senate might be unhappy with the present application of the law, but it had no right to alter it in order to reach desired results in the present case.[102]

The year before the trial, Columbia law professor Theodore Dwight had published a defense of a narrow interpretation of the impeachment power that emphasized not only the judicial quality of the Senate sitting for trial, but also the limited nature of the crimes that could be charged there. For Dwight, the Constitution did not simply draw upon British experience, but embodied it. The vague constitutional text "silently points us to English precedents for knowledge of the details." For the law professor, this was as much a point of difficulty as of assistance, for the British House of Lords had been unduly swayed "by the influences which beset a legislative assembly, of a kind unfavorable to the calmness of judicial action." Eliminating such extraneous influences led to the conclusion that impeachments, "like indictments, are methods of procedure in criminal cases, and nothing more." They were "purely judicial," and must be strictly distinguished from bills of attainder, which incorrectly "confound legislative and judicial power." The result is that the impeached possessed the same procedural guarantees as the criminally indicted, including a presumption of innocence, the existence of a prior known law, and ordinary rules of evidence. Separation of powers and the recognition of distinct, coordinate branches of government required that Congress not arrogate all powers to itself when sitting in its special capacity as a court.[103]

Dwight thought that British history supported the narrow construction, but the American context made that construction even more plausible to others. Dwight made clear that his primary concern was in justifying his construction, not in discovering British practice, for he carefully limited his field to exclude those "extreme cases favoring an opposite view," including most early impeachments and articles that were not tried or did not result in convictions.[104] The Constitution's impeachment power had to be construed in light of the American context, where Congress' powers were carefully limited. For the defense, one of the great achievements of the founders was to abandon the system of parliamentary supremacy favored by the managers. As William Groesbeck emphasized, "we have teachings of our own," and those taught that not only the executive and judicial branches were limited, but also the legislative branch.[105]

If Congress was to be limited, the nature of impeachable crimes must be limited. Unlike the tenure of judges, the president's tenure was not contingent upon "good behavior," and thus the impeachment power had to be regarded differently when directed at the president. The fact that the president was responsible to the electorate seemed to undercut both the necessity for and the appropriateness of executive accountability to Congress. By directing a broad impeachment power at the president, Congress claimed to be able to exercise the powers that had been reserved to the people, to judge the fitness of presidential candidates for office. For the defense it was this element of elected tenure, not differences in power, that distinguished the president from a monarch, and thus rendered the visions of British battles between the king and representatives of the people inappropriate.[106]

Without the guidance of fixed law, impeachments would enter "a limbo, a vacuum," leading at the most trivial level to the Congress' becoming a "school of manners" to "teach decorum of speech," as in the case of the tenth article. For this reason the defense insisted that the impeachment be tried in terms of the narrow criminal law, explicitly rejecting the *lex parliamentaria*. Limited government and a fixed constitution demanded that the American Senate be seen as a "tribunal different from any tribunal that the world ever saw," one that was constrained by genuine law, not by

"every species of offense which the Parliament chose to treat as such."
The constitutional requirement of "high crimes and misdemeanors" was a
"term of art" setting "true technical limits" on the impeachment power.[107]

Though agreeing that high crimes must be indictable offenses in order
to avoid subjecting civil officers to the whim of Congress, the advocates of
a narrow construction diverged on the specific indictable crimes that were
also impeachable. The common law provided a model of technical legality
with which to define the nature of high crimes, but it had been adopted
piecemeal by some of the states and not at all by the federal government.
This jurisdictional accident rendered the common law too uncertain to
serve as an adequate basis for an impeachment.[108] Thomas Nelson, on the
other hand, took an even more extreme view. If "high crimes and misdemeanors" were technical terms at common law, then their inclusion in the
Constitution sealed their meaning at that historical moment. The Constitution was not simply a political system that relied on subsidiary organiza-
tions to create and define law, but was itself the supreme law with a technical meaning. Nelson doubted "whether the Congress . . . has a right to
create a new crime . . . that was not known . . . at the date of the adoption
of the Constitution."[109] He not only would bind Congress in its judicial
function as a court of impeachment, but also hoped to constrain Congress
as a legislative body.

Nelson's argument was extreme even for Johnson's counsel, but he
indicated the tendency of the construction that the defense hoped to
establish. If the Constitution did not detail impeachable crimes, either
explicitly or implicitly, it at least characterized them. At a mere level of
interpretation, William Evarts, who had been Johnson's attorney general
before resigning to defend the president, insisted that "high crimes" was a
substantive, not a formal, category. Thus, when Congress defined a violation of the Tenure in Office Act as being a "high crime," Evarts noted that
"it means nothing to a lawyer." The term described law, but was not
embodied in law. Congress was limited to recognizing the substantive
meaning of constitutional crimes and could not add new categories of
purely political crimes. Congress' attempt to create an impeachable offense
in the Tenure Act did not touch the "substance" of presidential action,
"but only the form," and thus the House was attempting to remove a
president over a mere technicality of administrative procedure.[110] The
practical operation of the government required that impeachments be undertaken only in the most extreme circumstances, represented by the commission of serious indictable crimes by government officials.

These inconsistencies in Johnson's defense were relatively minor, given the nature of the charges. The defense offered a consistent construction that the Senate proceedings had to be regarded as a criminal trial and the Senate as a judicial body. Moreover, Johnson's defenders all maintained that mere political offenses, even if subversive of fundamental political norms, were not impeachable but had to be left with the electorate. By any version of the "high crimes" standard, as opposed to the broad "political" standard offered by the managers, Congress was limited in its impeachment powers to pursuing severe criminal conduct as recognized by preexisting law.[111]

The evolution of the Johnson impeachment indicated the weakness in the support for the broad construction. Though the Radicals garnered numerous victories in their quest to remove the president, many of those victories were strained and marginal, so that their political value was undercut. Lack of evidence killed the first impeachment investigation in the summer of 1867, and the House Judiciary Committee only narrowly supported a political impeachment in the fall of that year, which was not backed by the whole House. Although the House finally approved the impeachment with 128 affirmative votes, it rejected Butler's original political article and approved a reformulated tenth article only after the moderate Bingham was given the lead of the managers. Even then, the article was approved with only 88 votes.[112] The House accepted the broad construction and bound its managers to it in presenting the case before the Senate, but did so only reluctantly.

The Senate was also reluctant to accept the broad construction. The Senate rejected Sumner's motion, which would have abandoned evidentiary rules entirely, though many senators voted in a highly partisan manner in admitting evidence. Moreover, Chief Justice Salmon Chase, presiding over the Senate for the impeachment, orchestrated a reversal of the Senate's earlier resolutions in order to recognize the proceedings as a formal trial under a distinct and judicial body. On the other hand, the Senate behaved more politically in agreeing to administer the oath to Benjamin Wade, who as president *pro tempore* of the Senate would gain the White House upon Johnson's removal, and David Patterson, who was the president's son-in-law, both of whom were clearly interested in the outcome of the case and could hardly be impartial judges. The Senate determined that the states' political right to be represented in the trial overrode any consideration of personal interest relative to the judges or the accused.[113]

The outcome of the impeachment reflected this ambivalence toward the broad construction, establishing instead a more moderate construction. The Senate voted on only three of the eleven articles. Each was approved thirty-five to nineteen, with seven Republican defections to the side of acquittal causing them to fall one short of the two-thirds needed for conviction. The Senate began voting with the final, summary article. Following a ten-day recess, the Senate voted the same way on the second and third articles before adjourning *sine die,* abandoning the remaining articles. The narrow margin of defeat was intentionally symbolic; a number of moderate senators stood ready to cast a vote for acquittal if necessary but purposefully voted to convict in order to keep the margin close.[114] The president's narrow construction would have excluded all of the articles of impeachment, and the capacity of the Republicans to muster thirty-five votes for conviction even on the eleventh article clearly indicated that most of the Senate was unwilling to accept such a restriction on its power. Such a result was not surprising, given that the Senate had already passed the Tenure Act with its "high crimes" clause over a presidential veto. Nonetheless, the actual impeachment carried greater consequences than earlier legislative votes and required more deliberate consideration of the constitutional issues at stake relative to the nature of impeachable crimes.[115]

Unlike the Chase impeachment, the senators offered written opinions justifying their votes in the Johnson case. Though not conclusive, these opinions indicate that an articulate minority in the Senate fully accepted the broad construction and would have supported it in the voting. The majority, however, expressed much greater doubt as to the propriety of the broad construction and specifically condemned the tenth article for inappropriately charging Johnson with an unimpeachable offense. Even such a supporter of a relatively broad construction as John Sherman indicated the dilemma. At the same time that he held that "we are not bound to technical definitions of crimes" but must also look to any "gross and palpable breach of moral obligations tending to unfit an officer for the proper discharge of his office or to bring his office into public contempt," Sherman also argued that the Senate could not consider "other offenses" not explicitly charged in the articles and that individual senators must resist "political, personal, or partisan demands, or even grave considerations of public policy" in reaching their conclusions. Having accepted the judicial nature of the proceedings, however, few senators could reconcile the exclusion of public policy considerations and political demands with the necessity of judging whether the president had breached a political obligation or brought the office into disrepute. In practice, the necessity of finding "gross and palpable" political offenses became too difficult even for Sherman, who would not have convicted Johnson on the tenth article for fear of trespassing "on the jurisdiction of the people," who "alone may convict and condemn for such offenses."[116]

Sherman was by no means a Radical, however, and others were more willing to commit themselves fully to the broad construction. Timothy Howe thought the impeachment power comparable to the removal power, and therefore that the issue reduced to whether the president's actions were "so prejudicial to the state as to warrant his removal." To answer this question, a senator could be guided by either "written law" or his "own conscience." Even without the existence of the Tenure Act, Johnson might be impeached for removing a department head if "the people could . . . resent" such an action. Not surprisingly, Charles Sumner offered the most extensive senatorial argument in favor of a broad construction, asking only that the House "show me an act of evil example or influence committed by the President," and he would "show you an impeachable offense." Once the president had been impeached, the burden was on him to prove that his "continuance in office is not inconsistent with the *Public Safety.*"[117]

For these senators the implications of the broad construction were clear. Not only was the president, and especially the president, removable for political offenses, but such a decision was inherently political. Indeed, Sumner gave the boldest formulation of this conclusion. He refused to heed the "jargon of lawyers" or to "shut out from view that long list of transgressions explaining and coloring the final act of defiance." For Sumner, "this is a political proceeding, which the people at this moment are as competent to decide as the Senate," and he insisted that senators should consider the expected electoral repercussions in deciding how to cast their vote. Even while expressing their support for the broad construction, however, the Radicals were "surprised to find so many holding the opinion that the President is not impeachable for anything that the law does not declare a crime or misdemeanor" and disturbed to hear references to the Senate's judicial oath or the need for impartial deliberation.[118]

Despite their aggressiveness and visibility, the Radicals were in the minority and were unable to stamp the impeachment with their mark. Johnson's guilt under the broad construction was so evident, and the Radical pressure for removal so strong, that the Senate's acceptance of that construction would have assured his removal. The narrow weighing of evidence characteristic of many voting to convict as well as those voting to acquit indicated that the majority of the Senate was unwilling to embrace a political removal.[119]

The Republicans who voted to acquit relied on the lack of evidence to support an impeachment on the removal articles, rather than on an absence of a charged impeachable crime. Moreover, numerous senators voting to convict similarly weighed the evidence on the removal charges, while dismissing the political aspects of the impeachment as irrelevant. James Patterson of New Hampshire, for example, admitted that the president's 1866 speeches indicated Johnson's unfitness for high office, and yet were not impeachable. Even while examining the record for violations of known rules, however, these senators did not require a violation of a specific law. Without specifying the nature of impeachable crimes, more moderate Republican senators found abuse of presidential powers or breach of fundamental constitutional principles to be impeachable, with minimal regard for whether such abuses were defined in statutory law as opposed to constitutional text or presidential oath. Impeachments required culpable acts. But the president needed to be guilty only of crimes against clear and fundamental political principles, not of violation of the criminal law. The resulting construction established a narrow standard for impeachable crimes, but not the narrowest standard of serious indictable crimes advocated by the president's defenders.[120]

Overall, the Johnson impeachment rejected both the broad and narrow constructions, though the Radicals had managed to push the moderate position closer to the broad construction than it had been the year before. Political failings alone could not justify removal, and Congress remained bound by constitutional standards in approaching an impeachment and could not regard itself as possessed of full discretion and as a "law unto itself." The relatively broad nature of impeachable crimes, however, did not render the impeachment a political proceeding. *The Nation* captured mainstream Republican opinion in evaluating the impeachment, which it had ultimately favored, not as a political contest but as a form of legal trial, with the outcome representing a judicial acquittal, not a political vindication.[121] Johnson had been disciplined and his actions repudiated, even if he had not been removed.

Conclusion

The impeachment of Andrew Johnson was the culmination of a congressional effort to redefine the place of the executive branch in the federal

separation of powers. In this effort, the impeachment itself was less important for its attempt to remove Johnson or even to define the impeachment power than it was for its representation of the larger congressional
construction developed around and through the trial. The congressional
power to remove the president was the ultimate expression of the general
supremacy of the legislative branch. Contrary to the dire expositions of
later commentators, the impeachment power was clearly too unwieldy to
be used on a regular basis to reduce the president to a minister serving at
the will of the Congress. Rather than becoming a regular instrument of
interdepartmental relations, the impeachment power served as a crucial
symbol for congressional proponents, which could be invoked to fix the
appropriate role of the executive branch.[122]

The substantive construction of the executive power contained in the
impeachment made clear what congressional Radicals hoped to achieve.
Though not holding office at the behest of Congress, the president was
not a fully coordinate official. The executive branch possessed only an
inherently limited function of enforcing the legislative will. Moreover, the
branch was not a hierarchical organization under the command of the
president, but rather a conglomeration of semiautonomous officers responsible for particular administrative functions. Rather than being a distinct political representative of the national will, the president's relationship to the sources of political authority was secondary and mediated. Not
only did this effort build upon the growing strength of Congress emerging
from the Civil War; it also was a reaction to the expansive construction of
presidential powers offered by Johnson on the foundations of wartime and
antebellum precedents.

The struggles between the president and the Congress over these various constructions indicate the degree to which they depended on noninterpretive tools. The textual basis for the constructions at stake was quite
thin. Though superficially clear, the impeachment clause relied on a con
tradictory and ambiguous British practice, but modified that practice in
unclear ways while implanting it in an American republican context. The
federal history of impeachments provided some guidance by the time of
the Johnson trial, but remained uncertain in both its narrow substance and
its methodological implications. The removal power was not included in
the text at all, and depended on the degree of overlap at the very margin of
the separation of powers. Even the First Congress had been sharply divided over the location and nature of the removal power, and the development of subsequent political norms regarding political patronage strained

the meaning of that first settlement in a new context. The remaining substantive constructions flew even further from the constitutional text and its immediate history, while nonetheless dealing with essential features of the basic structures of government, their relative powers, and their relationships to each other and the citizenry. Though the traditional tools of interpretation could shed light on the issues at stake and define boundaries of discussion, they could not penetrate to the core of the debate and decisively settle those controversies.

Moreover, the particular nature of these controversies tended to put them beyond the reach of the judiciary and its legalistic approach. The Republicans specifically argued that Congress was the appropriate court in which to try these constitutional issues, denying the relevance of normal judicial standards and proceedings. Assuming Johnson's sincerity in his desire to test the Tenure Act in the court system, the Radicals emphatically rejected the authority of the judiciary on the issue and took action to circumvent a judicial hearing by orchestrating the dismissal of the charges against Lorenzo Thomas. The Court was unwilling to address the removal issue directly until well into the twentieth century, and even then did so unsatisfactorily and in a highly political manner. On other issues of Reconstruction and executive-legislative relations, the Court specifically withdrew from the arena, citing its own institutional incapacity to address such political questions.[123]

Without significant guidance on the discoverable meaning of the executive powers, the political branches were left to use the political tools at their disposal to reach an adequate settlement. Primary among these tools was the threat of removal itself, which the Radicals used to attempt to force presidential compliance with their construction of the executive power. Similarly, the president engaged Congress in a long series of maneuvers as each sought to outflank the other, with statutes, vetoes, overrides, removals, reinstatements, reassignments, circumventions, threats, and deals. Though often accompanied by discursive defenses of the competing constructions, such actions were also exercises in brute political force. Moreover, the threat of physical force loomed in the background, as each side feared the other's control over the military. Ultimately each contestant appealed to the people to rally behind a favored construction—an appeal that was less concerned with public discourse over constitutional meaning than with mustering the political strength to remove the opponent from power. Even in the context of the impeachment trial, senators and interested advocates were not above influencing senatorial votes by demonstrations of electoral, as well as argumentative, prowess.[124] While such blunt instruments were necessary to establish the political will to enforce a settlement of constitutional meaning, they were clearly ill suited for the rationalistic discovery of textual meaning required for interpretation.

Even at the level of pure discourse, however, the president and Congress routinely violated such accepted interpretive norms as reliance on moderation and reasoned argument. In line with the mustering of political force, the participants in the political debate often relied on extreme rhetoric, ad hominem attacks, and mere name-calling. In securing the construction, however, such rhetorical devices actually served an essential purpose that interpretive arguments could not. Not only did such flourishes help motivate political supporters, but they established the construction itself at the symbolic level. Successful invective tapped into a common store of political beliefs and understandings. To the extent that they were plausible, harsh metaphors linked individuals and particular events with larger constitutional issues, and thus created and connected the proffered constructions. Metaphorical arguments had the further advantage of making the case for the construction without requiring a detailing of exactly what was required by the constitutional text or what was entailed by the prospective construction. Johnson's defenders could invoke racial and national prejudice by labeling the congressional construction an attempt to "Mexicanize" the Constitution and federal government, while calling forth myriad more positive connotations by ranking Johnson with Jefferson, Jackson, and Lincoln. Similarly, persistent congressional characterizations of the president as King George, King James, or Napoleon cast Congress in the role of republican representatives of the people, without requiring an explicit test of the strength of the comparisons or the relevance of such references to determining who possessed the removal power under the Constitution. Successfully labeling the opposition carried political weight, while avoiding the difficult if not impossible task of explicating and defending the exact meaning of the labels under the circumstances or their implications for future practice.

Both sides in the conflict often depended on assertions of traditional institutional prerogative, necessary political interest, and general political principle to support their positions. In debating the removal power, Johnson was unwilling to surrender a right that had been formally recognized and exercised by all his predecessors, while senators explicitly complained that the president had trampled on accepted traditions of senatorial privilege and electoral necessity. Similarly, Johnson seemed bewildered that Congress would question his exercise of powers used by Lincoln, while the legislature insisted that presidential practice had always depended on congressional acquiescence, which could end at any time. The occupants of both branches worried aloud that the outcome of the conflict could reduce their own power and that of their successors.

Claims of institutional prerogative, rooted simply in tradition and institutional pride, were closely connected to political interests and goals. Johnson well knew that his position in the Republican party was too marginal to secure his renomination and that his hopes for a full term of his own depended on his building a separate party centered on his own presidency. Johnson's efforts to construct a unified executive branch under his command and with its own political will was an essential part of his larger effort to weaken the Republican hold over his administration and the federal government generally. Motivated by political ideals as well as personal ambition, Johnson's construction of the executive branch was instrumental to securing his policy goals as well as his own reelection, and this instrumental concern entered into his public justifications for his exercise of his executive powers. Members of Congress and their allies similarly mixed partisan interest and constitutional understandings. Radicals exhorted one another that an impeachment, and thus a broad construction of the impeachment power, was essential to ensuring Radical dominance of the party, the Congress, and the nation. Republicanism generally and Radicalism specifically became identified not only with union but also with the Constitution, such that any necessary means for advancing Republican interests were *ipso facto* constitutional. To many Republicans, Johnson's betrayal of party interests was as heinous as any other of his impeachable offenses, and it was Johnson's use of his powers to advance his personal interests at the expense of the party and nation that rendered those powers illegitimate.

The close identification between partisan and national interests, however, indicates that political principle remained a prominent part of the construction of the executive powers. Nonetheless, many of the principles advocated bore only a tenuous connection to the constitutional text, and textual authority was distinctly secondary in advancing and defending those principles. Congressional insistence that it was the legislature that best represented the popular will connected to well-developed and sweeping understandings of politics and republican government, but required little specific support from the Constitution itself. Proponents of executive power similarly developed their constructions as implications of the need for administrative efficiency, executive accountability, governmental strength and energy, and checks on legislative majorities. Though principled and related to concerns contained in the constitutional text, such considerations were independently valued and supplemented textual requirements. Both sides hoped not simply to vindicate the constitutional schema of the founders, but to adjoin and perfect it for a new, postbellum age. The question was not primarily what the Constitution had been, but what it would be.

In this constructive context, some individuals emphasized interpretive or legalistic concerns more than others did. Not surprisingly, the president hoped to enlist the courts in his effort to reduce the power of Congress. The defense counsels' approach to the impeachment clause reflected the president's efforts in other substantive areas, construing the constitutional text as a clear law that was binding on Congress in accord with judicial principles. Success in emphasizing the legal aspects of the Constitution would not only prohibit a turn to the *lex parliamentaria* in giving meaning to the impeachment clause, but could also authorize presidential refusal to enforce unconstitutional laws and a general reduction in the congressional role in reinventing the postbellum government. In other cases, however, even a legalistic constitution could offer little guidance as to what was included in the president's "executive powers," and Johnson relied as heavily as Congress on historical example and general political norms to provide a sustainable conception of the presidency within the system of separated powers.

The constitutional norms established by the Johnson impeachment were varied and somewhat vague. Failing to persuade some more moderate Republicans that the impeachment power should be regarded as a general power to remove incompetent presidents between elections or that the executive branch generally was simply a tool of congressional politics, the advocates of congressional power did manage to defeat Johnson's plans to build the executive branch into a centralized political unit under the control of the president and his efforts to clothe the presidency with a constitutional authority equivalent to that of the legislature and the judiciary. In condemning Johnson's effort to gain control of executive patronage for his own partisan benefit, congressional Radicals fatally undermined the entire spoils system, making fundamental concessions to the normative position of the emerging reformist movement. Not until after the turn of the century and another war would a president cease trying to prevent further erosion of his power and again begin to build the constitutional basis for a fully coordinate executive branch, but one still shaped by the Johnson experience.

5

Richard Nixon and the Leadership of the Modern State

On August 9, 1974, Richard Nixon became the first president to resign from office, avoiding the otherwise almost certain fate of becoming only the second president to be impeached. Though involving recognizably criminal activity by individuals in and around the Nixon White House, the events collectively known as Watergate also formed a defining political moment of the late twentieth century. Doubts about the modern national state that had been building prior to Nixon's ascendancy coalesced and were given new impetus by Nixon's own efforts to use the inherited and invented tools of the modern presidency to consolidate control over the apparatus of state power. Nixon's systematic efforts to challenge the Democratic party for control over the national government it had created brought to a head congressional efforts to regain influence over the state.

Unlike the earlier impeachment efforts directed at Chase and Johnson, the movement to impeach Richard Nixon was foreshortened by the president's own decision to withdraw from the dispute. The effect of this decision was to divert the building stream of congressional antipathy to presidential power into several more limited eddies of reform. The division of the constructions of national political leadership was already well under way by the time of Nixon's resignation, however.[1] In order to make a sweeping construction of the presidency as a whole, the reformers needed not only a suitable platform but also an alternative vision of the American presidency and its role within the constitutional order. Although there were elements of such a vision available, influential political actors were unwilling to take them up and defend a new type of presidency. The constructions at stake during this period were primarily about the control of the modern national state, not about its fundamental nature.[2]

Similarly, changing strategic understandings of world politics allowed greater congressional involvement in foreign policy, but did not touch the more basic acceptance of America's postwar role as global superpower. As the Vietnam war escalated, the "vital center" fragmented, limiting the political willingness to delegate to the president the power to conduct foreign policy in accord with agreed-upon goals.[3] As the Cold War metaphor broke down, the process of foreign policymaking became more complicated and less decisive. On the other hand, the maintenance of the national security state even in the face of these strategic changes sustained the importance of the commander-in-chief. Congressional reforms were to allow legislative penetration into national security debates and to expand the circle of participants in foreign policymaking.

As president, Nixon found a match between his office and his executive perspective. The primary lessons he drew from his legislative experience were that Congress was a weak, indecisive, and largely expendable institution. Before his successful 1968 campaign, Nixon told an interviewer, "I've always thought this country could run itself domestically without a President, all you need is a competent Cabinet to run the country at home. You need a President for foreign policy."[4] Even in domestic affairs, the legislative branch was absent, replaced by executive administration. Nixon's conception of the relative stature of the branches of the federal government was representative of the rising wing of his party. Though Dwight Eisenhower maintained a more limited theory of the president's proper place in the constitutional order, his presidency witnessed the defeat of the congressional wing of the Republican party.[5] The new conservatism associated with Barry Goldwater abandoned many of the concerns that the Old Right had developed during the 1930s and 1940s. The overriding requirements of anticommunism encouraged foreign interventionism and quieted earlier concerns over the consolidation of power within the federal government.[6]

If the Republican party was unwilling to challenge the existence of the modern presidency, the Democratic party of Jackson and Roosevelt had been complicit in its birth and growth. There had been a gradual shift toward administrative government throughout the early twentieth century, but it was FDR who recast the president as leader of the modern national state.[7] Though members of the party had begun to challenge presidential power as exercised by Lyndon Johnson and Richard Nixon, the party was unwilling to shed its presidential perspective so quickly, and most congressional Democrats favored more limited reforms rather than a radical reorientation of the separation of powers.

The actual growth in presidential power was both reflected and encouraged in the scholarly literature. For those reared on the successes of the New Deal, an activist president was seen as the keystone to an effective federal government. In contrast to the ossified and regressive Congress, the president represented the national will, was forward-looking, and drew upon the expertise of the "best and the brightest." As one commentator summarized, "One of the few political truths about the American system of government is that the President alone can give the nation an effective lead." As late as the 1960s, textbook writers, journalists, and scholars were calling for a removal of constraints from the president and a greater willingness on the part of the chief executive to use his available powers to their fullest.[8]

These developments both reached their pinnacle and came under increasing strain in the latter half of the 1960s and early 1970s. Lyndon Johnson not only controlled the legislative agenda with a myriad of new social programs; he also monopolized the framing of these programs under the direct auspices of the presidential office. Similarly, Johnson escalated American involvement in Vietnam under presidential direction, easily securing from Congress a recognition of a sweeping power for military action. Antiwar activism did not coalesce into an institutional challenge to the presidency itself until Johnson's successor laid down a broader challenge to the constituencies that had previously created the modern presidency.[9]

Despite Johnson's personal difficulties at the end of his term, Nixon determined not only to maintain the strength of the presidency but to increase it. While articulating a strategic vision that actually contributed to the breakdown of the Cold War consensus, Nixon conducted foreign policy in the institutional mode of his predecessors, who could rely on that basic agreement about ultimate goals. Domestically, Nixon acted upon a plebiscitary conception of the presidency, building on the idea of a presidential electoral mandate. Nixon's 1968 victory, however, marked the first time since 1848 that a president had come to power with a Congress dominated by the opposing party. Thus, to the Nixon administration, the presidential mandate did not so much direct Congress to follow the president in pursuing a single agenda as it authorized the president to take independent action without reference to Congress.[10]

Closely following from this conception of electoral investiture were Nixon's aborted efforts to develop an administrative presidency that could take action by hierarchical commands to the executive bureaucracy. Through a variety of measures designed to use the executive branch to achieve substantive policy outcomes, the administration hoped to realize its aims "free from the glare of publicity [and] congressional control." Given an increased reliance on executive action alone, however, Nixon was faced with an intensified version of the familiar problem of controlling the executive branch itself. He reacted with a more centralized White House structure that was more immediately responsive to presidential needs, while "trying to move the line between policy and administration in government" by penetrating further into the bureaucratic structure with his own political appointments and giving a greater implementation role to staff advisers.[11]

Such an extrapolation of the logic of the postwar presidency in the context of divided government and uncertain policy commitments contributed to a disillusionment with the presidency itself. New efforts emerged, not to redefine the presidency, but to place safeguards on the power the president exercised. As James MacGregor Burns argued after Watergate, "the cardinal problem is not the amount of power but the control and accountability of power." After all, presidential power remained the "power to do great good."[12] Reformers eventually settled on recognizing "that the presidency has become the dominant political institution in our system, but do[ing] everything possible to keep it within the Constitution and guided by the doctrines of constitutionalism"—that is, constitutionalism as presently conceived in the modern state.[13]

Examination of the Nixon era usefully carries our consideration of constitutional discourse into the modern era. Both the institutional tools of political conflict and the ubiquitous presence of the judiciary created potentially significant changes in the nature of constitutional construction in the late twentieth century. Moreover, placing the Nixon-era conflicts in the framework of constitutional construction highlights the historical backdrop for what is too often taken as a unique event. This analysis emphasizes the interrelationship between policy, partisanship, political ideology, and constitutional principle in these debates, with the consequence that the particular history of the period can be understood in a somewhat new light. The reforms of the period did not simply mark a return of Congress to its rightful constitutional role, but rather were part of a series of efforts to reconceptualize the separation of powers in the context of the modern administrative state. In this context, the results of these disputes were not as clear-cut as many participants had hoped and some commentators have suggested.

Among the many reforms passed during the mid-1970s, budgeting, war powers, and intelligence investigations stand out as particularly significant and representative of the constitutional debates of the period. Nonetheless, each of these reforms possessed a largely independent history and developed in accord with the dynamics of a particular dispute. In all three policy areas, the president had previously claimed predominance in the field, and Congress had accepted, if not encouraged, that understanding of the constitutional division of powers. As presidential leadership became problematic, these settlements came under question, and presidential authority was reconsidered. Congress institutionalized a leadership position in determining budget priorities, but it merely sought greater participation and monitoring in presidential war powers and intelligence activities.

Control over Budgeting

One area of significant constitutional construction to be developed during the Nixon presidency was the reform of the budgeting process, embodied legislatively in the Budget and Impoundment Control Act of 1974. Nixon provoked a crisis by developing and asserting executive budgetary powers clearly implied by earlier presidents but doing so to an extent and purpose that were unprecedented. The president's challenge to the congressional power of the purse resulted in judicial intervention in the dispute between the two elected branches. The case of the budget, however, indicates both the limits of judicial involvement in constitutional construction and the manner in which political processes push the government to develop constitutional meaning beyond that which the courts articulate in the legal process. The resulting measure provided a more extensive, more flexible, and fundamentally more political gloss on the constitutional requirements than that provided by the judiciary.

Budget Management and Presidential Impoundment

The strictures of constitutional interpretation suggest that presidential impoundments could and should be evaluated in isolation—either the power to impound is constitutionally permissible, or it is not. The conflict over Nixon's impoundments, however, indicates that this approach is flawed. The environment in which Nixon operated and the manner in which he used his powers were critical in determining not only the nature of his impoundments but also the appropriate congressional response to his actions. As the Watergate crisis deepened, Nixon's impoundments became both more disturbing and more solvable by congressional action.[14]

Most narrowly, impoundments involve the permanent refusal to spend funds on a given program as a result of policy disagreements between the executive and legislature. More broadly, the concept of impoundments includes any executive refusal to spend appropriated funds, regardless of whether funds are subsequently released for expenditure or of the specific rationale behind the deferral. While both forms of impoundment had historic precedent, the latter was not only common but had become routinized in the twentieth century. Nonetheless, the distinction between the two was often blurred and was not strongly pressed until Nixon.

The Nixon administration quickly committed itself to using the executive's role as the final spender of governmental funds as a tool of presidential policymaking. This decision was eased by the legislative setting of aggregate spending limits requiring the president to withhold funds for purely budgetary reasons. Despite the abandonment of fixed ceilings in 1971, the administration continued and even increased the pace of its impoundments. Nixon's impoundments went against tradition by falling particularly heavily on nondefense spending. They went against congressional policy by cutting Democratic programs particularly deeply, especially after the 1972 elections.[15]

The impoundment controversy was the focal point for a larger debate over budget management. For the president, impoundments necessarily resulted from the confluence of the executive task of administering governmental policy, limited fiscal resources, and congressional abdication from responsibility or meaningful participation in the budget. In order to press this claim, Nixon built his defense of the impoundment power in two parts. The first and narrower argument specifically legitimated the impoundment power itself. The broader element of his defense, however, downplayed the particulars of impoundment in favor of building a context in which such an action would be the necessary consequence. Thus, the second element of Nixon's defense built up the special place of the president in formulating the budget while criticizing the existing congressional budgetary process as inherently deficient. These two prongs of the Nixon defense were mutually reinforcing, and the overwhelming success of the latter in putting Congress on the defensive helped preserve elements of the former.

The case for the impoundment power was left quite vague by the administration, which relied heavily on precedent and institutional prerogative. When questioned at a press conference on the constitutional basis of presidential impoundment, Nixon replied that "the constitutional right of the President of the United States to impound funds—and that is not to spend money, when the spending of money would mean either increasing prices or increasing taxes for all people—that right is absolutely clear." The response was adroit both in expanding the traditional impoundment power by defining the constitutional claim in terms of Nixon's own fiscal policy goals and in relying on the absolute power of precedent. The most powerful defense of impoundments was the assertion of the right itself, which in turn depended upon the asserted right of earlier presidents. The "absolute clarity" of the president's constitutional right was supported not by extensive textual analysis or theoretical discussion, but by the Office of Management and Budget's list of previous presidential impoundments.[16] The Constitution is as the president has done.

Beyond the brute fact of past impoundments now cherished as institutional privilege, the administration spoke only vaguely of a constitutional duty on the part of the president to exercise discretion over spending. In part, the president's difficulty in this regard was in articulating the effects of a past construction. Deputy Attorney General Joseph Sneed maintained in congressional hearings that any restrictions on domestic impoundments would deprive "the President of a substantial portion of the 'executive power' vested in him by the Constitution," which itself placed the burden and obligation of administering the national budget exclusively on the president. It was this discretion over budgeting that rendered the president the "Chief Executive" and not the "Chief Clerk" bound only to spend congressionally appropriated funds without reference to larger policy goals. The OMB added to these claims by pointing to a variety of potential statutory sources for impoundment authority, which invoked the "President's constitutional duty to 'take care that the laws be faithfully executed.'"[17]

The Progressive shift toward executive control over budgeting specifically and the administrative state generally was exacerbated by the modern president's control over military planning.[18] Earlier justifications for impoundments reflected this dual concern. Even in the "peacetime" of the Cold War, the president made the first and final decision as to military budget priorities. In doing so, presidents emphasized less their special constitutional role as commander-in-chief than their special administrative capacity as chief executive.[19] It was the president, as head of the executive branch, who was capable of orderly strategic planning, adequately evaluating new technologies, and reviewing defense needs and budget outlays as a whole.

Such logic was not limited to military spending. As new demands for federal funds began to outstrip incremental growth and both prioritization within the budget and concern over the macroeconomic effects of aggregate expenditures became paramount considerations, the president made similar claims in the domestic sphere. Thus, in refusing to implement a congressional budget, the Johnson administration emphasized that the president's unique administrative position and capacity to take immediate action in the face of prevalent macroeconomic conditions overrode what would otherwise have been "a proper exercise of congressional prerogative" by the legislature in modifying the executive's budget proposal.[20]

The Constitution apparently delegated the power of the purse to the Congress. Nonetheless, by the mid-1960s one prominent commentator concluded that the "Constitution is silent" on the issues directly relevant to impoundments and that ultimately budgeting was "one of shared power between the legislature and the executive."[21] This sharing of powers was an incident of the inherent executive function to spend the funds appropriated by the legislature. During the twentieth century, this intrinsic executive role had been constructed as one of wide discretion and policymaking. Until relatively late in the dispute with Nixon, Congress had actively encouraged the executive to take the lead role in setting budget priorities, making macroeconomic policy, and using federal funds with discretion to achieve broad policy aims.[22]

Impoundments were simply the last stage in a process that favored executive budgeting. Progressive budget reformer William Willoughby had argued that "accountability can be enforced and efficiency secured only when responsibility is definitely located in a single authority," which could only be the "executive alone." The Budget and Accounting Act of 1921 sought to put this vision into practice, creating a unified executive budget that located responsibility squarely with the president. The later transformation of the Bureau of the Budget into the Office of Management and Budget reinvigorated the budget office as a tool for presidential control over fiscal policy.[23] Nixon hoped to build on this institutional legacy in order to emphasize the president's dominance in budgetmaking. While the administration's specific defense of the impoundment power was often vague and defensive, the president personally took the initiative in creating a political climate that would support impoundments and presidential leadership.

First, the president distinguished between particular federal programs of benefit to specific "constituent groups" from a general concern with tax rates and inflation, which were of concern to "all the American tax-payers." Congress represented those particularized interests favoring increased spending, but the president stood in defense of the general or national interest. Nixon did not vilify such "constituent groups" as special interests hostile to the true public good, but in fact recognized that particular spending programs had "attractive features," served "worthwhile purposes," were favored by "many people," and were not just an alien or parasitic element in society. Presidential rhetoric primarily benefited his constitutional position as national leader, rather than his particular policy positions.[24] As Congress bogged down in programmatic parts, only the president, as unique representative of the entire nation, could guard the macroeconomic whole.

The very deliberative and representative features of Congress that traditionally gave it the constitutional strength to set policy were turned against it in executive budgeting. Congress designedly "represents special interests." Nixon portrayed himself as differently situated. Although both Congress and the president had "a clear duty to protect the national interest in general prosperity," only the president could do what was "best for *all* the people." The unity of the executive branch and its national constituency contributed to the decisiveness of the president, in contrast to the endless divisions within the Congress. Only the president was able to look over the entire budget and make the "hard choices" that the fiscal and economic crisis required, while congressmen were unable to "deliver on the promises they make to the American people."[25]

This inherent deficiency was compounded by Congress' flawed internal organization, which Nixon used as the centerpiece of his attack. By dividing budget authority among multiple committees, and by combining budgeting power with substantive legislative jurisdiction in many committees, Congress not only had abdicated its constitutional power over the purse but had rendered itself incapable of recovering that power. Primary responsibility over the budget had fallen to the executive branch out of practical necessity, regardless of the implications of the formal distributions of powers prescribed in the constitutional text. While Nixon did note that this congressional structure intrinsically favored budget deficits, his primary claim was not so goal oriented.[26] Rather, the key to Nixon's construction of the presidential power over the budget was that Congress could not be responsible for any budget outcome. Like the Progressive reformers, Nixon assumed that responsibility required unified, identifiable leadership, which the executive branch obviously possessed but that the existing congressional structure prevented. The president not only could be held accountable for fiscal policy, but also had the institutional capacity to take responsibility for the budget as a whole.

Congressmen, let alone the Congress, could not know whether their votes would result in a deficit and thus could not take responsibility for the results. The "Congress suffers from institutional faults," possessing no "mechanism" for judging the "total financial picture." The result of these "hoary" procedures was that "Congress arrives at total Federal spending in an accidental, haphazard manner." The necessary result was "irresponsible spending," unless Congress either reformed its budget process or withdrew further from the formulation of budget policy. Although Nixon urged the former, he asserted the immediate necessity of the latter. In order "to have responsibility, you have to be responsible," but Congress could not be "responsible on money." The president stood alone in determining fiscal policy, though he was willing to challenge the legislature to become a "partner."[27]

Congressional Responsibility and Budget Reform

The response to Nixon's effort to solidify and extend the presidential construction was both vigorous and varied. Even as Congress began to deliberate on Nixon's impoundments and to consider the most appropriate response, the judiciary intervened, but with mixed results and limited constitutional success. Ultimately, judicial intervention served more to highlight the necessity for congressional action to construct the budget powers than to demonstrate the supremacy of the courts, the legal method, or constitutional interpretation as such. Although the courts nullified several specific impoundments on statutory grounds, they were unable either to create a practical mechanism for federal budgeting or to respond effectively to Nixon's broader claims to budgetary leadership. A political construction proved necessary to resolve these difficulties and to institutionalize the constitutional distribution of budget powers.

In fact the Supreme Court did not hear the impoundment issue until Congress had already taken action with the budget reform act, and that ruling was written quite narrowly.[28] Of somewhat greater influence were a number of lower court decisions that had been rendered as Congress deliberated. With few exceptions, the lower courts construed statutory intent as mandating expenditures.[29] Except by implication, these cases did not address the larger construction at issue in the Nixon impoundments by questioning the degree of legislative delegation intrinsic to the modern administrative state or the place of these specific project funds in the larger fiscal and macroeconomic context.

The fate of the impoundment controversy in the courts bolstered congressional convictions that several specific impoundments were legally questionable, but primarily it indicated the inadequacy of relying upon a judicial resolution of the issue. Published legal analysis tended to favor judicial intervention.[30] In formal terms the issue seemed clear: "Congress retains the power of the purse, and to the degree that it states its spending intent with some clarity, it may rely on the courts to enforce its will." As Congress itself recognized, however, the problem was not so simple. Judicial doctrine was designed to recognize "practices" inherent in the constitutional text itself and had difficulty accommodating the more slippery nature of constructions, which could emerge and disappear within the interstices of the text. Moreover, the legal analysis offered by the law reviews and the courts could not grapple with either the cumulative weight of modern statutes providing for executive discretion or the significance of the legislature's inability to express its will on the budget.[31] Depending on the judiciary to check impoundments would be "cumbersome, slow, and dangerously inflexible in constituting the federal courts as the arbiters of national spending policy."[32] Controlling the constitutional budgeting process required institution building more than it required judicial pronouncements.

The system of delegated discretion inherent in executive budgeting depended on an overall consensus on budget priorities and comity between the executive and legislative branches. Under Democratic administrations, particular disagreements were submerged under a broader consensus on the direction of American politics and were worked out informally in a context of plentiful federal revenues. Under Nixon, this informal process of accommodation broke down, as declining revenue growth and expanding spending commitments put new and less amenable pressures on the budget. The two branches themselves exacerbated these tensions by spurning efforts at informal negotiation and compromise. As a result, Congress was required to formalize the relationship between the two branches and to assume a larger role in budgeting.[33]

The congressional alternative to the presidential construction began with an admission that Nixon was right in his assessment of the congressional structure. Though not going so far as to admit that Nixon was right to impound, congressmen were willing to admit that the impoundments were a natural outgrowth of the executive budgeting that had been encouraged by Congress. As one proponent of reform argued, "I know what the Constitution says, but it is a principle of physics that when a vacuum develops, something will rush in to fill the void." Nixon had "not seized control of the budget," for Congress had "abdicated."[34] Though some were willing to conclude that such impoundments were unconstitutional, in the sense of being illegal, others found Congress complicit in an impoundment power that was constitutionally inappropriate but of ambiguous origin and legality. The perceived connection between Nixon's impoundments, the failure of the congressional budgeting process, and the varied nature of presidential supremacy indicated to Congress, if not to the courts, that resolution of the impoundment controversy was inescapably linked to the success of more general budget reform.[35]

In order to attack the root cause of impoundments, Congress had to reform its own procedures to take responsibility for budget results. Moreover, simply declaring impoundments to be illegal would undermine continuing congressional interest in the maintenance of the administrative state. One sponsor of budget reform instructed his colleagues that "budget reform and impoundment control have a joint purpose: to return responsibility for the spending policy of the United States to the legislative branch. One without the other would leave Congress in a weak and ineffectual position." Impoundment control was not enough; "Congress must be more than a check on the executive"; it must also be a positive force in developing the budget. Fortunately, a Senate committee concluded, there was "room within the interstices of the Constitution for that type of pragmatic accommodation to the pressure of modern government." The burden of the construction was not simply to define the limits of the presidential budgeting power, but to create "machinery to carry out [Congress'] responsibility." Budget reform was a "vital prerequisite of effective exercise of the power of the purse in this day and age."[36]

Given that the impoundment issue and the constitutional control of the purse more broadly were intimately connected, the congressional construction required the building of a new set of legislative institutions to regain budget leadership. Contrary to those who favored judicial resolution of the issue, congressional advocates of the new construction argued that policy decisions would inevitably be entangled in each case of impoundment. The link between the constitutional and policy issues required the creation of political institutions to make, monitor, and enforce budgeting decisions.[37] The difficulty of distinguishing legal from policy issues in impoundment and budgeting disputes also suggested the need for a more flexible mechanism than the judiciary. Though Nixon had eventually lost his legal effort to impound pollution control funds, he had been largely successful in achieving his policy aims because of the time and effort required to litigate the relevant cases in several courtrooms. But even as the legislature regretted the loss of comity between the two elected branches, it did not wish to reconstruct the budget powers on rigid, legal terms. Rather, congressional reformers sought to institutionalize a partnership between the branches that would recognize a more significant legislative role, without unalterably tying the hands of the president.[38]

Finally, institution building was essential if Congress was to respond effectively to the presidential construction advocated by Nixon. Congressional opponents of the president recognized the force of his contention that Congress lacked the organizational structure to take responsibility for budgeting. The extent of the executive power and its hold over the power of the purse depended on the existence of a viable alternative far more than it did on a formal division of powers. The reform provided Congress with a plausible claim to neutralizing the institutional advantage of the executive. Congress reduced the significance of the presidency's executive power by participating in it with its own instruments of executive decisionmaking.[39]

Political and institutional control over appropriations depended on the ability of Congress to assume "responsibility" for the budget. Earlier Congresses had systematically undermined legislative responsibility by internally dividing budget authority and cutting themselves off from essential information, while consolidating both in the presidential office. The congressional construction began by inserting greater congressional participation in executive budgeting. Budget reforms gave Congress direct access to the budget requests of a number of executive agencies, while requiring the OMB to provide justifications for proposals contained in the executive budget.[40] The formation of the Congressional Budget Office provided Congress with the institutional capacity for systematic budget planning.[41] The new Budget Committee gave Congress the means to consider individual spending programs in the context of the entire budget, including recognition of effects on the deficit. Through the new reconciliation process, in which Congress would vote on the overall budget, the legislature formalized a method for accepting accountability for the budget as a whole, including its aggregates and priorities.[42]

These efforts not only responded to the president's claims to institutional superiority, but also argued for the positive advantage of enhanced congressional participation in budgeting. Having plausibly gained the virtues of planning, visible accountability, and decisiveness, Congress claimed the additional value of representativeness and deliberation. Where Nixon emphasized the general interest in controlling inflation and taxes and the necessity of decisiveness in an era of limited resources, Congress insisted that it was precisely in a period of difficult decisions that pluralist representation was essential. Contrary to Nixon's portrayal of budgeting as an executive function outside the diverting influence of the "political winds," the congressional construction suggested that, so long as final decisions could be made, it was precisely those political forces, or popular preferences, that should define budget priorities.[43]

The legislature served both to transmit the diverse preferences of the people and as a forum for public discussion and justification of budget decisions. The Budget Act offered a net gain in the openness of budgeting, despite its newly centralized procedure for congressional budgeting. Though a proposal to force the president to submit three different budget proposals with their justifications failed, it was representative of the goals of the reform package as a whole in attempting to force public deliberation on budget figures rather than relying on the pro forma approval of figures reached in secret within the executive branch. Congressional responsibility for the budget required understanding, and the legitimacy of budget priorities depended on the opportunity for public consideration and "meaningful" approval of budget figures. To the long-standing commitment to managerial efficiency that the president relied upon in extending the executive construction, Congress counterposed an emphasis on democratic values.[44]

In adopting these reforms, Congress rejected the conceptual dichotomy articulated by the president, and thus the particular understanding of the division of institutional roles that the dichotomy served to reinforce. Ultimately, advocates of the congressional construction rejected the notion that responsibility and responsiveness were separate and mutually exclusive virtues. In the administration's construction, only the president could stand above particular social interests and political pressures and make decisions on budget priorities. Responsible decisionmaking required a certain independence from the very political forces to which the legislature was, appropriately, most responsive. Advocates of the congressional construction rejected this choice, and in so doing reoriented the debate such that congressional reform could simultaneously achieve both goals. On the one hand, the new institutions and norms established by the Budget Act would provide the capacity for better decisionmaking within the Congress, allowing it to take responsibility for budget totals and priorities. On the other hand, Congress was more responsive than the executive branch to popular demands on spending. These two virtues were mutually reinforcing in the context of budget reform, as political responsiveness was seen as contributing to better budget decisionmaking, and greater congressional responsibility allowed budget decisions to be more responsive to public needs.

Although the Budget Act claimed to be silent on the question of the constitutional powers of the president in budgeting, it established a new construction of the distribution of budgeting powers between Congress' power to appropriate funds and the president's executive power to spend them. Though constitutional powers of budgeting were recognized as shared, it was a distinctly legislative task to determine budget priorities and fiscal policy.[45] Impoundments were not eliminated, but were rather brought under congressional control. The flexibility of the new mechanisms for the enforcement of the legislative will inserted the legislature into the administrative process of monitoring and approving individual funding deferrals, while clarifying and updating congressional intent on particular appropriations as events changed. The executive power of impoundment was retained as a budgeting tool, but brought under legislative direction.[46]

More important than the resolution of the particular issue that sparked the constitutional "crisis" was the general shift in power inaugurated by the new construction. Though the specific procedure detailed in the Budget Act has been amended since 1974, the basic framework of centralized, congressional budgeting has been strengthened. The president has not been eliminated from the budget process, but his role has been substantially altered and reduced. Standard prereform conceptualizations of budgeting emphasizing a highly fragmented incrementalism and ready division of labor between the legislature and executive are no longer sufficient. Core congressional commitments have been politically insulated in "nondiscretionary" spending, whether through entitlements or through indexation.[47] The remainder of the budget has been deeply "politicized," in the sense that expenditures are more likely to be a source of partisan conflict and incorporated into aggregate spending trade-offs. Congress is now designed to replicate executive budget analysis and decisionmaking in order to meet the president in budgetary negotiations rather than rely on presidential guidance and initiative in setting budget priorities.[48]

In evaluating the success of the construction of the budgeting powers, however, it is important to bear in mind the nature of the construction itself. Although deficit spending was the trigger for both Nixon's impoundments and his claims of congressional irresponsibility, in developing its own construction of the budget powers Congress reoriented "responsibility" away from that context.[49] "Responsibility" in the congressional construction was defined in terms of accountability, not in terms of fiscal economy. Since the congressional construction centered on legislative responsibility for budget results, persistent deficits, the growth in "nondiscretionary" spending, and the relative stability of budget aggregates do not indicate the failure of the construction. The contending constructions of the president and Congress hinged on who would control the budget, not on the specific direction of budget policy.[50] By ending executive budgeting and shifting ultimate responsibility to Congress, the reformers were not pursuing immediate and radical programmatic changes relative to earlier budgets, but ensuring that any change in budget policy would primarily reflect legislative, and not just executive, commitments. Subsequent budgetary drift is, in fact, indicative of the success of the construction, which ensured that federal expenditures would reflect the diverse interests represented by Congress even at the cost of the managerial efficiency advocated by President Nixon. The changing political calculus created by divided government and limited fiscal resources fed a reconsideration of operative constitutional practices. As institutionalization replaced accommodation, resources were made available to advance some political goals, even as other objectives, such as deficit reduction, became more difficult to achieve.[51]

Constraining the War Powers

The first major construction of the Watergate period was the passage of the War Powers Resolution over a presidential veto in late 1973. While strong opponents of the Vietnam war and the presidential control of it found the resolution to be a disappointment, it marked the reentry of Congress into warmaking and signaled the end of congressional deference to the president's Cold War military actions. Advocates of congressional dominance in warmaking failed to institutionalize constitutional meaning in a detailed legal document that was judicially enforceable, but they succeeded in forcing a political compromise in which the president was constrained in taking unilateral military action.

The war powers claimed by Presidents Johnson and Nixon had roots in the earliest history of the Constitution, but their primary characteristics were developed only with the modern presidency. Judicial restraint relative to separation-of-powers controversies in foreign policy was set, however, even before the Court abandoned its objections to the activist state. Though appearing only as dicta in a case regarding an arms embargo, Justice Sutherland's 1936 claim of a "very delicate, plenary and exclusive power of the President as the sole organ of the federal government in the field of international relations—a power which does not require as a basis for its exercise an act of Congress" has been widely cited as justification for executive dominance of foreign relations generally.[52] Having elevated the president to a special place in foreign affairs, at least in constitutional rhetoric, the Court used the political questions doctrine to refuse to decide such issues as the legality of the war in Vietnam.[53]

The effective result of this judicial withdrawal was to leave the arena to political resolution, which in turn resulted in executive aggrandizement of warmaking powers. Although presidents had in the past instigated wars without extensive or prior congressional deliberation, the pace of American involvement in foreign military action increased after World War II, and engagements became more extensive, more dangerous, and more global in scope. With occasional hesitation, Congress supported and encouraged the growth of presidential power in the interest of foreign policy consensus.[54] This pattern of congressional deference was not seriously challenged until late in the Johnson presidency. While the specific attacks on Johnson and his policies were severe, they did not contribute to institutional reform of the basis for presidential warmaking.[55]

Neither presidential action nor congressional antagonism to the war allowed for a reduction in interbranch hostilities during the Nixon administration. As the president denounced his opponents as averse to any rational foreign policy, the Senate approved in 1969 the National Commitments Resolution, which contended that defense commitments could be made only by the joint action of the legislature and executive, and in 1970 the legislature distanced itself from presidential policy by repealing the Gulf of Tonkin Resolution. Having disengaged from the pretense that Vietnam was anything other than a presidential war, Congress began a more general effort to constrain the presidential power to initiate and conduct war independently of legislative influence. Nonetheless, the president insisted on his sole authority to determine the extent and pace of the withdrawal from Southeast Asia and denounced congressional opponents for undermining American national security and encouraging Communist insurgents.[56]

Congressional Reform and the War Powers

Reformers first had to establish that the war powers had in fact shifted to the executive during the preceding decades. Although there could be little question that the president had been taking the lead role in foreign policy, it was less immediately clear that this was problematic, alterable, or anything less than natural. Congressional endorsements of executive action plausibly indicated that the legislature was in fact fully engaged in the conduct of foreign policy. Thus, congressional reformers repeatedly stressed that presidential direction of the Vietnam war was a result of a particular historical evolution, that Congress had abdicated its role in foreign policy, and that it now must reassert itself to recover what it had lost.

Senator J. William Fulbright, chairman of the Senate Committee on Foreign Relations, was the most forceful voice in asserting that Congress had lost control over foreign policy. As early as 1967, Fulbright combined a demand for a formal statement of America's commitments to foreign powers with the contention that foreign policy had become the sole providence of the executive branch. Fulbright traced the decline of congressional influence over national security to the nation's "emergence as a major and permanent participant in world affairs" with its entrance into World War II. Subsequent events had intensified the distancing of the legislature from substantive decisionmaking, while creating "devices" to give the "appearance but not the reality of Congressional participation." The resulting "constitutional imbalance" was both historically contingent and relatively new. Recognition of these circumstances paved the way for a "constitutional change in the making." Such a historical narrative not only portrayed the coming constitutional construction as a return to an earlier constitutional balance, but had the added benefit of deemphasizing congressional complicity in executive policymaking.[57]

Though the recognition of a constitutional imbalance was essential to returning Congress to its proper role, the practical operation of the separation of powers did not depend on formal categorizations of duties. Rather, constitutional responsibilities responded to institutional practice. In order to reassert its place in defining and safeguarding national security, Congress had to develop appropriate structures of participation. The War Powers Resolution was intended to provide Congress with those necessary tools by creating more effective avenues for consultation between the legislative and executive branches, while imposing constraints on the president's ability to take unilateral action.[58]

In order to create new procedural mechanisms to realize the war power, however, congressional proponents had to recognize a certain flexibility and ambiguity in the constitutional text. While the fundamental aims of the Constitution relative to the war powers seemed clear enough, the operationalization of those goals was less clear. Recognizing that the president had overstepped his bounds in exercising the war powers did not, in itself, establish where those boundaries lay or how they were to be patrolled. Congressional action was needed to clarify the constitutional meaning of the legislature's power to declare war and raise and support the military. Interestingly, Raoul Berger, not known for his expansive view of constitutional flexibility, supported the War Powers Resolution in congressional hearings as a return to appropriate constitutional roles. Ignoring the specifics of the bill, Berger saw the proposed legislation as being primarily negative in nature, prohibiting unconstitutional presidential action. The bill was "a constitutional construction by Congress of its powers," eliminating the "'murkiness' created by a long series of self-serving Presidential assertions of power." Overturning presidential practice would simply "restore the original design" and "go back to the Constitution." For Berger, there could be no veneer of legitimacy for Cold War presidential leadership, but only a correction of unconstitutional action. Significantly, Berger viewed congressional action primarily as an opportunity for judicial review, which would truly establish correct constitutional meaning.[59]

Others were less certain of the clarity of the case. These more restrained assessments of the resolution and its likely effects grew from greater emphasis on the positive aspects of the legislation and on its political nature. In the same hearings, Alexander Bickel informed the senators that "Congress does not know it own place, so to speak; it has lost its bearings in this area. If Congress is ever again to take meaningful specific measures in matters of war and peace, it is apparent to me that it must first perform some quasi-constitutional act, an act of standing forth before the people as responsible, of declaring its responsibilities for itself and to the country with some clarity."[60] Whereas Berger supported the resolution as being similar to a judicial pronouncement of the unconstitutionality of presidential warmaking, Bickel understood it as an effort by Congress to grapple with the president for leadership of the national security state. Bickel's reading also implies congressional responsibility for the shifting constitutional balance. The Constitution could accommodate the legislature losing its own "bearings" and ceding authority to more active institutions. In order to regain a "meaningful" role in exercising the war powers, Congress must do more than declare the president to be in the wrong. It must also establish its own capacity and willingness to assume a position of authority. Constitutional roles could not simply be declared; they had to be constructed.

For congressional proponents of the new construction, both elements were present in the reconsideration of the war powers. The resolution was to "fill the lacuna resulting from the constitutional structure," specifying mechanisms for congressional involvement in the decisions that initiated military action, while defining the limits of legitimate presidential action. Although a determination of the limits of the presidential war powers was needed, it would also be insufficient. Given that the shift in war powers from the legislature to the executive had occurred as a result of congressional unwillingness to assume a position of leadership in foreign policy, those powers could be recovered only if Congress made clear its determination to define national security priorities in its own terms and created mechanisms to do so.[61]

As the Vietnam war increasingly seemed to have been misguided from its inception, congressional proponents of reform emphasized the deliberative benefits that could be garnered from involving the legislature in the decisionmaking. Although the war itself provided reformers with their primary example of erroneous executive action, the changing strategic thinking of the period provided the background for greater congressional deliberation. As long as the goals of Cold War foreign policy were clear and agreed upon, the "tactical" decisions of diplomatic and military action could be left to the expertise of the executive branch. A changing strategic environment, however, placed a premium on thoughtfulness, not on immediate action, and thus invoked the traditional strengths of the legislative branch. Senator Albert Gore, for example, was increasingly unwilling to defer to the commander-in-chief, noting that "I surely do not claim to be an authority on military strategy. I have no more experience in that regard than Secretary Laird or Secretary McNamara. We all have to do the best we can in the field, in which none of us can claim expertise." Given civilian control of the military, executive branch officials possessed no greater claim to expertise than did political officials in the legislative branch.[62] Even in the specific context of the war, executive leadership had not appreciably clarified the political and military goals of the conflict. In light of such concerns, Fulbright added that "public—and, I trust, constructive—criticism is one of the services that a Senator is uniquely able to perform." Such public criticism and discussion was necessary to the formulation of the "direction and purpose and philosophy" of American foreign policy, leaving its "day-to-day conduct" to executive managers.[63] Even more radical voices, however, argued that regardless of the level of expertise to be discovered in the Pentagon, executive officials were essentially agents to give concrete effect to legislative policies. In sharp contrast to the Republican reformers who had challenged Lincoln and Johnson a century before, however, such proponents of congressional supremacy had little effect on the direction of the constitutional construction taken in this area in the aftermath of Vietnam.[64]

Most fundamentally, reformers argued that collective decisionmaking was inherently preferable to that of a single individual. While events might require the president to make immediate judgements without the benefit of lengthy discussion and consultation, such a decisionmaking process was prone to errors and should be avoided whenever possible. The textual delegation to Congress of the power to declare war was made in recognition of this basic truth. The particulars of that collective decisionmaking were also important, however. As Fulbright noted, presidential consultations with individual legislators tended to devolve into the unidirectional transmission of decisions already made, rather than to become genuine debates over the merits of alternatives. Similarly, decisionmaking within the executive branch took on the same quality, as the aura of the office of the president stifled dissent among advisers. A valuable debate could flourish only by transferring the discussion into a public forum with independent actors, which meant that Congress should be a full participant in the formulation of policy.[65]

The second benefit of legislative participation in the war powers was one of representation and consent. Given the sacrifices that war inevitably required, the usually restrained Senator John Stennis argued that "the only stable basis for continual confidence in our government is to have people participate in the major decisions of whether we are to have peace or war." For congressional reformers, legislative participation in the leadership of the national security state was tantamount to popular participation in such decisionmaking.[66] As the governmental representatives of the people, legislators could provide the popular support that sustained military conflict required. Alternately, in the context of the war under Nixon, legislators served as conduits of public dissatisfaction with the war effort.

This dual function of Congress, to mobilize popular support and to reflect popular dissent, was a direct result of the close electoral connection between the representatives and their constituents. The Senate majority leader, Mike Mansfield, emphasized that "as a Senator I have a direct responsibility to the people of my State and that as a Senate we have responsibilities to the entire Nation." In the face of national division, electoral self-preservation required that the senators protect their institutional position. With the Senate's "responsibility and authority . . . at stake," Mansfield was "surprised that there are Senators who would place the position of this body in a secondary position." Far from giving consent to the war, Congress had been reduced to the purely supportive and passive function of "supply sergeant." Returning to its representative function meant taking a lead role in the "basic policy decisions."[67]

Though a distinct minority, some supporters of the congressional construction primarily hoped to throw up impediments to the exercise of any war powers. Although dissatisfaction with the executive exercise of those powers in Vietnam was critical to the construction as a whole, most proponents of reform merely articulated the desire to participate in those decisions, with the expected side effect that the decisions made under the new procedures would be better. For the pacifist wing of the reform movement, however, the overarching goal was to render warmaking more difficult. The glacial pace of congressional deliberation and legislative inactivity in the face of foreign crisis were positive goods to be contrasted advantageously to presidential isolation and haste, not difficulties to be overcome or excused. Rather than simply participating in the future course of the Cold War, this congressional construction would impose a disengagement from that conflict.[68]

National Security and Presidential Power

Unlike his congressional opponents, Nixon attempted to remove the debate from its contemporary context and to place it within a scenario of a future crisis in an antagonistic global environment. Proponents of a presidential construction made two claims about the nature of the war powers grounded in the constitutional text. Although the two arguments were superficially antagonistic, they shared a common legalistic approach to constitutional meaning and complemented each other. First, proponents claimed that the Constitution actually gave the president the dominant position in exercising the federal government's war powers, such that the Cold War presidency was consistent with constitutional design. Second, they argued that usage supplemented the bare bones of the constitutional text, and therefore the strong presidency that had evolved since the founding of the nation was now embedded in the Constitution itself. The combined force of these two points rendered the War Powers Resolution illegitimate as being in conflict with the existent Constitution.

Administration spokesmen relied on the first argument, though suggesting the second and without developing either extensively. Structurally, the administration argued, the Constitution was designed to strengthen the military prowess of the nation after a period of weakness under the Articles of Confederation. In order to realize that military strength, however, the government needed a powerful executive officer capable of mustering and directing that force. As State Department attorney Charles Brower testified before a Senate committee, the "President as Chief Executive and Commander in Chief is the officer bearing the responsibility and possessing the authority to insure that defense." The president was the functional equivalent of the United States government "in the sense" of national security concerns. Ultimately, "I would say that the President's authority with regard to the case we are discussing rests on his general authority under Article II of the Constitution. I think it would be difficult for anyone to be more precise than that. The Constitution is not such a precise document." For the administration, such imprecision cemented the broad presidential powers suggested by the text rather than allowing later refinements.[69]

The second legalistic claim for an inherent presidential war power was advocated not by the administration itself, but rather by interested proponents of the presidential position. In this reading, although the original text might have provided the president with extensive war powers, that text was less important than subsequent practice in defining constitutional meaning. Constitutional meaning was determined not only by the text, but also by an unbroken tradition of usage. Thus, former American Bar Association president David Maxwell informed the Senate that "changing conditions and the vastly different mores make it no longer acceptable to limit the President in exercising war powers." Those changes, however, were defined not by current political judgment, but by "usage and practice," that is, the accumulated evidence of prior acts of presidential warmaking. Where the text was vague in delegating the war powers, practice had made it determinate. Senator Barry Goldwater clarified this settled practice by presenting extensive lists of instances in which the president had ordered American troops into combat, with special emphasis on historical consistency and increasing global reach.[70]

Evidence of this "living Constitution" was advanced not as an indication of its force as a political document, but as a further extrapolation of its proper legal interpretation. James Madison had noted that the Constitution was "so new, and so complicated, [that] there should be occasional difficulties & differences in the practical expositions of it" as specific cases arose that had not been clearly foreseen and accounted for by the Philadelphia Convention delegates. Such "contested meanings" were to be settled by "a course of practice of sufficient uniformity and duration to carry with it the public sanction." For Madison, such practices were part of the contemporaneous expression of the founders' understanding of constitutional requirements. The "early, deliberate & continued practice" of the first legislatures supplemented the text, the historic purpose of the text, and the "comments prevailing at the time it was adopted" in providing the necessary material for a legal interpretation of the Constitution.[71] Early practice did not indicate the fluidity of constitutional meaning or an avenue of constitutional change, but rather made express the implicit meaning of a complicated text.

Later the Court institutionalized this understanding as legally applicable doctrine. In a different context, Felix Frankfurter explained that the plain text must be understood in terms of the "gloss" placed on it by "systematic, unbroken, executive practice, long pursued to the knowledge of the Congress and never before questioned, engaged in by Presidents who have also sworn to uphold the Constitution, making as it were such exercise of power part of the structure of our government."[72] Such "glosses" were among the interpretive tools available to the courts and were legally enforceable along with more directly discoverable constitutional meaning. Moreover, unlike constructions, there could be no recognition that such usage could change over time. The usefulness of practice for judicial interpretation was precisely its systematic, consistent, unchallenged character, which provided an unbroken link between present judicial interpreters and the practical expositions of the founders themselves. Goldwater, who was the primary advocate of this argument in the Senate, was emphatic that his lists of executive military actions were not evidence of a still-evolving or politically flexible document, but rather were designed to meet the Court's legal interpretive doctrine of "usage" to establish settled constitutional meaning. The War Powers Resolution was a "serious attack on the Constitution" precisely because usage had permanently defined constitutional meaning to legitimate presidential warmaking.[73]

Although the Constitution had favored the executive branch in its delegation of the war powers, it was also characterized by an essential elasticity. The proponents of the presidential construction were admittedly vague about how the president was to exercise the war powers. For the president, this vagueness was best characterized as "flexibility." The tension within this executive formula was again displayed by the State Department, which argued that because the "Constitution is a fundamentally flexible document which through fundamental political processes adapts to the changing times of history, we must accept the proposition that you would be changing the Constitution and altering this scheme by trying to outline very detailed rules" with the War Powers Resolution. In the executive construction, the Constitution was simultaneously flexible and fixed, broad yet specific. Though the changing Constitution could adapt to increased presidential warmaking, Congress could not "change the Constitution, amend the Constitution, by legislation." The Constitution was purposefully not a "precise document," and thus Congress could not "attempt to fix in detail, and to freeze, the allocation of the war power between the President and Congress."[74] For the administration, the Constitution was flexible in the same sense that it had been for Henry Clay and John Marshall. The fixed text delegated an area of discretion within which the president could make policy without the burden of additional constitutional values or procedures.

Maintaining the "flexibility" of the war powers in the Constitution had a tactical benefit for the proponents of the presidential construction. The congressional construction could be understood as an attempt to alter not simply recent presidential practice but the fundamental text itself. What Fulbright perceived as an "imbalance" was actually Alexander Hamilton's "energetic" executive in action in the modern world. Flexibility also offered substantive benefits under the presidential construction. More-detailed procedures than the broad authorizations of Article II would hamper the ability of the nation to respond adequately to a variety of diplomatic and military crises and would create a perception of American weakness among potential enemies.

The advocates of the presidential construction also emphasized the traditional strengths of the executive branch that indicated that the legislature should not take a leadership position in protecting the national security. Secretary of State William Rogers made the point most concisely:

Unlike the Presidency, the institutional characteristics of Congress have not lent themselves as well to the requirements of speed and secrecy in times of recurrent crises and rapid change. Its numerous members and their diverse constituencies, the complexity of its decision making processes, and its constitutional tasks of debate, discussion, and authorization inevitably make Congress a more deliberative, public, and diffuse body.[75]

The changing Cold War order only increased the need for executive response to instability. Although speed was an essential characteristic in the modern world, even for dealing with broad policy directions, unity and expertise supplemented and contributed to the benefits of executive responsiveness. The lines between larger policy decisions and immediate tactical decisions were often blurred in the military context. As long as the president made "a judgment that is within reason—that would not apply in a case of a man that happened to be insane," then it would not be the proper function of Congress to "convert the Senate into a war room."[76]

Indecisiveness not only slowed decisionmaking, with fatal consequences in regard to the war powers; it also undermined the decisions that were actually made. The secrecy maintained by the executive branch was necessary not only to preserve tactical surprise, but also to present a united front to the enemy. The public direction of foreign policy could be made clear as long as the president acted as "the sole organ of the Nation, both as Executive and Commander in Chief." As the Vietnam experience suggested, merely airing public dissent would undermine the war effort and give an impression of weakness. Although debate and criticism might be conducive to good decisionmaking, such disagreements must be kept out of so public a forum as the legislature.[77]

Finally, as the specifics of the resolution took shape, the proponents of the executive construction insisted that constitutional responsibility for the war powers could be taken only through positive action. As Nixon argued in his veto message, "one cannot become a responsible partner unless one is prepared to take responsible action."[78] In fact congressional reformers themselves were divided on this issue. Ultimately, a majority accepted the legislative veto as an adequate mechanism for preventing the president from altering the status quo. Without positive authorization from Congress, a presidential exercise of the war powers would be short-lived, and a state of peace would be reaffirmed. A significant minority, however, was unconvinced that congressional inaction could really result in a return to the status quo ante. A successful congressional construction of the war powers—that is, an assertion of legislative participation in the leadership of the national security state—required that Congress be willing to take a position on key foreign policy questions. Without the legislative will to reach a positive decision, the public would continue to look to the president when faced with an international crisis.[79] Although this division among congressional reformers was overcome for the purpose of passing the War Powers Resolution, the ultimate reliance on the legislative veto to implement the congressional will indicates the limited nature of the construction.

Participation without Leadership

The final construction of the war powers ensured an increased role for Congress in foreign policy, but left intact the president's primary leadership position. The mixed commitments of congressional reformers, the disparity between their final actions and their constitutional position, and the unwillingness of Congress to question the foundation of the imperial presidency—the postwar national security state—limited the effect of the construction. The War Powers Resolution signaled the end of the Cold War consensus and indicated the newly politically charged environment of foreign policy debates, ushering in a greater congressional role in determining defense priorities and the direction of foreign policy. Nonetheless, the specific procedures contained in the resolution reflected the unwillingness of Congress to curtail sharply presidential warmaking and have only marginally constrained presidential action in the decades since.

By allowing ninety days of presidentially initiated military action before triggering a response by legislative veto, Congress left the president with substantial discretion in the exercise of the war powers. Moreover, by refusing to detail the circumstances in which the president could use military force without prior congressional approval, the legislature implicitly sustained the extensive Article II powers advocated by the postwar presidents. Far from being a surprising failure of the resolution, the continuing presidential discretion to use military force in a variety of situations was pointed out at the time by the disappointed advocates of stronger congressional reform and defended by moderate reformers and the presidentialists.[80]

The War Powers Resolution was a culmination of a number of reforms enhancing congressional involvement in foreign policy, including foreign aid, defense appropriations, and treatymaking. It is a false choice to characterize the resolution as either "symbol or substance," for the resolution signaled the extent of the congressional resurgence in foreign policy. If war is the one instance in which Congress has not gained a leadership position in foreign policy, the resolution is nonetheless important in indicating the legislative claim to the entire policy area and has ensured congressional participation in military action. Certainly it allowed Congress to strike a blow against the imperial presidency at the height of Watergate, expressing the congressional resolve that presidential power would be lowered from its Nixonian heights.[81]

Even in the narrow context of military action itself, Congress has been involved in the types of activity at stake in the congressional construction. A minority of congressional reformers hoped to make war difficult to initiate, and to create a constitutional understanding that only Congress through positive action could authorize a military offensive. Viewed from this standard, as many later opponents of the presidential war power have done, the resolution has been a clear failure. Many of the reformers who took this view of constitutional powers were dissatisfied with the resolution from its inception, however. The more common congressional sentiment was not pacifist, but rather was concerned with the lack of legislative deliberation over major and sustained changes in the direction of American military policy. The Vietnam war and shifting strategic objectives, not the use of the American military per se, were the concerns of the reformist Congress. Even as later presidents have been able to undertake relatively "surgical" operations such as the invasions of Grenada and Panama and the bombing of Libya, more-sustained military operations at the margins of the current foreign policy agreement, such as the Lebanon incursion, paramilitary operations in Central America, and the Persian Gulf war, have evoked explicit congressional deliberation and authorization. More-recent efforts in Somalia and Haiti have reflected congressional pressure, if not formal authorization, after presidential hesitation to take action.[82]

The resolution did not force a severe shift in the exercise of the war powers, but it did mark a more limited expansion of congressional participation in national security concerns. Congress has been more active in involving itself in national security debates and has abandoned the deferential attitude of the postwar legislatures in favor of a more self-assured and antagonistic stance. Although presidents have been resistant to congressional demands, they have been unable to avoid congressional concerns and participation.

In the context of a continuing congressional commitment to the national security state and to America's role as a global superpower, the presidency has retained the leadership of the constitutional war powers. In passing the resolution, Congress recognized inherent presidential powers to use military force to defend American security interests. Further, Congress implicitly recognized the primary presidential claims to possess an advantage in secrecy and rapidity of action. The legislature, however, insisted on its own authority to determine the appropriate balance of decisiveness and deliberation. By insisting that unilateral presidential action operate under a preset time limit, Congress rejected the Nixonian claim that the initiation of hostilities justified any and all military action consistent with the president's judgment of national security. To the disappointment of some reformers, the congressional construction was not an effort to define the legal boundaries of presidential power, and thus did not authorize judicial action. As a consequence, Congress has maintained control over the interpretation and application of the resolution, and discretion over when to check presidential actions.[83]

Accountability in Intelligence

Closely related to the construction of the war powers was a final aftershock of the Watergate episode: the reform of intelligence policymaking. If the war powers had indicated the extreme difficulty of congressional participation in the far reaches of the foreign policy arena, foreign and domestic intelligence activities indicated the extreme delicacy of such participation. Moreover, whereas the war powers debate began with a relatively coherent goal of correcting an imbalance in the separation of powers and securing congressional leadership of military affairs, the debate over intelligence reforms was less purposive. Nonetheless, the eventual results were consistent in focusing less on defining and enforcing civil liberties against federal intelligence operations than on ensuring executive accountability to Congress for any operations undertaken.

Political Intelligence and Executive Government

Like the war powers, American intelligence activities have been largely the prerogative of the executive branch. Similarly, congressional deference was particularly pronounced and the executive particularly active during the uneasy peace of the Cold War. However, the nature of the enterprise, the extraordinary length of the Cold War, and advances in technology served to shield intelligence operations from both public and legislative notice to a degree impossible for the presidential exercise of the war powers or other aspects of foreign policy. Moreover, the postwar growth in intelligence capabilities occurred in both foreign and domestic service, and the boundaries between national security and domestic order were often blurred and crossed.

The executive apparatus of intelligence gathering had its roots in the administration of Franklin Roosevelt. J. Edgar Hoover was first appointed director of the Bureau of Investigation in 1924, but his agency greatly benefited from the nationalization of law enforcement under Roosevelt. With the expansion of the Bureau, Hoover set about establishing an independent base of public support for the agency and creating a relationship of mutual benefit with the occupant of the White House. As early as 1933, Hoover honored administration requests for information on Roosevelt's political critics and opponents. As the president's interests shifted from domestic to foreign policy, the Bureau's investigations expanded from such targets as the American Civil Liberties Union, the Communist party, and Father Charles Coughlin to Charles Lindbergh, Senator Gerald Nye, and former president Herbert Hoover. In authorizing the use of wiretaps, Roosevelt expanded the means as well as the subject of domestic surveillance.[84]

The expansion of both domestic and foreign intelligence-gathering capacity was accomplished almost entirely at presidential direction. As the FBI moved into internal national security, Hoover recommended against legislative authorization for fear of subjecting the Bureau to unwanted "attention" and "criticism or objections." Nonetheless, when Bureau activities became public at the end of the decade, Congress not only approved of the surveillance but encouraged its expansion. The legislature also gave the president relatively free rein in developing tools for foreign intelligence gathering. The National Security Act of 1947 was the only legislative charter for a foreign-intelligence-gathering agency, leaving the executive branch to supplement the Central Intelligence Agency on its own authority. The main congressional concern was to ensure civilian control over intelligence gathering, not to define its nature, purpose, or limits.[85]

Presidential directives tended to take the same broad approach. Unlike Congress, however, the president and his immediate subordinates maintained close contact with the intelligence community. Having committed intelligence to the executive branch, Congress chose to benefit occasionally from acquired information but to maintain a respectful deference as to the specific goals and methods of intelligence gathering. By the 1960s, various presidential administrations were routinely using intelligence agencies not only to gather information about dissident groups, political opponents, and journalists, but also to engage in positive action to disrupt disfavored groups ranging from the Ku Klux Klan to the Communist party to the Congress on Racial Equality.[86]

As executive use of the intelligence agencies grew more sophisticated and extensive, Congress offered its encouragement while minimizing its oversight. First during World War II and then in the Cold War, Congress aided the expansion of federal domestic intelligence by criminalizing and officially disfavoring certain political activities and groups. As fear of communism was replaced by concerns about domestic lawlessness, first from racial divisions and then from the New Left, congressional requests for information and executive action against agitators remained high.[87] More important to the growth of intelligence than such instances of active legislative support was the general attitudinal and structural orientation of congressional deference to the executive branch. One senator encapsulated the dominant congressional attitude in 1956, noting that "it is not a question of reluctance on the part of CIA officials to speak to us. Instead it is a question of our reluctance, if you will, to seek information and knowledge on subjects which I personally, as a Member of Congress and as a citizen, would rather not have." Legislative deference was not simply a matter of individual squeamishness, but was part of a constitutional understanding that placed intelligence operations under the exclusive control of the president. Senator Carl Hayden, chairman of the Senate Appropriations Committee, argued that congressional involvement in intelligence "would tend to impinge upon the constitutional authority and responsibility of the President in the conduct of foreign affairs." Senator Richard Russell informed his colleagues that intelligence activities must be taken "on faith," without congressional "examination." In 1971, when the subcommittee chairman responsible for CIA funding in the Senate was questioned about a 36,000-man covert operation in Laos, he admitted that "I did not know anything about it . . . I never asked . . . It never dawned on me to ask about it. I did see it published in the newspaper some time ago."[88]

The transmission of information to Congress was not routinized; instead, congressional curiosity and occasional concern over intelligence programs were satisfied through informal discussion with individual legislative leaders. The appropriate relationship between the legislative and executive branches on intelligence was well understood by both, and they behaved accordingly. CIA Director William Colby, the last before the reforms, did not know how to respond to Representative Les Aspin's request to know how the agency had traditionally handled a congressional objection to a CIA operation. No such contingencies had been expected or included in executive procedures. Director Allen Dulles informed the Warren Commission in 1964 that he felt obliged to tell only the president the truth about CIA activities, though he later privately amended the list to include the chairman of the oversight committee, if he ever actually wanted to know. Examining the era, Colby determined that "the old tradition was that you don't ask. It was a consensus that intelligence was apart from the rules." When congressional investigations threatened to encroach upon intelligence operations, legislators were quietly informed so that they would hedge their inquiries, and the occasional reform measures were overwhelmingly and quickly defeated. Congress both accepted and contributed to the presidentialist construction that made intelligence the prerogative of the executive branch alone.[89]

In this context of executive domination of intelligence gathering, presidents encountered the constraints of bureaucratic politics. By servicing the needs of his political superiors and by cultivating other sources of power, Hoover was free to impose on the Bureau his own vision of intelligence priorities and professional norms. The CIA similarly developed its own institutional practices and perspectives independently of the transitory presidencies. Though this institutional hardening complemented the loose presidential leadership of the intelligence community, it resulted in occasional tensions between the White House and the intelligence agencies. These divisions led to increasing efforts to personalize intelligence operations, whether by making the CIA more compliant with presidential wishes or by supplanting existing bureaucratic structures with new devices such as Nixon's "Plumbers," the administration's "dirty tricks" experts.[90]

Watergate special prosecutor Archibald Cox castigated the Nixon White House for "a neurotic passion for spying," articulating a standard theme of analyses of the Nixon presidency and suggesting that the uses of executive power under Nixon were unique and personal.[91] In fact, although the personalities of Nixon and his associates clearly exacerbated the problems of domestic intelligence, the Nixon administration was more the culmination of the systematic growth of presidential control over intelligence than an aberration. Both the means and ends of Nixonian surveillance were well grounded in the practices of the modern presidency, though the particular institutional mechanisms were new.

A number of factors undercut that consensus, leaving Nixon unprepared and exposed and laying the groundwork for a new constitutional construction of intelligence responsibilities. The CIA's prestige, competence, and influence had been gradually undermined since the abortive Bay of Pigs operation in 1961. Similarly, Hoover's political and then physical withdrawal from domestic intelligence left a vacuum filled by relatively inexperienced and politically naive operatives. By the mid-1970s the intelligence community no longer possessed the political capital to sustain itself in the face of scandal.[92] Second, the breakdown of the Cold War foreign policy consensus fractured intelligence gathering generally. The national security state gave substantial deference to the president to exercise his own discretion in doing what was necessary to defend American interests, but it also tolerated an expansive understanding of what threatened those interests, justifying investigations of such marginal threats as Charles Lindbergh, Martin Luther King Jr., and journalist Daniel Schorr. The dissolution of agreement on foreign policy goals required both a reduction in presidential discretion to act on those goals and a reassessment of previously perceived threats.[93] Third, changes in the electoral climate posed a particular threat to the intelligence activities of the Nixon White House. Nixon's law-and-order campaigns of 1970 and 1972 built support for executive action against various left-wing groups, but also set the president up for a congressional attack on the administration's own violations of the law, especially those that seemed primarily self-serving. Meanwhile, previously marginal components of the Democratic coalition became its core, even as the party maintained control of Congress. The Kennedy and Johnson administrations could afford to investigate the leadership of the civil rights movement, but by 1972 the civil rights and antiwar movements had become firmly entrenched in the party, and the FBI had files on many of the delegates to the Democratic National Convention. Extensive political surveillance of the old "dissident" groups was no longer tenable. Exposure of such exploitation of the modern presidency by a Republican administration required congressional response to defend what had become key Democratic constituencies.[94]

Exposure of executive intelligence came as the modern presidency was at its weakest point. In August 1973 Nixon invoked the old understandings in his defense of the Watergate affair, asserting that previous presidents had used the FBI to engage in the same activities as the Watergate burglars. In doing so, Nixon simultaneously exposed the fragility of the earlier construction and connected the activities of his campaign committee with the larger executive structure, inviting an expansion of the probe. The formation of the Special Investigative Unit, or the "Plumbers," for their original task of stopping administration leaks, which was later colonized in Nixon's reelection campaign committee, both made intelligence activities more responsive to White House needs and made the White House more vulnerable to exposure and criticism. Nixon's resignation seemed to confirm that the types of illegal and questionable activities detailed in the Watergate investigation were no longer acceptable presidential prerogatives. The press tied subsequent exposure of FBI and CIA intelligence abuses directly back to Watergate.[95]

In the absence of extensive prior debate, congressional consideration of intelligence activities and their possible reform extended through the 1970s. In the earlier war power debates, Congress had already defeated proposals for radical change that would have placed the legislature in a role of determining policy for covert activities. As a place-holding measure, Congress reaffirmed presidential responsibility for intelligence in national security, requiring only that the legislature be made aware of presidential actions. Despite its tentativeness, the Hughes-Ryan Amendment was the first legislative action on intelligence in nearly three decades and signaled that the old construction of executive powers over intelligence was in flux.[96]

Secrecy and Presidential Reform

In the aftermath of Hughes-Ryan and the disclosures of the CIA's "family jewels," the recently compiled files on the history of CIA abuses, additional efforts at reform seemed inevitable. President Ford chose a proactive approach, admitting the need for reform but attempting to contain it within the executive branch. Some in the intelligence community grudgingly defended the old order, making little accommodation to the reformers and offering their defense only on direct attack. In the end, neither approach was pursued extensively or prevented congressional reform. The two approaches were complementary, however, in framing the direction of the debate and in moderating the eventual outcome.

On January 14, 1975, Ford appointed a presidential commission headed by Vice President Nelson Rockefeller to examine American intelligence and recommend reforms to the president. In formulating the presidential response to the intelligence scandals, Ford was only partially constrained by the judiciary. Though the presidential conduct of foreign intelligence enjoyed the same judicial deference as executive control of foreign policy generally, domestic surveillance raised problematic First and Fourth Amendment issues that the judiciary intermittently addressed. Nonetheless, the courts left substantial constitutional questions unresolved.

By the time of the debates of the 1970s, judicial intervention in intelligence was focused primarily on Fourth Amendment issues of warrant requirements for electronic surveillance.[97] The text of the Fourth Amendment and judicial decisions at least suggested that search-and-seizure requirements were designed to protect citizens from criminal prosecutions, not from nonpunitive intelligence gathering.[98] The Court imposed new warrant requirements in domestic national security cases in 1972, but still hesitated to equate the warrant procedures in criminal and security cases and suggested that different standards might govern the latter.[99] Though carving out individual rights against some methods of domestic intelligence, such cases did not attempt to restrain foreign intelligence, nor did they undermine domestic intelligence per se. The Court declared cases of noninvasive government surveillance nonjusticiable, for example.[100] By the mid-1970s the courts had largely left the field open to the political construction of civil liberties relative to intelligence gathering.[101]

President Ford's immediate efforts were aimed at creating the momentum for executive reform and preempting any congressional investigation. Previous high-profile commissions had provided useful information for action, but, more importantly, they had established presidential leadership and prevented independent congressional investigations. The post-Watergate Congress, however, was unwilling to cede authority and information on the issue, and each chamber appointed its own select investigatory committee. As one Ford adviser observed, Congress "simply disregarded the fact that there was a Rockefeller commission."[102]

The administration's approach to the growing scandal was to minimize abuses while emphasizing the president's support for an intelligence component to American national security and the executive branch's comparative advantage in conducting intelligence effectively. Ford's few public remarks on intelligence sought to contrast a presidency concerned with national defense with thoughtless radicals in Congress. When questioned on the progress of the congressional investigations, the president only threatened that "under no circumstances . . . will I permit the dismantling or the destruction of an intelligence agency or community, because that does involve our national security."[103] The alternative remained presidential leadership. In his 1976 address to Congress, Ford promised, "In the near future, I will take actions to reform and strengthen our intelligence community. I ask for your positive cooperation. It is time to go beyond sensationalism and ensure an effective, responsible, and responsive intelligence capability." Presidential reform emphasized the capacity for intelligence operations as much as the need for controls on intelligence. Former CIA director John McCone clarified the president's position, contending that it was now time "to extinguish . . . criticism" of the intelligence service.[104] Public legislative criticism of the intelligence agencies served only to undermine national security.

In the view of executive officials, congressional investigations were a sharp contrast to executive efforts. Whereas the executive proceeded quietly and carefully to consider ways to improve American national security, the legislature used intelligence scandals for personal grandstanding and individual political advantage.[105] Regardless of the truth of such characterizations, their widespread acceptance within the executive branch indicated the attitudes that shaped the presidential response to reform efforts. An apolitical intelligence policy required presidential leadership. Neutral competence and quiet reason were the monopoly of executive officials.

The political myopia of the legislature allegedly damaged national security not only by undermining the intelligence agencies, but also by presenting a persistent threat to the secrecy of intelligence operations. The fear of leaks became perhaps the primary theme of arguments for continued executive dominance of intelligence. The president himself struck this chord, arguing that the executive could not release documents to congressional investigators because of their penchant for "sensationalized public debate over legitimate intelligence activities" and because of their internal procedures, which made "the protection of vital information next to impossible." As the debate began over legislative control of intelligence activities, proponents of presidential control repeatedly stressed the danger of leaks if Congress increased its oversight activity.[106]

The secrecy argument was substantially bolstered by recent high-profile transgressions. In 1969 Senator Stuart Symington's investigations had produced a torrent of leaks on covert operations in Laos. In 1974, in violation of House rules, Representative Michael Harrington had revealed classified information on CIA activities in Chile. Most problematic, however, were the various leaks from the select investigatory committees themselves. Those problems culminated in the 1976 publication of the Pike committee report by the *Village Voice*, after the House, deferring to executive complaints about the inclusion of classified information, had specifically decided not to publish it. Individual congressmen had inherent political incentives to publicize their knowledge, and this political reality led many to conclude that Congress must be effectively excluded from extensive involvement in intelligence policymaking. The weight of these failures in congressional security led even many advocates of the congressional construction to admit that the problem of leaks had to be solved before greater congressional control over intelligence was viable.[107]

The administration preferred to fight legislative reform by emphasizing congressional faults and the value of intelligence to national security, while trying to reduce public attention to the issue. These efforts were supported by a few who chose to defend even the "abuses" of the past as necessary for national security. Nixon himself contended that "it is quite obvious that there are inherently governmental actions which if undertaken by the sovereign in protection of the interest of the nation's security are lawful, but which if undertaken by private persons are not," noting a variety of such actions ranging from assassinations to warrantless searches. Similarly, longtime head of CIA counterintelligence James Angleton admitted that "I find it inconceivable that a covert agency is expected to obey all the overt orders of the government." Ultimately, the Constitution provided for an exclusive presidential prerogative to protect national security through covert means, even at the expense of formal laws. The balancing of individual constitutional rights and governmental constitutional powers had been made within the presidentialist construction.[108]

Building on these efforts, Ford issued an executive order to implement the Rockefeller commission's recommendations. Recognizing past abuses, the commission advised the president to institute a number of additional checks within the executive branch to help monitor and control intelligence activities. Significantly, these reforms included expanding existing White House structures in order to increase presidential control over executive agencies, while further consolidating congressional oversight in a single joint committee. Overall, Ford's reforms reinforced exclusive presidential control over and responsibility for intelligence, making minimal modifications in the subjects or methods of intelligence gathering. As one scholar has concluded, they were "as much (and perhaps more) an attempt to maintain executive control of the reform movement as . . . an attempt to accommodate reform pressures."[109]

Accountability to Congress

As the president attempted to defend the old order by containing reforms, Congress carved a new role for itself in national security and law enforcement by publicizing past abuses. Although the opportunity for reform was clearly available in the mid-1970s, the particular shape that reform should take was substantially less clear. The very mechanisms of exposure contained the foundation for the ultimate construction, as justifications for congressional investigation bled into arguments for permanent legislative oversight of intelligence activities. Once accountability was achieved, however, further efforts to extend the construction to redefine individual rights in a democratic society collapsed.

The reassertion of congressional responsibility over war powers opened an avenue by which to approach intelligence operations. At best, however, this extrapolation of congressional responsibilities resulted in a joint responsibility with the executive branch. The public, initiating quality of congressional participation in the war powers could not be extended to the intelligence sphere. Rather, congressional reformers merely contended that the legislature could involve itself in and restrain executive intelligence activities, but could not prohibit actions independently authorized by Article II. Through its appropriating and legislative powers, Congress could "regulate the conduct" of intelligence activities but could not direct them.[110]

Congressional willingness to support such reasoning was given early form in the creation of separate House and Senate select committees. The Senate committee, chaired by Frank Church, approached the investigation with a mixture of publicizing past executive activities and working with executive agencies to ensure the secrecy of sensitive information and the adequacy of reforms. The House, on the other hand, approached the task with greater partisanship and interbranch hostility. The first House committee imploded under its own internal political strains. A second committee under Otis Pike pursued a path of extensive publicity and antagonism toward the executive branch and made frequent use of subpoenas and contempt citations.[111]

The power of Congress to regulate what remained primarily an executive responsibility manifested itself in legislative oversight of the intelligence community. Executive-branch intelligence gathering had to be brought under political control, which required a proliferation of external checks on executive action to ensure accountability. Republican Senator Charles Percy contended that the realization of "laws and constitutional procedures" required "adequate accountability" to the elected representatives of the people. Nonetheless, the legislature could not "overreact and, really, in a sense, assume unto itself executive branch responsibilities."

Congressional responsibility to ensure effective and proper intelligence authorized only monitoring, not direct involvement. As Democratic Senator Walter Huddleston observed, the "heart of the matter is oversight and accountability," not congressional determination of intelligence policy.[112]

If oversight was the extent of the legislature's available constitutional power over intelligence, it was nonetheless a necessary duty. Whereas some congressional reformers saw oversight responsibilities as the result of changed conditions, others contended that the Constitution had always required oversight and legislators had previously "abrogated their constitutional responsibilities." Congressional monitoring arose from a number of considerations. Most obviously, proponents of a congressional role pointed to the historic failure of internal executive controls. The brute fact of persistent abuse called for a new approach.[113] Moreover, proponents of the congressional construction charged, the failure of executive intelligence was a problem intrinsic to the reliance on purely internal controls, which ignored the constitutional principle of checks and balances.

In a related point, oversight proponents contended that external monitoring of the executive was necessary not only to prevent abuses, but also to ensure the proper direction of public policy. The claim made in this context, however, was much more limited than the celebration of the congressional power of deliberation pressed in the war powers debate. Congressional monitoring of intelligence was needed simply to provide a link between those activities and the public that they served. The external accountability of executive agents contributed to the penetration of the internal norms of the intelligence community by the norms and expectations of the larger populace, as conveyed by members of Congress. An important subtext of such external linkages was that the intelligence agencies were not the exclusive tools of the president, but were to be responsive to the political needs of the legislative branch as well. To congressmen, political control of intelligence meant legislative control.[114]

A second type of construction competed with the call for congressional involvement in intelligence, and that was the desire to redefine the relationship between government and the people entirely so as to curtail sharply, if not to eliminate, intelligence activities. This second construction was rooted in an understanding of democracy and the rights of the citizenry that made them inconsistent with continued intelligence operations. Domestic surveillance carried an inherent risk that government agents might act to crush legitimate dissent. As interested participants, government officials were likely to take an expansive view of what activities were "subversive" of the existing political order and of what actions were acceptable in preventing that subversion. Moreover, even the most benign political surveillance carried the implicit threat of a more extensive use of government powers, creating an unacceptable "chilling effect" on political dissent.[115]

The additional threat of covert operations emerged from the government secrecy around them, rather than from their effects on their targets. The necessity of keeping information from the people's representatives, as Allen Dulles noted, or of making congressmen complicit in misinforming the people undercut the very basis of democratic control over government. The "intelligence agencies are in effect a clandestine government operating within the executive branch of the federal government," forcing Americans to "give up their right to participation in the political process and to informed consent." The simplest solution required reconceiving the requirements of democratic government and national security in order that "covert action and spies . . . be banned."[116]

Such an extreme construction gained little support in Congress, however. Most reformers were careful to distance themselves from such proposals and to counteract the president's alternative by insisting on their own commitment not only to the preservation of national security but also to the specific use of intelligence. The need for active covert intelligence operations "is not subject to question" in congressional debates.[117] Instead of an outright ban on covert activities, congressional reformers influenced by this more radical construction sought to define citizens' rights and agency rules to curtail intelligence activities.

The formalization of this impulse was somewhat more difficult, however, once the simple expedient of banning covert activities was rejected. This conception of radical reform developed several expressions. First, a new congressional oversight mechanism would act less to provide political control and access to agency policymaking than to serve as a civil rights watchdog. The procedural reform of new oversight mechanisms was purely a means to a substantive change, the redefinition of appropriate intelligence under the Constitution. Second, intelligence agencies would be brought under statutory charter. Such charters would strengthen the separation-of-powers construction by shifting the locus of authority for intelligence from presidential directives to congressional statutes. Charters would also serve a more fundamental purpose of defining more-stringent operating rules for the agencies. Third, the constitutional requirements of the privacy rights of individuals relative to intelligence investigations would be legislatively specified, redefining the government's relationship with its citizens.

In the case of each of these specific measures, congressional involvement in intelligence was seen as necessary not simply to multiply the political controls on executive agencies but to bring them under the "rule of law and the will of the people." The executive was not only an incompetent manager, but also an inadequate representative. Further, congressional action would include both "substantive restraints" and "procedural safeguards" to preserve the "Constitution and our fundamental values" against the types of activities previously justified and accepted under the president's duty to protect the national security. All of which served to repudiate the strong presidential construction that intelligence operations occurred outside the normal legal strictures as part of a presidential prerogative, while also contradicting the weaker claim that traditional intelligence procedures were permissible so long as there was greater supervision to prevent abuse.[118]

The rights construction contributed to congressional reform in additional ways by specifying the particular need for legislative action. Congressional action supplemented the constraints placed on intelligence by the judiciary. Where the judiciary deferred to executive judgment as to the importance of particular national security interests, Congress was positioned to challenge those claims in the particular and to establish procedures for categorizing and weighing them in general. Further, congressional monitoring of intelligence could prevent or stop executive programs that threatened to cause even nonjusticiable damage to individuals or social mores, vindicating privacy and free speech rights left unrecognized and undefended by the courts.[119]

The rights construction also provided a legislative response to the fear of leaks by redefining the problem. Whereas the separation-of-powers construction could only admit the relative advantage of the executive branch and counterbalance the benefits of additional control mechanisms imposed on the intelligence agencies, the rights construction could challenge the virtue of executive secrecy itself. In doing so, one construction aided and blended into the other. In the rights construction, the presidential monopoly on determining the need for secrecy was at the heart of the problem with intelligence operations. Congressional participation promised not simply more "leaks," but a more democratic openness with information about government activities.[120]

The establishment of a permanent Senate select intelligence oversight committee in May 1976 marked the success of the congressional construction in establishing the appropriateness of legislative oversight. The establishment of the oversight committee was partially shaped by rights arguments, but the creation of the committee also removed much of the impetus for additional reform. Subsequent reforms to extend the rights of citizens against government surveillance were modest, with more extensive legislative efforts failing to attract significant support.

The permanent intelligence committees established first in the Senate and a year later in the House followed the model of the Church committee in their cooperative relationship with the executive, while shifting from an investigative mode to a stance of "institutional oversight." Although some reformers were motivated by elements of the rights construction, others used it as a foil, allowing them to portray the separation-of-powers construction as less extreme. Moderates such as Church and Huddleston could deflect presidential criticisms and position themselves as equal to the deliberate reformers within the executive branch. Criticisms of the executive monopoly on secrecy by radical reformers such as Pike set the stage for charges of executive hypocrisy as legislators pointed out that the executive branch was itself a fertile source of leaks. The traditional executive advantage of secrecy in action was eroded, and reformers shifted the debate toward constructive efforts at ensuring adequate congressional security.[121]

The new consensus on oversight has proved reasonably stable and has resulted in a real shift in control over intelligence. One aspect of that shift is attitudinal. Both Congress and the intelligence community have radically altered their perception of their relationship. In 1983 Barry Goldwater, chairman of the Senate intelligence committee, admitted that "the formation of this new committee is the only positive aspect to emerge from the [Church] investigation," since it established "greater accountability to Congress" without resulting in damaging sensationalism.[122] Goldwater had opposed the creation of the oversight committee when he served on the Church committee. Such conversions have not been isolated; both branches now largely accept the principle and reality of oversight, though some Reagan-era political appointees remained resistant. By the mid-1990s, one scholar could conclude, with some overstatement, that Congress had "emerged as an equal partner of the executive branch" in intelligence.[123]

Such attitudinal shifts have been accompanied by significant structural changes. The new oversight committees consist of a rotating fifteen-person membership, with a consolidated jurisdiction and budgetary powers.

As a consequence, intelligence responsibilities now fall on a larger and more representative set of legislators, who have more resources with which to challenge the intelligence agencies. The flow of information between the committees and the intelligence communities has been routinized and drastically expanded. Congress now has access to essentially the same intelligence analysis as the executive branch and is regularly informed of covert operations. Structural and attitudinal shifts are displayed in a new congressional aggressiveness in intelligence in confirmations and investigations, for example.[124]

The transformation of the congressional role in intelligence has been drastic but not complete. Moreover, there are inherent limits in the position Congress has chosen to occupy. In embarking on its reforms, Congress ultimately did not question presidential responsibility for intelligence. Congress was placed in a distinctly secondary position of monitoring executive activity.[125] Iran-Contra indicates both the effects and limits of this approach. Intelligence remains a matter of presidential policy and responsibility, so that legislative constraints appear ad hoc and inappropriate to those in the White House. Nonetheless, the established intelligence bureaucracies are now highly responsive to the legislative will; one result was to force the Reagan administration to turn to more personalized agents to advance presidential policy.[126] The reforms of the 1970s were a response to executive actions that threatened legislative interests. Within the new boundaries created by those reforms, however, the incentives for active oversight are limited. Although executive investigations of protected congressional constituencies are now effectively barred, the political salience of current executive actions is much less certain. As a consequence, Congress was slow to respond to initial reports of presidential efforts to fund the Contras and has difficulty identifying executive actions that may require further investigation or discouragement. Congress has raised the stakes for executive transgressions of legislative sensibilities, but it has limited capacity to prevent determined presidents from taking action when they are willing to risk the possible political repercussions.[127] Congress has altered the calculus, but has not sought to establish absolute control.

If there are limits to the oversight established by the reforms, the substantive construction sought by some reformers was effectively abandoned. The perceived failure of the Pike committee, the prioritization of the formation of oversight committees over the drafting of legislative charters, and the expected effectiveness of the new committees rendered substantive constraints undesirable. The very formation of the oversight committee required reformers to pledge their support for a strong covert component of the national security state at the very moment when the past abuses of intelligence had been laid bare, rendering further reforms un-likely. Congress remained "on the defensive regarding its ability to main-tain secrecy for classified information," and once accountability was estab-lished, there was little support for an additional construction expanding the rights of dissident political activists. Debate over a comprehensive 1978 charter was quickly subsumed in debates over the difficulty of con-ducting effective intelligence operations under codified restrictions. The Foreign Intelligence Surveillance Act of 1978 did establish a special court to issue warrants for national security electronic searches. Although the act did construct the meaning of the Fourth Amendment's "reasonableness" requirement for searches in a national security context, it did so in a manner favoring existing intelligence operations.[128]

The construction instituted during the mid-1970s shifted constitutional understandings of the nature of covert intelligence, but did so in a manner that emphasized political control, not legal limits. Although there was an apparent reduction in targets of domestic surveillance during the early and middle 1970s, these changes reflected a response to reformed political controls rather than a new understanding of the appropriate nature of intelligence operations. Such controls have ensured the intelligence agen-cies' responsiveness to Congress as well as the president but have not constrained the goals or methods of those agencies.[129]

Conclusion

The constructions surrounding the dénouement of the Nixon presidency were varied and ultimately separate. Rather than culminating in a sweeping redefinition of the separation of powers and the nature of the executive office in a republic, the debates of the mid-1970s centered on several distinct issues. The congressional uprising in these various areas shared certain commonalities, such as the political weakness of the Nixon/Ford administration after the exposure of Watergate, the strategic crisis of the Vietnam war and détente, and the themes of democratic deliberation and openness. These common threads were not woven together, however, but were pieced into separate material. The eventual constructions of war, intelligence, and budgeting powers each had independent histories of in-vestigation, debate, and reform and operated in accord with separate dy-namics. No individual or stable set of individuals emerged to challenge presidential leadership and represent the rise of congressional government. There was no defining moment to highlight the general failings of the modern presidency and to develop an alternative.

The substance of the constructions themselves discouraged the emergence of a general challenge to the modern presidency. There was no significant commitment to an alternative model that could rival the existing one. Rather, there were numerous particular objections to aspects of presidential power and the specific ways in which it had been used in the preceding decade. The emergent response to such concerns was not a redefinition of the nature and role of the presidency, but an effort to impose better constraints and controls on a strong executive.

This general commitment to the modern presidency reflected continuing support for the activist national state with which it was connected. In both foreign and domestic policy debates, the challenge was to presidential leadership of the modern state, not to the state itself. The goal of the reformers was to expand the avenues of influence and the number of participants in policymaking, not to reshape the available ends and means of federal government action. In such a context, the modern presidency remained an essential component of the larger state apparatus. The strong presidency had to be sustained, even if it surrendered its hegemonic status.

Domestically, Congress gained more control of the power of the purse. In foreign policy, Congress gained only limited participation in the decisionmaking surrounding the exercise of the war powers. In intelligence, the legislature merely established a role of oversight of executive policymaking, without significantly constraining the substantive nature of intelligence or expanding the rights of citizens to be free from it. The differing results of these three constructions were a function of the particular history and dynamics of the separate debates that led to them. Although together they increased the power of Congress vis-à-vis the president, efforts to combine them into a single constitutional moment would misrepresent their development and separate meanings.

The earlier construction of presidential powers that was modified by the reforms of the 1970s can be characterized neither as a congressional "abdication" of responsibility nor as a mere "delegation" of policymaking details to the executive branch under the watchful eye of Congress.[130] Rather, the postwar construction of presidential powers fell somewhere in between. In contrast to the abdication view, Congress was clearly complicit in the development of presidential power and actively encouraged its use to achieve political ends favored by the legislature itself. The delega-

tion view, however, distorts the nature and scope of congressional deference to executive decisionmaking in the postwar years. The decay of congressional institutions across a range of policy areas, combined with the
growth of executive institutions and expertise, undermined congressional
attempts even to be aware of executive actions, let alone successfully to
challenge them. When those charged with overseeing executive intelligence operations on behalf of the Congress announce that they regard it as
inappropriate to find out what those intelligence operations even are, then
the "means to discipline those in the executive branch charged with carrying out this delegated authority" have clearly decayed past the capacity of
the model to explain adequately.[131]

The nature of constructions highlights the fact that constitutional structures are not as fluid as a simple delegation model might suggest. The
modern president had substantial authority to develop and execute policy
not only autonomously of Congress, but often without its knowledge and
sometimes against its will. The postwar construction carried with it a host
of institutional and ideological supports that insulated the president from
legislative challenge and undermined the type of hierarchical conceptions
of interbranch relations assumed by an principal-agent relationship between Congress and the president. As a result, changes in that construction could be realized only in the context of extended and systematic
division between the executive and legislature over the direction of future
policy, and only after a not insignificant lag and with substantial effort and
internal division. The delegation model correctly emphasizes the utility of
the earlier construction for serving congressional ends, but also significantly oversimplifies both governmental operations under the construction and the process of changing interbranch relations in a political
context.

Despite the fact that these constitutional changes occurred during the
latter part of a historic wave of judicial activism, they developed almost
entirely within the political branches themselves. The existence of political
constructions within the context of a general rise in judicial activity is a
function of both an unusual judicial restraint in these specific areas and the
particular virtues of the political branches. In the case of the war powers
and aspects of intelligence gathering, such deference was consistent with
long-held judicial understandings of the political nature of foreign policy.
Moreover, as the Court implicitly recognized, the Constitution was unclear as to the precise boundaries of presidential power in each of these
areas. Claims of presidential power over budgeting and military policy had

some foundation in the ambiguous spaces of the constitutional text, institutional practice, and legislative language, rendering interpretation both difficult and inadequate to address fully the points at issue.

Even without such restraint, however, the political branches pursued these constructions in such a way as to indicate the limited capacity of the courts to resolve the issues. Although presidential impoundments seemed well suited to judicial resolution, legislators themselves expressed dissatisfaction with reliance on the courts. The need for a declaratory judgment was transformed into the need for institution building to realize constitutional meaning in practice. Similar patterns emerged in the war powers and intelligence debates as simple prohibitions and rulemaking gave way to the creation of new or enhanced devices for ensuring political control. Moreover, congressional resolution of these issues allowed for a greater flexibility in the results. The institutionalization of interbranch cooperation permitted the negotiated settlement of particular conflicts, rather than the application of fixed rules. Presidential actions could be submitted to legislative influence without sacrificing the potential benefits of presidential initiative. Constructed settlements could also reach the larger political issues at stake in the narrow conflicts between the legislature and executive. Given the fluid nature of political power, judicial clarification of the formal boundaries between the branches would not in itself advance larger congressional aims.

Having brought these constitutional issues into the political realm, Congress and the president could establish their preferred construction only by political means. In attempting to establish his own authority to impound funds, for example, President Nixon engaged in a lengthy process of shaping public attitudes about the existence and nature of the budget "crisis" and the executive's superior capacity to solve it. The determination of the impoundment crisis depended not only on the arguments of the immediate debate, but also on a prior debate about the budget more generally. Further, the authority of that presidential rhetoric was grounded in its electoral effects as well as its internal reasonableness. The president's budget arguments were specifically campaign statements in support of his own reelection. Nixon's 1972 electoral victory transformed his budget speeches from mere policy arguments into a mandate from the people themselves, emboldening the president to attempt the impoundments and putting Congress on the defensive in checking them.

The effectiveness of the available political weapons and the dynamics of their use determined both the success of the constructions and their particular form. The final passage of war powers legislation after years of debate depended critically on the desire of hesitant legislators to strike a blow at the president in the context of an impending impeachment, while the intelligence investigations were advanced by the massive victory of post-Watergate reformers in 1974. President Ford's criticism of the intelligence investigations and his fear of leaks were backed by the executive's physical control over critical information, which resulted alternately in the dumping of vast amounts of trivial intelligence data on congressional staffers and in the withholding of key sensitive documents. The Church committee's willingness to cooperate with the executive branch to minimize damaging disclosures enhanced the Senate's ability to allay fears of leaks from a permanent oversight role. In contrast, the Pike committee's unauthorized publication of its final report severely damaged the House's ability to match both executive claims of superiority and the Senate's leadership in intelligence oversight. Especially in the Senate, the existence of more-radical reformers desiring substantive changes in intelligence policy provided the political space for more-moderate senators such as Church to establish their hawkish credentials. Legislative control over appropriations, and the credible threat of its use to punish executive intransigence, underlay all three debates and helped force executive concessions.

Similarly, the ultimate success of the construction depended not only on the success of the arguments made at the time, but also on the institutionalization of their results. As contemporary critics predicted, the failure of the War Powers Resolution to require positive action by Congress in response to executive deployment of troops has hampered congressional efforts to match its claims of equal responsibility for national security. Similarly, the prioritization of the forming of a permanent intelligence oversight committee over the drafting of a statutory charter for the intelligence agencies led to the establishment of political controls on the executive and the dissolution of the pressure for substantive reforms. More positively, the formation of an oversight committee with a rotating membership and budgeting powers gave weight to the congressional assertion of independent authority over intelligence policy. Likewise, the creation of the budget committees and supporting resources such as the CBO specified the manner in which Congress would exercise its power over the purse. The structural supports for the congressional constructions clarified and represented the attitudinal shifts that accompanied them.

As political actors, the proponents of the various constructions advocated during the period did not rely on close interpretive analysis of the Constitution in order to determine its meaning. The discussions of the constructions were both heated and wide-ranging. Even as some senators pleaded with their colleagues for moderation, others insisted that belligerent tones were precisely called for by the shift in constitutional powers and how they were now being used without congressional control. Beyond such emotional rhetoric, advocates pursued both the concrete effects of the alternative constructions and the broad political principles they supported. At times, such portraits were drawn in sensationally harsh and particular terms. Thus, proponents of presidential control of intelligence accused their opponents of being responsible for the death of CIA operative Richard Welch in Greece and predicted more such murders if the congressional construction were adopted. Both to belittle and to vilify presidential control, legislative reformers countered by detailing CIA assassination attempts against foreign leaders and efforts by FBI operatives to break up the marriages of members of dissident groups and by displaying CIA weaponry for television cameras. At other times, advocates focused on broad political principles and their connection to political practice. Presidential assertions of the value of the secrecy, decisiveness, efficiency, and unity of the executive branch were contrasted to traditional legislative virtues of representativeness, openness, and deliberativeness. Although the values embodied in the different branches of government were suggested by the Constitution itself, the political debate focused directly on the political principles and the appropriate balance among them to determine how to weight institutional responsibilities under the ambiguous text.

The weak position of a Republican president facing a Democratic Congress at a time of a shifting consensus on foreign and domestic policy fostered various efforts to increase legislative participation in the leadership of the national state. Divided government did not result in stalemate, but rather provoked an institutional and ideological restructuring to advance political concerns in an altered environment. Though Nixon and Ford were unable to sustain an expansion of presidential power or to prevent an undercutting of their inherited powers, they did contribute to the ultimate shape of the constructions that were established. For the legislature's part, Congress was able to establish new understandings of its responsibilities in budgeting, the conduct of foreign policy, and intelligence gathering, as well as to establish the institutional supports to realize those responsibilities. As a result, the leadership of the national state was expanded and diversified. Executive stewardship was replaced by interbranch cooperation in order to accommodate the emerging reality of divided government and diverse policy commitments.

6

Building the
American Constitution

Despite the failures of constitutional theory adequately to take into account the elaboration of constitutional meaning outside the courts, political practice bears witness to a continuing effort to resist the judicial monopolization of the Constitution and its meaning. Many of these political efforts to give meaning to the constitutional text are best characterized in terms of constitutional construction. Although some efforts at construing constitutional meaning can be readily explained through reference to the jurisprudential model of constitutional interpretation, significant aspects of our historical constitutional development are not driven primarily by their fidelity to known textual meaning and are not bound by the strictures of a jurisprudential approach. Ambitious political actors will ultimately turn to the text in order to find support for their own political interests and will construct a vision of constitutional meaning that enshrines their own values and interests. In doing so, they will challenge not only claims of judicial supremacy over constitutional meaning, but also the uniqueness of the role of the founders as architects of the federal government.

The Constitution does more than specify rights and powers retained by the people. It also delegates power from the people to their chosen representatives in order to realize positive constitutional values. As the preceding cases indicate, construction plays a role in both aspects of constitutionalism, but it may play its most significant role in specifying the ends and means of government. As a source of power, the Constitution provides positive meaning to fill the vacant space hedged in by constitutional restrictions. Within this permissible range of government action, political agents must determine the particular goals to be pursued and the means by which they are to be attained. With regard to this task, the Constitution is sometimes suggestive and sometimes silent. In order to render constitutional values concrete, the text must be supplemented by something outside itself. Within the gaps left by the founders, current political actors must construct a Constitution of their own to structure future policy choices. Though more flexible than the original constitutional text, the constructed Constitution provides a stable and purposive system within which the normal work of daily politics is conducted. Constructions constantly add a denser web of values, institutions, procedures, and rights to the general framework established by the constitutional text and made clear by interpretation.

The abilities to shape public understandings, to build institutions, and to achieve compliance without the force of law are critical to the success of constructions. In adapting the Constitution to the changing political environment, including the interests and ideals of the political community, constructions provide an important vehicle for constitutional development and change. The structure of the political system initiated by the constitutional text itself tends to encourage such development. The competing ambitions and interests of various government institutions encourage conflict over the appropriate constitutional standards to guide the polity, sometimes by shaping the immediate interests of particular political actors and sometimes by providing openings for political movements to launch an effort to reshape dominant ideological and institutional commitments. Constitutional understandings are shaped through the interplay of the nation's multiple political institutions and the ambiguities of the fundamental text.

The various cases examined above demonstrate how a political process gives meaning to the Constitution, the process of constitutional construction. In each instance the political branches of government sought, by their own methods and forms of argument, to elucidate the meaning of the Constitution and to realize its terms in political practice. The following pages highlight some general features of the model of constitutional construction that emerge from consideration of these several cases and develop some of the uses of the approach for our understanding of constitutional theory, American political history, and the separation of powers.

Constitutionalism in Theory and Practice

A clearer understanding of constitutional construction compels us to revise our understanding of how the Constitution works in practice by reconsidering where constitutional deliberation takes place, how the Constitution is to be construed, and how constitutional meaning is stabilized. An important first step is the realization that nonjudicial actors engage in constitutional deliberation. Since John Marshall, arguments over judicial review have begged the question of whether the judiciary possesses unique insights into the constitutional text. The bridge from constitutionalism to judicial supremacy has been built on the contention that the courts are preeminently the American "forum of principle," whereas the non-judicial arenas are characterized by a politics of power driven by conflicting interests and assertions of will.[1] Unfortunately, that bridge depended more on caricatures drawn by academic lawyers than on the examination of historical political experience. The role of the Court will have to be situated within a context of competing claims to constitutional authority and alternative visions of appropriate constitutional meaning.[2]

Political actors not only engage in efforts to elaborate constitutional meaning, but they do so in a fashion that is inconsistent with standard jurisprudential models of constitutional interpretation. These episodes can be better understood and evaluated if they are seen as distinct pursuits building on the particular concerns and capacities of active government officials.

Although the constitutional text may supply the opening and initiative for a construction, the advocates of new constitutional understandings must add something from outside. Proponents of the constructions examined above found textual cover for their positions, but in advocating the adoption of their constructions they relied on external political principles, policy concerns, and political interests. As such, constructions are a kind of situated principle, a bridge between abstract constitutional requirements and concrete policy considerations. Protective tariffs were regarded not simply as bad policy, but as illegitimate. They were illegitimate not because the Constitution clearly prohibited them, but because their social and economic effects were contrary to constitutional norms. Similarly, the exclusive presidential prerogative over intelligence policy was grounded in no small part on the presumed institutional capacity of the executive branch to act in secret. Of course, a certain level of secrecy was deemed essential to the practical success of intelligence policies, but the ability of the executive to prevent leaks was also part of the putative institutional virtue of the branch to foster energetic, decisive, unified government.

The middle ground occupied by construction between the legal formulations of interpretation and the practical determination of policy is characterized by a different form of debate and decisionmaking than would be appropriate to either of the others. Construction shares with interpretation a constitutional subject matter, concerned with the organic structures of and the limitations on government that regulate future policy debate. It shares with those policy debates, however, the tools for creating political outcomes. The advocates of constructions employ the rational arguments, if not the legal instruments, that are at least normatively required by the jurisprudential model. They also employ a metaphorical rhetoric and appeal to political power that are not just deviations from the normative standard but also essential components for building constructions.

Given that constructions are not grounded in discoverable meaning and are not concerned primarily with the formulation of legal rules, there are genuine limits to the ability of rational argument to fulfill the needs of construction. When John Randolph compared Chase's courtroom to the Star Chamber and Gerald Ford condemned Congress for eviscerating national security, they were seeking to establish the political norms that would give substance to the eventual constructions without attempting to detail their requirements. Depending on political will, not judicial doctrine, to sustain the construction necessitates efforts to establish that will. Emotional rhetoric, the organization of political interests through compromise, and a deliberate vagueness as to the boundaries of the new construction all contribute to reaching the political agreement to support a new governing arrangement. Furthermore, such devices serve not only to secure the construction, but also to define its substance. The allegation of monarchical tendencies in Andrew Johnson served both to motivate political followers and to characterize the substance of the construction itself, and such characterizations helped clarify the substance of the construction in elevating the power of the legislature to a primary place in the republic. Similarly, the appeal to legislators to support the War Powers Resolution in order to strike a blow against Nixon in the wake of Watergate and on the eve of impeachment both pointed to the immediate stakes involved in the passage of the legislation and indicated the broader principles and values underlying the effort to pare back the modern presidency. The ubiquity of such arguments represents not the contamination of the deliberative process, but the necessary form of such deliberation.

Similarly, those engaged in constructive efforts display none of the objectivity valued in the jurisprudential model. Constructions are made by explicit advocates, not by disinterested arbiters. Those who advocate a given construction expect to benefit from it, and the arguments and resources they muster in support of their cause reflect that expectation. Self-interest is an intrinsic part of the arguments marshaled by various government actors seeking to construe the Constitution so as to favor their own institutional position. Interest in the outcome and sincere commitment to the substantive principle at stake are not mutually exclusive in these contexts, however. Far from making the Constitution irrelevant to American politics, the politicized nature of constitutional meaning links the text to an operative government. Constitutional institutions structure political battles, and constitutional principles infuse political thought. Thus, Andrew Johnson's defense of the office of the chief executive in the face of attack from Radical Republicans in the Congress combined the contingent fact that he, and not they, occupied the White House at that particular historical juncture and the Jacksonian belief that the presidency was a crucial instrument of democracy. Similarly, the Jeffersonian insistence that the judiciary could not be radically independent of the popularly elected legislature reflected the conviction both that the legislature was tantamount to the people in a republican form of government and that the Federalist party had occupied the courts as a fortress from which to attack Republican electoral and policy goals. Partisan and social interests were also readily incorporated into constructive efforts. Daniel Webster did not hesitate to enlist the support of Northern manufacturers in defense of the federal government's power to impose the protective tariffs that benefited them, even as John Calhoun represented the commercial agriculture interests of the South. Partisan calculation was on display in each of the constructions, whether in the form of the Federalists standing united against all Republican charges against abusive judges or congressional Republican efforts to regain control over executive spoils or Democratic concerns that Richard Nixon would no longer respect the budgetary priorities that the postwar presidents implicitly had. All the participants in these debates were genuinely convinced that their efforts would help determine the future security of the republic, but they did not feign disinterest in the means to that goal. Although these constructions may have been deeply concerned with determining the best principles of our constitutional tradition, those principles were highly contested and politicized. Determining what was best within the Constitution necessitated an examination of a variety of concerns from the most high-minded to the most immediate, and the effort to secure the resulting vision required the employment of both the usual and the extraordinary political weapons that might be available for the task.

These constructions also suggest a certain similarity of tactics adopted by those engaged in such debates, as well as the contingent nature of the interpretive methods adopted by political actors to support their constructions. In each instance, those defending a construction approximating the status quo attempted to portray that understanding as required by a legalistic Constitution, while those advocating constitutional changes stressed the contingent nature of constitutional provisions.

As might be expected, this defensive construction was most pronounced in the cases of impeachment. Defendants in impeachments not only strove to fend off criticisms of their actions, but also insisted that the constitutional specification of impeachable offenses was both narrow and legalistic. The tendency was broader than impeachment proceedings alone, however. Advocates of the protectionist tariff, for example, likewise expressed support for a legalistic standard for determining constitutional meaning. This approach was useful to its advocates, in part because it tended to provide support for their substantive position on the underlying issues.

The legalistic understanding not only provided support for particular positions, however; it also favored the stability of constitutional meaning and tended to deny the legitimacy of efforts to change existing constitutional practices by political means. Construing the Constitution as a legal instrument meant that its terms were closed, requiring only discovery in existing institutional practice to make its requirements clear. The erasure of the contingency of a construction's adoption is a crucial part of the process of institutionalizing a successful construction. Proponents of new constructions, in contrast, rarely accepted the legalistic approach to the Constitution, but rather insisted on the indeterminacy or political nature of the text. Abandoning the legalistic approach allowed the introduction of external political considerations into debates over constitutional meaning. It also suggested that the Constitution was adaptable in ways that a legal instrument was not, capable of shifting and evolving to take into account changed circumstances.

The variations in this tactical tendency are also instructive. Both sides, for example, adopted a variation of the legalistic approach in the debate over presidential war powers. For advocates of presidential power, the Constitution specifically left discretion to the president in conducting war, just as for protectionists the founders had delegated tariff policy to legislative discretion. Presidentialists also argued, however, that the exercises of presidential discretion were historically cumulative. To the extent that there were indeterminacies in the text, institutional practice displayed the implicit meaning of the document. The past was legally binding on the future. For congressional advocates of restraint on presidential war powers, however, the Constitution could also be understood as a legalistic instrument. For proponents of a new construction, such as Senator Fulbright, the Constitution possessed a known, fixed legalistic meaning, and current presidential practice was in violation of constitutional law correctly understood. Neither side in the debate relied exclusively upon the legalistic understanding, nor did either employ substantial interpretive arguments to support its claims. The adoption of the legalistic perspective was part of the effort at construction itself, and was as contingent as the adoption of a more explicitly political position.

If there was a tactical advantage for some in portraying the Constitution as an entirely legal document, there apparently was always an advantage in claiming to be an advocate of true constitutional meaning. Very few of the individuals who entered into the debates over these several constructions contended forthrightly that the Constitution was indeterminate in regard to the given subject and that the proffered construction was the best reading among several alternatives. Whether defending an existing construction or advocating its replacement with a new one, those engaging in constructions sought to identify themselves with the true and required meaning of the Constitution. Within the context of an existing Constitution, the creative element of construction had to be downplayed in order to emphasize that the construction was consistent with the text and that the authority of the Constitution favored one side over the other. Even in the context of detailed mechanisms, which clearly were not themselves required by the text, such as the Budget Act or War Powers Resolution, proponents of the new construction emphasized the larger principles motivating the reforms and the degree to which the particular institutional innovations were rooted in and necessary to that larger constitutional directive.

A final implication of these cases for constitutional theory is that political constructions matter to constitutional outcomes. This is true at multiple levels. Significant elements of our constitutional structure have been explicated by methods that are rather distant from our standard jurisprudential models of interpretation. The extensive debates over appropriate interpretive methods, and the application of such methods to particular interpretive problems, highlight only a portion of what is ultimately relevant for our ability to understand and evaluate our constitutional development. Similarly, substantial portions of our historical experience that should be relevant to our ability to understand constitutionalism have been excluded from constitutional theory and relegated to mere political science. A fully integrated constitutional theory must take into account not only such traditional subjects as individual rights and judicial review, but also presidential power and territorial governance. Such an integration will require a reconsideration of the extent and nature of constitutional governance.[3]

The Constitution in American Political History

The model of constitutional construction opens up new avenues for exploring how American political institutions have developed. The Constitution is relevant to both the process of political change and the extent of political stability in the United States. In order to examine these possibilities, we must analyze the Constitution as both an independent and a dependent variable in political development. The Constitution stands above and acts on political officials, making certain outcomes relatively difficult while privileging others. But the Constitution is also subject to political influence, and often it stands as both agent and subject in political events. The document has reshaped our conception of what is desirable as well as what is possible, affecting political preferences as well as political incentives.[4] If the number of textual amendments to the Constitution understates its flexibility over time, the formula of a "living constitution" overstates its mutability. The Constitution is a real and independent force in political events, but it is not beyond politics.

The cases of construction examined earlier also indicate the layered nature of constitutional meaning.[5] Relatively narrow constructions, such as the adoption of nullification, are often embedded in broader ones, such as a principle of decentralized federalism. Although constructions can often be considered and settled with reference to individual layers, these multiple layers of meaning are interconnected, and their effects are transmitted in both directions. Thus, the effort to establish the device of nullification was unsuccessful, but the nullification movement did effect a shift in broader understandings of the nature of federal-state relations toward a more decentralized model. Though narrow constructions can affect related layers of broader constitutional meaning, the unwillingness to challenge broader commitments can place constraints on the available narrow constructions. The effort of some to use the War Powers Resolution as a device to end the presidential initiation of military action foundered on the continued commitment of most participants in the debate to the posture of the United States as global superpower. The interaction of the multiple layers of constitutional meaning can also result in unintended consequences in adopting new constructions. Thus, many proponents of congressional power resorted to arguments against the executive consolidation of Andrew Johnson that ultimately undermined the spoils system, despite the fact that many advocates of congressional dominance accepted the spoils as an aspect of that position and a foundation for that power. The fact that constitutional meaning can be debated in layers, rather than as a seamless whole, makes it possible for constructions to be debated in less than revolutionary circumstances. Although placing one aspect of constitutional meaning in flux may have far-reaching consequences, it need not require a complete redefinition of the nature of American government. Significant constitutional change occurs within, and not simply through, sweeping regimes. The effort to divide American history into regimes, eras, or systems may uncover certain truths about American politics, but it buries the more varied and targeted changes in the Constitution brought to light by a model of constructions.

Disaggregating the layers of constitutional meaning also reveals that individual constitutional constructions can be developed in multiple directions. American constitutional development is not a story of movement along a single plane in a single direction. Although some constructions have built on the trajectory of earlier ones, and others have remained stable for long periods, still others have been reversed or deeply altered. The accumulation of multiple constructions over time has complicated the constitutional system, but has not progressively ratcheted the Constitution toward some designated end. The constructions of the 1970s did not merely temporarily disrupt a secular trend toward executive aggrandizement, but significantly altered the direction of earlier constructions and established modified understandings that entailed the lateral penetration of the executive branch by Congress. Similarly, the prohibition of protective tariffs reversed the previous understandings of the constitutional powers of the federal government, and that new construction was itself reversed later. Andrew Johnson's construction of presidential power, which in some ways foreshadowed the developments of the twentieth century, was nonetheless considered and rejected in the nineteenth. Moreover, the nature of that nineteenth-century construction of presidential power helped determine the contours of the twentieth-century constructions that built on but did not restore the powers advocated by Johnson. New constructions do not simply synthesize the achievements of earlier ones. The new constructions break along different fault lines from the old, are hedged in by a different layering of adjacent constructions, and respond to a fresh political dynamic that need not follow either the substantive or procedural patterns of earlier constructions.

Recognizing the multiple dimensions of political and constitutional development also highlights the fact that constructions are not advanced by a single instrument or regularly recurring set of factors, such as presidential leadership or critical elections. In part, this suggests that the opportunities for political change have not passed with the founding itself, the historical thickening of the political and institutional environment, or the decline of strong parties capable of controlling politicians and rallying mass publics.[6] The past is a critical factor constraining and structuring the present and future, but it has not fully determined the available space for political action. Although current debates over constitutional meaning take place within the framework of the existing constitutional text, they are not wholly limited to the discovery of textual meaning or the mechanical unwinding of the founders' plans. Similarly, the accumulation of past political decisions and the complication of the political environment continue to shape current political actions, but there is little reason to expect that we have reached a point where no room remains for other fundamental political changes. The history of constructions calls on us to redirect our focus in examining political change, to abandon a constant search for revolutionary transformations. Although Andrew Johnson did not achieve his vision of the presidency, later presidents did in fact reorient interbranch relations to create a presidency in keeping with Johnson's goals. Further, even though Johnson was not successful in achieving his particular reconstruction of the presidency, his struggle did result in substantial changes in the nature of presidential power, the place of the Congress in the national government, and the relationship between state and party.

The considered cases do suggest the punctuated character of much of constitutional development, which belies claims of the gradual evolution of American politics in response to broad socioeconomic changes.[7] Whether elaborated by interpretation or by construction, the Constitution not only accommodates political pressures, but also contains them by maintaining preexisting institutions and norms. Constitutional change does not occur until such pressures become sufficiently great to overcome that resistance. When the old settlements are reconsidered and in flux, change is not instantaneous but is nonetheless sudden. New settlements are formed and institutionalized to replace the old, and politics becomes once again resistant to change. The Constitution also mediates such social pressures, altering as well as delaying their influence. Independent actors are empowered by constitutional structures. Government officials may well have their visions and interests to pursue, in opposition to or regardless of other political officials or social interests. Andrew Johnson is perhaps the most dramatic case of an individual thrust into power and capable of reorienting political events despite substantial opposition. As such, Johnson is important not only for what he failed to achieve, but also for how he forced others to respond to his presence.

If constitutional change occurs in isolated moments, however, there is a multitude of such moments. Constructions are relatively targeted, redefining specific constitutional subjects. They arise out of the particular dynamics of a given issue and connect them to a larger constitutional and political context. Being less than revolutionary, they can become somewhat routinized. They are extraordinary within the context of their specific subject matter, reordering perhaps long-held understandings of how the Constitution operates in a given area. In the context of political history, however, they are relatively common.[8] Though highly dramatic political events, several of the constructions examined above occurred at the margins of the political agenda of their periods. By the time of those constructions the Jeffersonians, Jacksonians, and Republicans were well on their way to consolidating their political positions. The advocates of the new constructions were able to connect their concerns with larger political interests and ideals, yet their constructions were neither central to those interests nor developed by them. Elections were not won and the people were not mobilized over such issues as the extent of the presidential removal power or the legislative priority in the separation of powers, even though those constructions were advocated in the public arena and drew strength from electoral results. The developing constitutional changes cannot be adequately explained in terms of broader electoral shifts focusing on a separate agenda. The constructions operated in accord with their own political dynamics and are best understood within that context. No recurrent pattern of electoral cleavages or partisan posturing emerges in these instances of punctuated development. Although several of these cases fell near realigning elections, such elections provide only limited help in explaining subsequent events.[9]

The relatively focused nature of constructions both multiplies their occurrence and emphasizes their particular histories. The passage of the Budget Act and the War Powers Resolution both served to constrain presidential power and chip away pieces of the modern presidency as inherited by Richard Nixon. As they did so, the two pieces of legislation built upon each other in weakening the political ability of the president to defend his institution; however, they were not pulled together as part of a more general redefinition of the presidency. Underlying commitments to the modern state and American globalism made such a reconsideration of the nature of the presidency undesirable. Similarly, the redefinition of the Jacksonian political economy to include free trade emerged not only from the general context of Jackson's attacks on government intervention in the economy, but also from the particular complaints, arguments, and political prowess that advocates of free trade had acquired over the preceding decade. In order to establish their construction, the advocates of free trade had to overcome not only opponents of the emerging Jacksonian majority, but also the administration itself and many of its allies.

Constitutional constructions allow change in the effective meaning of the constitutional text, but they are not analogous to textual amendments. Constructions indicate that not all constitutional change ought to be reduced to an amendment framework. The constructions considered here enjoyed varying degrees of success, but neither their success nor their substantive development hinged on "ratifying" elections. Likewise, these constructions did not depend on judicial review for their enforcement. They altered constitutional practices but barely affected judicial doctrine. Their success did not depend on the ability or willingness of the courts to embrace them as constitutionally required or to enforce them against recalcitrant politicians. Although the amendment model may explain some forms of constitutional change, it must at least be supplemented with a more politically oriented model that is less reliant on a notion of an autonomous fundamental law and of judicial enforcement.[10]

Even as aspects of the Constitution are often being reconsidered, within their own domain constructions stabilize constitutional meaning where the text illuminated by interpretation leaves it indeterminate. Subjecting constitutional meaning to political determination does not necessitate the abandonment of constraints, as jurisprudential models of constitutionalism tend to assume. Constructions remain binding on future political actors, even if they are not legally enforceable. Order remains even in the absence of rules.

The stability of constructions varies. They serve as an intermediate point between the near permanence of the constitutional text itself and the transitory quality of policy decisions. Moreover, the Constitution does not convey a single political order from the founding to the present, but rather represents a collection of more particular settlements. The prohibition on protective tariffs, for example, lasted somewhat over thirty years, but the determination of impeachable crimes established in 1805 remains in effect. Furthermore, the particulars of a construction may change even as the whole remains fundamentally sound. Thus, the procedures for congressional budgeting established in 1974 have been modified in the past two decades, but the basic expansion of congressional responsibility for budgeting remains intact. The political handling of constructions allows for useful marginal adjustments to accommodate particular needs, without unduly threatening the basic infrastructure of the construction. Such durability that constructions do achieve relies on the restructuring of political institutions and beliefs. Even while operating from the inside of politics, however, constructions perform the role that constitutions are supposed to perform—they structure and constrain future political debate and government action.[11]

Consideration of these few cases provides a partial inventory of the mechanisms available for maintaining a successful construction through time. Recognition and examination of such mechanisms of constitutional order provide a more comprehensive portrait of how constitutional constraints on political action operate beyond judicial review.[12] These various mechanisms need not be regarded as mutually exclusive, and indeed the more successful constructions examined here employed several simultaneously. One vehicle for realizing the examined constructions is ideological, or the articulation of a persuasive conception of constitutional meaning that is then widely adopted among relevant political actors. In these cases, government officials are constrained by past constructions because they accept their strictures, whether by genuine conversion or by replacement of personnel. In an effort to restructure political thinking and behavior, advocates of a construction will attempt to gain control of the language and imagery of political discourse, conveying the complex understandings of the construction through ambiguous and dramatic metaphors.[13] By altering the discursive space of politics, a successful construction makes certain policy options more difficult to realize.[14] Advocates of increased presidential power, for example, may find themselves aligned against the legislative partisans identified with the spirit of the American Revolution and popular sovereignty. The principles developed and defended in this politicized context need not be either theoretically pure or rationally formalistic. Such principles may operate with unstated contradictions and logical blind spots, or be linked with economic advantage and institutional privilege, yet they are accepted as pervasive convictions that are perceived as real and binding.[15] The acceptance of such principles need not be complete in order for them to be successful. Even though some such as James Polk's secretary of the treasury, Robert Walker, embraced laissez-faire values as the appropriate understanding of constitutional principles and requirements, others such as Daniel Webster accepted the free trade construction on the basis of its institutional weight. For many Jacksonian Democrats, the constitutional commitment to free trade became an article of faith, supplementing and extending any policy preference for reduced tariffs. Perhaps even more deeply and extensively, the Jeffersonians managed to convince themselves, their contemporaries, and their successors that Congress' impeachment power was extensive enough to include specific abuses of office and that the judiciary's proper role in a republic was primarily legal and nonpartisan. Even for those who may wish to pursue a different set of policies, such conceptual barriers can be difficult to overcome.

A second mechanism for stabilizing constructions employed in these cases is the structuring of political support. Such a restructuring of political fortunes can occur at multiple levels, notably through electoral/partisan prowess and through legislative/coalitional power. Thus, advocates of a given construction may succeed through their integration into a dominant party, constraining subsequent policy as a consequence of their electoral importance. Similarly, a construction may be solidified through its integration into an internal, legislative coalition, its supporters becoming necessary members of an enduring logrolling relationship. Through such efforts, an advocated construction can be integrated into a dominant electoral coalition. The construction need not be widely believed, so long as its advocates are well positioned. Such relationships may be vulnerable to electoral fortunes, but not necessarily. Advocates of the construction may convince all parties that a commitment to the construction, or at least a lack of hostility to the construction, is necessary to their own enduring political success.[16] A construction may begin as a mere piece of a coalitional compromise, and yet grow deeper roots that allow it to survive an alteration in the original coalitional calculations. The gradual reduction in import duties established by the Compromise Tariff helped wean protected industries from their dependence on favorable government trade policy, undercutting future political support for protection. When the Whigs attempted to resurrect protectionism in the mid-1840s, they did not enjoy the grassroots support that had been a staple of trade policy in the 1820s. Likewise, Henry Clay's failure to persuade the Court to reestablish the status quo ante upon the completion of the Compromise's scheduled duty reductions eliminated the regular legislative vehicle and bargaining position that the protectionists had enjoyed before the Compromise. The advocates of free trade were in a better position to defend their construction by the end of the Compromise period than they had been when the compromise was initially struck.

The establishment of a given political position as a central commitment of the dominant political coalition is itself a difficult task, requiring an effort beyond the mere presence of the requisite policy preferences or available votes. Elevating a given position from the political periphery to a party priority can provide substantial stability and place a constraint on future government action even without converting others into believers in the merits of an advocated construction.[17] The efforts of the nullifiers are illustrative of this pattern. John Calhoun's willingness to lead his supporters into the "Free Trade Party" threatened the success of the Democratic coalition. The actions of South Carolina in initiating the nullification crisis sent a clear signal to the Jacksonian party managers that trade policy would have to be a key element of the Democratic platform. The nullifiers made trade policy a partisan issue, against the wishes of party leaders who hoped to make trade nonpartisan and thereby allow Democrats to compete for protectionist votes. The successful resolution of the nullification crisis helped establish Democratic hegemony through the antebellum period, but did so on the nullifiers' terms. Through manipulation of the emerging party system, the nullifiers restructured the policy options for all viable political actors for the next three decades.

A final mechanism for solidifying the constructions examined above was the creation of new institutional structures to support them. The institutionalization of constructions helps establish a base of support for the future political defense of constructions and a point of resistance that opponents of a given construction must subsequently overcome.[18] Institutionalization can help stabilize a construction by altering either the incentives facing future political actors or the distribution of resources available to such future actors.[19] Officials with no intrinsic interest in defending an established construction can be given incentives to sustain it in the face of future opposition. Similarly, those who are actively opposed to a given construction can be discouraged from attacking it or enticed into pursuing other issues instead. Beyond inducing behavior consistent with the construction, institution building can also provide the resources necessary to carry preferred actions into effect. Even if the desire to enforce a given construction is widespread, supporting activity may be prohibitively costly to pursue, or the awareness of such supporting actions may simply be lacking without an institutional base to identify violations of newly established norms and appropriate remedial steps. The formation of the permanent intelligence oversight committees with budgeting authority and legislative specifications of reporting requirements created the institutional base for executive accountability to Congress in the conduct of intelligence operations, for example. The continuing existence of the committee serves as a focal point for the legislative exercise of its newly understood constitutional duties. Moreover, the institutionalization of oversight puts pressure on those operating within the system to sustain the new construction, as Barry Goldwater did on assuming leadership of the Senate committee. Postwar congressional rules encouraged the rise of such deferential members as Richard Russell, who had little to gain from pursuing intelligence matters and few resources with which to gather information on intelligence activities. After the reforms, even old-guard stalwarts such as Goldwater adopted a more watchful posture, if only to maintain their own prestige within the chamber.

Although many of the Nixon-era reforms included the creation of new institutions such as the war powers reporting requirements, the budget committees, and the impoundment legislative veto, other constructions relied on the modification of existing institutions. The impeachment mechanism itself was embedded in the text of the Constitution, but the terms and likelihood of its use had not been immediately defined. As a consequence, judges were aware of the existence of the impeachment power, but until well into Jefferson's first term it was a distant threat at best. The threatened use of existing institutional powers by Congress resulted in an anticipatory response in the federal judiciary after the Chase impeachment, minimizing the need to carry out that threat in subsequent practice. Future judges would question not only the propriety but also the wisdom of Chase's actions. This use of the impeachment power depended on a new understanding of the power itself and on a number of legislators' belief in the ultimate substantive goal, but it did not require that judges be converted into true believers in the new substantive construction of appropriate judicial behavior.[20] Similarly, Andrew Johnson sought to strengthen presidential power by building on and modifying existing patronage practices. In the context of the party system, Johnson did not need to create the spoils system—he merely needed to redefine its appropriate use. If he could have done so, he could have expected the lower echelon of political officeholders and party loyalists to rally around his favored constructions. Johnson's failure, and that of the nullifiers, to establish the availability of their preferred instruments should emphasize that questions of institutional design are themselves political choices and cannot simply be assumed.

Constitutional Structures and Forms

The significance, purpose, and desirability of the structural features of the Constitution have been minimized in recent constitutional scholarship, which has focused instead on specifying individual rights.[21] As a consequence, the concerns and analytical strengths of specifically constitutional studies have been missing in the study of the behavior and interaction of the elective branches of government and of federalism. The elective branches are forums of principle and venues for deliberation as well, though they often offer different principles and modes of deliberation to examine. A number of the cases examined here included disputes over the nature of the separation of powers itself, further indicating that the separation of powers has been a source of continuing conflict in American history. Disputes over the particular powers to be exercised by different government actors have reflected external substantive concerns as well as intrinsic concerns with the distribution of power itself.

The balance of powers has been adjusted over time to match different political needs and different systems of political values. The coordinated powers have not simply served the negative purpose of fracturing power and providing veto points for minority factions. They have also served the positive purpose of instituting different concerns within the structure of the government and of securing different government functions.[22] The relative power and influence of the presidency, for example, has depended on the perceived need for political decisiveness and administrative efficiency. When political consensus has been threatened, the particular virtues of the executive branch have been devalued in favor of the more representative, diverse, and deliberative legislature. Neither the ordering of values represented by the different branches nor the institutional embodiment of those values is absolute and unchanging. Both are subject to political dispute. Andrew Johnson and Samuel Chase, for example, attempted to lay claim to many of the political functions normally associated with the legislative branch. Likewise, in order to enhance its own position, Congress responded to challenges from the president by building its own administrative capacity in order to draw executive functions and expertise within its own sphere. On a different level, Johnson and Nixon sought to elevate the virtue of administrative efficiency at the expense of legislative dissension and politicization, even as Congress portrayed executive machinations as evidence of an antidemocratic force to be resisted and controlled. Though not firmly fixed, the different institutions of government do represent different goals, values, and interests. Their separate existence is not only a source of conflict and administrative inconvenience, but also the basis for a more complete system of constitutional governance and political deliberation.

These episodes in constitutional construction also suggest that the separation of powers is a source of positive action as well as a possible contributing factor to gridlock. The larger implication of the "deadlock" vision of separated powers is that the constitutional division is an obstacle to political discourse and action, which can be overcome only through the artificial unification of what the founders have set apart.[23] The cases we have considered indicate that this vision is too narrow to encompass the entire operation of the constitutional system. Putative party unity between the legislative and executive branches did not prevent divisions from developing, even in the context of substantial party activity. Such divisions reflected not only different policy commitments held by important government officials, but also different institutional positions and values as well as constitutional visions of those holding different offices and positions within the overall constitutional system. The friction between these different visions created both the impetus for and possibility of substantial constitutional and political change.

The diversity of political actors created openings to agitate for change, as well as bastions from which to resist it.[24] The federal structure created by the Constitution provided a platform for the free trade movement to gain political influence and to force its concerns onto the national agenda, even as the major institutions of the national government were held by those who were indifferent, if not openly hostile, to those concerns. The special status of the president as a national officer fed Andrew Johnson's claims to represent the disfranchised South in the federal government, even as the Republican Congress consolidated its own power in the absence of Southern representatives. The congressional committee system provided a platform for legislators such as J. William Fulbright, Otis Pike, and Frank Church to advance diverse visions of the appropriate role of the Congress in foreign policy and intelligence activities against the claims of a secretive and unresponsive executive branch. If such divisions provided the catalyst for change, significant new understandings of constitutional meaning were established despite these divisions. Further, those new constitutional settlements were generally managed without the benefit of substantial electoral changes that removed recalcitrant actors. The separation of powers did not prevent the development of powerful political movements capable of overcoming entrenched opposition or the creation of new constitutional understandings that forged common links among diverse political agents. Thus, the partisan division of the executive and legislature under Nixon was an important, if not essential, precondition to reconsideration of the status of the modern presidency and the powers and mechanisms of control over the modern national state. Likewise, partisan tensions between the Republican Congress and the relatively independent President Johnson forced a transformation of the presidency and presidential powers that had been deferred during the more amenable Lincoln administration. Political changes occur both within and through the constitutional fragmentation of power. Institutional diversity is the source of productive conflict, as well as a vehicle for carrying forward and protecting earlier political achievements.

The history of constructions also undermines the persistent story of presidential dominance and leadership in American governance. In some of the considered instances, the president was a prominent player in the debate over constitutional change. In other instances, however, the president ranged from interested bystander to marginal participant. Moreover, even when the president played a prominent role in these constructions, it was often as an initiator of action, but not as a leader or determiner of the final results. Thus, for example, even when Nixon and Andrew Johnson purposefully sought to extend their powers and initiated efforts to redefine the nature of their offices, they were quickly challenged for control over not only the eventual outcome of the debate but also the terms of the debate itself. If a clear pattern of dominance emerges in these cases, it is rather one of congressional resolution of constitutional meaning, not of presidential leadership of the direction of American politics. Although it would be too much to conclude that Congress is actually the dominant branch of American politics, these cases do indicate that Congress plays an important and persistent role in leading and settling debates over the future of American governance and that the president is not and need not be the primary focus of political action in order for significant governmental changes to take place.

A tentative final point can be made about the use of constitutional construction. Even though constructions are an instrument of constitutional development, that instrument itself has changed little over time. Advocates of construction have adopted new tools, such as Andrew Johnson's "Swing around the Circle" Richard Nixon's radio addresses, or Frank Church's televised hearings, but the basic characteristics of constructions have remained relatively stable. Constructions employed the political resources available at the moment, from party patronage to bureaucratic expertise, while remaining a recurrent activity in American politics. Even the rise of judicial activism has not eliminated the political construction of constitutional meaning. Critics of presidential power under Nixon did not rely on the courts to articulate rules to constrain the president, but developed their own institutions and understandings of constitutional principle to reshape the relations between the branches in these areas. The limitations on those modern constructions can be found in the conflicting commitments of the reformers rather than in any fear of or deference to judicial interpretation, or construction, of the Constitution. The political necessity of construction can be found in two primary factors. On the one hand, political actors have their own incentives to engage in constructions. The outcomes of constitutional debates are too significant to political actors' own concerns to leave such decisions exclusively to the judiciary.[25] On the other hand, judicial decrees are unlikely to be able to resolve many of the issues at stake in these disputes. The definition of constitutional values and the structuring of future political action are often dependent on the efforts of political actors themselves. The Taney Court could have declared itself in favor of a more decentralized federalism, but it could not have substituted for the state governments' own efforts to accept constitutional responsibilities. One explanation for the relative weakness of the War Powers Resolution, for example, is its adoption of a juristic model of constitutional enforcement and meaning. In the political context, however, the absence of positive congressional action in military crises merely serves to emphasize further the relative power of the president in this area. The success of constructions depends not on legal judgments, but on a structure of political action.

One change of potential significance, however, is the shifting of forums of constitutional dispute. In both historical and modern contexts, public debate over constitutional meaning has been a significant component of developing the constructions. Proponents of the various constructions have debated their nature in newspapers, journals, books, and public speeches from the beginning of the republic. Moreover, in each case, the final establishment of the constructions has occurred on the floor of the Congress, as the legislature has determined the extent and shape of the new consensus. In the modern constructions, however, a substantial amount of the necessary building of the arguments and movement toward a legislative understanding has been done in committee, rather than on the floor of the Congress. This new focus has several implications. The modern constructions display a much greater emphasis on technical mechanisms and detailed procedures than earlier constructions. Although such legislation as the establishment of the tariff duties in support of the Compromise Act could be quite detailed, the basic understandings of such constructions were established primarily through public agreements on principle, with only sketchy procedural mechanisms to carry them to realization. The constructions of the Nixon era, on the other hand, centered on the details of such legislation as the intelligence charters and the Budget Act. The politics of technique and process often obscured the politics of principle.

Furthermore, the reliance on committees suggests the possibility of more limited participation in and understanding of the proffered constructions. Such a possibility cannot be overstated, however. Congressional action has always depended on the extraordinary work of a handful of leaders, often meeting in private. Moreover, the modern committees have conducted much of their work in public, if not on television, with participation from noncommittee members encouraged. Nonetheless, the most extensive public expression of the new constitutional understandings and the arguments for them are contained in committee hearings or reports. Though the trend is less pronounced in the Senate, modern House floor debates are characterized more by brief displays of public position taking than by the careful articulation of principles by individual members. Such brevity calls into question the depth of the new commitments and the extent of congressional understandings of articulated principles, perhaps explaining the modern reliance on institutions to effectuate new constructions. Such considerations only qualify the nature of modern constructions. They do not vitiate the reality of them. The shifts in government practice that followed in the wake of the modern constructions have been identifiable and reasonably persistent, as they were for earlier efforts.

The Constitution operates as both a legal and a political document. In doing so, it constrains government action both by providing external checks on politics and by penetrating political practice itself. None of these constraints is self-enforcing, however. The Constitution in both senses is realized through current government institutions. Its service as a legal check on government depends on its interpretation and application, primarily by the courts. These legal constraints, however, are supplemented by purely political ones, imposed through and understood by construction, and maintained and modified within the political system itself. It is in the realm of construction that the Constitution adapts and evolves to accommodate and to cause external change. In this mode, the Constitution operates not merely as a constraint on government, but also as a source of political action. The fundamental text serves as an inspiration to political movements, the foundation of institutional growth, and a locus of political values. This positive dimension of constitutional governance is not fully captured by our current jurisprudential approach to constitutional meaning. It requires a more integrative approach that connects the Constitution to the actual operation of government institutions and to continuing political conflicts. Constitutional theory must recognize the multifaceted nature of the Constitution and the importance of divided powers for realizing its meaning. In doing so, we can begin to recapture some of the richness of the Constitution and to understand the complexity of constitutional government.

NOTES

1. The Political Constitution

1. See also John Brigham, *The Cult of the Court* (Philadelphia: Temple University Press, 1987); Robert Nagel, *Constitutional Cultures* (Berkeley: University of California Press, 1989); Stanley C. Brubaker, "The Court as Astigmatic Schoolmarm: A Case for the Clear Sighted Citizen," in *The Supreme Court and American Constitutionalism*, ed. Bradford P. Wilson and Ken Masugi (Lanham, Md.: Rowman & Littlefield, 1998).

2. Philip Bobbitt, *Constitutional Interpretation* (Cambridge: Basil Blackwell, 1991), 11–22.

3. Stephen M. Griffin, *American Constitutionalism* (Princeton: Princeton University Press, 1996); Bruce Ackerman, *We the People*, vol. 1 (Cambridge, Mass.: Harvard University Press, 1991); Wayne D. Moore, *Constitutional Rights and Powers of the People* (Princeton: Princeton University Press, 1996). See also Sanford Levinson, *Constitutional Faith* (Princeton: Princeton University Press, 1988); Barry Friedman, "Dialogue and Judicial Review," *Michigan Law Review* 91 (1993): 577; Mark A. Graber, "Constitutional Failures and Constitutional Theory," paper presented at the annual meeting of the Midwest Political Science Association, Chicago, April 10–12, 1997.

4. Ackerman, *We the People,* 230–294.

5. Martin Shefter, "Party, Bureaucracy, and Political Change in the United States," in *Political Parties,* ed. Sandy Maisel and Joseph Cooper (Beverly Hills: Sage, 1978).

6. E.g., Ronald Dworkin, *A Matter of Principle* (Cambridge, Mass.: Harvard University Press, 1985), 9–103.

7. E.g., Donald Morgan, *Congress and the Constitution* (Cambridge, Mass.: Harvard University Press, 1966); Susan R. Burgess, *Contest for Constitutional Authority* (Lawrence: University Press of Kansas, 1992); Ronald Dworkin, *Freedom's Law* (Cambridge, Mass.: Harvard University Press, 1996), 29–31, 343–346.

8. E.g., Larry Alexander and Frederick Schauer, "On Extrajudicial Constitutional Interpretation," *Harvard Law Review* 110 (1997): 1363–69.

9. See also Karl Llewellyn, "The Constitution as an Institution," *Columbia Law Review* 34 (1934): 7; Edward S. Corwin, "The Constitution as an Instrument and as Symbol," *American Political Science Review* 30 (1936): 1071; Stephen M. Griffin, "Bringing the State into Constitutional Theory: Public Authority and the Constitution," *Law and Social Inquiry* 16 (1991): 659; Walter M. Murphy, "Who Shall Interpret? The Quest For the Ultimate Constitutional Interpreter," *Review of Politics* 48 (1986): 406.

10. See also William F. Harris II, *The Interpretable Constitution* (Baltimore: Johns Hopkins University Press, 1993), 186–187.

11. See also Calvin Jillson, "Patterns and Periodicity in American National Politics," in *The Dynamics of American Politics*, ed. Lawrence C. Dodd and Calvin Jillson (Boulder: Westview Press, 1994), 26–28; Samuel P. Huntington, *American Politics* (Cambridge, Mass.: Harvard University Press, 1981), 112–113.

12. Ronald Dworkin, for example, argues that there are no legal "gaps"—Herculean judges can always "interpret" the law in order to find a determinative meaning even in hard cases. These judges, however, pursue an essentially two-step process, in which hard cases are decided by a rather different means from the easy cases. Whether or not this is regarded as "interpretation" makes a more than semantic difference, since he uses this jurisprudential theory to justify a dominant role for the judiciary in setting the government's course. Dworkin, *Taking Rights Seriously* (Cambridge, Mass.: Harvard University Press, 1978), 1–130. Cf. E. Philip Soper, "Legal Theory and the Obligation of a Judge: The Hart/Dworkin Dispute," *Michigan Law Review* 75 (1977): 473; C. L. Ten, "The Soundest Theory of Law," *Mind* 88 (1979): 522.

13. Accepting the distinction between text and its interpretation, and a hierarchy of the two, need not entail unmediated access to the text. It is enough that the two be seen as analytically distinct, even if the text is known only through its interpretation. Cf. Stanley Fish, *Doing What Comes Naturally* (Durham, N.C.: Duke University Press, 1989).

14. The categorization offered here between interpretation and construction does not seek to reopen the debate over the distinction between interpretation and "noninterpretation." The latter distinction was first advanced in Thomas Grey, "Do We Have an Unwritten Constitution?" *Stanford Law Review* 27 (1975): 710–714, and was adopted by several others. For an influential critique, see Dworkin, *A Matter of Principle*, 34–38. The interpretation/construction categorization does not map onto the interpretation/noninterpretation distinction. The latter distinction hinged on the acceptance of originalism as the only possible method of "interpretation." No such assumption is made here. Additionally, the interpretation/noninterpretation debate simply sought to locate the proper source for judicial pronouncements. The concern here, however, is with the degree of determinacy and the

nature of the answers that different methods of construing meaning can provide different institutions in order to create a multitiered elaboration of constitutional meaning. Thus, it is possible that the same "interpretive method" could provide different answers in the context of construction than it could in the context of interpretation, where it must necessarily integrate such considerations as textual details, historic origins of the text, and overall constitutional structure. The interpretation/construction distinction emphasizes the essential connection between Walter Murphy's several and separate questions of what, whom, and how to interpret, whereas the interpretation/noninterpretation debate accepts their separation and revolves around the question what. For a recent effort to address such questions but one still hampered by the old model, see Michael J. Perry, *The Constitution in the Courts* (New York: Oxford University Press, 1994).

15. Such resources as precedent and authorial intent are best regarded as tools of interpretation rather than a plurality of distinct interpretive methods. Different approaches to interpretation will give different weight to such tools, but few, if any, require the exclusive use of a single interpretive resource. For defenses of "interpretive pluralism," see Philip Bobbitt, *Constitutional Fate* (New York: Oxford University Press, 1982), esp. 230–249; Stephen M. Griffin, "Pluralism in Constitutional Interpretation," *Texas Law Review* 72 (1994): 1768; Richard H. Fallon Jr., "A Constructivist Coherence Theory of Constitutional Interpretation," *Harvard Law Review* 100 (1987): 1217; Robert Post, "Theories of Constitutional Interpretation," in *Law and the Order of Culture*, ed. Robert Post (Berkeley: University Press of California, 1991).

16. Harris, *The Interpretable Constitution*, 118. Harris' phrasing is useful here, though his understanding of constitutional elaboration is rather different from mine.

17. Frederick Schauer, "The Occasions of Constitutional Interpretation," *Boston University Law Review* 72 (1992): 740–743.

18. Griffin, *American Constitutionalism*, 13; Sylvia Snowiss, "From Fundamental Law to the Supreme Law of the Land: A Reinterpretation of the Origin of Judicial Review," *Studies in American Political Development* 2 (1987): 1.

19. E.g., Edward B. Foley, "Interpretation and Philosophy: Dworkin's Constitution," *Constitutional Commentary* 14 (1997): 151; Dworkin, *Taking Rights Seriously*, 131–149. See also Mark A. Graber, "Our (Im)perfect Constitution," *Review of Politics* 51 (1989): 86.

20. The current conception of judicial interpretation owes much to the now abandoned "process school" of the 1950s and 1960s. See also G. Edward White, "The Evolution of Reasoned Elaboration: Jurisprudential Criticism and Social Change," *Virginia Law Review* 59 (1973): 279.

21. These are all issues of constitutional inadequacy or irrelevancy. The issue of a clear constitutional flaw raises rather different concerns that cannot be re-

solved through constitutional elaboration. On this problem, see Mark V. Tushnet, "The Hardest Question in Constitutional Law," *Minnesota Law Review* 81 (1996): 1.

22. The political question doctrine raises similar concerns. This doctrine requires that the judiciary not intervene when a subject is specifically delegated to another branch for determination, when no clear standards for decision can be determined, or when deciding a case is inextricably related to policy concerns. One application of the idea of constitutional construction is to suggest that constitutional considerations have a role even in deciding "political questions." Baker v. Carr, 369 U.S. 186 (1962); Goldwater v. Carter, 444 U.S. 996 (1979); Luther v. Borden, 48 U.S. (7 How.) 1 (1849); Coleman v. Miller, 307 U.S. 433 (1939). For critiques of how the Court has employed the doctrine, see Louis Fisher, *Constitutional Dialogues* (Princeton: Princeton University Press, 1988), 110–116; Daniel N. Hoffman, *Our Elusive Constitution* (Albany: State University of New York Press, 1997), 13–45; Philippa Strum, *The Supreme Court and "Political Questions"* (University: University of Alabama Press, 1974).

23. A prohibition on taking "human life," for example, may not provide sufficient guidance to determine whether a fetus is included in the prohibition even though the ban establishes an otherwise clear legal rule. See also Alexander Hamilton, James Madison, and John Jay, *The Federalist Papers,* ed. Clinton Rossiter (New York: Mentor, 1961), No. 37, 228.

24. E.g., Thomas Aquinas, *The Political Ideas of St. Thomas Aquinas,* ed. Dino Bigongiari (New York: Hafner Press, 1953), 58–59, distinguishing between "conclusion from premises" and the "determination of certain generalities" in transferring the natural law into positive law; W. B. Gallie, "Essentially Contested Concepts," in *Philosophy and the Historical Understanding* (New York: Schocken Books, 1964), 157–191; William E. Connolly, *The Terms of Political Discourse* (Lexington, Mass.: D. C. Heath, 1974), 6–10. E.g., Charles O. Lerche Jr., "Congressional Interpretation of the Guarantee of a Republican Form of Government during Reconstruction," *Journal of Southern History* 15 (1949): 192.

Were the text is silent, it should come as no surprise that the first Congress made little use of original intentions in creating the executive departments, for example. That was a constitutional decision left for future generations of political actors. Cf. Kent Greenfield, "Original Penumbras: Constitutional Interpretation in the First Year of Congress," *Connecticut Law Review* 26 (1993): 79. On areas of unsettled meaning in constitutional systems, see also Michael Foley, *The Silence of Constitutions* (New York: Routledge, 1989).

25. Constitutions often contain prescriptive statements that are not legally binding, such as preambles, the "necessary and proper" clause in the U.S. Constitution, and the use of the word "ought" rather than "shall" in many early state constitutions. On the latter, see Donald S. Lutz, *Popular Consent and*

Popular Control (Baton Rouge: Louisiana State University Press, 1980), 65–66.

26. Though our analysis of this hermeneutical task has become highly sophisticated. E.g., Sanford Levinson and Steven Mailloux, eds., *Interpreting Law and Literature* (Evanston: Northwestern University Press, 1988).

27. Woodrow Wilson, *Congressional Government* (New York: Meridian Books, 1956), 31.

28. On the substantive definition of the constitution in the British tradition, see F. W. Maitland, *The Constitutional History of England* (New York: Cambridge University Press, 1941), 527; A. V. Dicey, *Introduction to the Study of the Law of the Constitution* (New York: Macmillan, 1915), 22–30; J. Harvey and L. Bather, *The British Constitution* (New York: Macmillan, 1972), 6; E. C. S. Wade and A. W. Bradley, *Constitutional Law* (London: Longmans, 1965), 1.

29. Thus the First Amendment guarantees freedom of speech, press, and petitioning of the legislature, all of which are not just limitations on political power but also positive designations of avenues of civic participation.

30. For similar but less detailed lists, see Samuel Freeman, "Original Meaning, Democratic Interpretation, and the Constitution," *Philosophy and Public Affairs* 21 (Winter 1992). 13; Donald S. Lutz, *The Origins of American Constitutionalism* (Baton Rouge. Louisiana State University Press, 1988), 16.

31. While these issues include all policy, they are not reducible to all policy debates. International posture depends on the numerous individual decisions that make up foreign policy, and yet no single decision moves the nation from isolationist republic to interventionist empire. Nonetheless, the mass of such issues has weight, and its momentum can be characterized even when no individual policy debate can be identified as decisive. Further, the participants in these debates recognize these shifts in momentum as well, and thus some debates tend to take on symbolic significance, marking the construction of the whole even if they do not themselves make the whole.

32. See also Donald S. Lutz, "The United States Constitution as an Incomplete Text," *Annals of the American Academy of Political and Social Science* 496 (March 1988): 23; Joseph Cropsey, "The United States as Regime and the Sources of the American Way of Life," *Political Philosophy and the Issues of Politics* (Chicago: University of Chicago Press, 1977); H. Jefferson Powell, *The Moral Tradition of American Constitutionalism* (Durham, N.C.: Duke University Press, 1993), 4, 49.

33. U.S. Constitution, Art. IV, §4; Luther v. Borden, 48 U.S. (7 How.) 1 (1849); Pacific States Tel. & Tel. Co. v. Oregon, 223 U.S. 118 (1912); U.S. Constitution, Art. I, § 8, 9, 10.

34. E.g., Richard Leopold, "The Emergence of America as a World Power: Some Second Thoughts," in *Change and Continuity in Twentieth-Century America*, ed. John Braeman, Robert H. Bremner, and Everett Walters (Columbus:

Ohio State University Press, 1964), 3–34; David Healy, *U.S. Expansionism* (Madison: University of Wisconsin Press, 1970); Walter LaFeber, *The New Empire* (Ithaca: Cornell University Press, 1963). For a contemporary statement, see Willson Beckles, *The New America* (London: Chapman & Hall, 1903). The construction was planted by the end of the nineteenth century, but did not reach full blossom until World War II and the subsequent Cold War.

35. Lochner v. New York, 198 U.S. 45 (1905). E.g., U.S. v. E.C. Knight Co., 156 U.S. 1 (1895); Hammer v. Dagenhart, 247 U.S. 251 (1918); Bailey v. Drexel Furniture Co., 259 U.S. 20 (1922); Adkins v. Children's Hospital, 261 U.S. 525 (1923); Muller v. Oregon, 208 U.S. 412 (1908); Pennsylvania Coal Co. v. Mahon, 260 U.S. 393 (1922); U.S. v. Butler, 297 U.S. 1 (1936); Panama City Refining v. Ryan, 293 U.S. 388 (1934).

36. Brown v. Board of Education, 347 U.S. 483 (1954). E.g., Sweatt v. Painter, 339 U.S. 629 (1950); McLaurin v. Oklahoma State Regents, 339 U.S. 637 (1950); Bolling v. Sharpe, 347 U.S. 497 (1954); Brown v. Board of Education, 349 U.S. 294 (1955); Cooper v. Aaron, 358 U.S. 1 (1958); Swann v. Charlotte-Mecklenberg Board of Education, 402 U.S. 1 (1971).

37. At least in the nonjudicial arena, however, broad constructions are compelling without any formal support of doctrines of precedent or *stare decisis*. Broad constructions are compelling because of their substantive force within the existing political context, not because of any prior commitment to stability, a notion that like cases should be decided alike, or belief in the epistemological value of prior decisions.

38. Similarly, interpretations or policymaking may surround a constitutional construction. The New Deal, for example, was not a single constitutional moment, but contained a variety of interrelated but distinct activities, only some of which created genuine constitutional change. Further, particular statutes passed during the period that represented new constitutional constructions were also likely to make policy as well.

39. Cf. Ackerman, *We the People*, 266–294; Michael Klarman, "Constitutional Fact/Constitutional Fiction: A Critique of Bruce Ackerman's Theory of Constitutional Moments," *Stanford Law Review* 44 (1992): 768–775.

40. The vast majority of the arguments considered here are best characterized as efforts at construction rather than interpretation. Some of the arguments made in these cases are more narrowly interpretive in their orientation. I do not evaluate the accuracy of those interpretive claims; my primary interest in them centers on their relationship with the broader political context. In some instances, it is a fundamentally political move to adopt an interpretive stance. My focus is on that political decision, rather than on the details of the interpretations that that decision produces. Moreover, purely interpretive efforts are insufficient fully to determine constitutional meaning in these cases, thus the insistent reliance on interpretive tools is more clearly for political effect in these circumstances.

41. The nature and pace of constitutional construction suggest that sociopolitical crisis generates such innovation as much as a progressive path of socioeconomic development, cycles of electoral transformations, or moments of political unity. The causes of constitutional construction are much more specific and limited than theories of systemic change would suggest. Divergent and useful discussions of the nature and utility of institutional change and critical moments include Karen Orren and Stephen Skowronek, "Beyond the Iconography of Order: Notes for a 'New Institutionalism,'" in *The Dynamics of American Politics,* ed. Lawrence C. Dodd and Calvin Jillson (Boulder: Westview Press, 1994); Walter Dean Burnham, *Critical Elections and the Mainsprings of American Politics* (New York: W. W. Norton, 1970); Louis Galambos, "The Emerging Organizational Synthesis in Modern American History," *Business History Review* 44 (Autumn 1970): 279; Robert Higgs, *Crisis and Leviathan* (New York: Oxford University Press, 1987); David Mayhew, *Divided We Govern* (New Haven: Yale University Press, 1991); Jillson, "Patterns and Periodicity," 24–58; Martin Sklar, "Periodization and Historiography: Studying American Political Development in the Progressive Era, 1890s–1916," *Studies in American Political Development* 5 (Fall 1991): 173.

42. Given our current understanding of the relationship between nonjudicial actors and the Constitution, success in this modest goal would be a significant advance. The effort to gain an intensive understanding of the category precludes to some degree a more abstract sense of constructions as an aggregate. The cases considered in depth here are simply too few to provide an adequate portrait of the timing of constructive activity or general trends in either the form or substance of the average construction. Relatedly, these cases, though highly suggestive, do not conclusively demonstrate what factors cause constructions to emerge or make them successful.

    The reader should be cautioned against inferring too much from incidental absences in case selection. Civil liberties are as much the subject of construction as is the separation of powers, but questions of individual liberty happen to play a background role in the cases considered here. Similarly, no cases were selected from an extended period encompassing the late nineteenth century and early twentieth centuries, though these were also periods of substantial constitutional ferment.

43. The selected cases do, however, avoid instances of purely judicial construction of constitutional meaning. Given the desire to emphasize the involvement of nonjudicial actors in American constitutional development, it is necessary to redress the imbalance in the literature as a whole by focusing on those actors. In addition, judicial acts of construction are not highly illustrative of the range of resources and arguments that are often employed in construction, and therefore are not very useful in establishing a sense of the category. Finally, the judiciary has particular institutional imperatives that lead it to minimize the distinction between construction and interpretation

and to deny that it ever goes beyond interpretation in rendering its decisions. Thus judicial efforts at construction present a special case that is better explored elsewhere, despite its obvious ultimate importance.

44. E.g., Richard E. Neustadt, *Presidential Power and the Modern Presidents* (New York: Free Press, 1990), 29; James MacGregor Burns, *The Deadlock of Democracy* (Englewood Cliffs, N.J.: Prentice-Hall, 1967); Samuel P. Huntington, *Political Order in Changing Societies* (New Haven: Yale University Press, 1968), 109–139; David W. Brady and Joseph Stewart Jr., "When Elections Really Matter: Realignments and Changes in Public Policy," in *Do Elections Matter?* ed. Benjamin Ginsberg and Alan Stone (Armonk, N.Y.: M. E. Sharpe, 1986), 19–34. See also Harvey C. Mansfield Jr., *America's Constitutional Soul* (Baltimore: Johns Hopkins University Press, 1991), 1–17, 115–127, 137–162.

45. See also Joseph Bessette and Jeffrey K. Tulis, "The Constitution, Politics, and the Presidency," in *The Presidency in the Constitutional Order,* ed. Bessette and Tulis (Baton Rouge: Louisiana State University Press, 1981), 3–30; Tulis, "The Two Constitutional Presidencies," in *The Presidency and the Political System,* ed. Michael Nelson (Washington, D.C.: CQ Press, 1995), 91–123; Michael L. Mezey, "The Legislature, the Executive, and Public Policy: The Futile Quest for Congressional Power," *Congress & the Presidency* 13 (Spring 1986): 1–20.

46. Cf. Hamilton et al., *The Federalist Papers,* No. 49.

2. The Chase Impeachment and Shaping the Federal Judiciary

1. Brief histories of the federal impeachments and their targets are provided in Eleanore Bushnell, *Crimes, Follies, and Misfortunes* (Urbana: University of Illinois Press, 1992). For specific analysis of the narrowly disciplinary nature of judicial impeachments in the 1980s see Mary L. Volcansek, *Judicial Impeachment* (Urbana: University of Illinois Press, 1993); Michael J. Gerhardt, *The Federal Impeachment Process* (Princeton: Princeton University Press, 1996). Although Gerhardt's examination is narrowly focused, his basic understanding of the political construction of constitutional meaning is generally consistent with the argument presented here.

2. Bushnell, *Crimes, Follies, and Misfortunes,* 57–58; Stephen B. Presser, *The Original Misunderstanding* (Durham: Carolina Academic Press, 1991), 23–27; Richard E. Ellis, *The Jeffersonian Crisis* (New York: W. W. Norton, 1971), 76–79.

3. In 1798, when sitting in Philadelphia with the district court judge Richard Peters, Chase ruled in a split decision that there was no federal common law of crimes and thus no basis for a prosecution for the attempted bribery of a federal officer. Chase was apparently alone among the Federalist justices in holding this opinion and seems to have changed his mind the next year as the party closed ranks. Chase also distinguished himself in a sharply worded

exchange with his fellow justices in *Calder*, in which Chase argued for the Court's authority to strike down state legislation in the name of the "great first principles of the social compact," even without specific constitutional restrictions. United States v. Worrall, 2 U.S. (2 Dall.) 384, 392–94 (1798); Calder v. Bull, 3 U.S. (3 Dall.) 386, 388 (1798); Presser, *Original Misunderstanding,* 67–99; Leonard Levy, *Emergence of a Free Press* (New York: Oxford University Press, 1985), 278; Julius Goebel Jr., *History of the Supreme Court,* vol. 1 (New York: Macmillan, 1971), 623–633.

4. On Federalist activities during the period, see John C. Miller, *The Federalist Era, 1789–1801* (New York: Harper & Row, 1960), 210–277; James Morton Smith, *Freedom's Fetters* (Ithaca: Cornell University Press, 1956); Stanley Elkins and Eric McKitrick, *The Age of Federalism* (New York: Oxford University Press, 1993), 691–754; James Roger Sharp, *American Politics in the Early Republic* (New Haven: Yale University Press, 1993), 163–225.

5. Charles Warren, *The Supreme Court in United States History,* vol. 1 (Boston: Little, Brown, 1922), 156–157. Chief Justice Oliver Ellsworth was in France on a diplomatic mission and William Cushing was sick.

6. The Jeffersonian political organization had no fixed name, though "Democratic-Republican Societies" provided a common appellation. I follow convention in referring to the Jeffersonian "party" by the less cumbersome title "Republican." It should not be confused with the later, antislavery Republican party.

7. Francis Wharton, ed., *State Trials of the United States during the Administrations of Washington and Adams* (Philadelphia: Carey and Hart, 1849), 668–679; Thomas Cooper, ed., *Proceedings in the Circuit Court of the United States Held in Philadelphia, April 11, 1800* (Philadelphia: Thomas Cooper, 1800).

8. Elkins and McKitrick, *Age of Federalism,* 696–700; Miller, *Federalist Era,* 247–248.

9. U.S. Constitution, Art. III, §3.

10. Adams later pardoned Fries from his capital sentence. The case is reported in Wharton, *State Trials,* 458–648. See also *Trial of Samuel Chase, An Associate Justice of the Supreme Court of the United States,* vol. 1 (Washington, D.C.: Smith and Lloyd, 1805), 139.

11. Wharton, *State Trials,* 697–712.

12. *Trial of Chase,* 1:7.

13. Chase had privately called for a public act of defiance on the part of the justices to the Jeffersonian repeal of the prior lame-duck legislature's Judiciary Act of 1801, which created Adams' "midnight appointments." He ultimately abided by the more cautious judgment of his brethren. The repeal was subsequently upheld in Stuart v. Laird, 5 U.S. (1 Cranch) 299 (1803). On Chase's reaction to the repeal, see his letter to Marshall in *The Papers of John Marshall,* ed. Charles Hobson, vol. 6 (Chapel Hill: University of North Carolina Press, 1990), 109 116; see also Warren, *Supreme Court,* 1:271.

14. *Trial of Chase*, 2:vi.

15. *Writings of Thomas Jefferson*, ed. H. A. Washington, 9 vols. (New York: John C. Riker, 1857), 4:486; Ellis, *Jeffersonian Crisis*, 80–81.

16. Lynn W. Turner, "The Impeachment of John Pickering," *American Historical Review* 54 (April 1949): 485; Bushnell, *Crimes, Follies, and Misfortunes*, 43–55; Peter Charles Hoffer and N. E. H. Hull, *Impeachment in America, 1635–1805* (New Haven: Yale University Press, 1984), 206–220; Ellis, *Jeffersonian Crisis*, 69–75.

17. *William Plumer's Memorandum of Proceedings in the United States Senate, 1803–1807*, ed. Everett S. Brown (New York: Macmillan, 1923), 101. Plumer later admitted that Pickering's friends should have sought his resignation; Turner, "Impeachment of Pickering," 491. Jefferson had been threatened with impeachment while serving as governor of Virginia, and rumors of a federal impeachment had circulated during prior administrations.

18. Kathryn Turner, "Federalist Policy and the Judiciary Act of 1801," *William and Mary Quarterly*, 3d ser., 22 (January 1965): 9, 20.

19. E.g., William H. Rehnquist, *Grand Inquests* (New York: William Morrow, 1992), 15–134; Albert Beveridge, *The Life of John Marshall*, vol. 3 (New York: Houghton Mifflin, 1919), 157–222; Irving Brant, *Impeachment* (New York: Alfred A. Knopf, 1972), 58–83; Raoul Berger, *Impeachment* (New York: Bantam, 1974), 234–262; Henry Adams, *History of the United States of America during the First Administration of Thomas Jefferson*, vol. 2 (New York: Charles Scribner's Sons, 1921), 218–244; Warren, *Supreme Court*, 1:269–298. Cf. Ellis, *Jeffersonian Crisis*, 17–107; idem, "The Impeachment of Samuel Chase," in *American Political Trials*, ed. Michael R. Belknap (Westport, Conn.: Greenwood Press, 1981), 57–78; Richard B. Lillich, "The Chase Impeachment," *American Journal of Legal History* 4 (1960): 49; Alexander Humphrey, "The Impeachment of Samuel Chase," *American Law Review* 33 (1899): 827.

20. Ellis, "Impeachment of Chase," 61. John Taylor was similarly warning his correspondents even before the election that they "were not entirely right in directing their efforts towards a change of men, rather than a change of principles"; Taylor, "Letters of John Taylor," *John P. Branch Historical Papers of Randolph-Macon College* 2 (June 1908): 269.

21. *Memoirs of John Quincy Adams*, ed. Charles Francis Adams, vol. 1 (Philadelphia: J. B. Lippincott, 1874), 322–323. The Republican Philadelphia *Aurora* commented on the Judiciary Act: "the *Judiciary Bill* gives the nomination of 25 *new Judges* besides Marshall, Clerks, etc. to the amount of 100 offices in all! Why are these measures pushed forward now? Is it for the public good or for *party purposes?*" Quoted in K. Turner, "Judiciary Act," 13. Strangely, Presser finds the limited nature of the Republican impeachments to be an indication that they were designed to create vacancies, rather than change behavior or correct principle; *Original Misunderstanding*, 12.

22. Henry Adams, *John Randolph* (Greenwich, Conn.: Fawcett, 1961), 96. Chief Justice Rehnquist is probably more astute in positing a causal relationship between the impeachment and the fact that judges "stopped including political harangues in their charges to grand juries"; *Grand Inquests,* 125. See also Lillich, "Chase Impeachment," 71.
23. Presser, *Original Misunderstanding,* 14.
24. Hoffer and Hull, *Impeachment in America,* 3–4; Berger, *Impeachment,* 70.
25. U.S. Constitution, Art. I, §2, 3; Art. II, §4; Art. III, §1.
26. On whether the Court could intervene, compare Charles L. Black Jr., *Impeachment* (New Haven: Yale University Press, 1974), 53–63, with Berger, *Impeachment,* 108–126.
27. U.S. v. Nixon, 418 U.S. 683 (1974). For criticism, see Robert A. Burt, *The Constitution in Conflict* (Cambridge, Mass.: Harvard University Press, 1992), 316–327.
28. U.S. Constitution, Art. I, §3; Art. II, §4; Art. II, §2.
29. Compare Berger, *Impeachment,* 56–107, with Hoffer and Hull, *Impeachment in America,* esp. 266–270.
30. Cf. Bushnell, *Crimes, Follies, and Misfortunes,* 9–23, esp. 13; Lillich, "Chase Impeachment," 72.
31. Bushnell, *Crimes, Follies, and Misfortunes,* 25–55.
32. Ellis, "Impeachment of Chase," 70; Forrest McDonald, *The Presidency of Thomas Jefferson* (Lawrence: University Press of Kansas, 1976), 89. Chase's effort to construct the trial as a legal, rather than a political, event was aided by Vice President Aaron Burr's decision to decorate the Senate chamber and conduct the trial in the extravagantly ceremonious manner of the British courtroom. Burr assured Chase that legal and judicial procedures would be followed in the trial. McDonald, 91–92; Beveridge, *Life of Marshall,* 3:179–180; *Trial of Chase,* 1:15, 22; 2:251.
33. *Trial of Chase,* 1:14, 97. Spelling has been modernized throughout.
34. Ibid., 25, 40, 48, 78–80. John Marshall implicitly supported this view of the impeachment, writing to Chase that giving Congress an appellate power would be preferable to the use of impeachments over "a Judge giving a legal opinion"; Marshall, *Papers,* 6:347.
35. *Trial of Chase,* 1:47, 97, 96. Such an argument not only excluded mere questions of temperament, judgment, and civility but also reminded the like-minded Republicans of his own opinion in *Worrall* that disallowed a bribery prosecution in the absence of specific statutory authorization; Presser, *Original Misunderstanding,* 157.
36. Cf. Ellis, who regards Chase's reading as simply "literal"; "Impeachment of Chase," 72.
37. U.S. Constitution, Art. I, §3.
38. *The Writings of Thomas Jefferson,* ed. Paul Leicester Ford, 10 vols. (New York: G. P. Putnam's Sons, 1892–1899), 7:474.
39. *Annals of Congress,* 7th Cong., 1st sess. (1802), 525.

40. *Trial of Chase,* 2:255, 134. Martin also made explicit that removal from office was a punishment; ibid., 140. Likewise, John Marshall's analysis in *Marbury* can be read as regarding judicial office as a "private right"; e.g., George L. Haskins, "Law versus Politics in the Early Years of the Marshall Court," *University of Pennsylvania Law Review* 130 (November 1981): 12.
41. Quoted in L. W. Turner, "Impeachment of Pickering," 494.
42. *Trial of Chase,* 2:141.
43. Ibid., 257, 13, 11, 14.
44. Ibid., 12–13, 134–140, 144–146, 257–262. On state precedents, compare 145–146 with 259–162.
45. Ibid., 263–264.
46. Ibid., 12, 138–139, 145.
47. Ibid., 14, 20, 327.
48. Giles quoted in Ellis, "Impeachment of Chase," 61; William Plumer, quoted in ibid., 63. See also Noble E. Cunningham Jr., *The Jeffersonian Republicans in Power* (Chapel Hill: University of North Carolina Press, 1963), 80–81.
49. Quoted in Adams, *Memoirs,* 1:322.
50. Warren, *Supreme Court,* 1:230.
51. Randolph quoted in *Annals of Congress,* 7th Cong., 1st sess. (1802), 658; *The Papers of James Madison,* ed. Charles Hobson and Robert Rutland, vol. 12 (Charlottesville: University Press of Virginia, 1979), 235, 238.
52. Hoffer and Hull, *Impeachment in America,* 119. Even the Federalists had once advocated a broad reading, James Bayard informed the Senate during the Blount impeachment that a judge could be removed not only for abusing his power but also for neglecting to use it energetically enough; Brant, *Impeachment,* 43.
53. Clinton quoted in Ellis, *Jeffersonian Crisis,* 102; Smith quoted in Adams, *Memoirs,* 1:322, 323.
54. Adams, *Randolph,* 95, 96, 97.
55. Plumer, *Memorandum,* 280. Adams wrote that Randolph's speech must be analyzed "from the point of view which lawyers must take," without seriously asking whether that was either the appropriate point of view or Randolph's; *Randolph,* 100.
56. *Trial of Chase,* 1:124.
57. Ibid., 352, 350, 370, 367–368.
58. Ibid., 352–353, 370.
59. *Annals of Congress,* 7th Cong., 1st sess. (1802), 532, 556; Taylor, "Letters," 286.
60. *Trial of Chase,* 2:335.
61. Ibid., 336, 338, 342. See also 378, 383, 399–400.
62. Ibid., 339–340, 336–337, 342. See also 385–386. The recent Pennsylvania impeachment of Alexander Addison provided useful encouragement for removing a judge for bad behavior, even absent criminal intent or the violation of criminal law. The example was particularly compelling because Pennsylva-

nia had the option of removal by address, which did not require any imputation of "high crimes and misdemeanors," but chose to remove Addison by impeachment instead; ibid., 397; Hoffer and Hull, *Impeachment in America*, 198–199, 204.

63. *Trial of Chase*, 2:339, 336, 337, 342.

64. Ibid., 453, 372–373, 388, 389, 391, 403. See also Hoffer and Hull, *Impeachment in America*, 234.

65. *Trial of Chase*, 2:386, 402.

66. Lillich, "Chase Impeachment," 55.

67. Ellis, "Impeachment of Chase," 101–102; Warren, *Supreme Court*, 1:294–295. The votes are tabulated in *Trial of Chase*, 2:493.

68. The Sedition Act specified that the relevant state law should be used in certain procedural matters.

69. E.g., Adams, *History*, 2:224–225; Ellis, "Impeachment of Chase," 67.

70. At several points the managers themselves disavowed this construction; *Trial of Chase*, 1:367–368; 2:342, 399–400.

71. Ibid., 2:366, 446, 456, 335.

72. Ibid., 255, 326–329.

73. Republicans charged that Marshall "exhibited a culpable partiality towards the accused," while also complaining that his rulings in the trial had been "wrapt . . . in obscurity." Republicans were certain that Marshall had manipulated the law to advance his political ends, but had done so in a manner more scheming than the overzealous Chase; Beveridge, *Life of Marshall*, 3:534, 532.

74. E.g., Stuart S. Nagel, "Court-Curbing Periods in American History," *Vanderbilt Law Review* 18 (1965): 925.

75. Bushnell, *Crimes, Follies, and Misfortunes*, 7, 19; Hoffer and Hull, *Impeachment in America*, 254–255.

76. Bushnell, *Crimes, Follies, and Misfortunes*, 91–113; cf. Brant, *Impeachment*, 128–129.

77. For useful exceptions, see Ellis, *Jeffersonian Crisis* and "Impeachment of Chase"; Presser, *Original Misunderstanding*.

78. E.g., Lillich, "Chase Impeachment," 71; Adams, *Randolph*, 96; Hoffer and Hull, *Impeachment in America*, 254.

79. Ellis, *Jeffersonian Crisis*, 12–14; Dumas Malone, *Jefferson the President: First Term, 1801–1805* (Boston: Little, Brown, 1970), 114–115; Marshall, *Papers*, 6:46–47, 89; Julian P. Boyd, "The Chasm That Separated Thomas Jefferson and John Marshall," in *Essays on the American Constitution*, ed. Gottfried Dietze (Englewood Cliffs, N.J.: Prentice-Hall, 1964), 3–20.

80. See generally Richard Hofstadter, *The Idea of a Party System* (Berkeley: University of California Press, 1969), esp. 74–169; Ralph Ketcham, *Presidents above Party* (Chapel Hill: University of North Carolina Press, 1984), esp. 215–235; Ronald P. Formisano, *The Transformation of Political Culture* (New York: Oxford University Press, 1983), 3–106. For a sympathetic read-

ing of the Judiciary Act, see K. Turner, "Judiciary Act"; for the Sedition Act, see Presser, *Original Misunderstanding,* 119–121.

81. Quoted in K. Turner, "Judiciary Act," 9, 13, 18, 19, 20.

82. Quoted in Warren, *Supreme Court,* 1:192–193.

83. Elkins and McKitrick, *Age of Federalism,* 691–754; Miller, *Federalist Era,* 210–277; Smith, *Freedom's Fetters*; Levy, *Free Press,* 220–308.

84. Quoted in Levy, *Free Press,* 300; *Annals of Congress,* 5th Cong., 2d sess. (1798), 2093, 2115–16.

85. Levy, *Free Press,* 299–301.

86. The Pickering trial had also featured judicial partisanship; L. W. Turner, "Impeachment of Pickering," 489–490.

87. Quoted in Smith, *Freedom's Fetters,* 384; Peters quoted in Presser, *Original Misunderstanding,* 11.

88. Smith, *Freedom's Fetters,* 342–343, 355. On the organized and systematic nature of the pre-election sedition prosecutions, controlled from Secretary of State Timothy Pickering's office, see Smith, 186–187.

89. Ellis, *Jeffersonian Crisis,* 44, 66; Warren, *Supreme Court,* 1:264. Cf. Haskins, "Law versus Politics," 7–10.

90. Quoted in Warren, *Supreme Court,* 1:166; see the various charges lecturing on such topics as the Jay Treaty, the French Revolution, and the Republican party, 166 n. 2. Boston Federalists praised Judge Francis Dana's political jury charges as at least as valuable as his judicial rulings; Simon E. Baldwin, *The American Judiciary* (New York: Century, 1905), 47. See also Ralph Lerner, "The Supreme Court as Republican Schoolmaster," in *The Supreme Court Review, 1967,* ed. Philip B. Kurland (Chicago: University of Chicago Press, 1970), 129–155. On sedition prosecutions, see Smith, *Freedom's Fetters,* 369; Warren, 1:195. On electioneering by judges, see Warren, 1:273–274.

91. Quoted in Warren, *Supreme Court,* 1:193. A Republican paper noted in 1803 that "The Federal Judges were partial, vindictive, and cruel . . . They obeyed the President rather than the law, and made their reason subservient to their passion"; ibid., 191.

92. Jefferson, *Writings,* ed. Ford, 7:447; *Writings,* ed. Washington, 4:424–25. See also ibid., 370; Boyd, "Chasm."

93. Jefferson, *Writings,* ed. Washington, 4:386; Malone, *Jefferson: First Term,* 144; Jefferson, *Writings,* ed. Ford, 8:25. See also Cunningham, *Jeffersonian Republicans,* 14–15, 60–62.

94. *Annals of Congress,* 7th Cong., 1st sess. (1802), 804, 583, 658; see also 581, 597–598, 659.

95. Levy, *Free Press,* 304–346; Smith, *Freedom's Fetters,* 426; Lance Banning, *The Jeffersonian Persuasion* (Ithaca: Cornell University Press, 1978), 256–261, 275–278; Adrienne Koch and Harry Ammon, "The Virginia and Kentucky Resolutions: An Episode in Jefferson's and Madison's Defense of Civil Liberties," *William and Mary Quarterly* 3d ser., 5 (1948): 147; James Morton Smith, "The Grass Roots Origins of the Kentucky Resolutions," ibid., 27

(April 1970): 221. Though Jefferson later tolerated, and even encouraged, isolated state sedition prosecutions, the Republican prosecutions did not result in the systematic persecution of the Federalists, and Jefferson, unlike the Federalists, took pains to distance himself from any prosecutions; Jefferson, *Writings,* ed. Ford, 9:30–31, 253; 8:139, 217–218; 7:448; *Writings,* ed. Washington, 4:485; Levy, 341, 344–346.

96. *Annals of Congress,* 5th Cong., 2d sess. (1798), 2009, 2140, 2144; 3d sess. (1799), 2996, 3000–01, 3006, 3010; 7th Cong., 1st sess. (1802), 584.

97. Ibid., 5th Cong., 2d sess. (1798), 2148–50, 2163–64. Notably, John Marshall ran for Congress as a Federalist, but in explicit opposition to the Sedition Act, even as Justice Chase praised and utilized its terms, indicating both the direction of the successful construction and Marshall's relative safety from future impeachments; Elkins and McKitrick, *Age of Federalism,* 729.

98. Levy, *Free Press,* 211; Hoffer and Hull, *Impeachment in America,* 192–195, 204. The construction of a politically impartial judiciary may have been necessary to the impeachment of Chase, but some Republicans perhaps pursued it with mixed emotions; e.g., Macon, quoted in Ellis, *Jeffersonian Crisis,* 81.

99. *Trial of Chase,* 1:6–9.

100. Ibid., 193, 194, 209.

101. Ibid., 347–348, 354, 385–386.

102. Ibid., 2:363–364, 375–376, 398–399, 449, 446–447; Jefferson, *Writings,* ed. Ford, 8:25

103. *Trial of Chase,* 2:141, 144–146, 158, 262–264.

104. Ibid., 1:97–101; 2:213, 326, 328–329.

105. Cocke quoted in Ellis, "Impeachment of Chase," 72; Clinton quoted in ibid., 73; anonymous note in *National Intelligencer,* ibid., 105.

106. Haskins, "Law versus Politics"; Sylvia Snowiss, *Judicial Review and the Law of the Constitution* (New Haven: Yale University Press, 1990), 109–175; G. Edward White, *The Marshall Court and Cultural Change* (New York: Oxford University Press, 1991), 53–60, 196–200; Charles F. Hobson, *The Great Chief Justice* (Lawrence: University Press of Kansas, 1996), 51–54, 150–155. See also Walter F. Murphy, *The Elements of Judicial Strategy* (Chicago: University of Chicago Press, 1964), 123–197.

107. Cf. Presser, *Original Misunderstanding,* 178–179; Ellis, "Impeachment of Chase," 73. Randolph repeatedly expressed admiration for Marshall; William Cabell Bruce, *John Randolph of Roanoke,* vol. 1 (New York: G. P. Putnam's Sons, 1922), 201.

108. Ellis, *Jeffersonian Crisis,* 238. The federal government did not reenact the sedition law until the wartime measure during World War I and the subsequent Cold War Smith Act; Smith, *Freedom's Fetters,* 432.

109. See also Formisano, *Transformation,* 86–106; Bruce Allen Murphy, *The Brandeis/Frankfurter Connection* (New York: Oxford University Press, 1982), 357.

110. Quoted in Donald G. Morgan, *Justice William Johnson* (Columbia: University of South Carolina Press, 1954), 264.

111. Justice Smith Thompson allowed himself to be placed on the ballot for the governorship of New York in 1828, though he expressed little interest in the position; White, *Marshall Court*, 316. Such ambitions for high executive office were made somewhat easier by early and mid-nineteenth century practices that largely separated the political candidate from the campaign, allowing the candidate to remain "above politics" even as his supporters immersed themselves in the contest.

112. Carl B. Swisher, *History of the Supreme Court of the United States,* vol. 5 (New York: Macmillan, 1974), 222–224, 235, 237. Catron may have found such explanations particularly necessary given his unusually close ties to Polk and his political career. William J. Cibes Jr., "Extrajudicial Activities of the Justices of the United States Supreme Court, 1790–1960" (Ph.D. diss., Princeton University, 1975), 512–516, 521–530. Similarly, Rufus King wrote Martin Van Buren that joining the Court "forever divorce[d] [one] from the political world." Van Buren agreed. White, *Marshall Court*, 312.

113. Louis Fisher, *Constitutional Dialogues* (Princeton: Princeton University Press, 1988), 153–161.

114. Hofstadter, *Idea of Party System,* esp. 74–211. See also Formisano, *Transformation,* 305–343; Ketcham, *Presidents above Party,* 120–140, 215–236; James Ceaser, *Presidential Selection* (Princeton: Princeton University Press, 1979), 41–122. Cf. White, *Marshall Court,* 196–200.

115. U.S. Constitution, Amends. V, VI, VII.

116. Mirhan R. Damaska, *The Faces of Justice and State Authority* (New Haven: Yale University Press, 1986), 16–71, 214–239; Thomas Andrew Green, *Verdict According to Conscience* (Chicago: University of Chicago Press, 1985), 105–199; K. Turner, "Judiciary Act"; Warren, *Supreme Court,* 1:209–122; George Lee Haskins and Herbert A. Johnson, *History of the Supreme Court of the United States,* vol. 2 (New York: Macmillan, 1981), 107–135, 163–181.

117. Presser, *Original Misunderstanding,* 11–12, 47–54; Wharton, *State Trials,* 670–672. The British common law gave judges extensive powers to instruct juries and comment on facts as well as the law, and many state constitutions explicitly defined rights to a fair trial in accordance with the common law. The states only gradually modified this particular British inheritance. Nonetheless, American colonial judges generally assumed a more limited role, and state practice varied. Kenneth A. Krasity, "The Role of the Judges in Jury Trials: The Elimination of Judicial Evaluation of Fact in American State Courts from 1795 to 1913," *University of Detroit Law Review* 62 (1985): 595–598, 606–607; Mark DeWolfe Howe, "Juries as Judges of Criminal Law," *Harvard Law Review* 52 (1939): 591–595; Shannon C. Stimson, *The American Revolution in the Law* (Princeton: Princeton University Press, 1990).

118. Respublica v. Oswald, 1 Dallas 318, 325, 326, 329, 329b (Pa. 1788). The legislature declined to impeach for lack of evidence; ibid., 329g. One of the complaints leading to the Addison impeachment was the judge's rejection of the Pennsylvanian consensus that the jury determined both law and fact; Howe, "Juries as Judges," 595.

119. *Annals of Congress,* 5th Cong., 2d sess., 1798, 2150. See also Lerner, "Supreme Court"; Smith, *Freedom's Fetters,* 420; Elkins and McKitrick, *Age of Federalism,* 713.

120. Goebel, *Supreme Court,* 635–636, 646; Levy, *Free Press,* 128, 212, 285; Green, *Verdict,* 318–355.

121. Wharton, *State Trials,* 628, 630. Peters intervened to suggest that the prosecutor simply summarize the facts of the case.

122. Ibid., 698, 708; quoted in Presser, *Original Misunderstanding,* 112. See also *Trial of Chase,* 1:68.

123. Wharton, *State Trials,* 710–717, 635, 674, 676, 677; see also Presser, *Original Misunderstanding,* 50–53, 103, 111–13, 135–36; *Trial of Chase,* 1:44; 2:51–52.

124. *Trial of Chase,* 1:33, 34–35; 2:166.

125. Ibid., 2:38, 44, 159; 2:157–158, 19–20, 246–147. See also *Works of Fisher Ames,* ed. W. B. Allen, vol. 1 (Indianapolis: Liberty Fund, 1983), 317.

126. *Trial of Chase,* 2:46, 50, 150–151, 167, 170, 200–201, 246–247, 272–274. See also White, *Marshall Court,* 187–188, 198–199.

127. *Trial of Chase,* 2:355, 413–417.

128. Ibid., 363–364, 471–472; 1:114; Cooper, *Circuit Court 1800,* 66, 59.

129. *Trial of Chase,* 1:109–110, 112, 141; 2:322–323, 327–328, 332, 381.

130. Presser, *Original Misunderstanding,* 109–111, 64–65, 105, 107.

131. Sparf v. U.S., 156 U.S. 51 (1895); Howe, "Juries as Judges," 589. Jefferson had earlier written that questions of law were best determined by the judge unless "judges may be suspected of bias," in which case the "jury [should] undertake to decide both law and fact"; *Notes on the State of Virginia,* in *Writings,* ed. Merrill D. Peterson (New York: Literary Classics, 1984), 256.

132. Presser, *Original Misunderstanding,* 171–189; Ellis, *Jeffersonian Crisis,* 233–284. Though sharply curtailed from the strong British prerogative advocated by Chase, state practice has varied. See Curtis Wright, "Instructions to the Jury: Summary without Comment," *Washington University Law Quarterly* 1954 (1954): 177; idem, "The Invasion of Jury: Temperature of the War," *Temple Law Quarterly* 27 (Fall 1953): 137; Damaska, *Faces of Justice,* 44–46, 232–234; Krasity, "Role of Judges," 595; "Note: The Changing Role of the Jury in the Nineteenth Century," *Yale Law Journal* 74 (1964): 170; Lawrence M. Friedman, *A History of American Law* (New York: Simon & Schuster, 1973), 137. State civil trial practice differed even from criminal trial norms; see Morton Horwitz, *The Transformation of American Law, 1780–1860* (Cambridge, Mass.: Harvard University Press, 1977), 28–29, 84–85, 141–143, 228.

133. Chase, in Marshall, *Papers,* 6:111, 112; *Trial of Chase,* 2:vi, viii.
134. K. Turner, "Judiciary Act," 18, 19, 16; Ames, *Works,* 1:284. See also Warren, *Supreme Court,* 1:210; *Annals of Congress,* 7th Cong., 1st sess. (1802), 529; Ames, *Works,* 1:126.
135. *Trial of Chase,* 1:44; 2:19–20, 46, 51–52, 156–159, 166.
136. Adams, *Memoirs,* 1:322.
137. Again, Giles set the tone, arguing in Congress that he "found, from the general character of the Constitution, that the general will was its basis, the general good its object, and the fundamental principle for effecting this object was the responsibility of all public agents, either mediately or immediately to the people"; quoted in Warren, *Supreme Court,* 1:216; *Annals of Congress,* 7th Cong., 1st sess. (1802), 585; see also 531–532, 562, 583–593, 658, 661.
138. Taylor, "Letters," 275, 285–287. Similarly, Edmund Pendleton suggested making federal judges removable by the address of the two congressional houses and barring judges from accepting additional offices from the executive; *Letters and Papers of Edmund Pendleton,* ed. David John Mays, vol. 2 (Charlottesville: University Press of Virginia, 1967), 698.
139. Jefferson, *Writings,* ed. Ford, 10:141; see also 7:474; *Writings,* ed. Washington, 4:386, 425; William Plumer, *Life of William Plumer,* ed. A. P. Peabody (New York: Da Capo Press, 1969), 253.
140. Quoted in Warren, *Supreme Court,* 1:292.
141. U.S. Constitution, Art. II, §§2, 4.
142. Jefferson, *Writings,* ed. Ford, 8:25; *Writings,* ed. Washington, 4:485, 386.
143. *Trial of Chase,* 2:371–373, 410, 471; Ellis, "Impeachment of Chase," 61; idem, *Jeffersonian Crisis,* 26, 41, 52, 65.
144. Warren, *Supreme Court,* 1:119, 167, 178, 200–201, 275; Jefferson quoted on 167; see also 167 n. 1. In contrast to the judiciary, members of the federal legislature were specifically forbidden from holding executive appointments; U.S. Constitution, Art. I, § 6. The Jeffersonians sought to annex this provision to the judicial branch as well.
145. Ellis, "Impeachment of Chase," 64; *Trial of Chase,* 2:339, 371, 410; *Annals of Congress,* 7th Cong., 1st sess. (1802), 583.
146. Levy, *Free Press,* 275–278; Goebel, *Supreme Court,* 623–633; Presser, *Original Misunderstanding,* 95–97; *Annals of Congress,* 5th Cong., 2d sess. (1798), 2146–47; 3d sess. (1799), 2989.
147. *Trial of Chase,* 1:44; 2:41–43, 46, 50–52, 153, 156–159, 166–167, 272–274.
148. Pendleton, *Letters and Papers,* 2:699; Jefferson, *Writings,* ed. Ford, 8:57; Levy, *Free Press,* 304–305, 311, 316; *Annals of Congress,* 5th Cong., 2d sess. (1798), 2141–42, 2157; 3d sess. (1799), 2999, 3012; 7th Cong., 1st sess. (1802), 554. The managers' concern over Chase's attitude toward the place of juries in criminal trials reflected these considerations. The Republicans argued that the law was always at least partially open and could never be

decisively determined by precedent. Given that conception of law, Chase's attempts to constrain the jury's consideration of all available arguments over the meaning of the law and his specific directions as to the law's meaning only served to remove the popular role from lawmaking and transfer final legislative authority to the judge. Recognition of a federal common law of crimes would likewise vastly expand the role of the federal judiciary, which would therefore require closer judicial responsibility to the people. The Republicans were willing to recognize relative judicial independence, but only in the context of a judiciary separated from the lawmaking function.

149. *Trial of Chase*, 2:493.
150. Ellis, *Jeffersonian Crisis*, 106–107; Bruce, *John Randolph*, 1:201. Similar constitutional amendments were introduced in the Senate after the Burr trial, but were buried in committee with little party or presidential support. Dumas Malone, *Jefferson the President: Second Term, 1805–1809* (Boston: Little, Brown, 1974), 367.
151. This also suggests that John Adams had not simply "misunderstood the meaning of the Constitution" in arguing for a representative balance of social orders rather than a functional separation of powers. The ratification of the Constitution did not simply lock in a single constitutional trajectory, and future political struggles were necessary to define and secure "the Federalist persuasion." Cf. Gordon S. Wood, *The Creation of the American Republic, 1776–1787* (New York: W. W. Norton, 1969), 567.
152. The curtailment of judicial service within the executive branch was particularly noticeable in the several decades immediately following the Chase impeachment. Cibes, "Extrajudicial Activities," 287–288, 449–50; Murphy, *Brandeis/Frankfurter*, 345–364.
153. U.S. v. Hudson and Goodwin, 11 U.S. (7 Cranch) 32 (1812).
154. Sylvia Snowiss, "From Fundamental Law to the Supreme Law of the Land: A Reinterpretation of the Origin of Judicial Review," *Studies in American Political Development* 2 (1987): 1; Hobson, *Great Chief Justice*, 51–54, 150–55; Haskins, "Law versus Politics."

3. The Nullification Crisis and the Limits of National Power

1. The phrase is the title of William W. Freehling's detailed study of the nullification crisis; *Prelude to Civil War* (New York: Harper & Row, 1966). Freehling's book has become the standard work on the controversy, though his title also suggests his thesis that nullification was essentially a conflict over slavery, which he also accepts as the cause of the war. For critiques of that connection, see Paul Bergeron, "The Nullification Controversy Revisited," *Tennessee Historical Quarterly* 35 (Fall 1976): 263–275; J. P. Ochenkowski, "The Origins of Nullification in South Carolina," *South Carolina Historical Magazine* 83 (April 1982): 121–153. Other useful histories include David Franklin Houston, *A Critical Study of Nullification in South*

Carolina (Gloucester, Mass.: Peter Smith, 1968); Chauncy Samuel Boucher, *The Nullification Controversy in South Carolina* (Chicago: University of Chicago Press, 1916); Frederic Bancroft, *Calhoun and the South Carolina Nullification Movement* (Baltimore: Johns Hopkins Press, 1928). On particular political moves to resolve the controversy, see Merrill D. Peterson, *Olive Branch and Sword: The Compromise of 1833* (Baton Rouge: Louisiana State University Press, 1982); Richard E. Ellis, *The Union at Risk* (New York: Oxford University Press, 1987).

2. Some also considered a bill, vetoed by Jackson, that provided for the distribution of revenue from the sale of public lands as part of the compromise; Peterson, *Olive Branch,* 82–83.

3. U.S. Constitution, Art. I, §8.

4. For the former, see Freehling, *Prelude;* for the latter, see Peterson, *Olive Branch.* Charles Sellers adopts a similar perspective but does not take into account the significance of the Compromise Tariff in inaugurating an era of free trade; *The Market Revolution* (New York: Oxford University Press, 1991), 330–331.

5. See David F. Ericson, *The Shaping of American Liberalism* (Chicago: University of Chicago Press, 1993), 76–78, 205–206. The debate over material versus ideological explanations of the nullification crisis mirrors the debate over the competence of the political branches to engage in constitutional interpretation. In both debates, the "contamination" of ideal concerns with political interests has served to draw the whole into the latter (lower?) sphere.

6. As Donald S. Lutz has argued, "Although details of the federal form remained incomplete in the Constitution, that does not detract from the importance of federalism. Details of almost every important aspect of the Constitution were left to future generations. The struggle over states' rights, judicial interpretation of the Bill of Rights as it applies to the states, and even the decline of state power versus national power operate within a framework defined by federalism"; *The Origins of American Constitutionalism* (Baton Rouge: Louisiana State University Press, 1988), 153. Cf. Ericson, *American Liberalism,* 75; Sellers, *Market Revolution,* 305, 306; Theodore J. Lowi, "Foreword," in *The Dynamics of American Politics,* ed. Lawrence C. Dodd and Calvin Jillson (Boulder: Westview Press, 1994), xiv.

7. The Kentucky resolutions, including Jefferson's original drafts, may be found in *The Writings of Thomas Jefferson,* ed. Paul Leicester Ford, 10 vols. (New York: G. P. Putnam's Sons, 1892–1899), 7:289–309; for the Virginia resolutions, see *The Writings of James Madison,* ed. Gaillard Hunt, 9 vols. (New York: G. P. Putnam's Sons, 1900–1910), 6:326–331. See also Adrienne Koch and Harry Ammon, "The Virginia and Kentucky Resolutions: An Episode in Jefferson's and Madison's Defense of Civil Liberties," *William and Mary Quarterly,* 3d ser., 5 (April 1948): 145–176; James Roger Sharp, *American Politics in the Early Republic* (New Haven: Yale University Press, 1993), 187–207.

8. Herman V. Ames, ed., *State Documents on Federal Relations* (New York: Da Capo Press, 1970), 16–25. Notably, there were no condemnations from the Southern states, though no state joined Virginia and Kentucky in their official denunciation of the Alien and Sedition Acts, and Massachusetts, Connecticut, New Hampshire and Pennsylvania explicitly endorsed those acts in their replies.

9. Madison, *Writings,* 6:331–406.

10. One notable distinction is that the Kentucky resolutions relied on the Tenth Amendment and federalism, whereas the Virginia resolutions referred specifically to the First Amendment to challenge Congress' power over seditious speech, though Jefferson's own draft of the Kentucky resolutions also made use of the First Amendment; Jefferson, *Writings,* 7:293–295; Madison, *Writings,* 6:328–329.

11. Madison, *Writings,* 6:329; Jefferson, *Writings,* 7:292. Compare John Locke, *Two Treatises of Government,* ed. Peter Laslett (New York: Cambridge University Press, 1988), §§13, 19.

12. Jefferson, *Writings,* 7:304. John Taylor, who sponsored the Virginia resolutions, provided the "sentinel" designation; *An Inquiry into the Principles and Policy of the Government of the United States* (New Haven: Yale University Press, 1950), 557. For similar imagery see James Madison, in *The Debates in the Several State Conventions on the Adoption of the Federal Constitution,* ed. Jonathan Elliot, vol. 3 (New York: Burt Franklin, 1964), 35.

13. Cf. Marbury v. Madison, 5 U.S. (1 Cranch) 137, 176–177 (1803).

14. Jefferson, *Writings,* 7:288–290. The Virginia resolutions called for the states "to interpose for arresting the progress of the evil, and for maintaining within their respective limits the authorities, rights, and liberties appertaining to them"; Madison, *Writings,* 6:326. Jefferson's draft specifically supplemented the suffrage with the "natural right" of each state "to nullify on their own authority all assumptions of power by others within their limits" as the appropriate check on the federal government; Jefferson, *Writings,* 7:301.

15. Rhode Island, for example, thought the Virginia legislature had inappropriately blended "together legislative and judicial powers" and was threatening the use of "the strength of its own arm"; Ames, *State Documents,* 17.

16. For example, in protesting the embargo in 1809, Rhode Island, which had opposed Virginia and Kentucky in 1798, declared itself "one of the parties to the Federal compact" with a "right to express their sense of any violation of its provisions" and "to interpose for the purpose of protecting" citizens from "usurped and unconstitutional power"; ibid., 43–44.

17. Ibid., 54–87. For a general history, see James M. Banner Jr., *To the Hartford Convention* (New York: Alfred A. Knopf, 1970).

18. The growth of Southern particularism is documented in Charles S. Sydnor, *The Development of Southern Sectionalism, 1819–1848* (Baton Rouge: Louisiana State University Press, 1948); Jesse T. Carpenter, *The South as a Conscious Minority, 1789–1861* (Columbia: University of South Carolina Press, 1990).

19. Fairfax's Devisee v. Hunter's Lessee, 11 U.S. (7 Cranch) 603 (1813); Hunter v. Martin, 4 Munford 1 (Va. 1814); Martin v. Hunter's Lessee, 14 U.S. (1 Wheat.) 304 (1816).

20. Roane's essays are collected in Gerald Gunther, ed., *John Marshall's Defense of McCulloch v. Maryland* (Stanford: Stanford University Press, 1969), 106–154. On the imperfection of the Constitution, see 130, 146–147. In his essays Roane also made use of his own decision in *Hunter v. Martin* and a similar decision by Pennsylvania's high court, which had also shown resistance to judicial nationalism; ibid., 149.

21. Ames, *State Documents,* 103–113.

22. Ibid., 119–121, 122–123, 125.

23. Ellis, *Union at Risk,* 102–122; Edwin A. Miles, "After John Marshall's Decision: *Worcester v. Georgia* and the Nullification Debate," *Journal of Southern History* 34 (November 1973): 519–544.

24. South Carolina was relatively slow among Southern states in rejecting the Federalist party and nationalism more generally. As late as December 1824, the legislature passed resolutions denying the authority of a state to "impugn the Acts of the Federal Government or the decisions of the Supreme Court of the United States," which was the "proper tribunal" for determining constitutional meaning. In the same year George McDuffie, later a leading nullifier, denied in the U.S. House of Representatives that the states were "sentinels" or "watch-towers of freedom"; Ames, *State Documents,* 137–139; Houston, *Nullification,* 30. On the failure of principled localism to shape national politics during the Jeffersonian era, see Norman K. Risjord, *The Old Republicans* (New York: Columbia University Press, 1965).

25. Brutus, *The Crisis* (Charleston, S.C.: A. E. Miller, 1827), 12–13.

26. Though not advocating Brutus' solution, Publius had argued similarly that federalism was a political, rather than legal, concept reliant upon political definition and maintenance; David F. Epstein, *The Political Theory of The Federalist* (Chicago: University of Chicago Press, 1984), 52–53.

27. Brutus, *Crisis,* 25, 109–110, 97, 104, 152–166; quotation p. 110.

28. Ibid., 47, 23, 82, 139.

29. For a somewhat different analysis of these divisions, see Major L. Wilson, "'Liberty and Union': An Analysis of Three Concepts Involved in the Nullification Controversy," *Journal of Southern History* 33 (August 1967): 331–355; David F. Ericson, "The Nullification Crisis, American Republicanism, and the Force Bill Debate," *Journal of Southern History* 61 (May 1995): 249.

30. In the summer of 1827 Thomas Cooper had called upon the South "to calculate the value of our Union" and insisted that the alternatives were "submission or separation." Similarly, some in the 1832 convention favored immediate secession, but they were unsuccessful in November and were routed by March. Houston, *Nullification,* 138–140; Peterson, *Olive Branch,* 87–88. For nullification's commitment to states' rights within union, see *The Papers of John C. Calhoun,* ed. Clyde N. Wilson, vol. 11 (Columbia: University of South Carolina Press, 1978), 276.

31. For Calhoun's appeals to the "spirit of '98," see John C. Calhoun, *Union and Liberty*, ed. Ross M. Lence (Indianapolis: Liberty Press, 1992), 370–371, 380; Calhoun, *Papers*, 11:447, 453, 464, 466, 564. Calhoun's innovation with regard to state conventions was not immediately recognized. For example, the famous Webster-Hayne debate in the U.S. Senate in 1830 assumed that the "South Carolina doctrine" held that the state legislature had the right to nullify; *Congressional Debates*, 21st Cong., 1st sess. (1830), 31–50, 58–83.

32. Calhoun, *Union and Liberty*, 345–346, 380–381; *Papers*, 11:281. The veto was only provisional, since three-fourths of the states could authoritatively interpret or add to the Constitution via amendment or convention; Calhoun, *Union and Liberty*, 356; *Papers*, 11:278, 634–636.

33. Calhoun, *Union and Liberty*, 419, 426.

34. Cf. Paul W. Kahn, *Legitimacy and History* (New Haven: Yale University Press, 1992), 35, 42–45.

35. Calhoun, *Union and Liberty*, 352, 356–359, 384–385, 407–408; *Papers*, 11:271–273, 492–493.

36. Calhoun, *Union and Liberty*, 342–343, 371, 373, 374, 390, 433, 436, 460.

37. Calhoun, *Papers*, 11:495.

38. Publius had argued that such influence was the guarantor of state authority in a federal system; Alexander Hamilton, James Madison, and John Jay, *The Federalist Papers*, ed. Clinton Rossiter (New York: Mentor, 1961), No. 32, 197.

39. Calhoun, *Union and Liberty*, 340, 343–344, 348, 359, 378, 433; *Papers*, 11:615, 619, 625, 645; Thomas Cooper, *Consolidation* (Columbia, S.C.: Times and Gazette, 1830).

40. *Writings and Speeches of Daniel Webster*, 18 vols. (Boston: Little, Brown, 1903), 2:59; 6:184. Nullification was thus nothing more than treason; *Congressional Debates*, 21st Cong., 1st sess. (1830), 79.

41. *Congressional Debates*, 21st Cong., 1st sess. (1830), 78; Webster, *Writings*, 6:201, 2:57.

42. *Congressional Debates*, 21st Cong., 1st sess. (1830), 76–77; Webster, *Writings*, 2:60. Of course, the reliance on constitutional law made the selection of judges a critical political issue; 2:62.

43. Webster, *Writings*, 6:219, 222, 197–198, 215; quotation p. 229; *Congressional Debates*, 21st Cong., 1st sess. (1830), 74, 77.

44. Webster, *Writings*, 6:219; *Congressional Debates*, 21st Cong., 1st sess. (1830), 74.

45. Webster, *Writings*, 6:185, 192; quotation p. 187.

46. *Congressional Debates*, 21st Cong., 1st sess. (1830), 64; Webster, *Writings*, 2:57–58, 47. See also John Quincy Adams, "Society and Civilization," *American Review* 2 (July 1845): 878; *Congressional Debates*, 22d Cong., 1st sess. (1832), app., 81, 88–89.

47. James Madison, *Federalist Papers*, No. 39, 240–246.

48. Connecticut Senator Samuel Foot's proposal would suspend land surveys,

given a current surplus of several million acres of already surveyed land. Cheap land was an important benefit to Western interests, both enriching Western constituents and encouraging Western development. Land sales also figured into fiscal policy. High tariff rates were quickly amortizing federal debt. A budget surplus, however, would create pressure to reduce the protectionist tariffs, threatening Northern interests. Thus, Northern representatives advocated distributing the surplus to the states for use in internal improvements, creating a new interest in maintaining or even increasing federal revenues from tariffs and land sales. Missouri's Thomas Hart Benton attacked the resolution as an effort to raise acreage price by restricting the supply of salable land, which in turn threatened western development and growth. Benton's charge threatened the American system's North-West coalition, potentially aligning the West with the South in order to maintain cheap land in exchange for a reduction in protection. South Carolina's Robert Hayne seized the opportunity to make such an offer. In order to cut off further exploration of that possibility, Daniel Webster changed the subject by taking the floor to attack South Carolina's nullification doctrines and to invoke nationalist sentiment against the South and shore up the protectionist coalition.

49. *Congressional Debates,* 21st Cong., 1st sess. (1830), 248, 264, 265.
50. Ibid., 265–267.
51. Madison, *Writings,* 9:391–392; Andrew Jackson, *Presidential Messages and State Papers,* ed. Julius W. Muller, vol. 3 (New York: Review of Reviews, 1917), 893; *Congressional Debates,* 21st Cong., 1st sess. (1830), 268–269. See also Madison, *Writings,* 9:355.
52. *Congressional Debates,* 21st Cong., 1st sess. (1830), 267; Madison, *Writings,* 9:341–357, 382–403, 479–482, 489–492; idem, *Letters and Other Writings of James Madison,* 4 vols. (Philadelphia: J. B. Lippincott, 1865), 4:334–337. See also Agricola, *Virginia Doctrines not Nullification* (Richmond: S. Shepherd, 1832). This was not simply an effort at face-saving by Madison, for the resolutions were at the base of the Republican understanding of the Constitution, and placing nullification in line with that earlier construction would make the nullifiers' task far easier. Madison's research led to some concessions to the nullifiers on Jefferson's views; Madison, *Writings,* 9:395–396. Prominent Virginia editor Thomas Ritchie concluded that "the *South Carolinians* were right as to Mr. Jefferson's opinions"; quoted in Merrill Peterson, *The Jefferson Image in the American Mind* (New York: Oxford University Press, 1960), 56. See also Abel Parker Upshur, *An Exposition of the Virginia Resolutions of 1798* (Philadelphia: Alexander's General Printing Office, 1833); and the South Carolina pamphlets cited in Peterson, 466.
53. *Congressional Debates,* 21st Cong., 1st sess. (1830), 271, 249–250. See also Madison, *Writings,* 9:479–480; Andrew Jackson, *The Statesmanship of Andrew Jackson,* ed. Francis N. Thorpe (New York: Tandy-Thomas, 1909), 27; Jackson, *Presidential Messages,* 3:1067.

54. Miles, "Marshall's Decision"; Richard Latner, "The Nullification Crisis and Republican Subversion," *Journal of Southern History* 43 (February 1977): 19–38; Jackson, *Statesmanship*, 20.

55. *The Correspondence of Andrew Jackson*, ed. John Spencer Bassett, 7. vols. (New York: Carnegie Institute, 1926–1935), 4:241–242; quotations, ibid., 462–463; Jackson, *Statesmanship*, 22.

56. *Congressional Debates*, 21st Cong., 1st sess. (1830), 267; Jackson, *Presidential Messages*, 3:1034–36, 1043, 1050, 1068.

57. Jackson, *Presidential Messages*, 3:1052, 1054, 1056, 1055, 1059, 1060, 1062. Jackson's strong nationalism was somewhat balanced by his conciliatory fourth annual message delivered days before. Alternating between the carrot and the stick in dealing with the nullifiers was characteristic of the centrist position, given that both the centrists and the nullifiers drew upon the same states' rights tradition.

58. Ellis, *Union at Risk*, 83–91, 111–112, 129–132, 147–149. Martin Van Buren likewise questioned the nationalism of the proclamation, but in this Jackson explicitly went against Van Buren and other states' rights critics; Sellers, *Market Revolution*, 328; Jackson, *Correspondence*, 5:2–4, 11–12.

59. E.g., *Letter from George M. Troup to a Gentlemen in Georgia* (Milledgeville, Ga.: Prince & Bagland, 1834); Littleton Waller Tazewell, *A Review of the Proclamation of President Jackson of the 10th of December, 1832* (Norfolk, Va.: J. D. Ghiselin, 1888).

60. *Congressional Debates*, 21st Cong., 1st sess. (1830), 132–145; Ellis, *Union at Risk*, 171–172, 176.

61. Abel Parker Upshur, *A Brief Enquiry into the True Nature and Character of Our Federal Government* (New York: Da Capo Press, 1971). The South Carolina legislature declined to act on the governor's call for a nullification convention after passage of the tariff of 1842, and the Wisconsin legislature rather insincerely "nullified" the Fugitive Slave Law in 1859 as part of a more general effort at undermining the law; Houston, *Nullification*, 154–155; Ames, *State Documents*, 63–65. Although the federal government was firm in denying the power of nullification, executive branch officials were much more solicitous of Wisconsin than Jackson had been of South Carolina. Presidential response to such challenges is much less determined than many commentators have suggested; Carl B. Swisher, *Roger B. Taney* (New York: Macmillan, 1936), 531.

62. The replies to South Carolina are collected in *State Papers on Nullification* (New York: Da Capo Press, 1970). Calhoun's final treatise on the Constitution barely mentions interposition; *Union and Liberty*, 217–218. On the decline of nullification generally in Southern thought, see Carpenter, *Conscious Minority*, 136–141, 235–236.

63. Jackson, *Presidential Messages*, 3:1072. Cf. Sellers, who emphasizes the rejection of nullification and ignores the broader acceptance of states' rights federalism; *Market Revolution*, 330–331.

64. E.g., "Memorandum by James H. Hammond," *American Historical Review* 6 (July 1901): 742; Jackson, *Correspondence,* 4:109.

65. On the extremes impinging on this new center, see Richard Current, *Daniel Webster and the Rise of National Conservatism* (Boston: Little, Brown, 1955); and John McCardell, *The Idea of a Southern Nation* (New York: W. W. Norton, 1979).

66. Calhoun, *Papers,* 13:636–640; Ellis, *Union at Risk,* 141–157; Charles Wiltse, *John C. Calhoun: Nullifier, 1829–1839* (Indianapolis: Bobbs-Merrill, 1949), 358–361; Martin Van Buren, *Messages and Papers of the Presidents,* ed. James Richardson, 20 vols. (New York: Bureau of National Literature, 1897–1922), 4:1531, 1533–36.

67. Wiltse, *Calhoun,* 369–373; *Congressional Globe,* 25th Cong., 2d sess. (1838), 74; app., 53, 70, 74; Webster, *Writings,* 18:33; James K. Polk, *Messages and Papers,* 5:2224–25.

68. Cf. Robert Lowry Clinton, "Judicial Review, Nationalism, and the Commerce Clause: Contrasting Antebellum and Postbellum Supreme Court Decision Making," *Political Research Quarterly* 47 (December 1994): 857. Clinton's particular concerns obscure the degree of difference in the constitutional logic employed by the Marshall and Taney Courts and the degree to which the changing discourse reflected changes that had occurred in the political arena. Similarly, Howard Gillman attributes the divisions on the Taney Court over federalism to the inadequacy of Marshall's doctrinal elaboration. But those divisions are traceable to the disintegration of the political consensus on federalism that fed shifts in the Court's docket, rendered earlier doctrines inadequate, required a shift in judicial reasoning, and legitimated the more extreme states' rights position. Gillman, "The Struggle over Marshall and the Politics of Constitutional History," *Political Science Quarterly* 47 (December 1994): 883 n. 8.

69. Taney himself had been uninvolved in the nullification crisis, having been preoccupied with Jackson's conflict with the Bank; Swisher, *Taney,* 207–208.

70. McCulloch v. Maryland, 17 U.S. (4 Wheat.) 316, 403, 405, 410 (1819). Marshall later expanded on the history, admitting that the states were independent before ratification but insisting that the "whole character in which the States appear, underwent a change" with ratification. In essence, the states of the Union were not the same states that existed before ratification. Gibbons v. Ogden, 22 U.S. (9 Wheat.) 1, 187 (1824). See also R. Kent Newmyer, *The Supreme Court under Marshall and Taney* (New York: Thomas Y. Crowell, 1968), 41, 50.

71. Gibbons v. Ogden, 189. Marshall insisted that, though rarely encountered, there were judicially cognizable limits to federal power; e.g., ibid., 203; Marbury v. Madison, 5 U.S. (1 Cranch) 137, 176–177 (1803); McCulloch v. Maryland, 405.

72. Gibbons v. Odgen, 194, 196, 210–211; see also Brown v. Maryland, 25 U.S. (12 Wheat.) 419 (1827). Compare Jeffersonian Justice William Johnson's

opinion, arguing that the legitimate use of the states' police powers, as opposed to their powers over commercial regulations, could not come into conflict and therefore be overridden by the congressional regulatory powers; ibid., 235.

73. Willson v. Black Bird Creek Marsh Co., 27 U.S. (2 Pet.) 245, 252 (1829). On Marshall's flirtation with exclusivity, see Newmyer, *Court under Marshall and Taney*, 52; Swisher, *Taney*, 393–394; Felix Frankfurter, *The Commerce Clause* (Chicago: Quadrangle Books, 1964), 50.

74. Newmyer, *Court under Marshall and Taney*, 115.

75. Dred Scott v. Sandford, 60 U.S. (19 How.) 393, 434, 410, 411 (1857); Ohio Life Insurance and Trust Co. v. Debolt, 57 U.S. (16 How.) 416, 428 (1853).

76. "And the powers of the general government, and of the State, although both exist and are exercised within the same territorial limits, are yet separate and distinct sovereignties, acting separately and independently of each other, within their separate spheres"; Ableman v. Booth, 62 U.S. (21 How.) 506, 516 (1858). Such language borrowed from and was consistent with Marshall's earlier opinions. However, Taney approached such conclusions from the opposite direction and explicitly reached them only in the context of a significant challenge to federal authority. The *Ableman* decision also emphasized *Martin*'s holding that a state court could not contradict a federal ruling on constitutional law; ibid., 516; Martin v. Hunter's Lessee, 14 U.S. (1 Wheat.) 304 (1816). See also Charles W. Smith Jr., *Roger B. Taney* (Chapel Hill: University of North Carolina, 1936), 82–105.

77. The License Cases, 46 U.S. (5 How.) 504, 579, 574 (1847). See also Frankfurter, *Commerce Clause*, 50–52; Newmyer, *Court under Marshall and Taney*, 116. In *Cooley* the Court asserted that there were some aspects of navigation that were implicitly removed from state jurisdiction, but at the same time it upheld Pennsylvania's regulation of the port of Philadelphia, explicitly reaffirmed concurrent state jurisdiction over and interest in interstate commerce, and did not extend federal authority beyond a narrow issue of navigation regulations or indicate what exclusive federal jurisdiction would mean outside the context of an existing federal law; Cooley v. Board of Wardens of the Port of Philadelphia, 53 U.S. (12 How.) 299 (1851). In addition, *Cooley* went beyond *Willson* by recognizing in the states an inherent concurrent power over commerce, not just a residual claim to a dormant federal power.

78. Charles River Bridge v. Warren Bridge, 36 U.S. (11 Pet.) 420, 547 (1837). Taney's comments came in the context of a state-corporation conflict, but the views expressed there are representative of his conception of the states and federalism more generally.

79. Bank of Augusta v. Earle, 38 U.S. (13 Pet.) 519, 590, 598 (1839).

80. Ironically, because the immediate effect of the decision was to support a bank against a state, the Democratic press was critical of Taney and the Whig

press was supportive; Charles Warren, *The Supreme Court in United States History,* vol. 2 (Boston: Little, Brown, 1922), 57–62. As a later observer noted, however, the case represented a "change in trend from the Marshall court" on federalism issues toward a more states' rights stance; Swisher, *Taney,* 385. On a different application of state extraterritoriality, see Arthur Bestor, "State Sovereignty and Slavery: A Reinterpretation of the Proslavery Constitutional Doctrine, 1846–1860," *Journal of the Illinois State Historical Society* 54 (Summer 1961): 117.

81. The License Cases, 579; Prigg v. Pennsylvania, 41 U.S. (16 Pet.) 539, 628 (1842); Kentucky v. Dennison, 65 U.S. (24 How.) 66 (1861). Contrast, for example, Story's nationalist *Prigg* opinion; Prigg v. Pennsylvania, 611–612, 615–616.

82. Ableman v. Booth, 62 U.S. (21 How.) 506, 517–520 (1858). Jackson's response to state challenges to federal authority more closely resembled Story's than Taney's.

83. The compromised nature of the post-nullification construction of federalism was also reflected on the Court. As *Ableman* makes clear, the Court was not willing to reopen federal judicial supremacy over the state courts; but other issues were less settled. *Miln* put the Court on record as supporting state exclusivity over police powers, allowing the states to trump even active use of the federal commerce powers. Taney demonstrated the more centrist position by retreating to a position similar to Johnson's: that commercial regulations were distinct from the proper subject of the police powers. Newmyer, *Court under Marshall and Taney,* 103; Swisher, *Taney,* 374–376, 394–396, 404–405; New York v. Miln, 36 U.S. (11 Pet.) 102 (1837). Similarly, in keeping with the post-nullification settlement, Taney avoided ruling on the constitutionality of old internal improvements as a dead issue, but Justice Peter Daniel asserted the radical position in a concurrence; Searight v. Stokes et al., 44 U.S. (3 How.) 151, 163, 166, 180–181 (1844). In the judiciary as elsewhere, the radical federalist position was not adopted, but the terms of the debate and the new centrist position had shifted in response to its demands.

84. On American trade policy during this period, see Edward Stanwood, *American Tariff Controversies in the Nineteenth Century,* 2 vols. (New York: Russell & Russell, 1967); F. W. Taussig, *The Tariff History of the United States* (New York: G. P. Putnam's Sons, 1931); Judith Goldstein, *Ideas, Interests, and American Trade Policy* (Ithaca: Cornell University Press, 1993); Sidney Ratner, *The Tariff in American History* (New York: D. Van Nostrand, 1972); Davis Dewey, *The Financial History of the United States* (New York: A. M. Kelley, 1968).

85. In a vain attempt to slow the 1816 juggernaut, a Southern congressman suggested that to the extent that high tariffs served to constrict the cotton trade, they were also an impermissible tax on exports. The charge was

neither answered nor renewed. Stanwood, *Tariff Controversies,* 1:293–94; U.S. Constitution, Art. I, §9.

86. Daniel Webster, "Free Trade Speech and Resolutions at Faneuil Hall, in 1820," in *Southern State Rights, Free Trade and Anti-Abolition Tract No. 1* (Charleston, S.C.: Walker & Burke, 1844), 14, 15, 23.

87. *Annals of Congress,* 18th Cong., 1st sess. (1824), 3075, 3078, 3095. See also 3440, 648, 1564.

88. Charles Mercer of Virginia made the unique suggestion that the import tax on cotton baggings, essential for the cotton trade, was equivalent to a tax on exports; ibid., 688. During the 1820s Taylor authored a number of works vindicating orthodox Jeffersonian principles against various nationalist and "aristocratic" foes. On the tariff, see Taylor, *Tyranny Unmasked* (1822) (Indianapolis: Liberty Fund, 1992).

89. *Annals of Congress,* 18th Cong., 1st sess. (1824), 620–621, 648.

90. Ibid., 623–624, 648–649; quotation p. 649. See also Taylor, ibid., 600; and P. P. Barbour, ibid., 1918.

91. Stanwood, *Tariff Controversies,* 1:190.

92. *Annals of Congress,* 18th Cong., 1st sess. (1824), 1994; Stanwood, *Tariff Controversies,* 1:224. Although the opinion was never cited in congressional debates and did not address the protection issue directly, Clay was working against John Marshall's off-handed remark that imposts fell under the revenue clause and were a tax, not a regulation; Gibbons v. Ogden, 201.

93. Drew McCoy, *The Elusive Republic* (New York: W. W. Norton, 1980), esp. 209–259.

94. Madison, *Writings,* 9:317–333; quotations pp. 327, 372, 334.

95. McCulloch v. Maryland, 400.

96. Ibid., 407–409, 401 402. Marshall's opinion reflects both a broad substantive reading of constitutional powers, which allowed a range of policy instruments to the government, and a willingness to view the choice of government instruments as being essentially a subconstitutional issue. The constitutional text positively creates an active national government and negatively refrains from specifying the actions that should be taken by that government.

97. Jackson, *Presidential Messages,* 3:993, 1003. See generally Marvin Meyers, *The Jacksonian Persuasion* (Stanford: Stanford University Press, 1960).

98. *Niles' Weekly Register,* 12 June 1824, 245. The Jacksonian attempt to capture the tariff issue from Adams is detailed in Robert V. Remini, *The Election of Andrew Jackson* (New York: J. B. Lippincott, 1963).

99. Andrew Jackson, *Messages and Papers,* 3:1013–14, 1078, 1086–87, 1160–62; quotations pp. 1165, 1169. Adams thought that in this fourth annual message, Jackson had yielded completely to the nullifiers. Adams' assessment is accurate only to the extent that it correctly recognized the dynamics of political events—Jackson could no longer sustain protectionism in the

face of the nullifiers' attack; John Quincy Adams, *Memoirs of John Quincy Adams*, ed. Charles Francis Adams, vol. 8 (Philadelphia: J. B. Lippincott, 1876), 503.

100. Calhoun, *Union and Liberty*, 356; *Papers*, 11:645, 269, 673.

101. For an interpretive approach by an antiprotectionist, see *Congressional Debates*, 22d Cong., 1st sess. (1832), 306–311. For an interpretive defense of protection, see 195–201.

102. E.g., Calhoun, *Union and Liberty*, 336; *Congressional Debates*, 22d Cong., 1st sess. (1832), 307.

103. Calhoun, *Union and Liberty*, 453.

104. Ibid., 316, 327–328, 363; quotation p. 343; Calhoun, *Papers*, 11:269, 502, 674. The uniformity limitation particularly resonated with the taxing power, for the imposition of unequal tax burdens effectively taxed the minority section without its consent. Only the uniformity requirement allowed the possibility of leaving the imposition of taxes to majoritarian voting.

105. Calhoun, *Papers*, 11:514–515, 558.

106. Calhoun, *Union and Liberty*, 315; quotations in "Memorandum by James Hammond," 743–744; and Calhoun, *Union and Liberty*, 423, 415.

107. *Congressional Debates*, 22d Cong., 2d sess. (1833), 463, 466, 468, 724, 730–731, 734, 808.

108. Ibid., 727–729, 698, 707, 793–794, 1043, 732; quotation p. 808. Clay's hope was that the protective principle would gain converts in the future and could be resuscitated then.

109. Ibid., 464, 692, 696, 704, 793, 797; quotations pp. 466, 467.

110. Ibid., 467–469, 731, 735–736, 738.

111. Jackson, *Messages and Papers*, 4:1458–65; 3:1337–41, 1247–48. Cf. 3:1014–15, 1072, 1074, 1076–78.

112. Clay in *Congressional Debates*, 24th Cong., 2d sess. (1837), 882; Webster, *Writings*, 8:214, 217.

113. Stanwood, *Tariff Controversies*, 2:22, 80, 94; Dewey, *Financial History*, 237–238, 247–250; Taussig, *Tariff History*, 113; Peterson, *Olive Branch*, 118; Ratner, *Tariff*, 21–24; Sellers, *Market Revolution*, 412–413.

114. *Congressional Globe*, 27th Cong., 2d sess. (1842), 575, 580, 588, 664–666, 674, 680, 771.

115. *Correspondence of James K. Polk*, ed. Wayne Cutler, vol. 7 (Nashville: Vanderbilt University Press, 1989), 267; Polk, *Messages and Papers*, 5:2226–29, 2253–56. In protectionist Pennsylvania, however, this message of incidental protectionism was at least occasionally spun as the Democratic endorsement of protectionism proper, including the tariff of 1842; Charles Sellers, *James K. Polk, Continentalist* (Princeton: Princeton University Press, 1966), 116–128; Nathan Sargent, *Public Men and Events*, vol. 2 (Philadelphia: J. B. Lippincott, 1875), 232–241. Sellers finds Polk's letter to be a clear endorsement of protectionism, but this interpretation is questionable given the text of the letter itself, the varying interpretations given to the letter both within

and without Pennsylvania, the inconsistency of that position with Polk's known views and oral communications with others, and Sellers' misunderstanding of the nature of the 1833 construction, which established incidental protection as a distinct "free trade" position. Nonetheless, it cannot be denied that protectionism remained a potent political force in Pennsylvania in 1844, even if it gained little national backing.

116. *Congressional Globe,* 29th Cong., 1st sess. (1846), 1004–05, 1156, 761, 747; appendix, 9–11; see also 731, 740, 754, 761, 993–994, 1020–21, 1035, 1045.

117. Internal taxes were often used to legitimate increased tariffs, both by offsetting of the costs of the former on business and by using the first to buy support for the second; Ratner, *Tariff,* 28–31; Robert Stanley, *Dimensions of Law in the Service of Order* (New York: Oxford University Press, 1993), 15–58.

118. Marshall L. DeRosa, *The Confederate Constitution of 1861* (Columbia: University of Missouri Press, 1991), 89–99; C.S.A. Constitution, Art. I, §8, clause 1.

119. Tariffs were passed in 1816, 1824, 1828, 1832, and 1833, and only the last reduced protection. After the Compromise, tariffs were passed in 1842, 1846, and 1857, with the last two bringing substantial reduction in tariff rates. The country's first reciprocal trade agreement, in 1854, was negotiated with Canada; Ratner, *Tariff,* 12 27.

120. *Congressional Debates,* 22d Cong., 1st sess. (1832), 267; Jackson, *Statesmanship,* 23.

121. The Supreme Court ruled that the terms of the Compromise tariff survived the last revision contained in the original schedule, siding with the Tyler administration against Clay; Aldridge et. al. v. Williams, 44 U.S. (3 How.) 8 (1845).

122. Jackson, *Presidential Messages,* 3:995. Such a ratcheting effect might be avoided if early precedent in fact ruled a given power out of bounds. As a practical matter, however, it is uncertain if there could be a "negative" weight of uniform precedent to prevent later claims to power. Jackson could make use of the Bank's controversial history to deny the uniformity of precedent, but what would be the meaning of a simple "failure" to establish a bank during the early years of the republic? Would this serve as a precedent against the existence of such a power, or simply as a continuing constitutional gap not yet filled in by positive state action?

4. Andrew Johnson and Executive Construction

1. Johnson's historical reputation has gyrated wildly over the last century, as he recovered from his postbellum nadir to be lauded as a defender of the Constitution in the early twentieth century and then berated as a racist obstructionist in the new revisionism of the last three decades. See Larry Kincaid,

"Victims of Circumstance: An Interpretation of Changing Attitudes toward Republican Policy Makers and Reconstruction," *Journal of American Studies* 57 (June 1970): 48. For the early reinterpretation of Johnson see John W. Burgess, *Reconstruction and the Constitution* (Westport, Conn.: Negro Universities Press, 1970); William A. Dunning, *Reconstruction, Political and Economic, 1865–1877* (New York: Harper & Brothers, 1962); idem, *Essays on the Civil War and Reconstruction, and Related Topics* (New York: Macmillan, 1898); Howard K. Beale, *The Critical Year* (New York: Frederick Ungar, 1958); George F. Milton, *The Age of Hate* (Hamden, Conn.: Archon Books, 1965). Leading revisionist works include David Donald, "Why They Impeached Andrew Johnson," *American Heritage* 8 (December 1956): 21; Eric L. McKitrick, *Andrew Johnson and Reconstruction* (Chicago: University of Chicago Press, 1960); W. R. Brock, *An American Crisis* (New York: St. Martin's Press, 1963); Michael Les Benedict, *The Impeachment and Trial of Andrew Johnson* (New York: W. W. Norton, 1973); Hans L. Trefousse, *Impeachment of a President* (Knoxville: University of Tennessee Press, 1975); Eric Foner, *Reconstruction* (New York: Harper & Row, 1988). The standard narrative of the impeachment remains David Miller DeWitt, *The Impeachment and Trial of Andrew Johnson* (New York: Russell & Russell, 1967).

2. Republican ranks had been fortified between the vetoes by the expulsion of a Democratic senator from New Jersey and his replacement with a Republican.

3. The congressional Republicans were aided by the addition of a new state, Nebraska, which was admitted over a presidential veto. Congress failed to override a veto in order to admit the severely underpopulated Colorado.

4. Recent revisionists have characterized Johnson as an imperial president bent on overturning the gains made during the Civil War and virtually reestablishing a slavocracy; e.g., Trefousse, *Impeachment;* Benedict, *Impeachment of Johnson.* Earlier historians portrayed Congress as determined to overturn the constitutional system and introduce parliamentary governance; e.g., Burgess, *Reconstruction;* Dunning, *Essays,* 253–303. In the transition, historians have pronounced both sides to have been overtaken by their own paranoia and psychological straitjackets; e.g., McKitrick, *Johnson and Reconstruction;* George C. Rable, "Forces of Darkness, Forces of Light: The Impeachment of Andrew Johnson and the Paranoid Style," *Southern Studies* 17 (Summer 1978): 151.

5. Stephen Skowronek, *The Politics Presidents Make* (Cambridge, Mass.: Harvard University Press, 1993). Skowronek does not discuss the case of Andrew Johnson in any detail, but Johnson would fit his description of a "preemptive" president fighting against a resilient regime.

6. On Lincoln's ambiguous relationship with his own power, see David H. Donald, *Lincoln Reconsidered* (New York: Vintage, 1961), 187–208.

7. Jeffrey K. Tulis, *The Rhetorical Presidency* (Princeton: Princeton University Press, 1987), esp. 87–93.

8. The Progressive historians argued that the impeachment marked the defining

moment for the American domestic regime in a conflict between Northern capitalists and agrarian populists, but such a cleavage misrepresents the actual divisions in the dispute. See Charles Beard and Mary Beard, *The Rise of American Civilization,* vol. 2 (New York: Macmillan, 1930), 52–121; Robert P. Sharkey, *Money, Class, and Party* (Baltimore: Johns Hopkins University Press, 1967). Disputes over federalism had largely taken place elsewhere; e.g., Michael Les Benedict, "Preserving the Constitution: The Conservative Basis of Radical Reconstruction," *Journal of American History* 61 (June 1974): 65; Harold M. Hyman, *A More Perfect Union* (New York: Alfred A. Knopf, 1973), 364–444. More recent revisionists have emphasized the role of race in the conflict. Such concerns are an important component of the impeachment politics. The substantive commitments of the two sides helped shape the contours of their dispute, though an exclusive focus on race obscures the real conflict over separation of powers that was at stake as well. Institutional power was both an immediately instrumental and an independent concern here. Cf. Trefousse, *Impeachment;* Martin E. Mantell, *Johnson, Grant, and the Politics of Reconstruction* (New York: Columbia University Press, 1973).

9. Theodore J. Lowi, "Foreword," in *The Dynamics of American Politics,* ed. Lawrence C. Dodd and Calvin Jillson (Boulder: Westview Press, 1994), xii.

10. The 1868 impeachment may be seen as a continuation of the struggle between Hamiltonian/Jacksonian and Whig theories of the presidency; Alfred H. Kelly, "Comment on Harold M. Hyman's Paper," in *New Frontiers of the American Reconstruction,* ed. Harold M. Hyman (Urbana: University of Illinois Press, 1966), 51.

11. Acting under the "war power of the Government" and the executive's duty to enforce the law, Lincoln effectively initiated a war against the new Confederacy, including the institution of a blockade of Southern ports, the mobilization of additional troops, and the suspension of the right to habeas corpus; Roy Basler, ed., *Abraham Lincoln: His Speeches and Writings* (New York: Da Capo, 1990), 594–609. Unlike Johnson, Lincoln did eventually convene a special session of Congress, though like his successor, Lincoln presented Congress with a slate of presidential actions simply to be ratified. Characteristically, Lincoln admitted that some had questioned the "legality and propriety of what has been done," but then strongly asserted his right to act on his own authority, "trusting then as now that Congress would readily ratify them." Though accepting a Jacksonian conception of the presidency, the late antebellum Democratic presidents were relatively weak; Kelly, "Comment," 47–48.

12. *Congressional Globe,* 37th Cong., 2d sess. (1862), 2972; James M. McPherson, *Battle Cry of Freedom* (New York: Oxford University Press, 1988), 348–365; Skowronek, *Politics,* 216–219. The increasing power of the presidency was indicated the next year, however, by Lincoln's simultaneous denial of regular congressional power under the Constitution to emancipate the

slaves and assertion of presidential authority to do the same; Skowronek, 210–215, 220–221.

13. See generally James G. Randall, *Constitutional Problems under Lincoln* (Urbana: University of Illinois Press, 1951), esp. 517–519; Edward S. Corwin, *The President* (New York: New York University Press, 1984), 263–269. Moreover, there was a growth of a Republican theory of a strong presidency, aided in part by the addition of former Democrats to the party; Harold M. Hyman, "Reconstruction and Political-Constitutional Institutions: The Popular Expression," in *New Frontiers*, 29–34; Arthur M. Schlesinger Jr., *The Imperial Presidency* (Boston: Houghton Mifflin, 1989), 58–66; Richard J. Ellis and Stephen Kirk, "Presidential Mandates in the Nineteenth Century: Conceptual Change and Institutional Development," *Studies in American Political Development* 9 (Spring 1995): 165–175.

14. Lincoln's "Ten Percent Plan" gave a full pardon to Southerners who took an oath of future loyalty. New state governments could be formed as soon as a population equivalent to 10 percent of the votes cast in 1860 was so certified as "loyal"; Foner, *Reconstruction*, 35–37, 60–62.

15. McKitrick, *Johnson and Reconstruction*, 142–152; Foner, *Reconstruction*, 176–227; Edward McPherson, *The Political History of the United States of America during the Period of Reconstruction* (Washington, D.C.: Solomons and Chapman, 1875), 9–13, 64–67.

16. McPherson, *Political History*, 109–110.

17. Ibid., 60.

18. Ibid., 85.

19. On theories of Reconstruction, see Charles O. Lerche Jr., "Congressional Interpretation of the Guarantee of a Republican Form of Government during Reconstruction," *Journal of Southern History* 15 (May 1949): 192; John Hurd, "Theories of Reconstruction," *American Law Review* 1 (January 1867): 238; Burgess, *Reconstruction*, 1–8, 57–61; McKitrick, *Johnson and Reconstruction*, 93–119. The institutional implications of those different theories were ambiguous, however; e.g., Alfred Conkling, *The Powers of the Executive Department of the Government of the United States* (Albany: Weare C. Little, 1866), 72–88; Charles Ernest Chadsey, *The Struggle between President Johnson and Congress over Reconstruction* (New York: AMS Press, 1967), 35–42; Orestes A. Brownson, *The Works of Orestes A. Brownson*, ed. Henry F. Brownson, vol. 17 (New York: AMS Press, 1966), 459–460, 511–517.

20. McPherson, *Political History*, 68–74, 147–151, 178.

21. Ibid., 74–81.

22. Gregory Horness, ed., *Presidential Vetoes, 1789–1988*, (Washington, D.C.: U.S. Government Printing Office, 1992), ix. Although the percentage of overridden vetoes declined with later presidents, before Johnson only two presidents had had any overrides, whereas only five escaped overrides after Johnson. Similarly, six previous presidents had not used the veto power at all,

whereas after Johnson only the assassinated James Garfield neglected to use the power. The veto remained a potent weapon after Johnson but was none-theless a different instrument.

23. Richard E. Neustadt, for example, has argued that reliance on formal presi-dential powers, such as the veto, is an indication of presidential weakness; *Presidential Power and the Modern Presidents* (New York: Free Press, 1990), 10–28.

24. *Trial of Andrew Johnson, President of the United States, Before the Senate of the United States, on Impeachment by the House of Representatives for High Crimes and Misdemeanors,* 3 vols. (Washington, D.C.: U.S. Government Printing Office, 1868), 2:123. Somewhat oddly, Nelson began his defense of Johnson with a lengthy discussion of his character, but these discussions of the president's class background, loyalty to the Union, and commitment to Jacksonian constitutionalism arrayed the symbols of the larger contest to settle Johnson's ultimate construction; ibid., 118–124.

25. See also Aaron B. Wildavsky, "The Two Presidencies," in *The Presidency,* ed. Wildavsky (Boston: Little, Brown, 1969), 230–243.

26. The historical literature is divided between partisans of each branch. The traditional interpretation puts Johnson in a defensive position; e.g., Irving Brant, *Impeachment* (New York: Alfred A. Knopf, 1973), 133–153; William H. Rehnquist, *Grand Inquests* (New York: William Morrow, 1992), 250–251, 270; Eleanore Bushnell, *Crimes, Follies, and Misfortunes* (Urbana: University of Illinois Press, 1992), 161. Michael Benedict has forcefully argued the opposite view in *Impeachment* and "A New Look at the Impeachment of Andrew Johnson," *Political Science Quarterly* 88 (September 1973): 349. The early nationalist school took a more balanced view, consistent with that argued here; e.g., Dunning, *Essays,* 302–303; Chadsey, *Struggle,* 141.

27. McPherson, *Political History,* 176; Corwin, *The President,* 100–110.

28. Leonard D. White, *The Republican Era* (New York: Macmillan, 1958), 28; Stephen Skowronek, *Building a New American State* (New York: Cambridge University Press, 1982), 51, 55–56; Richard Franklin Bensel, *Yankee Leviathan* (New York: Cambridge University Press, 1990), 341–42.

29. McPherson, *Political History,* 176.

30. *Trial of Johnson,* 1:39, 55–56. The doctrine of implied powers "is just as applicable to the President of the United States as it is to any senator or to any representative"; 2:175.

31. Ibid., 1:47, 59, 61, 63–65.

32. Ibid., 207; see also 208, 316, 381. In his own response and veto message, Johnson emphasized the lessons of the Civil War, when Lincoln needed to remove executive officers of dubious loyalty in order to respond promptly and effectively to a threat to national security. The capacity of the executive to muster immediate, overwhelming, and certain force was the very hallmark of the executive powers; ibid. 39, 55–56.

33. "No single change in the practical operation of the executive branch gave

Presidents greater power than this"; Leonard D. White, *The Jacksonians* (New York: Macmillan, 1956), 34.

34. William Marcy, quoted in ibid., 313. On the increase in congressional control over appointments in the antebellum period, see 115.

35. Ibid., 341; see also 332, 337.

36. Harry J. Carman and Reinhard H. Luthin, *Lincoln and the Patronage* (New York: Columbia University Press, 1943), 164–165, 240, 281–282, 313–315; Joseph P. Harris, *The Advice and Consent of the Senate* (Berkeley: University of California Press, 1953), 71–72.

37. Harris, *Advice and Consent,* 73; Dunning, *Essays,* 255; Donald, "Why They Impeached," 103; Hyman, *More Perfect Union,* 304; James E. Sefton, *Andrew Johnson and the Uses of Constitutional Power* (Boston: Little, Brown, 1980), 114.

38. Milton, *Age of Hate,* 275–276, 311; quotation p. 275; Beale, *Critical Year,* 115–121.

39. McPherson, *Political History,* 60, 61. Johnson named Thaddeus Stevens, Charles Sumner, and activist Wendell Phillips. Johnson was not the first, even in the Republican party, to express such a sentiment, but his status as president gave a completely different significance to such statements; McKitrick, *Johnson and Reconstruction,* 62 n. 41.

40. McKitrick, *Johnson and Reconstruction,* 295.

41. Ibid., 377–420; quotation p. 390 n. 49; McPherson, *Political History,* 127–129.

42. McPherson, *Political History,* 140.

43. James Wilson's minority report refused to impeach Johnson over his use of the spoils for this very reason; *Reports of the Committees of the United States House of Representatives,* 40th Cong., 1st sess. (1867), no. 7, 86. As the Radicals realized, however, the scale and formal nature of Johnson's removals were not the key issues. Johnson threatened to revolutionize the patronage power by altering its intent, by attempting to replace rather than shore up congressional power; Carl Russell Fish, *The Civil Service and the Patronage* (Cambridge, Mass.: Harvard University Press, 1920), 188–190.

44. *House Reports* (1867), 34, 40–41.

45. *Trial of Johnson,* 1:96.

46. Cf. Clinton Rossiter, *The American Presidency* (New York: Signet, 1956), 9–30.

47. *Trial of Johnson,* 1:97, 99–100, 107; 2:44, 421, 424, 442, 447. See also Timothy Farrar, *The Manual of the Constitution of the United States* (Boston: Little, Brown, 1872), 538, 541–442, 545.

48. *Trial of Johnson,* 1:26, 112–113, 115, 676–677; 2:42–43, 112. Stanton had upheld the Radical construction in sending a plea for instructions to the Senate leadership when Johnson ordered his second removal. Senator Sumner took over executive responsibility in sending Stanton a one-word command, "Stick"; Benedict, *Impeachment of Johnson,* 101–102.

49. "When the officers of the government would not bend the knee and cry 'great and good prince,' they saw him attempt to hurl them from his courts"; *Trial of Johnson*, 2:63–64, 114, 228–229; quotations pp. 27, 81, 43; see also Farrar, *Manual of Constitution*, 453.

50. *Trial of Johnson*, 3:66, 217; see also 32–34, 60–64, 103, 137, 163, 310, 312, 318, 352.

51. Ibid., 200. Ralph J. Roske, "The Seven Martyrs?" *American Historical Review* 64 (January 1959): 329; Foner, *Reconstruction*, 488–499; Ari Hoogenboom, *Outlawing the Spoils* (Westport, Conn.: Greenwood Press, 1982), 111–119.

52. Hoogenboom, *Outlawing the Spoils*, 38–39.

53. John Norton Pomeroy, *An Introduction to the Constitutional Law of the United States* (New York: Hurd & Houghton, 1870), 422–439; quotation p. 438. For Pomeroy, this construction gave appropriate meaning to the president's role as chief executive; 416–418.

54. Conkling, *Executive Department*, 125, 98, 119, 139; see generally 95–139. See also Farrar, *Manual of Constitution*, 453–454. On Roscoe Conkling, see White, *Republican Era*, 33–35; Hoogenboom, *Outlawing the Spoils*, 155–171, 204–207; Wilfred E. Binkley, *President and Congress* (New York: Vintage, 1962), 191–197.

55. *Nation*, March 5, 1868, 181–182; ibid., May 14, 1868, 384; Hoogenboom, *Outlawing the Spoils*, 15–39; Fish, *Civil Service and Patronage*, 208; William B. Hesseltine, *Ulysses S. Grant, Politician* (New York: Dodd, Mead, 1935), 150–152. James Garfield later argued that politicized appointments were forever out of reach of the president; "A Century of Congress," *Atlantic Monthly* 40 (July 1877): 60–61.

56. Henry Brook Adams, "Civil Service Reform," *North American Review* 109 (October 1869): 443–475; idem, "The Session," ibid., 108 (1869): 615; Hoogenboom, *Outlawing the Spoils*, 47–48, 53–54, 65–67; Hesseltine, *Grant*, 159–160. By refusing to make an exception to the ethics laws, Congress did exclude Grant's first choice for Treasury and forced him to accept the former House impeachment manager, George Boutwell, demonstrating that even a nonpolitical cabinet was still beholden to Congress; Hesseltine, 147.

57. In his extensive commentary on the Constitution, George Boutwell did not feel compelled to make any reference at all to implied executive powers, even to criticize them; *The Constitution of the United States at the End of the First Century* (Boston: D. C. Heath, 1895).

58. Binkley, *President and Congress*, 171, 190–204; Fish, *Civil Service and Patronage*, 204. Fish's final chapters describe the period before, during, and after the impeachment crisis as "the spoils system triumphant," "the struggle for patronage," and the "period of civil service reform," respectively. Although the reform movement after Johnson did not make steady gains, its pressure was constant, and it was clearly the spoilsmen who were on the

defensive as the civil service construction was secured and elaborated. Grover Cleveland, for example, argued that the Tenure Act was unconstitutional, since it contradicted the authoritative construction of the removal power made by the First Congress. Though determining that the removal power belonged exclusively to the executive, he strained to justify his own removals as necessary for good administration and to punish those who had used their offices for partisan purposes. Political spoils were not an adequate rationale for the exercise of presidential discretion over removals. Grover Cleveland, *Presidential Problems* (New York: Century, 1904), 24–25, 28–32, 39–45.

59. See, e.g., Sidney M. Milkis, *The President and the Parties* (New York: Oxford University Press, 1993), 137–140.

60. McPherson, *Political History,* 71, 60, 83, 127, 172.

61. James W. Ceaser, *Presidential Selection* (Princeton: Princeton University Press, 1979), 123–169; Stephen A. Salmore and Barbara G. Salmore, *Candidates, Parties, and Campaigns* (Washington, D.C.: CQ Press, 1985), 23–24, 28–30; Marvin R. Weisbord, *Campaigning for President* (New York: Washington Square Press, 1966), 3–61. See also Tulis, *Rhetorical Presidency,* 61–93.

62. To emphasize his point, Lincoln transmitted the text of his proposed message to Congress even after his required changes had been made and he had signed the bill into law. Binkley, *President and Congress,* 146.

63. McPherson, *Political History,* 78, 127, 130, 128, 60, 71–72, 83. See also *Congressional Globe,* 40th Cong., 2d sess. (1968), 162, 179, 198–199.

64. Andrew Jackson, *Presidential Messages and State Papers,* ed. Julius W. Muller, vol. 3 (New York: Review of Reviews, 1917), 995–997; Basler, *Abraham Lincoln,* 585–586; Ex Parte Merryman, 17 Fed. Cases 144 (1861).

65. *Trial of Johnson,* 1:39–40. Previously Johnson had darkly hinted at a more energetic doctrine, contending that cases could arise in which the president would be required to "stand on his rights, and maintain them, regardless of the consequences." The extent to which the president might go in defending his rights and what exactly was included among them were left uncertain. In the tense political climate of the winter of 1867–68, Johnson envisioned the possibility of a congressional attempt to suspend him from office or to strip him of explicit powers prior to any impeachment, while some in Congress feared that Johnson was threatening the establishment of a military dictatorship; Andrew Johnson, *Messages and Papers of the Presidents,* ed. James Richardson, vol. 5 (New York: Bureau of National Literature, 1897), 3756–79.

66. *Trial of Johnson,* 1:387–388; see also Pomeroy, *Constitutional Law,* 444–445. See also Salmon Chase, quoted in Milton, *Age of Hate,* 564. It is significant that Johnson asserted at a minimum that the president could publicly agitate against Congress. He insisted on the direct connection between the people and the president, entitling the executive to speak directly

to the people, defend his constitutional vision, and stump for his own policy agenda; *Trial of Johnson,* 1:50–52, 412–413; 2:180, 183.

67. *Trial of Johnson,* 2:136, 126, 200, 272, 292–293. To the extent that such a judgment was inherently "judicial," however, the president only shared in a power primarily possessed by the courts. If the president could resist Congress over disputed authority, it was primarily in order to take the issue to the courts, where the law of the Constitution could be recognized and vindicated; ibid., 1:40, 428; 2:382–383.

68. Ibid., 2:166–167. Nelson's argument shifts ground, away from Curtis' and Johnson' initial claims that the president was merely acting as a citizen. Johnson also insisted that he was unwilling to abandon the claims made for the institution of the presidency by his predecessors, notably Jefferson, Jackson, and Lincoln; 126–127, 163, 167–168, 272, 296, 338, 340.

69. Ibid., 134, 123, 198.

70. Far from embracing "theories of congressional omnipotence," the people had sought to establish an executive branch equal in power to the legislature. Indeed, the defense asserted, the American Revolution had been fought against the "tyranny of Parliament," and that spirit actually required that the executive strictly check Congress; ibid., 271, 273–274; see also 181, 194, 298–305, 327, 378, 383.

71. Ibid., 1:96, 98, 115; 2:70, 72, 402. See also "The Shifting of Powers," *Atlantic Monthly* 27 (June 1871): 665–666; "The President on the Stump," *North American Review* 102 (March 1866): 534.

72. "The President on the Stump," 532–533, 537 538. Johnson's resistance to congressional policy could only be the beginning of an erosion of congressional power that would result in another Caesar, Napoleon, or Cromwell when the shift was complete; *Trial of Johnson,* 1:110–113, 115–117, 120–121; 2:62–63. See also Charles Mayo Ellis, "The Causes for Which a President Can Be Impeached," *Atlantic Monthly* 19 (January 1867): 88–91; *House Reports,* 40th Cong., 1st. sess. (1867), no. 7, 2, 37.

73. *Trial of Johnson,* 1:684; 2:27–28, 18. During the 1866 campaign Stevens had declared: "Congress is the sovergin power, because the people speak through them; and Andrew Johnson must learn that he is your servant and that as Congress shall order he must obey. There is no escape from it. God forbid that he should have one little of power except what he derives through Congress and the Constitution." Since Congress was the effective voice of the sovereign people, however, there was little difference between what Congress required of the president and what the Constitution allowed. Quoted in Binkley, *President and Congress,* 166. See also E. P. Whipple, "The President and Congress," *Atlantic Monthly* 17 (March 1866): 500, 503; "The President on the Stump," 540; *Congressional Globe,* 40th Cong., 2d sess. (1868), 177, 195, 199, 201, 214; Sidney George Fisher, *The Trial of the Constitution* (Philadelphia: J. B. Lippincott, 1862), 60, 142–143; Wil-

liam H. Riker, "Sidney George Fisher and the Separation of Powers during the Civil War," *Journal of the History of Ideas* 15 (June 1954): 397.

74. *Trial of Johnson*, 2:228, 427, 70, 91. Though Boutwell was explicitly arguing the level of deference due to Congress, the force of the managers' arguments indicated that the possibility of any unconstitutional law was so remote as to be virtually impossible.

75. Ibid., 467; see also 239, 246, 256, 465–467.

76. Ibid., 231, 42, 251–252, 397; see also 15–16, 42, 67–68, 105, 109–110, 230–231, 237–238, 251–252, 260–261, 390–392.

77. Ibid., 1:685, 687; 2:256; see also 2:26, 69, 228, 397–399; Farrar, *Manual of Constitution*, 535–545.

78. *Trial of Johnson*, 1:107–108, 122, 682–683, 668; 2:71, 74–75, 91, 223–224, 229, 405–406, 415. See also Farrar, *Manual of Constitution*, 535; Pomeroy, *Constitutional Law*, 443; Fisher, *Trial of Constitution*, 59.

79. Trefousse, *Impeachment*, 131, 151; *Trial of Johnson*, 2:118; McPherson, *Political History*, 366.

80. *Trial of Johnson*, 3:110, 126; see also 15–16, 70, 77–79, 110–111, 123, 134–135, 144, 151–152, 176–177, 193. There was limited support for Johnson's position among the acquitters; ibid., 57, 117–120, 176–177, 193–198, 303.

81. Milton, *Age of Hate*, 533–34; Mantell, *Johnson, Grant, and Reconstruction*, 89–90; Benedict, *Impeachment of Johnson*, 137–139.

82. McPherson, *Political History*, 365, 416, 417.

83. Tulis, *Rhetorical Presidency*, 64–66, 84–87; Binkley, *President and Congress*, 205–227; Woodrow Wilson, *Congressional Government* (New York: Meridian, 1956), 14, 31, 48–50; Henry Adams, "The Session," *North American Review* 111 (February 1870): 41. See also White, *Republican Era*, 20–25, 47; Schlesinger, *Imperial Presidency*, 77–79; James Bryce, *The American Commonwealth* (New York: Macmillan, 1924), 48–49, 156, 166.

84. E.g., Garfield, "Century of Congress," 60–62; "Shifting of Powers," 665–670.

85. Bushnell, *Crimes, Follies, and Misfortunes*, 115–124.

86. *Congressional Globe*, 40th Cong., 2d sess. (1868), 1387; Farrar, *Manual of Constitution*, 533–534. Senator Lyman Trumbull threatened to impeach any judges who interfered with Congress; Milton, *Age of Hate*, 543.

87. *Trial of Johnson*, 1:682. John Bingham concluded for the managers, "I waste no words upon the frivolous questions whether the articles have the technical requisites of an indictment. There is no law anywhere that requires it . . . they are well enough understood . . . that the President stands charged with usurpation of power"; ibid., 2:429–430; see also George Boutwell at 67, John Logan at 18. In advocating impeachment, one congressman assured his colleagues that the "people" would look beyond any technical language used or crimes charged in articles in order to try the real

issue of "grasping and domineering power"; *Congressional Globe,* 40th Cong., 2d sess. (1867), app., 201. Cf. Hyman, *More Perfect Union,* 509.

88. *Trial of Johnson,* 1:89–90. For the correlation between guilty votes and votes to exclude defense evidence, see Rable, "Forces of Darkness," 168–169. For Sumner's motion to admit all evidence, see *Trial of Johnson,* 1:589–590. Sumner wrote in his opinion after the trial: "An impeachment is not a technical proceeding, as at *nisi prius* or in a county court, where the rigid rules of the common law prevail . . . The precision of history is enough without the technical precision of an indictment . . . A mere technicality, much more a quibble . . . is a wretched anachronism when we are considering a question of history or political duty." The impeachment was a "trial of political offenses, before a political body, with a political judgment only"; ibid., 3:253.

89. Quoted in Milton, *Age of Hate,* 378. In the battle over Reconstruction, Thaddeus Stevens made clear that postbellum politics must be structured to guarantee the "perpetual ascendancy" of the Republican party, and preferably the Radical wing of that party. The impeachment served that goal; Brock, *American Crisis,* 100; Benedict, *Impeachment of Johnson,* 21–25, 61–88; Raoul Berger, *Impeachment* (New York: Bantam, 1974), 266.

90. *Congressional Globe,* 40th Cong., 2d sess. (1867), app., 55; McPherson, *Political History,* 177.

91. Farrar, *Manual of Constitution,* 437, 530, 532, 536. "Impeachment is what the law-making power of Congress chooses to make it, or to permit it to become"; Farrar, 529.

92. In contrast, the Federalists favored governmental power but distrusted the impeachment power as a limit on government. The Republicans embraced legislative supremacy, identifying the holder of general governmental power with the wielder of the impeachment weapon; the Federalists were less comfortable with the popular branch of government.

93. Pomeroy, *Constitutional Law,* 485. See also Ellis, "Causes," 89; William Lawrence, "The Law of Impeachment," *American Law Register* 15 (September 1867): 658; Hyman, "Reconstruction," in *New Frontiers,* 1–39; Kelly, "Comment," 40–58; Benedict, "Preserving the Constitution."

94. *Congressional Globe,* 40th Cong., 2d sess. (1867), app., 60–61; *House Reports* (1867), 1–2, 51–55. The managers emphasized that the Senate could not regard itself as any ordinary court, since the president could never be an ordinary defendant. An individual could never step out of the role of president and claim the ordinary rights guaranteed to and reserved for private citizens. Not only would the president overawe an ordinary jury, but he threatened to overwhelm even the Senate, and therefore Congress must always adopt an aggressive posture relative to the president, not the neutral stance of a judge or jury. As an inherently political institution, the Senate

could hope to do nothing else than take into account the effects of Johnson's presidency on the health of the polity; *Trial of Johnson,* 1:116, 26–28, 88–90; 3:208, 213, 280, 368–369.

95. *Trial of Johnson,* 1:135, 137–440; Lawrence, "Law of Impeachment," 646. Lawrence pointed out (659–660) that the power to impeach was given solely to the House, and the power to convict solely to the Senate, while the power to make legislation was given to both jointly. The implication he drew from this was that the two houses of Congress operated independently during an impeachment and could not be bound by the previous joint actions of the whole, notably including legislative definitions of high crimes.

96. *Trial of Johnson,* 1:88–89.

97. Lawrence, "Law of Impeachment," 650; *Trial of Johnson,* 1:94–95.

98. Pomeroy, *Constitutional Law,* 390; Farrar, *Manual of Constitution,* 531; Lawrence, "Law of Impeachment," 677–679; *Trial of Johnson,* 1:146; 2:23–25, 409–413.

99. Conkling, *Executive Department,* 119–120, 139; *Nation,* February 27, 1868, 164; March 5, 1868, 184; Ellis, "Causes," 89, 92; *Trial of Johnson,* 1:88–89, 94–95; 2:220; 3:67–69, 78–79, 151–152, 249–255, 352. For some Republicans the goal was even more narrow, to secure Radical Republicanism in the government; Berger, *Impeachment,* 266; Trefousse, *Impeachment,* 138–147; Benedict, *Impeachment of Johnson,* 21–25, 61–88.

100. For example, in Johnson's official reply to the impeachment, he included no general statement as to the proper scope of the impeachment power and called into doubt the impeachable nature of his speeches only in the context of defending his right to speak to his constituents without fear of "question, inquisition, impeachment or inculpation in any form or manner whatsoever"; *Trial of Johnson,* 1:51, 52.

101. Ibid., 26, 28. As "eminent judges" and not "mere politicians," the senators were required to "place yourselves in Andrew Johnson's position, and to look from his standpoint, and judge in the manner in which he judged"; ibid., 2:121–122.

102. Ibid., 1:377, 379.

103. Theodore Dwight, "Trial by Impeachment," *American Law Register* 15 (March 1867): 257–258, 261; see also 268–269; James Wilson in *House Reports* (1867), 61–63. Dwight's efforts were largely interpretive, but relied upon a prior effort to narrow the range of arguments and evidence that were to be regarded as legitimate. Dwight was explicit in his efforts to separate the appropriate "legal" precedents for understanding the impeachment power from the inappropriate "political" history of the use of the impeachment power. The law professor's article is exemplary of the effort to shift the debate into a legalistic rhetoric and an interpretive mode of argument.

104. Dwight, "Trial by Impeachment," 264; see also 263–267. Cf. Peter Charles Hoffer and N. E. H. Hull, *Impeachment in America, 1635–1805* (New Ha-

ven: Yale University Press, 1984), 3–4, who indicate that it was particularly these excluded cases that indicated the ambiguous and political potential of the impeachment power in the British context.

105. *Trial of Johnson*, 1:408–410; quotation, 2:190; see also 2:130–137.

106. *House Reports* (1867), 67, 105; *Trial of Johnson*, 2:189, 298. See also Dwight, "Trial by Impeachment," 282–83.

107. *Trial of Johnson*, 1:410, 411; 2:130, 142; *House Reports* (1867), 61–62.

108. *House Reports* (1867), 75–77.

109. *Trial of Johnson*, 2:134, 136, 140.

110. Ibid., 288–289, 380, 364. See also 190–191.

111. Three of the articles associated with the Stanton removal did charge violations of other laws, two of a wartime conspiracy act and one of the army appropriations provision that altered the military chain of command. All centered on the same set of actions, and failure to establish the illegality and impeachability of the Stanton removal would have effectively undermined all nine articles. The final article of impeachment was largely a summary of the earlier articles, and thus contained violations both of presidential duty and of statutory law.

112. Of the thirty-nine votes lost on the tenth article relative to the well-supported first eight, thirty-seven were abstentions. The ninth and eleventh articles also lost a significant number of votes to abstentions, eighteen and nineteen respectively; McPherson, *Political History*, 187–190, 264–282; Benedict, *Impeachment of Johnson*, 112–114. Thaddeus Stevens wrote Butler that the original articles lacked "any real vigor," prompting Butler to offer more political articles, in part to establish the broad construction. Butler defended the tenth article by citing the actions of the House against Chase, attacking his moderate detractors for supporting "this old dogma of non-liability for indictable crimes that I had supposed was dead and buried—I knew it stunk"; Benedict, *Impeachment of Johnson*, 112; *Congressional Globe*, 40th Cong., 2d sess. (1868), 1639–40. Frederick Pike had expressed the moderate view the year before: "It is one question whether he has discharged the duties of his office acceptably, and quite another whether, with him for a foot-ball, this house shall enter upon the game of President-making"; ibid., 1st sess. (1867), 587. Wilson changed his vote only because the impeachment was made "inevitable by [Johnson's] own deliberate criminal conduct" after the failure of the earlier impeachment attempt, but he resisted the tenth article as contradicting the construction of the Chase impeachment; ibid., 2d sess. (1868), 1386, 1640–41.

113. Not only did the chief justice insist that the Senate formally adjourn the "court" before considering legislative business, but also he maneuvered the Senate into approving his own right as presiding officer to make initial rulings on matters of law and form and to cast the deciding vote in case of ties. Thus Chase took an active role in the proceedings, emphasizing its judicial tone; *Trial of Johnson*, 3:388, 401; 1:12, 175–188; Benedict, *Impeachment of*

Johnson, 115–122. The right of the states to be represented in the Senate did not extend to the South, however; *Trial of Johnson*, 1:36.

114. *Trial of Johnson*, 2:486–497; Dunning, *Reconstruction*, 107. Though a guilty vote was clearly favored by the Republican party, it was not required; Roske, "Seven Martyrs?" 323.

115. The Tenure Act had been passed in the previous Congress by a Senate vote of twenty-two to ten, and passed again in a straight party vote over the presidential veto, thirty-five to eleven. All seven Republicans who voted for acquittal had supported the Tenure Act in the override; McPherson, *Political History*, 177. Though the specific inclusion of the tenth article forced the managers to adopt a broad construction of the impeachment powers, the Senate did not vote on this article, undoubtedly because of its perceived weakness.

116. *Trial of Johnson*, 3:3, 15.

117. Ibid., 68, 69, 249–255; see also 67, 78–80, 104, 215, 249–255. Howe would have convicted under the tenth article, for "by my own estimate of what the bearing of the Chief Magistrate should be," Johnson had brought the office into disrepute. This opinion was confirmed by the "opinion of the great majority of the American people as expressed at this time"; ibid., 79.

118. Ibid., 280, 352; see also 368–369.

119. E.g., ibid., 82, 95–101, 152, 156–161, 207, 319, 328, 370. The fact that few of the Democrats actually entered opinions for the record suggests the marginality of the narrow construction even if the Democrats matched the Radical strength in voting numbers. Whereas the Radicals could advocate and justify their position, the Democrats could merely cast their quiet votes and observe the proceedings.

120. Ibid., 317, 121–122, 127, 146, 188, 190–191, 213; see also 94, 142, 213.

121. *Nation*, April 30, 1868, 344; May 21, 1868, 404–405, 408.

122. Of course, the impeachment was not only symbolic. The Republicans also genuinely wanted to remove Johnson himself.

123. Myers v. U.S., 272 U.S. 52 (1926); Mississippi v. Johnson, 71 U.S. (4 Wall.) 475 (1867); Georgia v. Stanton, 73 U.S. (6 Wall.) 50 (1867). In his opinion in *Myers* former president William Howard Taft condemned the Tenure Act as an unconstitutional encroachment on the executive, but in order to reach that conclusion he relied heavily on noninterpretive claims about administrative efficiency and the binding quality of the First Congress' decision. The decision sparked sharp dissents at the time and was curtailed a decade later; Humphrey's Executive v. U.S., 295 U.S. 602 (1935). See also Corwin, *The President*, 100–110; William Howard Taft, *Our Chief Magistrate and His Powers* (New York: Columbia University Press, 1925), 56–62.

124. Republican operatives orchestrated massive letter campaigns to demonstrate the electoral consequences of a vote for acquittal, though many Republican papers gradually came to support "independent" voting, free from partisan pressures. If the dissenting Republicans were not actually punished for their

votes, there were clear efforts to convince them during the trial that they would be; Roske, "Seven Martyrs?" 324; idem, "Republican Newspaper Support for the Acquittal of President Johnson," *Tennessee Historical Quarterly* 11 (September 1952): 263; Benedict, *Impeachment of Johnson*, 171; Milton, *Age of Hate*, 552. Though Chase used his own influence to affect the voting, the chief justice was indignant over the operation of the Senate. Chase wrote to a friend: "Think of legislatures, political conventions, even religious bodies, undertaking to instruct Senators how to vote, guilty or not guilty . . . What would be thought of such attempts to drive the decisions of any other courts? All the appliances to force a measure through Congress are in use here to force a conviction through the Court of Impeachment"; quoted in Milton, 604.

5. Richard Nixon and the Leadership of the Modern State

1. Relatively clear evidence of criminality rendered discussion of the outer ranges of the impeachment power politically superfluous. Nixon's immediate resignation added to this sense of finality and contributed to a belief that "Watergate" primarily involved the criminal activities of identifiable individuals. For contrasting perspectives on the impeachment power, see Raoul Berger, *Impeachment* (New York: Bantam, 1974); Charles L. Black Jr., *Impeachment* (New Haven: Yale University Press, 1974). On the limited nature of the Nixon impeachment, see John R. Labovitz, *Presidential Impeachment* (New Haven: Yale University Press, 1978), 90–131; L. H. LaRue, *Political Discourse* (Athens: University of Georgia Press, 1988); John Robert Greene, *The Limits of Power* (Bloomington: Indiana University Press, 1992), 174–178; Philip B. Kurland, *Watergate and the Constitution* (Chicago: University of Chicago Press, 1978), 119–120; Stanley I. Kutler, *The Wars of Watergate* (New York: Alfred A. Knopf, 1990), 136; Dagmar S. Hamilton, "The Nixon Impeachment and the Abuse of Presidential Power," in *Watergate and Afterward*, ed. Leon Friedman and William F. Levantrosser (Westport, Conn.: Greenwood Press, 1992), 199–207. Compare the actual impeachment articles with the proposal of the American Civil Liberties Union, *Why President Richard Nixon Should Be Impeached* (Washington, D.C.: Public Affairs Press, 1973).

2. Joan Hoff, *Nixon Reconsidered* (New York: Basic Books, 1994), 17–144; A. James Reichley, *Conservatives in an Age of Change* (Washington, D.C.: Brookings Institution, 1981), 205–231, 408–409; Michael A. Genovese, *The Nixon Presidency* (Westport, Conn.: Greenwood Press, 1990), 60–95.

3. John Ehrman, *The Rise of Neoconservatism* (New Haven: Yale University Press, 1995), 1–62; Genovese, *Nixon Presidency*, 99–165; Reichley, *Conservatives*, 98–129; Hoff, *Nixon Reconsidered*, 147–273. For a contemporary statement of the end of consensus but also the limits of that fragmentation, see Henry Brandon, *The Retreat of American Power* (Garden City, N.Y.:

Doubleday, 1973); Robert W. Tucker, *The Radical Left and American Foreign Policy* (Baltimore: Johns Hopkins Press, 1971). On the limited congressional support for a positive reorientation of the American international posture, see Aage R. Clausen and Carl E. Van Horn, "The Congressional Response to a Decade of Change: 1963–1972," *Journal of Politics* 39 (August 1977): 652–659; Barbara Sinclair, "Agenda and Alignment Change: The House of Representatives, 1925–1978," in *Congress Reconsidered*, ed. Lawrence C. Dodd and Bruce I. Oppenheimer (Washington, D.C.: CQ Press, 1981), 236–242.

4. Quoted in Genovese, *Nixon Presidency*, 72. Later Nixon wrote: "the alternative to strong Presidential government is government by Congress, which is no government at all"; Richard M. Nixon, *In the Arena* (New York: Simon and Schuster, 1990), 207. Similarly, Nixon contended that he had to be an "activist President" in order to fill the "vacuum created when Congress failed to discipline itself sufficiently to play a strong policy-making role"; quoted in Kutler, *Wars of Watergate*, 127. Cf. Arthur M. Schlesinger Jr., *The Imperial Presidency* (Boston: Houghton Mifflin, 1989), 140, 151, 154.

5. "Having talked of 'restoring the balance,' Eisenhower quickly found himself to be a presidentialist—that is, a defender of the accrued responsibilities of the modern presidency"; Fred I. Greenstein, "Change and Continuity in the Modern Presidency," in *The New American Political System*, ed. Anthony King (Washington, D.C.: American Enterprise Institute, 1978), 59.

6. George H. Nash, *The Conservative Intellectual Movement in America since 1945* (New York: Basic Books, 1979), 84–130, 186–219; Michael W. Miles, *The Odyssey of the American Right* (New York: Oxford University Press, 1980), 47–93, 181–219; Jerome L. Himmelstein, *To the Right* (Berkeley: University of California Press, 1990), 35–45; John Patrick Diggins, *Up from Communism* (New York: Columbia University Press, 1994), 447–450.

7. Greenstein, "Change and Continuity," 45–53; Richard E. Neustadt, *Presidential Power and the Modern Presidents* (New York: Free Press, 1990), 3–9; Stephen Skowronek, *The Politics Presidents Make* (Cambridge, Mass.: Harvard University Press, 1993), 17–32, 288–324; Sidney Milkis, *The President and the Parties* (New York: Oxford University Press, 1993), 52–146.

8. Walter Johnson, quoted in William G. Andrews, "The Presidency, Congress, and Constitutional Theory," in *Perspectives on the Presidency*, ed. Aaron Wildavsky (Boston: Little, Brown, 1975), 26. Richard E. Neustadt advised, "The more determinedly a President seeks power, the more he will bring vigor to his clerkship. As he does so he contributes to the energy of government"; *Presidential Power* (New York: John Wiley and Sons, 1960), 185. See generally Andrews, "Presidency," 24–31; Thomas E. Cronin, "The Textbook Presidency and Political Science," in *Perspectives on the Presidency*, ed. Stanley Bach and George T. Sulzner (Lexington, Mass.: D. C. Heath, 1974), 54–74; idem, *The State of the Presidency* (Boston: Little, Brown, 1975), 23–84; Samuel P. Huntington, "Congressional Responses to the Twentieth

Century," in *The Congress and America's Future,* ed. David Truman (Englewood Cliffs, N.J.: Prentice-Hall, 1965), 5–31.

9. The New Left, for example, was a likely source for a new conceptualization of executive power, but instead it largely expended its efforts on socioeconomic, cultural, and tactical considerations; e.g., the "Port Huron Statement" of the Students for a Democratic Society, reprinted in James Miller, *"Democracy Is in the Streets"* (New York: Simon and Schuster, 1987), 329–374, esp. 337, 362–363. See also Miller, 141–154; Michael Harrington, *Toward a Democratic Left* (Baltimore: Penguin, 1969), 114–123.

10. Kutler, *Wars of Watergate,* 128–133; Schlesinger, *Imperial Presidency,* 254–255, 264–267; Stanley Kelley Jr., *Interpreting Elections* (Princeton: Princeton University Press, 1983), 72–74, 99, 126–129, 168; Theodore J. Lowi, *The Personal President* (Ithaca: Cornell University Press, 1985), 97–133, 143 146, 174–181; Robert A. Dahl, "Myth of the Presidential Mandate," *Political Science Quarterly* 105 (1990): 355. Chief of Staff H. R. Haldeman summed up the administration attitude: "I don't think Congress is supposed to work with the White House—it is a different organization, and under the Constitution I don't think we should expect agreement"; quoted in Kutler, 128.

11. Ronald Randall, "Presidential Power versus Bureaucratic Intransigence: The Influence of Richard Nixon on Welfare Policy," *American Political Science Review* 73 (September 1979): 808; Richard P. Nathan, *The Plot That Failed* (New York: John Wiley and Sons, 1975), 9; Howard Ball, *Controlling Regulatory Sprawl* (Westport, Conn.: Greenwood Press, 1984), 47–51; James P. Pfiffner, "White House Staff versus the Cabinet: Centripetal and Centrifugal Roles," *Presidential Studies Quarterly* 16 (1985): 669–670, 677–679; Fred I. Greenstein, "A President Is Forced to Resign: Watergate, White House Organization, and Nixon's Personality," in *America in the Seventies,* ed. Allan P. Sindler (Boston: Little, Brown, 1977), 68–81; Lowi, *Personal President,* 76–79; Kutler, *Wars of Watergate,* 82–96; Terry M. Moe, "The Politicized Presidency," in *The New Direction in American Politics,* ed. John E. Chubb and Peter E. Peterson (Washington, D.C.: Brookings Institution, 1985), 235–271; Godfrey Hodgson, *All Things to All Men* (New York: Simon and Schuster, 1980).

12. James MacGregor Burns, "Foreword," in Theodore C. Sorensen, *Watchmen in the Night* (Cambridge, Mass.: MIT Press, 1975), xii; Sorensen, *Watchmen,* 75. Similarly, Stanley Kutler concluded that "power and authority were not so much at issue during the Watergate years as were responsibility and accountability"; *Wars of Watergate,* 608. See also Rexford G. Tugwell and Thomas E. Cronin, eds., *The Presidency Reappraised* (New York: Praeger, 1974); Cronin, *State of the Presidency,* 85–116; idem, "Textbook Presidency," 66–74; Andrews, "Presidency," 29–31; Arthur Selwyn Miller, "Implications of Watergate: Some Proposals for Cutting the Presidency Down to Size," *Hastings Constitutional Law Quarterly* 2 (Winter 1975): 33;

Frederick C. Mosher et al., *Watergate* (New York: Basic Books, 1974); George E. Reedy, *The Twilight of the Presidency* (New York: New American Library, 1970), 160–182.

13. Thomas E. Cronin, "An Imperiled Presidency?" in *The Post-Imperial Presidency,* ed. Vincent Davis (New York: Praeger, 1980), 149. See also "Watergate Revisited: A Legislative Legacy," *CQ Almanac* 38 (1982): 387; James Sundquist, "Reflections on Watergate: Lessons for Public Administration," *Public Administration Review* 34 (September/October 1974): 453; idem, *The Decline and Resurgence of Congress* (Washington, D.C.: Brookings Institution, 1981), 199–414; Richard E. Neustadt, "The Constraining of the President: The Presidency after Watergate," *British Journal of Political Science* 4 (1974): 383; Frederick M. Kaiser, "Congressional Oversight of the Presidency," *Annals of the American Academy of the Political and Social Sciences* 499 (September 1988): 75; Lloyd N. Cutler, "A Proposal for a Continuing Public Prosecutor," *Hastings Constitutional Law Quarterly* 2 (Winter 1975): 21; Benjamin R. Civiletti, "Post-Watergate Legislation in Retrospect," *Southwestern Law Journal* 34 (1981): 1043.

14. William G. Munselle, "Congressional Reform: The Case of Impoundment," *Policy Studies Journal* 5 (Summer 1977): 481.

15. See generally Louis Fisher, *Presidential Spending Power* (Princeton: Princeton University Press, 1975); James P. Pfiffner, *The President, the Budget, and Congress* (Boulder: Westview Press, 1979); David A. Martin, "Note: Protecting the Fisc: Executive Impoundment and Congressional Power," *Yale Law Journal* 82 (1973): 1636; "Note: Impoundment of Funds," *Harvard Law Review* 86 (1973): 1505.

16. *Public Papers of the Presidents of the United States: Richard Nixon, 1973* (Washington, D.C.: Government Printing Office, 1975), 62; *Federal Register* 38 (February 6, 1973): 3474. See also Senate Ad Hoc Subcommittee on Impoundment of Funds of the Senate Committee on Government Operations and the Subcommittee on Separation of Powers of the Senate Committee on the Judiciary, *Impoundment of Appropriated Funds by the President: Hearings on S. 373,* 93d Cong., 1st sess. (1973), 369; House Committee on Rules, *Impoundment Control and 1974 Expenditure Limits,* 93d Cong., 1st sess. (1973), H. Rept. 336, 16.

17. The impoundment of funds for the military could be further justified on the basis of the "President's constitutional role as Commander-in-Chief"; Senate Ad Hoc Subcommittee, *Impoundment of Appropriated Funds,* 370, 369, 368; OMB quoted in Martin, "Note," 1637 n. 5. The OMB's claim can be analyzed as purely a question of statutory interpretation, adding little of substance to the president's constitutional authority; ibid., 1645–57; "Note: Impoundment of Funds," 1516–29. However, consideration of this clause and the host of statutes referenced by it also contributes to an understanding of the administration's conception of the "executive power" more broadly in the context of the twentieth century's modern, administrative presidency.

Sneed made clear that the administration regarded statutory language as supplementary to the inherent authority of the president under Article II, which was critical in the "last analysis"; Senate Ad Hoc Subcommittee, 371, 372.

18. On the growth of presidential control over the administrative state, see John Marini, *The Politics of Budget Control* (Washington, D.C.: Crane Russak, 1992); Milkis, *President and Parties,* 21–218; Naomi Caiden, "Paradox, Ambiguity, and Enigma: The Strange Case of the Executive Budget and the United States Constitution," *Public Administration Review* 47 (January/February 1987): 84; Jerry L. McCaffery, "The Development of Public Budgeting in the United States," in *A Centennial History of the American Administrative State,* ed. Ralph Chandler (New York: Free Press, 1987), 345–377; John A. Rohr, *To Run a Constitution* (Lawrence: University Press of Kansas, 1986), 55–194.

19. House Committee, *Impoundment Control,* 17. Because the Nixon controversy centered on domestic spending, critics of the administration were tentatively willing to grant the commander-in-chief's right to control defense spending. Though fed by the Cold War, the administrative presidency of midcentury was not so compartmentalized.

20. *Public Papers of the Presidents of the United States: Lyndon B. Johnson, 1966* (Washington, D.C.: Government Printing Office, 1967), 981. See also House Committee, *Impoundment Control,* 17–18.

21. U.S. Constitution, Art. I, §9; Arthur Selwyn Miller, "Presidential Power to Impound Appropriated Funds: An Exercise in Constitutional Decision Making," *North Carolina Law Review* 43 (1965): 505. See also Edward S. Corwin, *The President* (New York: New York University Press, 1984), 149–151.

22. See, e.g., A. S. Miller, "Presidential Power," 535–536; Martin, "Note," 1645–57; "Impoundment of Funds," 1516–29; Marini, *Budget Control,* 39–140; Munselle, "Congressional Reform," 480.

23. William F. Willoughby, *The Problem of a National Budget* (New York: D. Appleton, 1918), 29, 30; 42 U.S. Stat. 21, ch. 18, §206, 212. See also Caiden, "Paradox," 84–86; Allen Schick, "The Budget Bureau That Was: Thoughts on the Rise, Decline and Future of a Presidential Agency," in Wildavsky, *Perspectives on the Presidency,* 339–360; Herbert Stein, *The Fiscal Revolution in America* (Chicago: University of Chicago Press, 1969); Larry Berman, "The Office of Management and Budget That Almost Wasn't," *Political Science Quarterly* 92 (Summer 1977): 281–285; Hugh Heclo, "OMB and the Presidency—the Problem of 'Neutral Competence,'" *Public Interest* 38 (1975): 84–87, 93; Marini, *Budget Control,* 112, 117; Nixon, *Public Papers, 1973,* 540.

24. *Public Papers of the Presidents of the United States: Richard Nixon, 1972* (Washington, D.C.: Government Printing Office, 1974), 742, 1042. Nixon's proffered construction did favor spending cuts, but his emphasis was

on the "hard choices" that the president had to make in cutting programs, rather than establishing the particular programs or types of programs that should be cut. Indeed, Nixon emphasized that he had followed the desires of others in setting budget priorities, favoring domestic over defense spending; *Public Papers of the Presidents of the United States: Richard Nixon, 1970* (Washington, D.C.: Government Printing Office, 1971), 600–601. See also, Hoff, *Nixon Reconsidered,* 17–144.

25. Richard Nixon, *RN* (New York: Grosset & Dunlap, 1978), 762; *Public Papers, 1970,* 601; *1972,* 743, 965, 992, 1042; *1973,* 62. See also Senate Ad Hoc Subcommittee, *Impoundment of Appropriated Funds,* 367, 369.

26. Nixon, *Public Papers, 1970,* 600.

27. Nixon, *Public Papers, 1972,* 965–966, 741–742, 965–967, 991, 1010, 1042; *1970,* 601; *1973,* 62, 123–124. See also Senate Subcommittee on Separation of Powers of the Senate Judiciary Committee, *Executive Impoundment of Appropriated Funds: Hearings before the Subcommittee on Separation of Powers of the Senate Judiciary Committee,* 92d Cong., 1st sess. (1971), 135; Senate Ad Hoc Subcommittee, *Impoundments of Appropriated Funds,* 269.

28. Train v. City of New York, 420 U.S. 35 (1975).

29. The courts largely avoided the difficulty of a detailed analysis of the legislative history, which indicated much greater uncertainty as to the firmness of congressional appropriations, or of the statutory language itself, which was consistent with most other appropriations bills in seeming to grant great discretion to the executive branch. E.g., City of New York v. Ruckelshaus, 358 F. Supp. 669 (1973); City of New York v. Train, 494 F.2d 1033 (DC Cir. 1974); Minnesota v. Fri, 4–73 Civ. 133 (D.C. Minn. 1973); Florida v. Train, Civ. 73–156 (N.D. Fla. 1974); Brown v. Ruckelshaus, 364 F. Supp. 258 (D. Cal. 1973); Texas v. Ruckelshaus, C.A. no. A-73-CA-38 (W.D. Tex. 1973); Maine v. Train, Civ. 14–51 (D. Maine 1974); Campaign Clean Water, Inc. v. Ruckelshaus, 361 F. Supp. 689 (E.D. Va. 1973); Campaign Clean Water, Inc. v. Train, 489 F. 2d 492 (1973). See also Paul Gewirtz, "The Courts, Congress, and Executive Policy-Making: Notes on Three Doctrines," *Law and Contemporary Problems* 40 (Summer 1976): 46.

30. E.g., Martin; "Note: Impoundment of Funds"; "Note: The Likely Law of Executive Impoundment," *Iowa Law Review* 59 (1973): 50; Mark Cohn, "Note: Impoundment of Funds Appropriated by Congress," *Ohio State Law Journal* 34 (1973): 416; A. S. Miller, "Presidential Power," 505–506, 510, 512, 517, 524, 533, 544.

31. Martin, "Note," 1658. House Committee, *Impoundment Control,* 5–6; *Congressional Record,* 93d Cong., 1st sess. (1973), 39731; Frank Church, "Impoundment of Appropriated Funds: The Decline of Congressional Control over Executive Discretion," *Stanford Law Review* 22 (June 1970): 1252; Sundquist, *Decline and Resurgence,* 207.

32. David B. Frohnmayer, "The Separation of Powers: An Essay on the Vitality of a Constitutional Idea," *Oregon Law Review* 52 (Spring 1973): 226.

33. Caiden, "Paradox," 88; House Committee, *Impoundment Control*, 5; Greene, *Limits*, 206; Kutler, *Wars of Watergate*, 133–136; Allen Schick, *Congress and Money* (Washington, D.C.: Brookings Institution, 1980), 29, 44–45.

34. *Congressional Record*, 93d Cong., 1st sess. (1973), 39352–53, 25543, 39695. See also Church, "Impoundment," 1241–43; *Congressional Record*, 93d Cong., 2d sess. (1974), 7147–48; Senate Ad Hoc Subcommittee, *Impoundment of Appropriated Funds*, 1–2. Many linked budget reform to a more general effort to redefine executive power. *Congressional Record*, 93d Cong., 1st sess. (1973), 25548, 39344, 39348–50, 39364–71, 39557–58, 39696, 39710, 39729–30. See also Terry Sullivan, "Domestic Legislative Coalitions and Impeachment," in Friedman and Levantrosser, *Watergate and Afterward*, 209–218.

35. *Congressional Record*, 93d Cong., 1st sess. (1973), 25553, 25555, 25564–65, 25831–34, 39344, 39351; House Committee, *Impoundment Control*, 5.

36. Senate Committee on Government Operations, *Federal Impoundment Control Procedures Act*, 93d Cong., 1st sess. (1973), S. Rept. 121, 19; *Congressional Record*, 93d Cong., 1st sess. (1973), 39340, 39696, 25555, 39707; see also 25554, 39351–52, 39710, 39731; ibid., 2d sess. (1974), 7157.

37. *Congressional Record*, 93d Cong., 1st sess. (1973), 39710–11, 39348–53, 39725, 39731, 25551–52, 25555, 25560–61, 25566; ibid., 2d sess. (1974), 7157.

38. Schick, *Congress and Money*, 48; Fisher, *Presidential Spending*, 192–194; *Congressional Record*, 93d Cong., 1st sess. (1973), 25546, 25553–56, 25563, 39362, 39725–28, 39736; ibid., 2d sess. (1974), 7146; House Committee, *Impoundment Control*, 5–6.

39. *Congressional Record*, 93d Cong., 1st sess. (1973), 39696, 39710–16, 39737, 25553–55, 25822, 3061; ibid., 2d sess. (1974), 7145–48.

40. Heclo, "OMB," 80; Nixon, *Public Papers, 1973*, 540; Marini, *Budget Control*, 112, 117; Schick, *Congress and Money*, 20–22; Louis Fisher, *Constitutional Conflicts between Congress and the President* (Lawrence: University Press of Kansas, 1997), 228–231; 88 Stat. 323, P.L. 93–344 (1974), Title VI, §601. The Budget Act also required Senate confirmation of the directors of the OMB.

41. The creation of the CBO was the culmination of efforts to match executive evaluative capacity, which included the expansion of the General Accounting Office and the Office of Technology Assessment; Sundquist, *Decline and Resurgence*, 216, 404.

42. *Congressional Record*, 93d Cong., 2d sess. (1974), 7145–48; ibid., 1st sess. (1973), 25545–46, 25553–55, 25822, 39692–96, 39710–16, 39729–30, 39737; Schick, *Congress and Money*, 77–78; John B. Gilmour, *Reconcilable Differences?* (Berkeley: University of California Press, 1990), 7–8, 79; Sorensen, *Watchmen*, 90.

43. Nixon, *Public Papers, 1972*, 992, 744; *Congressional Record*, 93d Cong., 1st sess. (1973), 39554, 39548, 39697, 39706–07, 25544.

44. Senate Committee, *Impoundment Control,* 9; *Congressional Record,* 93d Cong., 1st sess. (1973), 39695–97, 39713–16, 39728, 25544, 25548; Schick, *Congress and Money,* 21; James A. Thurber, "The Impact of Budget Reform on Presidential and Congressional Governance," in *Divided Democracy,* ed. Thurber (Washington, D.C.: CQ Press, 1991), 166; Gilmour, *Reconcilable Differences?* 5. The relative openness of congressional deliberation had been further enhanced by reforms requiring open committee hearings and more recorded votes; Leroy N. Rieselbach, *Congressional Reform* (Washington, D.C.: CQ Press, 1994), 57–58.

45. 88 Stat. 323, P.L. 93-344 (1974), Title X, §1001; *Congressional Record,* 93d Cong., 1st sess. (1973), 39548.

46. Schick, *Congress and Money,* 406–407; idem, *The Capacity to Budget* (Washington, D.C.: Urban Institute, 1990), 111–113; Joel Haveman, *Congress and the Budget* (Bloomington: Indiana University Press, 1978), 181, 189; Thurber, "Impact," 161; Fisher, *Constitutional Conflicts,* 228–231; Caiden, "Paradox," 89–90; Munselle, "Congressional Reform," 483–444.

47. E.g., Aaron Wildavsky, *The Politics of the Budgetary Process* (Boston: Little, Brown, 1964); Richard F. Fenno Jr., *The Power of the Purse* (Boston: Little, Brown, 1966); R. Kent Weaver, *Automatic Government* (Washington, D.C.: Brookings Institution, 1988).

48. Dennis S. Ippolito, *Uncertain Legacies* (Charlottesville: University Press of Virginia, 1990); Donald F. Kettl, *Deficit Politics* (New York: Macmillan, 1992), 129–132; Schick, *Capacity to Budget,* 101–113, 159–93; Gilmour, *Reconcilable Differences?*

49. Cf. Louis Fisher, "Ten Years of the Budget Act: Still Searching for Controls," *Public Budgeting & Finance* 5 (Autumn 1985): 14; idem, "The Budget Act: A Further Loss of Spending Control," in *Congressional Budgeting,* ed. W. Thomas Wander, F. Ted Herbert, and Gary W. Copeland (Baltimore: Johns Hopkins University Press, 1984), 170–189.

50. Cf. Thurber, "Impact," 145–167.

51. See also Schick, *Congress and Money,* 72–74; idem, *Capacity to Budget,* 159–193; Ippolito, *Legacies,* 18–19. To this extent, the "line-item veto" represents an amelioration of the 1974 construction, though being subject to congressional override remains consistent with the flexibility of controlling executive discretion within the context of congressional budgeting.

52. U.S. v. Curtiss-Wright Export Corp., 299 U.S. 304, 328 (1936). Gordon Silverstein has usefully emphasized that the Court also sought to maximize national power to engage in foreign policy; *Imbalance of Powers* (New York: Oxford University Press, 1997), 36–42.

53. Mora v. McNamara, 389 U.S. 934 (1967); McArthur v. Clifford, 393 U.S. 810 (1968); Massachusetts v. Laird, 400 U.S. 886 (1970); Da Costa v. Laird, 405 U.S. 979 (1972); Velvel v. Johnson, 287 F. Supp. 846 (1968); Berk v. Laird, 317 F. Supp. 715 (1970); Orlando v. Laird, 443 F.2d 1043 (1971); Luftig v. McNamara, 373 F.2d 664 (1967).

54. E.g., Schlesinger, *Imperial Presidency*, 132–136; Louis Fisher, *Presidential War Power* (Lawrence: University Press of Kansas, 1995), 95–133. Senator Robert Taft was one of the few vocal opponents of this pattern of congressional deference; James T. Patterson, *Mr. Republican* (Boston: Houghton Mifflin, 1972), 197.

55. E.g., Johnson, *Public Papers, 1966*, 685; Leonard C. Meeker, "The Legality of United States Participation in the Defense of South Viet-Nam," March 8, 1966, reprinted in *Congressional Record*, 91st Cong., 2d sess. (1970), 20974–75. On Johnson's personalization of the war more generally, see Larry Berman, *Lyndon Johnson's War* (New York: W. W. Norton, 1989).

56. That Vietnam was a "presidential war" does not indicate that there was no congressional support for it. Rather, the Americanization of the Vietnamese conflict was undertaken in the context of congressional deference to the president, even if congressmen as well as the general public approved of the specific actions the executive took. The administration had already abandoned any reliance on the Tonkin resolution for legal justification for the war, and Congress refused to adopt more stringent measures that would have cut off funds and required a withdrawal from Vietnam or even from Cambodia.

57. *Congressional Record*, 90th Cong., 1st sess. (1967), 20703. See also ibid., 91st Cong., 2d sess. (1970), 13828, 13885, 15555, 15723, 37398, 37400, ibid., 93d Cong., 1st sess. (1973), 24662–64; Senate Committee on Foreign Relations, *National Commitments*, 90th Cong., 1st sess. (1967), S. Rept. 797, 5; idem, *War Powers Legislation, 1973: Hearings before the Committee on Foreign Relations on S. 440*, 93d Cong., 1st sess. (1973), 6, 112, 240; idem, *War Powers Legislation: Hearings before the Committee on Foreign Relations on S. 731, S.J. Res. 18, and S.J. Res. 59*, 91st Cong., 1st sess. (1971), 8–10, 31. See J. William Fulbright, "American Foreign Policy in the 20th Century under an 18th-Century Constitution," *Cornell Law Quarterly* 47 (Fall 1961): 1.

58. *Congressional Record*, 91st Cong., 2d sess. (1970), 37398; ibid., 92d Cong., 1st sess. (1971), 28873; ibid., 93d Cong., 1st sess. (1973), 24699–700; Senate Committee, *War Powers, 1973*, 61.

59. U.S. Constitution, Art. 1, §8; Senate Committee, *War Powers, 1973*, 5, 6, 11. Berger's use of the term "construction" is propitious, but he does not fully indicate its distinctive nature from interpretation.

60. Senate Committee, *War Powers, 1973*, 20–21.

61. William B. Spong Jr., "The War Powers Resolution Revisited: Historic Accomplishment or Surrender?" *William and Mary Law Review* 16 (1975): 844. See also Senate Committee, *War Powers, 1973*, 3–5, 64, 108, 110, 112; *Congressional Record*, 91st Cong., 2d sess. (1970), 37398; ibid., 92d Cong., 1st sess. (1971), 28873–75; ibid., 93d Cong., 1st sess. (1973), 24654–59, 24699–700.

62. *Congressional Record*, 91st Cong., 2d sess. (1970), 13887, 13885.

63. *Congressional Record,* 90th Cong., 1st sess. (1967), 20704, 20703.

64. E.g., Senate Committee, *War Powers, 1971,* 518–519; *Congressional Record,* 93d Cong., 1st sess. (1973), 25054–56; ibid., 92d Cong., 1st sess. (1971), 28873.

65. *Congressional Record,* 93d Cong., 1st sess. (1973), 20702–04; ibid., 91st Cong., 2d sess. (1970), 13828, 37400; ibid., 92d Cong., 1st sess. (1971), 28877; ibid., 93d Cong., 1st sess. (1973), 24699–703; Senate Committee, *War Powers, 1973,* 40; Senate Committee, *War Powers, 1971,* 516, 530; Senate Committee, *National Commitments,* 7–8.

66. Senate Committee, *War Powers, 1973,* 110; *Congressional Record,* 91st Cong., 2d sess. (1970), 13886; ibid., 93d Cong., 1st sess. (1973), 24697.

67. *Congressional Record,* 91st Cong., 2d sess. (1970), 13826, 15555, 37339–400.

68. Ibid., 93d Cong., 1st sess. (1973), 24657–64, 24697, 25052–53; Senate Committee, *War Powers, 1971,* 91–92, 516.

69. Senate Committee, *War Powers, 1973,* 56–57, 100. By identifying the presidential office with the nation for purposes of national security, the administration allowed the president to justify any military actions with reference to external events rather than domestic procedures. Thus, for example, Secretary of Defense Elliot Richardson gave on a Sunday morning interview show what became the official administration statement regarding its constitutional authority for the renewed bombing in Vietnam after the American withdrawal, stating that "Basically I believe that our Constitutional authority rests on the circumstances that we are coming out of a ten-year period of conflict. This is the wind-up." Good policy was equivalent to constitutional authority; ibid., 105. Similarly, American military failures were presidential failures. Resisting congressional dissent, Nixon argued: "if the United States at this time leaves Vietnam, and allows a Communist takeover, the office of President of the United States will lose respect, and I am not going to let that happen"; *Public Papers, 1972,* 561.

70. Senate Committee, *War Powers, 1973,* 59–60, 117; Eugene V. Rostow, "Great Cases Make Bad Law: The War Powers Act," *Texas Law Review* 50 (1972): 833; *Congressional Record,* 91st Cong., 2d sess. (1970), 20974–75, 15721–23; ibid., 93d Cong., 1st sess. (1973), 25056–57; J. T. Emerson, "War Powers Legislation," *West Virginia Law Review* 74 (1972): 53.

71. *The Writings of James Madison,* ed. Gaillard Hunt, vol. 9 (New York: G. P. Putnam's Sons, 1910), 372.

72. Youngstown Sheet & Tube Co. v. Sawyer, 343 U.S. 579, 610–11 (1952); see also U.S. v. Midwest Oil Co., 236 U.S. 459, 474 (1915).

73. *Congressional Record,* 91st Cong., 2d sess. (1970), 20974–75, 15721–23; Rostow, "Great Cases," 834. The administration made use of such lists with less facility. Ultimately the administration would only point to the brute fact of presidential warmaking without taking a stand on the significance of that fact. Thus, Secretary of State William Rogers "disavowed them as a prece-

dent. I was just citing what had happened throughout history . . . the way the Constitution has worked in fact over the years, right or wrong"; Senate Committee, *War Powers, 1971,* 529.

74. Senate Committee, *War Powers, 1973,* 93, 100; *1971,* 498, 525. See also William P. Rogers, "Congress, the President, and the War Powers," *California Law Review* 59 (1971): 1194; Nixon, *Public Papers, 1973,* 893.

75. Rogers, "Congress, President, and War Powers," 1208. See also, *Public Papers of the Presidents of the United States: Richard Nixon, 1971* (Washington, D.C.: Government Printing Office, 1972), 599.

76. *Congressional Record,* 91st Cong., 2d sess. (1970), 15555, 15720.

77. Ibid., 15723, 13827; ibid., 93d Cong., 1st sess. (1973), 25077. See also ibid., 91st Cong., 2d sess. (1970), 15553, 15719, 37403; ibid., 92d Cong., 1st sess. (1971), 28873

78. Nixon, *Public Papers, 1973,* 895.

79. *Congressional Record,* 93d Cong., 1st sess. (1973), 24654–78, 24697–99.

80. "Congress had answered the President's usurpation of its most solemn power by legitimizing it"; Thomas Eagleton, *War and Presidential Power* (New York: Liveright, 1974), 220. See also Sorensen, *Watchmen,* 21; *Congressional Record,* 92d Cong., 1st sess. (1971), 28878; ibid., 93d Cong., 1st sess. (1973), 24659–98, 25052–53.

81. Sundquist, *Decline and Resurgence,* 238–314; Fisher, *Constitutional Conflicts,* 309, 323–324, Greene, *Limits,* 205; Kutler, *Wars of Watergate,* 601; Philip Brenner and William M. LeoGrande, "Congress and Nicaragua: The Limits of Alternative Policy Making," in Thurber, *Divided Democracy,* 220 221.

82. Christopher J. Deering, "Congress, the President, and War Powers: The Perennial Debate," in Thurber, *Divided Democracy,* 172, 186–189; Louis Fisher, "President Clinton as Commander in Chief," in *Rivals for Power,* ed. James A. Thurber (Washington, D.C.: CQ Press, 1996), 214–224; Brenner and LeoGrande, "Nicaragua," 220–221; Kutler, *Wars of Watergate,* 602–603; *Congressional Record,* 93d Cong., 1st sess. (1973), 24703.

83. Louis Fisher, "War Powers: the Need for Collective Judgment," in Thurber, *Divided Democracy,* 199, 212–215; Deering, "War Powers," 187–188; Sundquist, *Decline and Resurgence,* 239, 263, 270–272; Howard E. Shuman, "National Security—Shared and Divided Powers," in *The Constitution and National Security,* ed. Howard E. Shuman and Walter R. Thomas (Washington, D.C.: National Defense University Press, 1990), 69–71; Michael J. Glennon, "The War Powers Resolution Ten Years Later: More Politics than Law," *American Journal of International Law* 76 (July 1984): 581; Thomas Mann, "Making Foreign Policy: President and Congress," in *A Question of Balance,* ed. Mann (Washington, D.C.: Brookings Institution, 1990), 1; Robert Katzmann, "War Powers: Toward a New Accommodation," in Mann, *Question of Balance,* 35; Barry Blechman, *The Politics of National Security* (New York: Oxford University Press, 1990), 167; Graham

T. Allison, "Making War: The President and Congress," *Law and Contemporary Problems* 40 (Summer 1976): 96–105; Thomas M. Franck and Edward Weisband, *Foreign Policy by Congress* (New York: Oxford University Press, 1979), 61–162; Susan R. Burgess, *Contest for Constitutional Authority* (Lawrence: University Press of Kansas, 1992), 65–108.

84. Tony G. Poveda, *Lawlessness and Reform* (Pacific Grove, Calif.: Brooks/ Cole, 1990), 15–40; Kenneth O'Reilly, "The New Deal and the FBI: The Roosevelt Administration, Crime Control, and National Security," *Journal of American History* 69 (December 1982): 638, 646, 647–651; Morton Halperin et al., *The Lawless State* (New York: Penguin, 1976), 95–99; Barton J. Bernstein, "The Road to Watergate and Beyond: The Growth and Abuse of Executive Authority since 1940," *Law and Contemporary Problems* 40 (Spring 1976): 64.

85. John T. Elliff, "Congress and the Intelligence Community," in *Congress Reconsidered,* ed. Lawrence C. Dodd and Bruce Oppenheimer (New York: Praeger, 1977), 195; O'Reilly, "New Deal and FBI," 651–656; Halperin et al., *Lawless State,* 97; Rhodri Jeffreys-Jones, *The CIA and American Democracy* (New Haven: Yale University Press, 1989), 24–41; Harry Howe Ransom, "Congress and Reform of the C.I.A.," *Policy Studies Journal* 5 (Summer 1977): 477; Glenn P. Hastedt, "The Constitutional Control of Intelligence," *Intelligence and National Security* 1 (May 1986): 255–258; Frank J. Smist Jr., *Congress Oversees the United States Intelligence Community, 1947–1994* (Knoxville: University of Tennessee Press, 1994), 4–6; 50 U.S.C. §430 (1970).

86. Bernstein, "Road to Watergate," 65–74; Poveda, *Lawlessness,* 44–55; Ransom, "Reform of C.I.A.," 477; Halperin et al., *Lawless State,* 61–236; Richard E. Morgan, *Domestic Intelligence* (Austin: University of Texas Press, 1980), 39–56; James Kirkpatrick Davis, *Spying on America* (Westport, Conn.: Praeger, 1992); Athan Theoharis, *Spying on Americans* (Philadelphia: Temple University Press, 1978).

87. Morgan, *Domestic Intelligence,* 40; Halperin et al., *Lawless State,* 97; Poveda, *Lawlessness,* 43–56.

88. Hastedt, "Control of Intelligence," 258; Elliff, "Intelligence Community," 196–97.

89. Loch Johnson, *A Season of Inquiry* (Lexington: University Press of Kentucky, 1985), 6–8; Elliff, "Intelligence Community," 195–197; Hastedt, "Control of Intelligence," 258–259; Ransom, "Reform of C.I.A.," 477; Smist, *Congress Oversees,* 4–6; Halperin et al., *Lawless State,* 114–115; John M. Oseth, *Regulating U.S. Intelligence Operations* (Lexington: University Press of Kentucky, 1985), 42–44; Loch Johnson, "Legislative Reform of Intelligence Policy," *Polity* 17 (Spring 1985): 551, 558–559; Senate Select Committee to Study Governmental Operations with Respect to Intelligence Activities, *Intelligence Activities and the Rights of Americans,* 94th Cong., 1st sess. (1976), S. Rept. 755v2, 280–281.

90. Poveda, *Lawlessness,* 43–70; Jeffreys-Jones, *CIA and Democracy,* 139–193; J.

Anthony Lukas, *Nightmare* (New York: Viking Press, 1976), 7, 20; Kutler, *Wars of Watergate,* 112.

91. Quoted in Elliff, "Intelligence Community," 198. See also, e.g., Sorensen, *Watchmen,* 15, 53; Lukas, *Nightmare,* 7, 20; Kutler, *Wars of Watergate,* 579; Genovese, *Nixon Presidency,* 1–19, 223; James David Barber, *The Presidential Character* (Englewood Cliffs, N.J.: Prentice-Hall, 1985), 299–388.

92. Jeffreys-Jones, *CIA and Democracy,* 118–193; Kutler, *Wars of Watergate,* 100–14; Lukas, *Nightmare,* 10–118.

93. Franck and Weisband, *Foreign Policy by Congress,* 115–134; Genovese, *Nixon Presidency,* 99–170; Greene, *Limits,* 78–127.

94. Bernstein, "Road to Watergate," 73–74; Greene, *Limits,* 56–64; Kutler, *Wars of Watergate,* 126–160; Poveda, *Lawlessness,* 52–69; Halperin et al., *Lawless State,* 7, 119, 124; Martin Shefter, "Party, Bureaucracy, and Political Change in the United States," in *Political Parties,* ed. Sandy Maisel and Joseph Cooper (Beverly Hills: Sage, 1978), 243–254. On the rhetoric of the "rule of law," see LaRue, *Political Discourse.*

95. Morgan, *Domestic Intelligence,* 4–5; Poveda, *Lawlessness,* 4–6, 68–70; Johnson, *Season,* 9–11; Franck and Weisband, *Foreign Policy by Congress,* 115–134; Jeffreys Jones, *CIA and Democracy,* 176–218; Kathryn S. Olmsted, *Challenging the Secret Government* (Chapel Hill: University of North Carolina Press, 1996), 11–27.

96. Ransom, "Reform of C.I.A.," 478; Elliff, "Intelligence Community," 199–201; Johnson, "Legislative Reform," 552–53; Hastedt, "Control of Intelligence," 259; Franck and Weisband, *Foreign Policy by Congress,* 117–118; *Congressional Record,* 93d Cong., 1st sess. (1973), 25079, 25092. The 1970 Case Act had barred CIA paramilitary operations in Cambodia, but Congress was unwilling to move from negating a particular policy decision to making a more general rule; Jeffreys-Jones, *CIA and Democracy,* 185.

97. On the limits of judicial involvement in intelligence, see Morgan, *Domestic Intelligence,* 104–125; Marc Palay, "Note: The Fourth Amendment and Judicial Review of Foreign Intelligence Wiretapping: *Zweibon v. Mitchell,*" *George Washington Law Review* 45 (November 1976): 55; Morton Halperin, "National Security and Civil Liberties," *Foreign Policy* 21 (Winter 1975–76): 125; Oseth, *Regulating Intelligence,* 53–57.

98. Mapp v. Ohio, 367 U.S. 643 (1961); Katz v. U.S., 389 U.S. 347 (1967); 18 U.S.C. §§2510–20 (1970).

99. U.S. v. U.S. District Court, 407 U.S. 297, 313–322 (1972).

100. Laird v. Tatum, 408 U.S. 1 (1972). Similarly, an appellate court took up the issue of a warrantless search for the purposes of foreign intelligence only to conclude that the judiciary was not competent to examine critically the administration's judgment of a national security interest in the case. The "reasonableness" of a national security search under the Fourth Amendment ultimately required a political, not judicial, determination. U.S. v. Butenko, 494 F.2d 593 (1974).

101. Cf. Morgan, *Domestic Intelligence,* 120.

102. Johnson, *Season*, 10–11; Smist, *Congress Oversees*, 26–27.

103. *Public Papers of the Presidents of the United States: Gerald R. Ford, 1975* (Washington, D.C.: Government Printing Office, 1977), 1555, 1508.

104. Quoted in Johnson, *Season*, 168, 38.

105. E.g., Smist, *Congress Oversees*, 173–174. Though apparently less of a perceived problem than the House, Senate Select Committee Chairman Frank Church's presidential campaign also caused persistent concerns; e.g., Johnson, *Season*, 164–165.

106. Quoted in Johnson, *Season*, 38–39. See also Ford, *Public Papers, 1975*, 1508; *Congressional Record*, 94th Cong., 2d sess. (1976), 14162–64, 14645, 13986, 13992.

107. The unrelated assassination of the chief CIA operative in Greece during the investigations served as a reminder of the stakes of unauthorized disclosures; Jeffreys-Jones, *CIA and Democracy*, 178–179, 185, 196–200, 211–212; Smist, *Congress Oversees*, 134–137, 155–157, 186–189; Johnson, *Season*, 184–214; *Congressional Record*, 94th Cong., 2d sess. (1976), 13683, 13978–79, 13981–82, 14645.

108. Halperin et al., *Lawless State*, 224–225; Johnson, *Season*, 86–87, 137; Smist, *Congress Oversees*, 72–75; Senate Select Committee to Study Governmental Operations with Respect to Intelligence Activities, *Supplementary Detailed Staff Reports on Foreign and Military Intelligence*, 94th Cong., 1st sess. (1976), S. Rept. 755v4, 157–158. See also Smist, 168; Johnson, 82; Oseth, *Regulating Intelligence*, 3–4, 65–67.

109. Oseth, *Regulating Intelligence*, 71–100, quotation p. 97; Smist, *Congress Oversees*, 79–80; Johnson, *Season*, 193–197; idem, "Legislative Reform," 554–555; Halperin et al., *Lawless State*, 245–252; Poveda, *Lawlessness*, 76–77, 85, 169; Olmsted, *Secret Government*, 172–175; Commission on CIA Activities within the United States, *Report to the President* (Washington, D.C.: Government Printing Office, 1975).

110. Senate Select Committee to Study Governmental Operations with Respect to Intelligence Activities, *Foreign and Military Intelligence*, 94th Cong., 1st sess. (1976), S. Rept. 755v1, 31–40.

111. Smist, *Congress Oversees*, 25–81, 134–213; Johnson, *Season*, 12–26.

112. *Congressional Record*, 94th Cong., 2d sess. (1976), 13683, 13687–88, 13690.

113. Ibid., 13974, 13693; Senate Select Committee, *Intelligence Activities and the Rights of Americans*, 266–268, 277–281.

114. *Congressional Record*, 94th Cong., 2d sess. (1976), 13977–79, 13974, 13689–95, 13683, 13687; House Permanent Select Committee on Intelligence, *Intelligence Oversight Act of 1980*, 96th Cong., 2d sess. (1980), H. Rept. 1153, 1–2; Senate Select Committee, *Intelligence Activities and the Rights of Americans*, 291–292; Barry Goldwater, "Congress and Intelligence Oversight," *Washington Quarterly* 6 (Summer 1983): 17–18; Johnson, *Season*, 31; Poveda, *Lawlessness*, 73–86, 167–180.

115. Halperin et al., *Lawless State*, 256–269; Robert Borosage, "Secrecy vs. the

Constitution," *Society* 12 (March/April 1975): 71; Paul W. Blackstock, "Political Surveillance and the Constitutional Order," *Worldview* 14 (May 1971): 11; Theohoris; Laird v. Tatum, 408 U.S. 1, 28 (1972); Morgan, *Domestic Intelligence,* 104–125.

116. Borosage, "Secrecy," 72; Halperin et al., *Lawless State,* 256, 263. Such understandings gained support from the New Left's ambiguous calls for a "participatory democracy"; Miller, *Democracy,* 141–154, 333.

117. *Congressional Record,* 94th Cong., 2d sess. (1976), 13688, 13683, 13981; Senate Select Committee, *Intelligence Activities and the Rights of Americans,* 289. Cf. *Congressional Record,* 94th Cong., 2d sess. (1976), 13996.

118. *Congressional Record,* 94th Cong., 2d sess. (1976), 13683, 13682, 13687, 13689, 13691, 13695; Senate Select Committee, *Intelligence Activities and Rights of Americans,* 292–293. The ease with which concerns about "democracy" could be rolled into reforms to enhance "accountability" to Congress via enhanced oversight can be seen in Arthur Macy Cox, *The Myths of National Security* (Boston: Beacon Press, 1975), esp. 1–3, 61–86, 150–210.

119. Halperin, "Civil Liberties," 130–131; Oseth, *Regulating Intelligence,* 64; Senate Select Committee on Intelligence, *Foreign Intelligence Surveillance Act of 1978,* 95th Cong., 1st sess. (1978), S. Rept. 701, 9–15; Morgan, *Domestic Intelligence,* 100; Halperin et al., *Lawless State,* 263–269.

120. Smist, *Congress Oversees,* 152, 155–157, 176; *Congressional Record,* 94th Cong., 2d sess. (1976), 13981–82, 13986–87; Halperin et al., *Lawless State,* 256–263.

121. Smist, *Congress Oversees,* 82–85, 214–217; Johnson, *Season,* 233; Ransom, "Reform of C.I.A.," 479; Loch Johnson, "The U.S. Congress and the CIA: Monitoring the Dark Side of Government," *Legislative Studies Quarterly* 4 (November 1980): 491–492; *Congressional Record,* 94th Cong., 2d sess. (1976), 13683, 14164, 13988, 13992, 13996 97, 13978–79.

122. Goldwater, "Intelligence Oversight," 17. See also Johnson, "Legislative Reform," 567; Senate Select Committee on Intelligence, *Intelligence Oversight Act of 1980,* 96th Cong., 2d sess. (1980), S. Rept. 730, 5.

123. Smist, *Congress Oversees,* 331. See also Johnson, *Season,* 252–267; Poveda, *Lawlessness,* 167–180; Elliff, "Intelligence Community," 202–205; Loch Johnson, "Playing Hardball with the CIA," in *The President, the Congress, and the Making of Foreign Policy,* ed. Paul E. Peterson (Norman: University of Oklahoma Press, 1994), 69; Gregory Treverton, "Intelligence: Welcome to the American Government," in Mann, *Question of Balance,* 70.

124. Smist, *Congress Oversees,* 214–331; Johnson, "Hardball," 49–73; Treverton, "Intelligence," 79–108; Elliff, "Intelligence Community," 202–205.

125. This is not simply the "war powers model." Congress has merely claimed that the executive branch should be responsive in the realm of intelligence, not that Congress holds authority over intelligence. The two debates followed related but ultimately distinct dynamics. Cf. Silverstein, *Imbalance,* 141–144.

126. See also Moe, "Politicized Presidency."

127. Johnson, "Hardball," 65–69; Treverton, "Intelligence," 80–93. See also Mathew McCubbins and Thomas Schwartz, "Congressional Oversight Overlooked: Police Patrols versus Fire Alarms," *American Journal of Political Science* 28 (February 1984): 165. The ambivalent nature of the congressional reforms suggests that Iran-Contra is better conceptualized as more akin to Vietnam than to Watergate; Koh, *National Security Constitution*, 3. Cf. Fisher, *War Power*, 178–181.

128. Ransom, "Reform of C.I.A.," 479–480; Poveda, *Lawlessness*, 73–88, 167–82; Oseth, *Regulating Intelligence*, 103–162; Jeffreys-Jones, *CIA and Democracy*, 216–228; Anne Karalekas, "Intelligence Oversight: Has Anything Changed?" *Washington Quarterly* 6 (Summer 1983): 23–30; Johnson, *Season*, 254–256; Halperin et al., *Lawless State*, 263–279; *Congressional Record*, 94th Cong., 2d sess. (1976), 13981.

129. Poveda, *Lawlessness*, 73–86, 127–143, 167–180; Davis, *Spying*, 176–180; Kutler, *Wars of Watergate*, 585–586. Recent events further confirm the nature and limits of the intelligence construction. Federal law enforcement agencies have been shown to have extensive intelligence networks in domestic but marginal religious and political communities, though such networks remain insufficient to prevent all criminal incidents related to such groups.

130. These are the choices offered by Mathew McCubbins, "Government on Lay-Away: Federal Spending and Deficits under Divided Party Control," in *The Politics of Divided Government*, ed. Gary W. Cox and Samuel Kernell (Boulder: Westview Press, 1991), 116. McCubbins favors the delegation view and rather uncharitably ascribes the "abdication" view to James Sundquist, who does not use the term himself; *Decline and Resurgence*, 12, 35–36. McCubbins has made clear elsewhere that the delegation model assumes conscious congressional decisions to employ an agent to perform duties unquestionably belonging to Congress; D. Roderick Kiewiet and Mathew D. McCubbins, *The Logic of Delegation* (Chicago: University of Chicago Press, 1991). Such assumptions are obviously inappropriate in cases of constitutional construction, where the locus of primary responsibility is precisely what is at stake in the conflict. Generalizing McCubbins' model to such disputes incorrectly presumes both legislative supremacy and relatively clear and inflexible constitutional meaning.

131. McCubbins, "Lay-Away," 116.

6. Building the American Constitution

1. Alexander M. Bickel, *The Least Dangerous Branch* (Indianapolis: Bobbs-Merrill, 1962); Ronald Dworkin, *A Matter of Principle* (Cambridge, Mass.: Harvard University Press, 1985).

2. On this theme, see also Susan R. Burgess, *Contest for Constitutional Authority* (Lawrence: University Press of Kansas, 1992); Walter F. Murphy, "Who Shall Interpret? The Quest for the Ultimate Constitutional Interpreter,"

Review of Politics 48 (1986): 406; Robert Nagel, *Constitutional Cultures* (Berkeley: University of California Press, 1989); Robert Burt, *The Constitution in Conflict* (Cambridge, Mass.: Harvard University Press, 1992); John Agresto, *The Supreme Court and Constitutional Democracy* (Ithaca: Cornell University Press, 1984); Sanford Levinson, *Constitutional Faith* (Princeton: Princeton University Press, 1988); Louis Fisher, *Constitutional Dialogues* (Princeton: Princeton University Press, 1988).

3. A better understanding of nonjudicial constitutional development may well help explain the judicial development of constitutional law; e.g., Bruce Ackerman *We the People,* vol. 1 (Cambridge, Mass.: Harvard University Press, 1991); Stephen M. Griffin, *American Constitutionalism* (Princeton: Princeton University Press, 1996); Howard Gillman, "The Collapse of Constitutional Originalism and the Rise of the Notion of the 'Living Constitution' in the Course of American State-Building," *Studies in American Political Development* 11 (1997): 191.

4. E.g., Rogers M. Smith, "If Politics Matters: Implications for a 'New Institutionalism,'" *Studies in American Political Development* 6 (Spring 1992): 14–30; Gerald Berk, *Alternative Tracks* (Baltimore: Johns Hopkins University Press, 1994); Michael W. McCann, *Rights at Work* (Chicago: University of Chicago Press, 1994); Susan R. Burgess, "Beyond Instrumental Politics: The New Institutionalism, Legal Rhetoric, and Judicial Supremacy," *Polity* 25 (1993): 445. Cf. Bert A. Rockman, "The New Institutionalism and the Old Institutions," in *New Perspectives on American Politics,* ed. Lawrence C. Dodd and Calvin Jillson (Washington, D.C.: CQ Press, 1994), 152, 157; William H. Riker, "Heresthetic and Rhetoric in the Spatial Model," in *Advances in the Spatial Theory of Voting,* ed. James Enelow and Melvin Hinich (New York: Cambridge University Press, 1990).

5. For a layered model of political development, see also Karen Orren and Stephen Skowronek, "Beyond the Iconography of Order: Notes for a 'New Institutionalism,'" in *The Dynamics of American Politics,* ed. Lawrence C. Dodd and Calvin Jillson (Boulder: Westview Press, 1994); Orren and Skowronek, "Institutions and Intercurrence: Theory Building in the Fullness of Time," in *Nomos, 38: Political Order,* ed. Ian Shapiro and Russell Hardin (New York: New York University Press, 1996).

6. E.g., Gordon Wood, *The Creation of the American Republic, 1776–1787* (New York: W. W. Norton, 1969), 519–615; Stephen Skowronek, *The Politics Presidents Make* (Cambridge, Mass.: Harvard University Press, 1993), 55–57; Walter Dean Burnham, *Critical Elections and the Mainsprings of American Politics* (New York: W. W. Norton, 1970), 175–193.

7. On punctuated change, see Stephen Jay Gould and Niles Eldredge, "Punctuated Equilibria: The Tempo and Mode of Evolution Reconsidered," *Paleobiology* 3 (1977): 115; Stephen D. Krasner, "Approaches to the State: Alternative Conceptions and Historical Dynamics," *Comparative Politics* 16 (January 1983): 240–243.

8. Cf. the few revolutionary "constitutional moments" outlined by Ackerman, *We the People.*

9. See Paul Kleppner, *Continuity and Change in Electoral Politics, 1892–1928* (Westport, Conn.: Greenwood Press, 1987), 226; Allan J. Lichtman, "The End of Realignment Theory? Toward a New Research Program for American Political History," *Historical Methods* 15 (1982): 184–186; J. Morgan Kousser, "Restoring Politics to Political History," *Journal of Interdisciplinary History* 12 (1982): 569. Explanations that rely on national electoral agendas overcoming normal parochial concerns overlook the extent to which political agendas can be driven by nonelectoral concerns, including institutional and ideological interests. Cf. David W. Brady and Joseph Stewart Jr., "When Elections Really Matter: Realignments and Changes in Public Policy," in *Do Elections Matter?* ed. Benjamin Ginsberg and Alan Stone (Armonk, N.Y.: M. E. Sharpe, 1986), 19–34. Finally, realignment theory, though useful in particular contexts, is historically limited, providing little leverage for comprehending such pre–party system activities as the Chase impeachment or "dealignment" activities as the Nixon-era conflicts. The approach can be generalized only at the expense of blurring the analytical mechanisms that gave it explanatory utility. See also Joel H. Silbey, "Beyond Realignment and Realignment Theory: American Political Eras, 1789–1989," in *The End of Realignment?* ed. Byron E. Shafer (Madison: University of Wisconsin Press, 1991). Cf. Sean Q. Kelly, "Punctuated Change and the Era of Divided Government," in Dodd and Jillson, *New Perspectives,* 162–190.

10. Ackerman is concerned not with elucidating the existing Constitution's ambiguous meaning, but rather with replacing inherited and known constitutional requirements with new ones. In the context of construction, the people have already ratified the Constitution that is to be construed. The question at hand is merely how they will construct its meaning and fill in the gaps that were previously left in it. As a consequence, deliberation on particular constructions is likely to be limited to interested constituencies, not the whole citizenry. See also Karl Llewellyn, "The Constitution as an Institution," *Columbia Law Review* 34 (1934): 7. Moreover, determining the intent of the electorate for the purposes of judicial enforcement is a task rife with indeterminacies. See also Robert Dahl, "Myth of the Presidential Mandate," *Political Science Quarterly* 105 (1990): 355; Richard McCormick, "Walter Dean Burnham and 'The System of 1896,'" *Social Science History* 10 (Fall 1986): 245; Stanley Kelley Jr., *Interpreting Elections* (Princeton: Princeton University Press, 1983); Michael Klarman, "Constitutional Fact/Constitutional Fiction: A Critique of Bruce Ackerman's Theory of Constitutional Moments," *Stanford Law Review* 44 (February 1992): 767–770.

11. Some commentators have emphasized the constraining function of constitutionalism to the exclusion of all others, with the consequence that the institution of judicial review is privileged as being nearly tantamount to constitu-

tionalism and that the connections between the ordering and limiting functions of constitutions are underanalyzed; e.g., Charles H. McIlwain, *Constitutionalism* (Ithaca: Cornell University Press, 1947); Giovanni Sartori, "Constitutionalism: A Preliminary Discussion," *American Political Science Review* 56 (1962): 853; Ronald Dworkin, "Constitutionalism and Democracy," *European Journal of Philosophy* 3 (1995): 2.

12. From the perspective of empirical study, an exclusive focus on judicial review as the enforcement mechanism for constitutional limitations begs the question of how that institution survives outside politics. Ackerman usefully bridges the gap between normative and empirical theory by asking exactly that question, and positing that judicial review is stabilized by the difficulty of forming a unified political force given the constitutional separation of powers; *We the People*, 255–270. On the problem of institutionalization, see also Robert A. Dahl, "Decision-Making in a Democracy: The Supreme Court as National Policy-Maker," *Journal of Public Law* 6 (Fall 1957): 279; William H. Riker, "Implications from the Disequilibrium of Majority Rule for the Study of Institutions," *American Political Science Review* 74 (June 1980): 432; Kenneth A. Shepsle, "Studying Institutions: Some Lessons from the Rational Choice Approach," *Journal of Theoretical Politics* 1 (1989): 131; idem, "Institutional Equilibrium and Equilibrium Institutions," in *Political Science: The Science of Politics*, ed. Herbert F. Weisberg (New York: Agathon Press, 1986); Martin Shefter and Benjamin Ginsberg, "Institutionalizing the Reagan Regime," in Ginsberg and Stone, *Do Elections Matter?*

13. Clifford Geertz, *The Interpretation of Cultures* (New York: Basic Books, 1973), 193–233; Kenneth Burke, *The Philosophy of Literary Form* (Baton Rouge: Louisiana State University Press, 1967), 1–137; Mark Johnson, ed., *Philosophical Perspectives on Metaphor* (Minneapolis: University of Minnesota Press, 1981); William F. Harris II, *The Interpretable Constitution* (Baltimore: Johns Hopkins University Press, 1993), 46–83; Anne Norton, *Alternative Americas* (Chicago: University of Chicago Press, 1986), 1–16; Lawrence C. Dodd, "Political Learning and Political Change: Understanding Development across Time," in Dodd and Jillson, *Dynamics of American Politics*.

14. At the most extreme, a successful construction could make alternatives literally unthinkable; e.g., Thomas S. Kuhn, *The Structure of Scientific Revolutions* (Chicago: University of Chicago Press, 1970); J. G. A. Pocock, *Politics, Language, and Time* (Chicago: University of Chicago Press, 1989).

15. On a similar point, William Browne notes: "Issues are not selected by member enterprises because they appear to be good ideas in some neutral policy sense. Although issues can be seen as good ideas, 'good' seems to be determined by a combination of enterprise appeal and certain strategic advantages associated with each issue"; *Cultivating Congress* (Lawrence: University Press of Kansas, 1995), 65. On the limitations of political ideology, see also Robert G. McCloskey, "The American Ideology," in *The Continuing Crisis in American Politics*, ed. Marian D. Irish (Englewood Cliffs, N.J.:

Prentice-Hall, 1963); Louis Hartz, *The Liberal Tradition in America* (New York: Harcourt, Brace & World, 1955), 3–14; Samuel Huntington, *American Politics* (Cambridge, Mass.: Harvard University Press, 1981); Nagel, *Constitutional Cultures*, 106–156.

16. Stephen Skowronek's enduring "regimes" reflect a similar sense. The combined commitments of institutions and ideas may be most strongly associated with a dominant party and yet require the "minority" party to accommodate itself to those interests. Franklin Roosevelt's Democratic New Deal order survived the Eisenhower Republican interregnum, in part by requiring the creation of the "New Republicans," who would not compete on central aspects of the New Deal commitments. Skowronek, *Politics Presidents Make*, 3–58.

17. There are substantial information and transaction costs associated with forming governing coalitions, making them more stable than a mere counting of policy preferences might suggest. See also John Aldrich, *Why Parties?* (Chicago: University of Chicago Press, 1995), 201–240; Gary W. Cox and Mathew D. McCubbins, *Legislative Leviathan* (Berkeley: University of California Press, 1993), 83–157; Howard Rosenthal and Keith Poole, "Congress and Railroad Regulation: 1874–1887," in *The Regulated Economy,* ed. Claudia Goldin and Gary D. Libecap (Chicago: University of Chicago Press, 1994).

18. Judicial review serves as such an institutional support for the Constitution itself, preventing it from becoming a "mere parchment barrier" by creating mechanisms and incentives to defend textual requirements against momentary policy preferences.

19. See also Douglass C. North, *Institutions, Institutional Change, and Economic Performance* (New York: Cambridge University Press, 1990); D. Roderick Kiewiet and Mathew D. McCubbins, *The Logic of Delegation* (Chicago: University of Chicago Press, 1991), 1–38; Jack Knight, *Institutions and Social Conflict* (New York: Cambridge University Press, 1992); Shepsle, "Studying Institutions."

20. More recently, some justices have cited the New Deal attack on the courts to discourage their colleagues from reconsidering inherited understandings of federalism; e.g., National League of Cities v. Usery, 426 U.S. 833, 868 (1976); U.S. v. Lopez, 131 L. Ed. 2d 626, 666, 669 (1995).

21. For useful exceptions, see Richard Bellamy, "The Political Form of the Constitution: The Separation of Powers, Rights, and Representative Democracy," *Political Studies* 44 (1996): 436; M. J. C. Vile, *Constitutionalism and the Separation of Powers* (New York: Oxford University Press, 1967); Louis Fisher, *Constitutional Conflicts between Congress and the President* (Lawrence: University Press of Kansas, 1997).

22. For a classic example of the homogenization view of the separation of powers, see Richard E. Neustadt, *Presidential Power and the Modern Presidents* (New York: Free Press, 1990), 29.

23. For examples of the deadlock view, see Woodrow Wilson, *Constitutional Government in the United States* (New York: Columbia University Press, 1908), 56–77; James MacGregor Burns, *The Deadlock of Democracy* (Englewood Cliffs, N.J.: Prentice-Hall, 1967); Samuel P. Huntington, *Political Order in Changing Societies* (New Haven: Yale University Press, 1968), 109–139; James L. Sundquist, "Party Decay and the Capacity to Govern," in *The Future of American Political Parties,* ed. Joel L. Fleishman (Englewood Cliffs, N.J.: Prentice-Hall, 1982).

24. On the emergence of policy from fragmented sources of power, see Martha Derthick and Paul J. Quirk, *The Politics of Deregulation* (Washington, D.C.: Brookings Institution, 1985). On political forces favoring the emergence of policy within the separation of powers, see David Mayhew, *Divided We Govern* (New Haven: Yale University Press, 1991).

25. See also James Meernik and Joseph Ignagni, "Judicial Review and Coordinate Construction of the Constitution," *American Journal of Political Science* 41 (1997): 447.

INDEX